W9-CWV-737

THE SOVIET DEFENCE-INDUSTRY COMPLEX FROM STALIN TO KHRUSHCHEV

STUDIES IN RUSSIAN AND EAST EUROPEAN HISTORY AND SOCIETY

Recent titles include:

Lynne Attwood
CREATING THE NEW SOVIET WOMAN

John Barber and Mark Harrison (*editors*)
THE SOVIET DEFENCE-INDUSTRY COMPLEX FROM STALIN TO KHRUSHCHEV

Vincent Barnett
KONDRATIEV AND THE DYNAMICS OF ECONOMIC DEVELOPMENT

R. W. Davies
SOVIET HISTORY IN THE YELTSIN ERA

James Hughes
STALINISM IN A RUSSIAN PROVINCE

Melanie Ilič
WOMEN WORKERS IN THE SOVIET INTERWAR ECONOMY

Peter Kirkow
RUSSIA'S PROVINCES

E. A. Rees (*editor*)
DECISION-MAKING IN THE STALINIST COMMAND ECONOMY

Lennart Samuelson
PLANS FOR STALIN'S WAR MACHINE
Tukhachevskii and Military-Economic Planning, 1925–1941

Vera Tolz
RUSSIAN ACADEMICIANS AND THE REVOLUTION

Studies in Russian and East European History and Society
Series Standing Order ISBN 0–333–71239–0
(*outside North America only*)

You can receive future titles in this series as they are published by placing a standing order. Please contact your bookseller or, in case of difficulty, write to us at the address below with your name and address, the title of the series and the ISBN quoted above.

Customer Services Department, Macmillan Distribution Ltd
Houndmills, Basingstoke, Hampshire RG21 6XS, England

The Soviet Defence-Industry Complex from Stalin to Khrushchev

Edited by

John Barber
Vice-Provost
King's College
Cambridge

and

Mark Harrison
Professor of Economics
University of Warwick

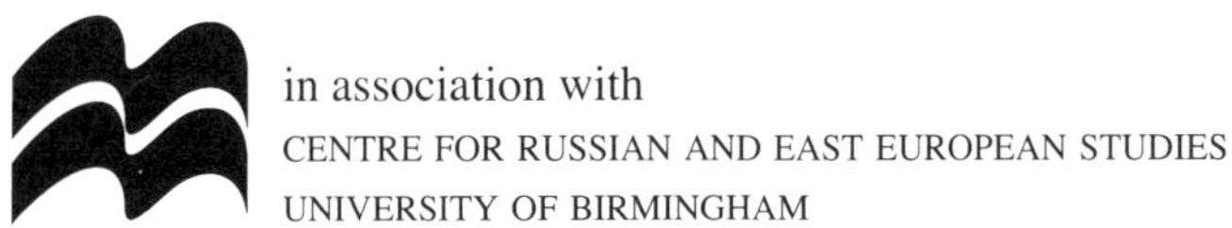

First published in Great Britain 2000 by
MACMILLAN PRESS LTD
Houndmills, Basingstoke, Hampshire RG21 6XS and London
Companies and representatives throughout the world

A catalogue record for this book is available from the British Library.

ISBN 0–333–72763–0

First published in the United States of America 2000 by
ST. MARTIN'S PRESS, INC.,
Scholarly and Reference Division,
175 Fifth Avenue, New York, N.Y. 10010

ISBN 0–312–22602–0

Library of Congress Cataloging-in-Publication Data
The Soviet defence-industry complex from Stalin to Khrushchev / edited by John Barber and Mark Harrison.
p. cm. — (Studies in Russian and East European history and society)
Includes bibliographical references and index.
ISBN 0–312–22602–0
1. Defense industries—Soviet Union—History. I. Barber, John, 1944– . II. Harrison, Mark, 1949– . III. University of Birmingham. Centre for Russian and East European Studies. IV. Series.
HD9743.S672S68 1999
338.4'76233'0947—dc21 99–16308
CIP

This book is printed on paper suitable for recycling and made from fully managed and sustained forest sources.

10 9 8 7 6 5 4 3 2 1
09 08 07 06 05 04 03 02 01 00

Printed and bound in Great Britain by Antony Rowe Ltd, Chippenham, Wiltshire

Contents

List of tables

List of figures

Preface

This book had its origins in a series of meetings between Nikolai Simonov, Boris Starkov, and the editors in England and Russia in the early 1990s. With the fall of the Soviet state, Russian archives were offering new opportunities for historical research on hitherto closed topics. Through the twists and turns of the Russian post-Communist transition, the political stock of the Russian defence-industry complex performed strongly. At the same time its true history remained unwritten. International collaborative teamwork seemed the most effective bridge between old-style Sovietology and the new prospect of path-breaking investigation of the primary documents held in state, military, and party archives.

In the course of this research the circle of our collaborators widened. We were joined by the senior British economic historian of the Soviet Union R.W. Davies, the Swedish military-economic historian Lennart Samuelson, and, from St Petersburg, members of Boris Starkov's group of researchers on the history of the defence industry. Our work was underpinned by financial support from the British Economic and Social Research Council in the period from the summer of 1994 to the late autumn of 1996.

The present book is the result of this collaboration. It deals with the history of the Russian defence complex in its formative years. In 1917 Soviet leaders had believed themselves to be at the forefront of a movement which would end in worldwide revolution and social transformations on a continental scale. Within a few years these expectations proved illusory. The book begins in the mid-1920s as the new Soviet state grappled with new realities – a world at peace, but full of hostility, and of enemies within as well as without. Soviet leaders found themselves still in power, but weakened and isolated. They launched their country into the process of building 'socialism in a single country'. In the 1930s under Stalin's rule the Soviet Union rearmed and its defence industry expanded, though at heavy cost. In the 1940s the country fought off Hitler's deep invasion, mobilised its economic and industrial resources, and played a major part in the eventual defeat of the Axis powers; then it had to face a postwar world of terrifying new weapons and new industrial requirements. By the 1950s, when Khrushchev assumed the leadership, the Soviet Union had transformed itself into a global military-industrial power. Thus the years which ran from Stalin to Khrushchev comprise an era in which the Soviet Union really did revolutionise the international economic and political order.

This book is organised in five parts. Part I presents an overview – a collective evaluation (Chapter 1) of the main themes of the book by the principal Russian and English participants in the project. Parts II and III cover various aspects of the defence-industry complex in two historical phases of its formation: the interwar years (Chapters 2 to 4), and the wartime and postwar phase (Chapters 5 to 7). Part IV reviews issues in the social history of the defence-industry complex, taking two cities as subjects of three case studies (Chapters 8 to 10). Part V considers how the defence-industry complex was regulated by military and economic planners and by the security organs (Chapters 11 to 13).

The historical documents on which this book is based are scattered through a dozen different archives. Russian archives, like the Russian economy, social order, and political system, are today in transition. The transition from secrecy to openness is just as difficult and painful as the transition from state socialism to a market economy, or from the one-party state to a pluralist democracy. This applies in particular to defence-related fields, even where the defence issues lie entirely in the past. Many such documents have been entirely declassified and are accessible to anyone. Others may be cited but not quoted, or quoted but not identified by their catalogue reference of *fond*, *opis'*, and *delo*. This explains much of the lack of uniformity in the style of archival references of the different chapters, which would otherwise be regrettable. Many more documents continue to be withheld from scholarly investigation. They will keep their surprises for future generations, perhaps even forever.

Acknowledgements

The editors wish to express their collective thanks to the Economic and Social Research Council for financial support under grant no. R000221176, to the Centre for Russian and East European Studies of the University of Birmingham, to King's College, Cambridge, and to the University of Warwick Research and Teaching Innovations Fund for other financial support, and to the University of Warwick for the grant of study leave; to Dr N.S. Simonov and Prof. B.A. Starkov for their indispensible collaboration; to Prof. J.M. Cooper, Prof. R.W. Davies, Dr E.A. Rees, Dr Lennart Samuelson, and the late Prof. P.J.D. Wiles, for advice and help over the long period in which this project was devised and executed (at the final stage, Prof. Davies and Dr Rees also read the whole typescript and contributed many valuable comments and criticisms); to the directors and staff of the following archives for assistance to the authors and access to documents: APRF (the Archive of the President of the Russian Federation, Moscow), Arkhiv Sluzhby Vneshnei Razvedki Rossiiskoi Federatsii (the Foreign Intelligence Archive of the Russian Federation, Moscow), Arkhiv Soveta Ministrov SSSR (the Archive of the Council of Ministers of the USSR (Moscow), Arkhiv UFSB (the Archive of the St Petersburg and Leningrad District Administration of the Federal Security Service, St Petersburg), Arkhiv UNKVD (the Archive of the St Petersburg District Administration of the People's Commissariat of Internal Affairs, St Petersburg), GARF (the State Archive of the Russian Federation), RGAE (the Russian State Economics Archive), RGVA (the Russian State Military Archive), RTsKhIDNI (the Russian Centre for Conservation and Study of Documents of Contemporary History), TsA FSBR (the Central Archive of the Federal Security Service of Russia, Moscow), and TsGA IPD (the Central State Archive of Historical Political Documents, St Petersburg); and to Carfax Publishers for permission to use material for Chapters 2 and 4 from articles previously published in *Europe-Asia Studies*. Chapter 2 is a revised version of Simonov, N.S., '"Strengthen the defence of the land of the Soviets": the 1927 "war alarm" and its consequences', *Europe-Asia Studies*, vol. 48(8), 1996, 1355–64; Chapter 4 is revised and substantially abridged from Harrison, M., and Davies, R.W., 'The Soviet military-economic effort under the second five-year plan (1933–1937)', *Europe-Asia Studies*, 49(3), 1997, 369–406.

The authors are additionally and separately grateful as follows: Lennart Samuelson (Chapter 3) to the Stockholm Institute for East European Economies, the Swedish Institute, and the Wallander Research Foundation for financial support; R.W. Davies and Mark Harrison (Chapter 4) to the ESRC for financial support of research on 'Economic development and centre-local relations in the Soviet command economy' (principal investigators: Prof. R.W. Davies and Dr E.A. Rees) under grant no. R000235636; Mark Harrison (Chapter 5) to the participants in the All-University of California economic history conference at UC Santa Barbara (especially Gregory Grossman, David Holloway, and Kerry Ellen Pannell) for discussion and comments; Mark Harrison (Chapter 6) to the members of economic history seminars at the University of Warwick and All Souls' College, Oxford (especially Naomi Azrieli, Stephen Broadberry, Nick Crafts, Charles Feinstein, and Avner Offer) for discussion and comments, and to Mike Berry, David Edgerton, and David Holloway for help with sources.

Notes on the contributors

John Barber is Fellow and Vice-Provost of King's College, Cambridge, Lecturer in Social and Political Sciences at the University of Cambridge, author of *Soviet historians in crisis, 1928–1932* (Macmillan, 1981) and co-author (with Mark Harrison) of *The Soviet home front, 1941–5: a social and economic history of the USSR in World War II* (Longman, 1991).

R.W. Davies is Emeritus Professor of Russian Economic Studies at the University of Birmingham, co-editor (with Mark Harrison and S.G. Wheatcroft) of *The economic transformation of the Soviet Union, 1913–1945* (Cambridge University Press, 1994), and author of *The Industrialization of Soviet Russia* (Macmillan) of which four volumes have appeared since 1980 and further volumes are now in preparation.

Viktoriia Glazyrina is a research student in the Department of History of the State University of Economics and Finance, St Petersburg.

Mark Harrison is Professor of Economics at the University of Warwick, co-author (with John Barber) of *The Soviet home front, 1941–5: a social and economic history of the USSR in World War II* (Longman, 1991), co-editor (with R.W. Davies and S.G. Wheatcroft) of *The economic transformation of the Soviet Union, 1913–1945* (Cambridge University Press, 1994), author of *Accounting for war: Soviet production, employment and the defence burden, 1940–1945* (Cambridge University Press, 1996), and editor of *The economics of World War II: six great powers in international comparison* (Cambridge University Press, 1998).

Natalia Lebina is Professor of Russian History at the State University of Economics and Finance, St Petersburg, chief editor of the "Russian everyday life" section in the journal *Rodina*, and author of books and articles on Russian social history including (with M.V. Shkarovskii) *Prostitutsiia v Peterburge, 40-e gody XIX veka-40e gody XX veka* [Prostitution in St Petersburg from the 1840s to the 1940s] (Progress-akademiia, 1994).

Aleksandr Losik is Professor of Russian History at the Aerospace Academy, St Petersburg.

Lennart Samuelson is Research Fellow in the Department of Strategic Studies of the National Defence College, Stockholm, and author of *Plans for Stalin's war-machine: Tukhachevskii and military-economic planning, 1925–41*, (Macmillan, in press).

Aleksandr Shcherba is Reader in Russian History at the Aerospace Academy, St Petersburg.

Nikolai Simonov, formerly Senior Researcher at the Institute of Russian History of the Russian Academy of Sciences, Moscow, is author of *Voenno-promyshlennyi kompleks SSSR v 1920–1950-e gody: tempy ekonomicheskogo rosta, struktura, organizatsiia proizvodstva i upravlenie* [The military-industrial complex of the USSR from the 1920s to the 1950s: rates of economic growth, structure, production organisation, and management] (Rossiiskaia politicheskaia entsiklopediia, 1996).

Boris Starkov is Professor of Russian History at the State University of Economics and Finance, St Petersburg, and author of *Dela i liudi Stalinskogo vremeni* [Affairs and people of the Stalin period] (Izdatel'stvo Sankt-Peterburgskogo universiteta ekonomiki i finansov, 1995).

Glossary and abbreviations

Note

The name adopted for ministries in Soviet Russia after the revolution was *narodnyi komissariat* or 'people's commissariat'. *Narodnyi komissariat* was usually abbreviated to *narkomat*, or *narkom–* (e.g. Narkomfin, the People's Commissariat of Finance), or to the initial letters NK– (e.g. NKVD, the People's Commissariat of Internal Affairs). On 15 March 1946 the people's commissariats were renamed *ministerstva* ('ministries'), abbreviated to *Min–* (e.g. Minfin) or to the initial letter M– (e.g. MVD).

GIRD	Jet Propulsion Research Group of *Osoaviakhim* (until 1933)
GIRT	State Institute for jet propulsion technology of *Narkomboepripasov*, 1942–44
GKO *or* GOKO	State Defence Committee, the war cabinet (1941–5)
Glavredmet	chief administration of rare metals of *Narkomtsvetmet/Mintsvetmet*
GNP	gross national product
Gosplan	State Planning Commission (of the Council of Ministers, formerly *Sovnarkom*)
Gulag	chief administration of corrective-labour camps of the *MVD (NKVD)*
GVMU	chief war-mobilisation administration of *Narkomtiazhprom*
KB	design bureau; also TsKB (central design bureau), OKB ('experimental' or 'special' design bureau), and so on
krai	territory – usually a group of national or ethnic autonomous regions within a Union Republic (e.g. the Krasnoiarsk *krai* of the Russian Federation)
MGB (NKGB)	Ministry (Commissariat) of State Security (1943–53)
Minaviaprom (Narkomaviaprom)	Ministry (Commissariat) of the Aircraft Industry
Minoboronprom (Narkomoboronprom)	Ministry (Commissariat) of the Defence Industry (1936–9 and 1953 onwards)

Minselmash	the postwar Ministry of Agricultural Machinery (in wartime, *Narkomboepripasov*)
Minsredmash	Ministry of Medium Engineering (1953 onwards)
Mintsvetmet (Narkomtsvetmet)	Ministry (Commissariat) of Nonferrous Metallurgy
Minvooruzheniia (Narkomvooruzheniia)	Ministry (Commissariat) of Armament
MO (NKO)	Ministry (Commissariat) of Defence (1934–46 and from 1953)
MVD (NKVD)	Ministry (Commissariat) of Internal Affairs (from 1934)
Narkomaviaprom	see *Minaviaprom*
Narkomboepripasov	the wartime Commissariat for Ammunition
Narkomfin	Commissariat of Finance
Narkommash	Commissariat of Engineering (1936–9)
Narkomoboronprom	see *Minoboronprom*
Narkomtiazhprom	Commissariat of Heavy Industry (1932–6)
Narkomtsvetmet	see *Mintsvetmet*
Narkomvooruzheniia	see *Minvooruzheniia*
NII	research institute
NKGB	see *MGB*
NKO	see *MO* (from 1934)
NKVD	see *MVD*
NKVM	Commissariat of Military and Naval Affairs (until 1934)
NMP	net material product
oblast'	region (formerly province) within a Union Republic, with a city as its capital (e.g. Leningrad *oblast'*, Sverdlovsk *oblast'*)
OGPU	Unified State Political Administration (security agency until 1934, predecessor of the *NKVD*)
OKB	*see* KB
Osoaviakhim	(1) Society for Cooperation in Air and Chemical Defence (i.e. civil defence) (2) the codename of the operation to deport German specialists to the USSR (October 1946)
PGU	First Chief Administration of the Council of Ministers (Sovnarkom)
R&D	research and development
raion	district – a neighbourhood or ward within a region or urban settlement

RNII	Jet Propulsion Research Institute of *Narkomtiazhprom* (lead design organisation for rocketry, 1933–8)
RVS *or* Revvoensovet	Revolutionary Military Council
RZ STO	the business sessions of *STO*
Sharashka	penal research or design establishment under the *NKVD-MVD*
Sovnarkom	Council of People's Commissars (renamed the Council of Ministers in March 1946)
STO	Council of Labour and Defence
TsAGI	Zhukovskii Central Aero-Hydrodynamics Institute of *Minaviaprom*
TsKB	*see* KB
VGU	Second Chief Administration of the Council of Ministers (Sovnarkom)
VSNKh	Supreme Council of the National Economy (1917–32)

Part I
Overview

1 The structure and development of the defence-industry complex

John Barber, Mark Harrison, Nikolai Simonov and Boris Starkov

INTRODUCTION

Defence was of paramount concern to the leaders of the Soviet state from its inception. The Bolshevik Revolution of October 1917 took place as World War I began its final climactic year, amid fears of a renewed German offensive against Russia on the eastern front. As the Soviet government entered into a humiliating peace with Germany, Russia descended rapidly into a bitter Civil War of Reds versus Whites. At the same time the former Allies of the old regime weighed in on the side of the Whites to oust the Bolsheviks and restore Russia to a state of war with Germany. Military issues continually crowded the Bolshevik agenda. The Civil War ended in a victory for the Soviet side, and a sharp contraction of the Red Army and of Soviet defence expenditures followed. At the same time the legacy of the civil war experience was of a siege mentality and a perception of unceasing threats from every quarter of the capitalist world. This legacy would persist throughout the entire Soviet period.

It was in the second half of the 1920s that the key decisions were taken to promote the development of the Soviet Union's industrial capacity for mass production of modern weapons and combat equipment. We now have a clear picture of the context and motivation of these decisions (for further evidence and discussion see Chapters 2 and 3). First, for Moscow the late 1920s were a period of renewed international tension, including specifically the 'war alarm' of 1927. At the same time Soviet leaders had no reason to anticipate, and did not anticipate, an immediate war. The war for which they began to plan lay, as yet, some years in the future – certainly beyond the five-year horizon of consecutive national economic plans. Uncertainty dominated their calculations. This was a war which they feared, expected others to initiate, and did not plan to initiate themselves. There was no plan to rearm in order themselves to undertake either a war of expansion, or a preventive war. A defensive motivation was strongly felt. At the same time they also wished to be ready to take advantage of any opportunities whether for expansion or for the export of revolution, which the aggressive action of others might present to them. At various times they also wished to be in a position to undertake pre-emptive action to forestall others' aggression if the need arose.

By the late 1920s, Soviet leaders had also thoroughly absorbed the lessons of European warfare since the Crimean War, and above all of World War I. In the modern era, the outcome of wars would be decided by industrial power as much as by fighting spirit. The quantities of guns, shells, tanks, and aircraft which each side could deploy on the front line would be critical. Moreover, given the murderous conditions of the twentieth-century battlefield, the decisive quantities would include not only those accumulated in peacetime and available when war broke out, but also those produced in wartime to replace initial losses and swell the numbers on the front line as counters to the enemy's economic mobilisation when the war was already in progress. In the Soviet Union these calculations formed powerful motives for the urgent development both of a specialised, large scale defence industry and of industrialisation of the whole economy in a more general sense.

The international tensions of the late 1920s were used to promote the radical transformation of the whole social and economic system under the first Stalinist five-year plan (1928–32). By the late 1920s the regime was locked in a struggle with the peasantry eerily reminiscent of the contradictions which had destroyed the economy of Imperial Russia in World War I. Russia had entered the war in 1914 a great power but a poor country, with a large surplus of food for export produced in low-income peasant agriculture. Mobilisation for the war diverted scarce resources from agricultural production and consumption to war production and military service. The result was a breakdown of urban–rural trade and a collapse of the rural food surplus. Russia could no longer feed its own soldiers and workers. This vicious circle was not broken by the 1917 Revolution. Soviet Russia survived the ensuing Civil War not having solved its food problem, and triumphed only because the enemy's weaknesses were even greater. Only the end of the Civil War in 1921 permitted recovery. By the end of the 1920s, however, a second mobilisation, not for war but for rapid industrialisation, was once again undermining Soviet urban–rural trade and the rural food surplus. With history fresh in their minds, military and political leaders were sharply aware that the Soviet Union was in no condition to face a renewal of international conflict.

From the late 1920s onwards the Soviet Union was engaged in preparation for war. The preparations were defensive, but also active. They were not limited to development of the armed forces themselves, but also embraced largescale construction of specialised defence industry facilities. The forced-march industrialisation programme could also be understood as contributing to the preparation of the country for war, by enlarging its potential for war production. Lastly, the new collective-farm system for food production and procurement was intended in part to break the power of the peasantry to hold the country to ransom in time of war. And it may be argued that, although the collectivisation of agriculture was costly far beyond Soviet leaders' expectations, and was disastrous for peacetime economic and social development, when the anticipated war finally broke out in 1941 the peasantry was no longer in a position to prevent the regime from imposing wartime priorities and mobilising everything for war, even when there was not enough food available to keep everyone alive.

It would be quite wrong to suppose, however, that purely military motivations are sufficient to explain the Soviet social and economic transformation of the interwar years in its entirety. The Soviet Union was never ruled by its military commanders. Behind rapid state-socialist industrialisation and farm collectivisation was clearly a coalition of interests which came together to form a distinct entity. Sometimes this coalition has been described as the Soviet 'military-industrial complex'. Whether or not this is the right term is a question to which we return at the end of the present chapter.

For the time being we employ the term 'defence-industry complex' to signify our own more limited agenda. Our main interest is in the Soviet defence industry – its production and R&D facilities, its workforce and management, its institutions and leaders and their interaction with others. We call it a 'complex' to the extent that its composite elements came together to form a complex unity differentiated from other elements of the Soviet social, economic, and political system. In the present state of our knowledge about Soviet history and society we believe that the defence industry is a prime subject for scholarly investigation, and the purpose of this chapter is essentially to explain why. Our first task is therefore the difficult one of defining the scope and limits of the defence-industry complex.

THE PRODUCTION OF THE MEANS OF DESTRUCTION

What made the defence-industry complex a special part of the Soviet economy? The most obvious way of distinguishing the Soviet defence-industry complex is by its product. The customer of defence industry was the Soviet armed forces, and the basic product which changed hands among them was 'the means of destruction'.

There are some subtle differences in what is implied by such a relationship in the divergent schools of classical economics, western and Marxist. In the Marxist scheme still widely employed by Russian historians, the economy is portrayed as a system producing two kinds of material commodities, the means of production (sometimes called group 'A') and of consumption (group 'B') respectively. The services sector, being 'nonproductive' from a material commodity standpoint, sits on top of the production base, and is enabled to provide services only because of the redistribution of material commodities to support its activities and workforce. Weapons do not fit easily into this classification, since they are means neither of consumption nor of production, and in the postwar period it became common among Soviet economists to define the defence industry as a third branch (group 'C', for argument's sake) engaged in the production of the material means of destruction.

Such distinctions are not made in present-day western classical (sometimes called 'neoclassical') economics. From a utilitarian standpoint, all goods and services are produced in order to satisfy needs. Society's need for weaponry and military services is not, in principle, different from household needs for consumer goods and services, or firms' needs for materials or investment goods. Thus defence outlays are simply classed as one among many possible final uses of the total output of goods and services.

Sometimes quite detailed practical implications are drawn from these rather philosophical starting points. Marxist economists have tended to view the commitment of resources to military-industrial enterprise as at best a diversion from the objectives of long-run economic development, certainly a fiscal burden on the state, and possibly also directly inflationary. This is because outlays on the means of destruction create incomes among those engaged in group 'C' activity, and therefore provide them with purchasing power which adds to demand, without contributing any equivalent means of production or consumption to the overall supply.

Western classical economists do not, of course, dispute the fiscal burden associated with heavy defence outlays. But they do not see defence spending as different in kind from any other form of government consumption. All forms of public expenditure contribute to the fulfilment of some kind of social need (not necessarily with equal efficiency), however defined, and all require financing.

Each of the alternative approaches has its strengths. On the side of the Marxist approach is anecdotal evidence of the postwar period which suggests that many of the worst performing economies have also carried relatively heavy military burdens (for example the USSR), while some of the most rapidly growing economies (for example Japan) have benefited from light spending on defence. A more systematic approach to the data suggests an inverse U-shaped relationship into which the Soviet case also fits quite well: increasing military spending from a low base boosts economic growth, but beyond a point (roughly 9 per cent of GDP) it starts to drag performance down again.[1]

The Western classical approach also has strengths. For example, the worst inflations of the twentieth century have not coincided with the periods of heaviest military spending, that is, with rearmament and war. Usually they have come in the aftermath of wars, when military spending fell sharply. The factor precipitating rapid inflation was not the expansion of group 'C' activity, but the explosion of pent-up civilian demands coupled with the collapse of the state's revenue-raising powers. Examples are Germany, Austria-Hungary, and Soviet Russia after World War I; Germany, Italy, Japan, and the Soviet Union after World War II (the Soviet postwar inflation however being successfully repressed and corrected); and the Russian and most other transitional economies after the ending of the Cold War.

Thus the distinctiveness of the sector producing the means of destruction is not entirely clear from a purely theoretical standpoint. As will be shown in more detail below, our ability to differentiate group 'C' from groups 'A' and 'B' is also rather limited in practice. Delineating the activities giving rise to the production of the means of destruction may be more complicated than would appear at first sight. If we consider the question from the product angle, it is not so hard to find the products which can be used only for armament. But they typically become so *only at the final stage of production*. Before that, they are represented by materials, components, fuels, and labour which have many possible uses, civilian as well as military. From the angle of the production establishment, this amounts to the same thing as saying that military industry is really just a collection of assembly plants which turn the materials, components, and energy produced by the civilian economy into finished weapons. Thus military industry, and that part of the value of finished weapons which represents its value added, are just the tip of the iceberg if we are looking for the entire production apparatus which supports military production. There is always more to group 'C' than meets the eye.

There is also less than meets the eye, in the sense that production establishments with a significant commitment to military production usually have significant sideline involvement in the supply of civilian commodities too. This may arise because it makes market sense (as producers' insurance against volatility in the level of government orders for weapons) or because it helps to defray the budgetary cost of maintaining reserve capacities available for mobilisation in an emergency.

In other words, the 'civilian' economy always participates in military production to the extent that its intermediate products end up embodied in weapons as well as consumer or investment goods. At the same time the 'defence industry' usually maintains a significant profile of products for civilian use.

In summary, neither economic philosophy nor the empirical workings of a specialised exchange economy provide secure grounds for differentiating the defence-industry complex from other components of the production system. Thus the reader should understand that, when we speak of the defence-industry complex, we are not referring to a physical thing which can be readily isolated. The 'defence-industry complex' is not so much a thing as a heuristic concept the validity of which must be judged empirically by its useful results.

CORE AND PERIPHERY

What we mean by the defence-industry complex in the Soviet case is best explained as follows. At its core, specialised defence production was administered by a powerful grouping of supply and user ministries (these were called 'people's commissariats' before 1946). Also within the defence-industry complex, but not, strictly speaking, of the defence industry, should be listed agencies such as *Glavvoenstroi*, the chief administration for defence industry construction, formed in 1941. As part of this complex should also be included the procurement agencies of the user departments, the ministries (or commissariats) of defence and the Navy.

Defence *production* and the defence-industry complex were, therefore, not coterminous. The defence-industry complex included agencies which monitored the work of (or, in the case of Glavvoenstroi, supplied services to) the defence industry without being part of it. It included firms with significant commitments to supply of civilian vehicles, aircraft, ships, and electrical goods. However, with the accelerated pace of rearmament before World War II, the civilian production of the defence-industry complex was probably less important than the growing military production of a widening circle of nominally civilian enterprises outside the defence-industry complex which were in fact being drawn into the defence industry.[2]

Of course some final products can really only be used in a military context, especially weapons and their modern platforms (aircraft, armoured vehicles, ships, and missiles). The specialisation of industrial processes gave rise to a core of defence industry enterprises which did little else than produce these specialised defence products. But this core shaded into a far wider peripheral circle of dual-purpose and general-purpose products. This is because almost every 'civilian' product, if not itself of potential direct military application, was composed of parts and materials which could be so used when recombined in some other form.

For example, according to an input–output table of the Soviet economy based on the 1941 plan, the goods and services purchased out of the defence budget were supplied *directly* by just 10 of the 22 material production sectors (of which 'defence industry' was the most important, but also including transport and communications, construction, and trade), and just one of the 5 service sectors, which together comprised the whole economy. But we only have to go back through *one stage* of intermediate processing to find *every single branch* of commodity production involved, if not in direct supply of final defence products, then in *indirect* supply of intermediate products for eventual defence use.[3]

Thus the defence industry was not a tightly defined group of enterprises, but could rather be thought of as a series of concentric rings. At the core lay the big assembly plants permanently specialised in producing finished weapons (guns, shells, aircraft, tanks, missiles, warships). But hundreds of smaller factories produced dual-purpose products which were immediately capable of or easily adaptable to defence use (e.g. road vehicles). Surrounding the assembly plants lay the subcontracting system. This included in particular the suppliers of specialized, weapons-related materials and components (e.g. armour steel, uranium ore), and of high-grade dual-purpose products (e.g. rolled and alloy steels, radio-electronic instruments, aviation fuel). Beyond the periphery, no longer part of the defence industry as such, lay the non-specialized civilian plants and farm enterprises supplying defence producers, defence subcontractors, and the armed forces with general-purpose goods and services – food rations and fuel, electric power, transport services, and general machinery.

There is an obvious sense, therefore, in which the growth of the Soviet Union's overall military-industrial potential was sustained by general economic development. In this sense it could be said that every aspect of the Soviet economic development strategy was of some kind of defence significance. For example, the promotion of the capital goods industries in the early 1930s certainly created additional possibilities for expansion of industrial capacity of kinds – including that of defence industry – later in the decade. Investments in roads, railways, and air transport each enhanced the economy's future potential for satisfying all kinds of needs – including those of defence. But developing a *future* military-industrial potential was not the same thing as developing defence production *in the present*. It would be an exaggeration to include every kind of economic activity in the defence-related sphere, as if farm work and aircraft assembly were of equal proximity and significance. The latter lay at the core, whereas the former lay beyond the periphery.

The institutional definition of the core could be blurred, however, by the fact that almost all the capacities specialising in producing narrowly military products were also potentially convertible to peaceful production. Indeed, to avoid the peacetime expense of reserve capacities standing idle, civilian and military products were often produced side by side by the big defence producers.

CADRE AND RESERVE

By the twentieth century all the great powers had developed specialised defence production facilities. These facilities provided an assortment of modern weapons, a base for research and development, and so on. But the traumatic experience of World War I in Russia, Germany, and Britain alike had also demonstrated the complete inadequacy of such specialised facilities – typically a few public ordnance factories and shipyards collaborating with a narrow 'charmed circle' of big private sector defence contractors – to meet the huge demands for munitions which transpired as soon as modern armies clashed on the battlefield. In light of this experience 'mobilisation' took on new meaning for the twentieth century – not just the mobilisation of men to the front line, but the mobilisation of all industrial resources to support war production.

Rethinking the mobilisation of Soviet industry gave rise to the concept of 'cadre' and 'reserve'.[4] The 'cadre' factories were to be the specialised producers of weapons, with the tasks of building up peacetime combat stocks, sustaining the military-technical innovation process, and (should war break out) replacing early losses in the period while the 'reserve' came into play. From 1927 cadre defence factories, and in the 1930s research institutes and design bureaux, were numbered like military units (rather than named like civilian enterprises – see further below). The 'reserve' factories were the defence-related and part-time defence producers designated under a prewar mobilisation plan, which could be swiftly converted to full-time war production when war broke out.

It might be expected that the pressures of interwar rearmament drove Soviet industry towards expansion of the cadre factories at the expense of the reserve. And we shall see below that the number of cadre factories rose at a rapid rate, while their workforce and output rose still faster. At the same time, Soviet military leaders were mindful that, once World War I had broken out, the great bulk of its demands had been met by factories of the reserve, not the cadre. Therefore the stress of rearmament was not limited to expansion of the cadre factories. Mobilisation planning became a major activity in its own right (see Chapters 3 and 11). There were various complicated schemes for categorising factories in groups according to their mobilisation tasks (see for example Chapter 8). There was a fluctuating emphasis on the possibility of building up cadre factories' reserve capacities through peacetime orders for civilian products, and on the dispersal of defence orders and subcontracting for defence products across a wide swathe of civilian industry suppliers in order to build up the reserve of potential defence producers.

At least a part of the growth in the number of cadre factories from the end of the 1920s through to the post-Stalin years is captured in the figures reported in table 1.1. These figures are certainly indicative of the general trend. However, the number of enterprises is a very incomplete measure of activity. Moreover, as the table suggests, the numbers are based on a varying and again usually incomplete administrative definition of defence production (for example, by 1956 there were many more than four ministries with core defence production tasks). Therefore, a fuller understanding requires quite a lot of additional explanation.

As far as the interwar period is concerned, in the ten years from 1929 to 1939 the number of defence factories grew roughly fivefold. Output and

Table 1.1. 'Cadre' defence factories and their ministerial subordination, 1929–56 (selected years)

	Ministry or other agency	*Number of factories*
1929	6 trusts: Orudiino-Arsenel'nyi (Gun and Arsenal), Oruzheino-Pulemetnyi (Rifle and Machine-Gun), Patronno-Trubochnyi (Cartridge and Barrel), Aviatsionnyi (Aviation), Voenno-Khimicheskii (Military-Chemical)	43
1936	Narkomoboronprom (People's Commissariat of the Defence Industry)	183
1939	4 people's commissariats: Narkomaviaprom (aircraft industry), Narkomsudprom (shipbuilding), Narkomvooruzheniia (armament), Narkomboepripasov (ammunition)	218
1956	4 ministries: Minaviaprom (aircraft industry), Minoboronprom (defence industry), Minsudprom (shipbuilding), Minradioprom (radio industry)	781

Sources: 1929: calculated from RGAE, 2097/1/1051, 64 (figures exclude military acids, military optics, military shipbuilding, and radio products). Other years: Simonov (1996), 38–42.

employment grew still more rapidly than this. On a comparable definition in 1940 there were roughly 1.2 million defence industry workers, a tenfold increase over 1929; the quantity of weapons produced had risen by between twenty and thirty times at least, probably more, over a similar period (see Chapter 4). Thus by the end of the interwar period there were many more defence factories than at the end of the 1920s, and at the same time the typical defence factory was much larger in workforce terms, and larger still in terms of production.

GROWTH AND REORGANISATION

In the late 1920s under VSNKh there were six military-industrial trusts (the Gun and Arsenal, Rifle and Machine Gun, Shell and Barrel, Aviation, Military-Chemical, and Military-Acid Trusts, of which the first five in November 1929 deployed 43 factories with 141 700 workers and 40 per cent civilian production.[5] In April–May 1930 these trusts were liquidated, and, apart from those directly involved in manufacture of guns and explosives, the enterprises were redistributed among civilian agencies. In 1932, however, with the dissolution of VSNKh and formation of Narkomtiazhprom, the defence producers of both cadre and reserve were brought together again under three chief administrations (for the aircraft industry, shipbuilding, and 'military industry', i.e. armament and ammunition), the Military-Chemical, Organic Products, Artificial Fibres, Cartridges, Arsenal, Shell, and Special Engineering (i.e. tankbuilding) Trusts, and the State Association of Optical Mechanics Factories.

In 1936 there began the process of breaking up the administration of heavy industry.[6] Just as VSNKh had become seen as too unwieldy for managing the early stages of forced industrialisation under the first Five-Year Plan, now it was the turn of Narkomtiazhprom. This was partly in order to improve ministerial controls on resource mobilisation in the enterprise, partly in order to undermine the minister, Sergo Ordzhonikidze. Both purposes were served by breaking up his ministry, creating a large number of fresh ministerial posts, and cutting out layers of bureaucracy between ministers and enterprises in the new, smaller ministerial units. From the standpoint of defence industry enterprise, therefore, the first step was one of concentration: 183 specialised producers were brought together under a new ministry for defence industry (Narkomoboronprom). Under the pressures of rearmament at a growing pace, however, the administrative fission process soon spread to the defence industry itself; in 1939, Narkomoboronprom was broken up into four new ministries for the aircraft industry (Narkomaviaprom), shipbuilding (Narkomsudprom), armament (Narkomvooruzheniia), and ammunition (Narkomboepripasov).

Before and during World War II, the relationship between the cadre and reserve factories went through sharp changes. In the last years before the war rearmament accelerated, cadre facilities were increasingly pre-empted by military orders, and the reserve was increasingly mobilised. Defence orders were widely subcontracted through civilian industry, and the supply of goods for civilian use declined. In the case of the aircraft industry, the cadre-reserve distinction was lost altogether as subcontractors were brought under the direct control of the ministry.[7]

These prewar trends were just a pale foretaste, however, of what transpired in the war years. The cadre-reserve distinction collapsed as the whole economy was mobilised, and industrial capacity was converted indiscriminately to the production of defence products and products for defence use. The Soviet Union was saved not only by the courage of its soldiers and workers but also by a production and productivity miracle (see Chapter 5). Munitions output soared while civilian branches of industry collapsed. The share of specialised defence industry in industry net value added rose from 14 per cent in 1940 to more than 60 per cent in 1942–3. Because this was accompanied by huge productivity gains, the workforce share of defence industry rose by much less, to a little over 30 per cent in the same period.[8] Thus there remained a substantial circle of apparently 'civilian' producers in wartime, but these were engaged to a significant extent in the supply of general-purpose final products to the army and intermediate goods to the defence industry.

World War II brought few changes in the ministerial structure; new commissariats were created for tankbuilding and mortar armament, but otherwise the general pattern of ministerial specialisation remained unchanged. More important than ministerial organisation was the tightening of supraministerial controls on key producers. The topic of supraministerial regulation is discussed further below.

The years after World War II were marked by twin processes of demobilisation, and rearmament based around new weapon technologies including atomic weapons, rocketry, jet propulsion, radar, and electronics (see Chapters 6 and 7). Some wartime ministries were civilianised. Some cadre factories were handed over to civilian agencies e.g. the ministries of transport engineering, agricultural engineering, heavy engineering, the vehicle and tractor industry) where they were grouped under special military administrations (e.g. ammunition and rocket artillery within agricultural engineering, tanks within transport engineering). Other ministries were conserved, e.g. Minaviaprom, Minvooruzheniia (renamed Minoboronprom in 1954), and Minsudprom. At the same time entirely new industries were being created both under existing ministries such as Minvooruzheniia (rocketry) and Minaviaprom (jet aviation), and under new chief administrations subordinated directly to the council of ministries (atomic weapons, the nuclear industry, radar, and radio-TV-infrared technology). In 1954 the latter were formed into new ministries for the radio industry, electronic industry, and 'medium engineering'.

The demobilisation of defence industry after the Second World War was accompanied by widespread reconversion of industrial capacity back to peacetime production, and by growth in the civilian output of defence industry facilities. Thus the peacetime 'reserve' was restored, along with the reserve capacities of the 'cadre' factories. By 1950 the civilian products of five military-industrial ministries were planned to account for half the gross value of their output, compared with 15 per cent in 1945 and a quarter in 1940.[9] But the simultaneous creation of new weapon systems and specialised industries to produce them meant that by the mid-1950s the specialised apparatus of the defence industry as a whole was larger than ever; just the four ministries represented in table 1.1 alone accounted for 781 factories, more than three times the number of prewar 1939.

REGULATION AND MONITORING

Before the revolution the Russian defence industry had operated in a market environment. Of course there were limits on the scope of market forces. Some were peculiar to a low-income, agrarian economy which had emerged only recently from its medieval phase, and which retained a centralised, bureaucratic mode of government. Other limits on the market for defence products were those which we find even in highly industrialised market economies – monopsony and monopoly, a significant element of public-sector ownership, barriers against the entry of new private-sector capital, cost-plus pricing, and accompanying tendencies to inflated costs and under-utilised capacity.[10]

The shortage economy which emerged under Stalin's Five Year Plans wrote most of these tendencies in large on Soviet economic institutions generally. Non-market resource allocation now characterised the whole economy, not just the defence industry. Self-interested industrial enterprises generally ceased to respond to price signals in their input choices and cost decisions, since inefficient decisions were no longer subject to economic penalties. They were regulated instead by non-price controls imposed from above. Non-price controls reflected the emergence of a widespread 'agency problem' which acquired systemic significance.

In the classic formulation of the principal-agent problem, knowledge is distributed unevenly.[11] Principals have good general knowledge, but poor local knowledge of the specific context in which their agents act on their behalf. As a result, in the course of carrying out higher orders, agents acquire scope for discretionary or opportunistic action to reallocate resources towards their own goals. At the same time principals aim to restrict the opportunities for agents' discretionary behaviour by establishing systems of monitoring, reward, and punishment. Meanwhile, agents seek to maintain their discretion while at the same time maximising the incentives and satisfying the performance criteria fixed by their principals. This model corresponded to many well known features of Soviet economic life. Managers and workers in the enterprise aimed to live quietly and get paid without too much effort, rather than to add to output or company profits. To counteract this tendency, the state imposed stringent quantitative controls, pressing the firm to raise output and effort even when external supplies could not be guaranteed. In turn, firms sought to protect their autonomy by producing to the letter of the plan, not its spirit, and also by accumulating excess stocks of machinery, labour, and materials, bargaining for increased input allocations, inflating costs, and insuring against external supply failure by unauthorised investment in vertically integrated processes so as to create hidden reserves of production capacity of all kinds.

These tendencies were at work in all spheres of economic life, whether or not they were defence-related, but defence production still had special characteristics. On the supply side, defence needs were given high priority. This gave the defence industry a degree of privilege, protecting it against the worst features of the shortage economy. It also gave defence producers ample scope to create hidden capacity reserves. While privileged on the supply side, however, the defence industry faced demand conditions more challenging than those facing civilian producers. This is because the users of the defence industry's final output were in a much stronger position than the users of civilian goods. Unlike civilian households, the military was technically knowledgeable and politically influential; unlike civilian industrial users, the military was also in a position to refuse defective output, through its military inspectors present in all major defence assembly plants. The military's ability to force industry to share its objectives thus helped to limit the opportunistic behaviour of defence industry management.

In this sense, the armed forces and the defence industry faced each other in the 'market place' for munitions as antagonists. The armed forces' interest in low-cost, combat-effective munitions did not complement the interest of the defence industry in ease of plan fulfilment, the inflation of claims on current resources, and the aggrandisement of capacity reserves.[12] At the same time, both the military and the defence complex shared common interests in the high priority accorded to defence needs, the prestige associated with defence work, and the identification of national security with military power.

The defence-industry complex was at the core of the Soviet regime's priorities. Government policies of public-sector industrial accumulation expressed a strong linkage of self-sufficient economic development with military security and industrialisation. Heavy industry and defence industry benefited alike. Defence industry got the best of everything, but in return suffered the most intense scrutiny from above.

The regulatory structure of the defence-industry complex was multi-dimensional and multi-layer. Some element of supraministerial regulation, involving both military and political leadership, was continually present. The most important strategic decisions were taken in the Politburo of the party Central Committee. Within the Politburo there was always a Central Committee secretary heading a department of the Central Committee apparatus responsible for military and military-industrial affairs.

At the next level, there was usually a government agency under the Sovnarkom (after 1946, the Council of Ministers) for supraministerial coordination of the army and defence industry. In the 1920s, for example, this was the function of the Council for Labour and Defence (*Sovet truda i oborony*, or STO). By the late 1930s the same job had been divided between two supraministerial committees, a Defence Committee (*Komitet oborony*), and an Economic Council (the *Ekonomsovet*). The Defence Committee supervised the work of the defence and navy commissariats; its military-industrial commission (*voenno-promyshlennaia kommissiia*, or VPK) had charge of the mobilisation readiness of both cadre and reserve industrial facilities.The Economic Council ran several production-branch subcommittees, including one for the defence industry.

During the Second World War the functions of the Politburo, Defence Council and Economic Council were merged in Stalin's war cabinet, the

GKO (*Gosudarstvennyi komitet oborony*) and under it from 1943 the Operations bureau (*Operativnyi biuro*). In the postwar period there was a return to a more conventional arrangement, with the Politburo and Central Committee secretaries on the one hand, and a government Defence Council (*Sovet oborony*) and VPK on the other, playing distinct roles.

The defence industry administrations and ministries themselves formed the hierarchical chain of command. The line of direct, personal, management responsibility for production outcomes (*edinonachalie*) ran from the minister or chief of administration to his deputies, assistant chiefs, and so on, down to the enterprise director. The detailed monitoring of their activity, the tasks of day-to-day co-ordination, and the troubleshooting of production programmes in case of need, were the prerogative of the defence sector of the State Planning Commission (*Gosplan*).

The regulatory institutions of the defence-industry complex so far described were special mainly in the degree of attention and supervision, not in kind. Civilian producers were also subject to strategic decision making in the Politburo, ministerial and supraministerial regulation, and detailed planning, monitoring, and trouble-shooting. The defence industry was special, however, to the extent that, to a degree unusual in the Soviet economy, the industry was regulated by its customer (NKVM-NKO-MO – the ministry or, before 1946 the commissariat, of defence).[13]

Civilian producers produced to satisfy government orders, not the requirements of final users. Final users of civilian products had little or no say in determining product quality or assortment, which were subject only to weak administrative controls, and they were usually grateful to receive anything rather than nothing. There were little or no incentives to reward the introduction of either new products or new processes. In defence industry, in contrast, by the 1930s regulation had evolved in the direction of quasi-market testing for both existing products and for new product designs. For neither case was there a real market, not even an internal one. Nonetheless there were real elements of consumer sovereignty, which were entirely absent from any other sphere of the economy.

As far as current production was concerned, in 1930, the defence commissariat had won the right to appoint its military representatives (*voennye predstaviteli*, or *voenpredy* for short) to work in all the important defence factories, where they were responsible for ensuring war readiness (see Chapter 11), and also for chasing the progress of defence orders and accepting (or rejecting) finished output (see Chapter 12). The power to reject output was real, and is attested both by persistently high rejection rates and by the strenuous efforts of defence industry managers to deflect the *voenpred* regime. A different system was applied to military R&D in industry which nonetheless had the same result of giving the military the power to pick and choose and giving industry an incentive to please the customer. This was the system of rivalry among competing design bureaux, which were set to compete with each other in coming up with new models and weapon systems to satisfy military specifications. The system did not work in all circumstances, as is shown for the case of long-range rocketry (see Chapter 6). Sometimes the required scale of technological development was too great for rivalry to be permitted; on other occasions, the outcome of rivalry was imposed by the security organs (the NKVD-MVD), a regulatory agency not mentioned yet which oversaw all branches of the economy, military or civilian. Still, subject to some exceptions the competitive R&D system worked reliably on the whole.

Thus institutionalised consumer influence on the defence industry had the effect of further mitigating the inherent tendencies of the shortage economy. In non-military branches indifference to customer requirements led to restricted assortment, low quality, and a conservative product technology. In Soviet defence industry these were avoided, with the result that the army had access to a wide range up-to-date, modernised weapons which were often at the forefront of global technology and were usually also serviceable in combat.

Although military themes were very prominent in the Soviet economy and political system from the 1930s onwards, civilian leaders (in the first place, Stalin) retained complete authority over the course of rearmament and military-economic policy. Military representation in the highest circles of party and government remained very limited. The supremacy of civilian leadership was reinforced by the extensive purges of 1937–8 in which the security organs stamped their authority on every sphere of public life and every public institution. In the military sphere the purges destroyed pre-emptively any leanings towards independent political ambition on the part of the Red Army officer corps, and severely weakened its professional autonomy.

At a lower level, however, there was already established and continued to be a pervasive military presence in defence industry, and military influence over its management.

INTEGRATION AND DISINTEGRATION

Once a specialised defence-industry complex administration had been established, to what extent could it free its production apparatus from dependence on the civilian economy? This issue has to be understood in relation to the tendency to production autarky in the economic system as a whole. Under the Stalinist five-year plans, despite far-reaching economic centralisation, many important areas of life were still regulated from below. Wherever needs were left unfilled by the planning system, workers, managers and consumers created decentralised mechanisms to fill the gaps and pursue their own objectives. In the machine-building industry a common such mechanism involved the autarkic development by the factory of its own sideline production of metals, components, fuels, tools or electric power. This pursuit of self-reliance may be understood as one more aspect of the agency problem already mentioned; self-reliance fostered the ability of the enterprise to meet objectives imposed from above while at the same time enlarging the opportunities for discretionary use of resources not derived from the plan and often concealed from the planners.

The defence industry certainly shared this tendency to a high degree. In the extreme case, it gave rise to the autarkic development of huge metallurgical, power, manufacturing, and assembly complexes in the remote interior of the country, and eventually the 'closed' cities which were secret at the time and are discussed further below (see also Chapter 10).

On the other hand there were also countervailing tendencies which limited autarky and which were expressed with particular force in defence industry. One thing which lowered the incentive to pursue autarkic development was the priority system itself, which placed defence producers first in the queue for scarce commodities, protecting them against the worst uncertainties of the shortage economy by making them less likely to suffer from interrupted or deficient supply than civilian producers. As a result defence producers were better able to tolerate dependence on external suppliers and faced a weaker incentive than civilian producers to develop a high degree of vertical integration. They could also afford to reap more benefits from specialisation.

A second factor which actively prevented defence producers from achieving autarky was the positioning of the defence industry at the forefront of the expanding Soviet technological frontier. The development and serial production of new products, the establishment of new technologies, and the birth of new largescale industries could not be achieved in an autarkic way on the basis of the existing resources of the defence industry. Each new product or technology turned out to require the wide involvement and collaboration of civilian agencies and suppliers. Every technological breakthrough in the design of tanks, aircraft, aeroengines, missiles, and atomic weaponry (see Chapters 6 and 7) required the unanticipated conscription of new cohorts of civilian specialists and enterprises to the ranks of the defence-industry complex.

A third factor which counteracted the trend to self-reliance was the requirements of mass production. When war loomed and the demand for weapons surged, the capacity of the cadre factories was insufficient, and the reserve had to be brought into play. Thus the mobilisation capacity of defence industry in peacetime depended upon a healthy civilian economy. At the same time the peacetime expenses of maintaining the specialised cadre defence factories were defrayed by requiring their participation in sideline production for civilian use.

PRIORITY, PRIVILEGE, SECRECY, TERROR

The defence-industry complex suffered intense scrutiny from above, but little or no scrutiny from below. This was ensured by the regime of secrecy. Secrecy was applied first of all to production. In 1927 the 'cadre' defence factories were anonymised, their traditional names being replaced by numbers 1 to 56. Thus the Aviakhim aircraft works (Moscow) became factory no. 1, the Kovrov machine-gun works became factory no. 2, the Volodarskii tube and explosive works (Ul'ianovsk) became factory no. 3, and so on. As the number of defence producers rose the numerical range of the list expanded accordingly. As ministries were created and reorganised, the numbered factories were passed from one subordination to another, and were occasionally renumbered, but more often the number once allocated stuck for many years. From the 1930s onwards many specialised defence research institutes and laboratories were added to the numbered list, sometimes attached to production enterprises and sharing their numbers for purposes of identification.[14]

For purposes of communication, defence producers were often allocated special postal and telegraphic codes which made no reference to real locations or street addresses. Thus, for example, in the 1930s the telegraphic address of aircraft factory no. 16 (Voronezh) was simply '*Krylo*' ('Wing'). In 1946 the production of the atomic bomb was entrusted to KB-11 (design bureau no. 11), '*pochtovyi iashchik* [Post Office box] Arzamas-16' (see Chapter 7). Arzamas was a town in the Volga region south of Gor'kii, and Arzamas-16 was somewhere nearby – but not in Arzamas. This – the creation of closed cities in the remote regions of the Volga, the Urals, and western Siberia, not marked on any map, entirely specialised in defence production and built for no other purpose – had its origins in the evacuation of defence industry from the western and southern regions threatened by German occupation to the remote interior in 1941 and 1942, but was greatly reinforced by the extraordinary secrecy attached to the postwar development of new strategic weapons. It became the most exaggerated expression of secrecy in the whole system (see Chapter 10).

Walls of secrecy were thrown up not only around the defence-industry complex, but also within it. Thus, in the 1930s defence industry managers waged a stubborn campaign to exclude military representatives from information relevant to the calculation of product costs and prices, on the grounds of 'need to know'; this, despite the defence ministry's right to verify costs and prices on site, previously enshrined in government statute. At the same time, the regulations governing the work of military representatives in defence plant insistently invoked their duty to guard and conceal secret documentation of production and mobilisation plans from all factory personnel not explicitly permitted to have oversight of them (see Chapter 12).

In the 1930s statistical secrecy shielded the public from any general knowledge of the scale, character, or direction of defence activity, with the sole exception of a single line in the state budget headed 'expenditures on defence'. The budget was approved annually in a public session of the Supreme Soviet. In the 1940s even this information disappeared temporarily from view. In the 1950s Soviet leaders began to make occasional revelations concerning, for example, numbers of armed forces personnel in various periods; with the 1960s, the pace of serious historical research began to include the disclosure of more detailed statistical information concerning the defence-industry complex in the prewar period and World War II, but not relating to the postwar period itself.

The published information was sometimes intended to mislead. The historical record now shows clearly that the pressure to distort was greatest when Soviet leaders found themselves involved with other states in disarmament processes. Thus in the context of its participation in the World Disarmament Conference at Geneva the Soviet Union published highly understated figures for budget defence outlays and military force levels for 1931–4 (see Chapter 4). The systematic and growing understatement of budget defence outlays which began in 1959 and persisted right through to the end of the Soviet period was likewise associated with the consecutive eras of 'peaceful coexistence' and 'detente'.[15]

On the other hand, in the period of prewar rearmament, World War II, and the early Cold War, what little was published was relatively truthful. Of course the published information was extremely scanty, and there was little need to distort since almost every kind of information was simply suppressed. Thus any information which might assist a calculation of the scale, activity, or location of the defence-industry complex was withheld. The statistical system became partially disintegrated; within each plannng, statistical, or financial agency, flows of defence-related information were channelled separately through a 'first department' (*pervyi otdel*), thus creating a segregation of military from civilian data. (The 'first department' was the point of contact for the security organs in every establishment.)

It was a serious methodological problem whether to reaggregate the military and civilian data flows at the apex of the statistical system for the purpose of calculating overall indicators and balances of sectoral, regional, and national economic activity. If defence-related flows were excluded altogether from totals (e.g. of the gross output of industry), then the integrity of the planning system would be jeopardised, and economic growth indicators would be seriously distorted. Thus on 8 January 1932 a Politburo resolution required that defence industry production *should* be included in the calculated totals for industry as a whole.[16] But this was still far less than was required for adequate monitoring of defence industry from within the apparatus. In March 1935 the statistical chief N. Osinskii complained that

Gosplan's statistical branch was starved of defence-industry data; at the end of that month, Sovnarkom adopted a complicated resolution on the subject which required defence industry to submit full reports of both real and financial outcomes to Gosplan at the centre; of real outcomes, but only in relation to civilian products, to local statistical agencies; and of financial outcomes alone to the Ministry of Finance.[17]

The strategy of partial revelation, for example including defence industry production in the totals for industry as a whole, but not as a separate item, was fraught with danger. The risk was that an intelligent observer could deduce the value of the defence component from the published statistics of the total compared with the sum of the subtotals relating to civilian items. Exactly this situation arose in the spring of 1937, when Narkomtiazhprom published figures for the gross output of its civilian products alone, while Gosplan published almost simultaneously the overall gross output of Narkomtiazhprom. There was an alarmed reaction from within Gosplan demanding strict punishment of those responsible.[18] The fears aroused were ironically justified, for an entire cohort of western scholars made its way in the postwar period by analysing exactly such indiscretions, whether noticed or unnoticed by the Soviet regime itself.

The purposes of secrecy were many. Among them was the legitimate strategic purpose of denying sensitive national security information to potential enemies. The strategy of war avoidance pursued by the Soviet Union required secrecy for two reasons. One was the concealment of weaknesses which might give an advantage to some potential aggressor, or tempt an enemy to engage in opportunistic aggression. This consideration was clearly a factor in the interwar period, becoming stronger as the likelihood of war with Japan and Germany increased, and the traumatic experience of Germany's surprise attack in June 1941 magnified it tremendously in the postwar period. The other reason was to make it more difficult for potential aggressors to formulate realistic war plans, by denying them the information which would enable them to predict likely Soviet actions in the event of war. This became especially significant in the context of postwar nuclear deterrence. Additionally, the Soviet Union's own war plans themselves also rested on secrecy, as a condition for the achievement of strategic and tactical deception and surprise.

At the same time it is clear that secrecy in the Soviet defence-industry complex went beyond what was required by strategic considerations alone. Secrecy was used also to prevent popular scrutiny and defend privilege. For example, once Soviet military 'secrets' were known in the west (for example, from defectors' reports) there was no basis in national security to prevent such information from reaching the Soviet population; however, the Soviet censorship was as keen to prevent the leakage of militarily sensitive information into the Soviet public arena from western public sources as it was to prevent leakages from its own closed official circles. Secretiveness was therefore one of the defences protecting the priority and privilege of the military sector generally, and of the defence industry in particular.

The favourable position of the defence industry in the Soviet economy's priority system became entrenched in the 1930s. Probably the formation of Narkomoboronprom in 1936, and the subsequent emergence of still more specialised defence industry ministries, marked a decisive stage in the entrenchment of this priority.[19]

The economic priority accorded to Soviet defence agencies has sometimes been viewed in an oversimplified way. For example, the regime was often ready to allocate a disproportionate share of new resources to military goals in its strategic plans and perspectives, so there were many periods when the share of defence in the state budget, or in GNP, drifted upwards (for more detail see Chapter 4). On the other hand, there were also times when such trends appeared to be against the spirit of the policies written into the plans in advance, the first Five-Year Plan (which anticipated a *declining* defence share) being a case in point. Another period when a peace dividend was anticipated (and not just anticipated but also realised) was the years after the Second World War. Often enough, when the defence share of total output rose sharply, it disrupted the economy and diverted resources away from other government goals. When overall resources were short and the economy was overstrained, soldiers sometimes had to take a turn in the queue, tailor their designs to the resources available, and make a few sacrifices. But still, the belt-tightening done by the military was usually metaphorical. When famine came it was peasants, not staff officers, who starved to death.

Thus the defence industry was generally privileged relative to other branches. The fact that such privilege remained unquestioned for five decades is surely attributable in significant part to secrecy and censorship. Thus an important function of secrecy was to allow decisions to be taken which gave expression to the priority of defence industry interests and sustained their privilege, without the need to render any public account, or engage in informed discussion other than within the confines of the Politburo and high-level defence agencies.

However, not all aspects of Soviet military-industrial secrecy can be understood as a government conspiracy to subvert public accountability. The walls of secrecy *within* the defence-industry complex do not fit this description. The production data deemed too secret to release to the central planners, the cost data considered too secret to reveal to the soldiers, and so on, reflected the more general agency problem faced by the regime. In the defence-industry complex, secrecy aided agents in their search for discretion and struggle for autonomy at every level. Military secrecy prevented public questioning of regime priorities. At the same time, economic secrecy prevented planners from questioning producer demands for resources, and also stopped soldiers from questioning producer demands for cash. Thus producers eagerly coopted the institutions of secretiveness to increase their opportunities of gaining access to resources and relaxing external constraints on their behaviour.

The dangers of excessive secretiveness were very real. One was the increasing difficulty of mobilising resources and ensuring high performance. Beyond a point, secretiveness inhibited regulation from above as well as scrutiny from below. Another result which followed directly was the increasing powers assumed by the only special agency with the right to inquire into everything, and before whom there could be no secrets – the security police. Thus secretiveness and terror were also connected. The cycle was completed when those with specialist responsibility for the administration of terror such as Beriia in turn became leaders of defence industry (see Chapters 9 and 13).

In the Stalin years the distinction between civilian and military information became blurred. Between 1938 and 1956 virtually anything was liable to be made secret. To this extent the defence-industry complex ceased to be special from the standpoint of secretiveness. In wartime such secretiveness may have been tolerable, and its negative consequences offset at least in part by countervailing forces such as increased national feeling, which made opportunistic behaviour less likely and the need for terroristic repression less self-evident. In peacetime, however, an efficient economy could not be run indefinitely on the basis of secretiveness and terror. Khrushchev in some sense recognised the link between secretiveness and terror in 1956 when he lifted simultaneously the veil of secrecy and the threat of mass repression from civilian affairs. So from 1956 onwards, although neither secretiveness nor repression were eliminated, secrecy was restricted to its previously 'normal' sphere of defence and national security interests (defined rather more broadly than in many other states), and repression was limited to the public critics of the regime.

CONCLUSION: A 'MILITARY-INDUSTRIAL COMPLEX'?

What was special about the Soviet defence industry? First, was the defence-industry complex really separate from the civilian economy in the sense of specialised institutions, particular behaviours, and separate resources? Our answer is that this was the case to a considerable extent, but not absolutely. In many ways the special features of the defence-industry complex were just the basic tendencies of the Soviet economy writ large. The multi-layer hierarchical controls, the tendencies of secretiveness and of autarky, were special in degree, not in kind.

Second, what is implied by our inability to be precise in defining the limits of the defence industry? Does it lend support to the idea that the whole economy was driven by the requirements of military activity and was characterised by a primarily military motivation at its core? It is true that there was an interpenetration of civilian and military industrial production. Defence factories relied on the civilian economy for supplies and produced civilian products as well as weapons. Civilian producers were involved in defence industry as suppliers of intermediate products and sideline final military products as well. These were permanent features of Soviet industry, although to a varying degree. But in our view this does not mean that the whole economy should be seen as just a supportive apparatus for the defence industry and nothing more.

For one thing, not all parts of the civilian economy were involved in production for defence to the same degree; some were entirely separate or were involved, if at all, incidentally (for example to the extent that soldiers purchased consumer goods or used civilian services which had not been specifically designated for them). For another, while some major aspects of civilian economic development were undoubtedly influenced by military considerations, some aspects of defence industry development such as the 'excessive' secretiveness described above were really expressions of civilian public interest or even private self-interest for which military justifications were no more than a convenient cloak, while still others had entirely nonmilitary rationales.

The collusion of military and economic interests in the pursuit of common goals and to the detriment of society as a whole has sometimes been described in the west as giving rise to a 'military-industrial complex'. In a Soviet setting this term has been applied in at least three or four different ways. Many such uses are completely inappropriate and arise from a mistranslation. In English the term 'military-industrial complex' carries the clear implication of a coalition of industrial interests with the interests of the defence ministry and armed forces – 'military' and 'industrial' carry equal weight as adjectival qualifiers of the 'complex'. It is usually translated into Russian as *voenno-promyshlennyi kompleks* ('VPK' for short). However, the Russian is ambiguous where the English is not, and may be understood not as referring to the military-industrial complex in the broad western sense, but to a narrower complex *of the 'military' (i.e. defence) industry alone* – the adjectival *voenno-* (meaning military) qualifies *promyshlennyi* (meaning industrial), not the 'complex'. In that case the Russian 'VPK' should be translated back to English as our own, narrower 'defence-industry complex'. This rule has been followed in the translation of Chapters 8, 9, 10, and 13 (but see further discussion in Chapter 9).

Here we are interested only in those interpretations of the Soviet military-industrial complex which adhere to the western sense of a broad coalition between military and industrial interests. Most sweeping is the interpretation of Mikhail Agursky and Hannes Adomeit; they found 'a core of truth in the aphorism that "the USA *has* a military-industrial complex, the USSR *is* a military-industrial complex"'.[20] They based this distinction on the contrast between the United States political structure, open to pressure from interests outside itself, civilian as well as defence-related, and the closed Soviet political structure from which independent civilian interests and values capable of resisting military-industrial pressures were excluded. They went on to say, however, that 'to consider the whole of the Soviet Union as a military-industrial complex is far too broad to be meaningful', a conclusion with which the present authors are certainly in agreement.

A more differentiated view was that of Vernon Aspaturian, who presented two alternative versions or 'prototypes', one weaker and the other stronger.[21] The weaker sense is that of the Soviet military-industrial complex as:

> a deliberate and symbiotic sharing of interests on the part of the military establishment, industry, and high-ranking political figures, whose collective influence is sufficient to shape decisions to accord with the interests of these groups at the expense of others in Soviet society.

A somewhat stronger interpretation would present the Soviet military-industrial complex as:

> an interlocking and interdependent structure of interests among military, industrial, and political figures, that enables or impels them to behave as a distinctive political actor separate from its individual components. A complex of this type . . . would exhibit a high degree of policy unity and act as a single input into the political system.

The second is stronger than the first because of the requirement that the influence of the military-industrial complex is exerted by its representatives acting in unison. In the first, weaker version, its influence arises from the sum of actions of the military, industrial, and political leaders acting separately, although deliberately. Aspaturian's own preference was for something 'much more than the first prototype and something less than the second'.

The post-Soviet Russian scholar Irina Bystrova would appear to agree with Aspaturian when she stresses that 'despite its traditional prioritisation, the [military-industrial complex] was hardly the "alpha and omega" of Soviet society'. In correspondence with his stronger prototype, however, she refers to the Soviet military-industrial complex as '*a powerful corporation which represented the common interests of social and political groups* connected with the provision of national security of the USSR: the professional soldiers, the defence industry sector, the party and state officials, and the representatives of the security agencies and scientific and technical circles'.[22] Her idea of the military-industrial complex as a corporate entity matches Aspaturian's hypothesis that it 'acted as a single input into the political system'. However, she limits the application of this concept to the post-Stalin period because Stalin's policy of 'divide and rule' prevented the emergence of a military-industrial complex before that time.[23]

We ourselves would reject Aspaturian's stronger version, and might accept his weaker one only with some qualifications. Some of these qualifications were suggested by Peter Almquist. He concurred with Aspaturian in the idea that shared interest must underlie the idea of a military-industrial complex:

> For a military-industrial complex to exist in a meaningful way, the military and its supporting industries must have, first, complementary interests. By this it is meant that one of the 'partners' generally benefits from the self-interested actions of the other...

As distinct from shared *interest*, however, Almquist suggested that shared *purpose* must be capable of independent and separate expression:

> Second, and equally important, both the military and the industry must have a means of influencing the political decision makers. In a military-industrial complex, a 'silent partner' is an irrelevant partner...[24]

Our research shows that, in the period which we have covered, the conditions for existence of a Soviet military-industrial complex proposed by both Aspaturian and Almquist were met only to some extent. First, the armed forces and defence industry certainly shared a common interest in increasing resources for military as opposed to civilian uses. However, when it came to practical decision making about resource allocation, there were different levels and stages to consider. At a very general, strategic level, a decision to allocate more resources to the armed forces carried the implication of more resources for defence industry, and conversely. Once decisions at this level had been taken, however (for example, over budgetary allocations), there was a large potential for conflict between soldiers and industrialists at the next level, since higher costs and less exacting standards implied more resources and an easier life for defence producers at the expense of resources for the military, while cheaper, better weapons could only be bought by means of direct pressure on the producers. The day-to-day correspondence between the supply and service departments within the defence-industry complex which we have seen speaks eloquently of the mutual tensions, frustrations, suspicions, and antagonisms generated by this relationship. Thus the interests of the two sides were complementary in part, but there was also an irreducible element of conflict.

Secondly, there is evidence of independent voice of the armed forces and of defence industry in the process of resource allocation; thus, neither was 'silent'. But were they partners? When they pressed for higher production and mobilisation targets, soldiers knew that more resources would be required for defence industry production and construction. But is there evidence of military-industrial collusion in pressing for more joint resources? This step in the argument remains unsupported by evidence. The voice of the armed forces was conspicuous only by its absence. Thus when M.G. Pervukhin, minister for the chemical industry, fought the planning chief N.A. Voznesenskii for more resources for the uranium industry after the Second World War, it was within a bureaucratic framework which excluded the military (the Special Committee appointed by Stalin to take charge of atomic weapons development had no armed forces representatives). When in the same period D.M. Ustinov, minister for armament, fought G.M. Popov, chief of Mossovet (the Moscow city administration), for factory space for jet and rocket armament, the dispute was settled by Stalin, not prcssure from the armed forces.[25]

To the extent that it was possible, each interest group, military and industrial, fought its own corner. Moreover, the extent of pressure which each could bring to bear was strictly constrained by the political system in which they operated. The interests of Soviet society were already strongly identified with military and defence-industry interests, but the concentration of decision making in the central party organs and the ubiquitous role of the party-state apparatus meant that military and defence-industry interests had little or no freedom of independent action. Civilian leaders from Stalin onwards retained complete authority through prewar rearmament, World War II, and postwar military confrontation and standoff. The political influence of outstanding soldiers was always tenuous, from Marshal M.N. Tukhachevskii (the Red Army chief of armament, executed by Stalin in 1937) to air force Marshal A.A. Novikov (imprisoned by Stalin in 1946) and Marshal G.K. Zhukov (sacked first by Stalin in 1946, then by Khrushchev in 1957). If any other branch of the state apparatus developed an organic relationship with the defence industry at this time, it was the security organs under the leadership of the civilian minister for internal affairs and deputy prime minister L.P. Beriia. Beriia, like Stalin's postwar commander of ground forces N.A. Bulganin, also possessed the military rank of Marshal, but neither was a professional military man. Beriia shared Stalin's distrust of the professional soldiers, even to the point where in the early 1950s he stood in the way of the armed forces' acquisition of the nuclear weapons developed under his own leadership at such cost in industrial resources (see Chapter 13).

These considerations do not conclusively refute the arguments for the emergence of a Soviet military-industrial complex, particularly in the last three decades of the Soviet state which are not covered by our research. But they do justify our decision to focus our historical investigations on the Soviet defence industry as such (see further Chapters 8, 9, and 10).

At the end of the day it makes sense to look back on the Soviet defence-industry complex as a distinct part of the economy, and not the whole, but not entirely separate from the other parts either. This complex consisted of the specialised defence producers, combined with the regulatory bodies to which they were subordinate, formed a distinct element in the Soviet political economy, weighty and influential to be sure – but not all-encompassing or all-determining, not really autonomous, and characterised by inner fault-lines as well as by unifying themes. The study of this defence-industry complex is therefore a particularly fascinating route to enlightenment as to the nature of the Soviet economy and society more generally. We hope that the reader will find the Soviet defence-industry complex further illuminated, if not fully, then at least in many aspects for the first time, in the chapters which follow.

NOTES

1 Daniel Landau, cited by Easterly and Fischer (1995), 347.
2 See Tupper (1984).
3 Harrison (1996), 241–7 (table F-5).
4 This basic principle was outlined by the head of the VSNKh chief administration of military industry P.I. Bogdanov and his assistant professor V.S. Mikhailov in a report 'On the organisation of military industry' to a joint session of Revvoensovet, Sovnarkom, and STO, 2 March 1924 (RGAE, 2097/1/64, 8–24).
5 As source to table 1.1.
6 The following account of ministerial reorganisation draws mainly upon Harrison (1985), 267–86, and Crowfoot and Harrison (1990).
7 Tupper (1984).
8 Harrison (1996), 81, 87.
9 RGAE, 4372/6/693, 161–2. The 1950 targets appear to have been somewhat undershot. By 1950 civilian output was accounting for only a quarter of Minaviaprom output (compared with the 40 per cent plan), which was back to the level of 1940. For Minvooruzheniia the share was 55 per cent compared with planned 60 per cent, and both were well above the 15 per cent 1940 level. RGAE, 4372/97/536, 29.
10 Gatrell (1994), 260–90.
11 For discussion of agency problems in the Soviet administrative setting, see Gregory (1990).
12 This type of conflict is emphasised by Almquist (1990), 126–7.
13 The Soviet defence ministry underwent several nominal transformations and reorganisations during the period under review. The People's Commissariat of Military and Naval Affairs (NKVM – *narodnyi komissariat voennykh i morskikh del*) was established on 23 November 1917, but between January 1918 and 12 November 1923 it was divided into two commissariats responsible separately one for military affairs (including aviation), the other for the navy. On 15 March 1934 NKVM was renamed the People's Commissariat of Defence (NKO – *narodnyi komissariat oborony*). On 30 December 1937 responsibility for the navy was again removed from NKO to a separate commissariat (NKVMF – *narodnyi komissariat voenno-morskogo flota*); this division was maintained until 25 February 1946 when a unified People's Commissariat of the Armed Forces (NKVS – *narodnyi komissariat vooruzhennykh sil*) was once more created. In March 1946, all the people's commissariats were renamed ministries (hence, MVS – *ministerstvo vooruzhennykh sil*). On 25 February 1950 the MVS was renamed the 'War

Ministry' (*voennoe ministerstvo*), and the navy was hived off for a third time to a new Navy Ministry (*voenno-morskoe ministerstvo*). A unified Ministry of Defence (MO – *ministerstvo oborony*), finally re-established on 15 March 1953, was then maintained without alteration of name or principal functions until 1991. See SVE (1978), vol. 5, 294–5 ('Ministerstvo oborony'). The Defence Minister through most of the interwar period was the long serving (1925–40) K.E. Voroshilov.

14 For a new listing of the numbered factories over the period of this study see Cooper, Dexter, and Harrison (1999).

15 On the problem of the postwar budgetary accounting for defence allocations see Jacobsen (1987).

16 RGAE, 1562/329/120, 37.

17 RGAE, 7297/38/91, 28.

18 RGAE, 7297/38/91, 66–8.

19 Thanks to Julian Cooper for making this point.

20 Agursky and Adomeit (1978), 6.

21 Aspaturian (1973), 103.

22 Bystrova (1997), 32, 35 (emphasis added).

23 Bystrova (1996), 4–5.

24 Almquist (1990), 12–13.

25 Bystrova (1996), 5, 6, 10.

Part II
The Formative Phase

2 The 'war scare' of 1927 and the birth of the defence-industry complex

N.S. Simonov

INTRODUCTION

The system of international relations formed in the 1920s on the basis of the Versailles peace treaty and the League of Nations protected the USSR – though none too reliably – from military confrontation with the West. The Soviet Union's security was also reinforced by its emergence from international political isolation through the establishment of diplomatic and consular relations with all the European countries, including those where the Russian White Guard emigration was based. Industrial and financial circles in the West were interested in penetrating the vast Russian market, and therefore turned a blind eye to the subversive activities of the Comintern which was giving moral and material encouragement to extremist political groups throughout the world, and to the calls emanating from Moscow for the international solidarity of the workers and a world proletarian revolution. It was not the communist character of the ruling political regime in the USSR (the West was almost reconciled to this and, recalling the French Revolution, was calmly awaiting the hour of the 'Russian Thermidor') but the Soviet government's attempts to interfere in the internal affairs of colonial and dependent countries that complicated the USSR's international position. A particular cause of irritation (primarily to Britain and Japan) was Soviet support for the national-democratic revolution in China.

As the Soviet economy, and hence its military-industrial capacity, recovered from the destruction of World War I and the Civil War, the West began to make efforts to strengthen the defence capability of the states bordering the Soviet Union, in order to remove any temptation for the Bolsheviks to repeat the autumn 1920 'Warsaw campaign'. Nor did the Soviet government's feverish preparations for armed intervention in support of the 'German socialist revolution' in October 1923 go unnoticed in the West. One way or another, in the mid-1920s there began to form a military-political bloc opposed to the Soviet Union – the so-called 'little Entente' (Poland, the Baltic states, Romania, and Finland). When, in the event of a border dispute or some other conflict, this bloc was supported by the 'large Entente' (Britain,

France, and the USA), the Soviet Union really found itself in an extraordinary military and political situation, greatly exacerbated by the growing probability of renewed civil war if there were a prolonged or unsuccessful external war.

Historians of international affairs have now shown convincingly that neither in the middle nor at the end of the 1920s was anybody preparing to attack the USSR.[1] Public opinion in the countries which had been the victors in World War I was generally pacifist. Under the terms of the Versailles peace treaty, Germany, where there was a strong revanchist mood, did not have armed forces capable of conducting an aggressive war. The Soviet Union's closest neighbours did not have strategic and operational plans co-ordinated at general staff level for a surprise attack and destruction of the 'first socialist state in the world'. Britain, with which the Conservative government was prepared to break off diplomatic relations in 1927, had no common land frontier with the USSR. The situation may have been a little more complicated in the Far East in the Chinese Eastern Railway (KVZhD) region, but the gathering armed conflict with Manchuria was strictly local in character.

The alarm of the party–state leadership in the USSR about an imminent large-scale foreign war had no foundation, therefore, in the military plans of potential aggressors and the possibilities perceived by them.[2] The war scare was perhaps amplified by the 'psychological trauma' connected with memories of the Red Army's defeat at Warsaw in 1920. It was also exaggerated and played upon for purposes of internal politics. At the same time the left opposition emphasised the dangers of the Soviet Union's isolation in order to attack the regime for its complacency, while the regime did the same in order to foster the image of the left opposition (and subsequently, too, the right deviation) as unpatriotic. To concentrate on these factors to the exclusion of others would, however, be a mistake. Without in the least underrating their significance, they should all the same be relegated to the second rank. The principal factors for the USSR party–state leadership in the matter of the growing threat of war were quite real: the state of the armed forces, the readiness of the economy for mobilisation, and the political mood of the peasantry which was the chief mass of the country's population.

Twenty years ago E.H. Carr wrote:

> Critical British and American writers commonly dismiss Soviet fears in the summer of 1927 of hostile action engineered by Great Britain not only as groundless (which they were), but as artificially worked up for internal purposes (which in this period they were not).

Subsequently a consensus emerged among western scholars, summed up by Robert C. Tucker in the view

> ...that the leaders' fears, however unjustified, were real and that they contributed to the determination to build Soviet military defences in a

hurry through the heavy-industry-oriented Five-Year Plan. At the same time the war danger was deliberately exaggerated in connection with the anti-Trotskyist campaign then in its culminating phase...

That these invocations served [Stalin's] interests in the contests against the Trotskyist and Bukharinist oppositions is certainly true. But they likewise expressed his political purpose. His foreign policy, it must be emphasised, was anything but warlike during those years and even after. Operating as he did on the assumption that a war was inevitable, it was Stalin's purpose to postpone it and make use of the time thus gained for creating a powerful Soviet heavy industry and war industry with all possible speed.[3]

In this chapter I examine these ideas in the new light cast by the formerly secret official analyses, evaluations, and decisions of the time.

THE RELATIONSHIP BETWEEN EXTERNAL AND INTERNAL THREATS

On 30 March 1925 M.V. Frunze, Chairman of the Revvoensovet (RVS) and People's Commissar for Military and Naval Affairs (NKVM), presented a report to the Politburo on the state of the Soviet armed forces in connection with the growing British military-political and military-economic influence in Poland, Romania, and the Baltic states.

His report drew attention to the poor material position of the Red Army, and its obsolete and outworn weaponry. First, beside the positive factor of the territorial system of armed forces recruitment (savings in the maintenance cost of army personnel, the number of which otherwise would have had to be reduced to 1.2 million men), the report noted deepseated shortcomings: poor preparation of the contingents called up, the 'peasant mood' among servicemen, the extended deadlines for general mobilisation, and so forth. Frunze proposed reducing the number of men in the USSR armed forces to 700 000, so that on this basis, in the event of war, an army of 2.5 million could be deployed more rapidly and less painfully – which would still be somewhat fewer in number than the army deployed by the USSR's nearest neighbours in the West. In order to carry out urgent measures to improve the material position of the Red Army and develop defence industry, Frunze asked the top party leadership to increase the war department's budget by 60 per cent from 412 million rubles in 1924/25 to 656 million rubles in 1925/26.[4]

The Soviet armed forces were not so weak, of course, that they could not perform the task of strategic deterrence of a probable opponent. On 1 January 1926 the RKKA (Red Army) had 70 infantry divisions, 22 reserve regular infantry divisions and 7 territorial infantry reserve regiments,

11 cavalry divisions and 8 cavalry brigades, numbering 610 000 men in all. For weapons it had 6987 guns of all calibres, 30 162 machine guns, 60 tanks, 99 armoured vehicles, 42 armoured trains and 694 combat aircraft. The Soviet naval forces in the Baltic consisted of 3 battleships, 2 cruisers, 8 destroyers, 9 submarines and 12 patrol boats. In the Black Sea there were 2 cruisers, 4 destroyers, 6 submarines and 21 patrol boats.[5]

For direct military resistance the Soviet armed forces were less powerful, since in this case the factor of mobilisation readiness (the speed of and time needed for mobilisation and deployment of the armed forces and defence industry) came into play. Assessing the state of Soviet defence readiness from this point of view, RKKA chief of staff M. Tukhachevskii had cause to state in his report to the Politburo on 26 December 1926: ‘Neither the Red Army nor the country is prepared for war. Our meagre material combat mobilisation stocks are scarcely sufficient for the first period of war. Thereafter our position will worsen (especially in conditions of blockade)’.[6] According to a NKVM requisition compiled for the event of war, in the first year of fighting 32 million shells and 3.25 billion rifle rounds would be required. If war broke out, however, the Red Army would receive only 29 per cent of its requirements for rifle rounds and 8.2 per cent of the shells it needed from Soviet defence industry as it then was. Moreover, when compiling this requisition the NKVM had started from extremely modest assumptions: that fighting would be conducted for not more than six months in the year and that rates of ammunition consumption would remain at the same level as in the last year of the Civil War.[7]

In the course of defining more precisely the military-industrial potential of the probable adversary, and establishing the country’s budgetary and resource possibilities, NKVM increased its demands for material and financial provision for its operational and mobilisation plans. On 5 April 1927 the Presidium of VSNKh reported:

> The production capacity which defence industry plants have at present does not at all match the volume of current mobilisation requirements of the war department [*Voenved*]. For most basic items of weaponry defence industry plants, even at full stretch, can cover only a certain portion of the requirements issued by the war department. In some cases this proportion is very low and amounts to only 10–15 per cent. For more than half the items the figure is not more than 50 per cent.[8]

The weakest link in the supply of NKVM requirements remained the production of ammunition and of complex military equipment (the tank and armoured vehicle and aviation industries were at an embryonic stage).

The low level of mobilisation readiness of military industry, however, was not the weakest point in the plans for defence preparation of the USSR. The party–state leadership could not fail to be concerned about the general condition of the rear, and especially the morale and the political mood of the population. If it found itself fighting a civil as well as an external war, for example, as a result of the inevitable return to requisitioning and confiscation in the countryside, this would mean a threat to the very existence of the communist regime. All private property owners, to whom the Soviet regime, even under NEP, denied the opportunity to prosper as well as they could otherwise have done, were potential enemies in such circumstances. And not only they. For a regime calling itself 'proletarian' the defeatist political mood in genuinely proletarian circles was discouraging enough. Thus, an OGPU summary dated 20 August 1927 gives the following highly revealing list of workers' negative opinions on the regime in the context of a forthcoming war:

> If there is war the workers won't go to it, because they are persuaded that Soviet power has [only] a 'seductive charm' and will itself try to start a war since it has no other way out.
>
> We are threatened by war because of communist propaganda abroad.
>
> Like many others I'm not going to defend. There aren't any more fools, we've defended enough and what did we get for it? Nothing. A worker now lives much worse than under the tsarist regime.
>
> Let those who are better off fight; it's all the same to us.
>
> Kill all the communists and Komsomol members who want a war.
>
> If there's a war we'll kill the administration first, then we'll fight.
>
> If you give us war we'll get weapons and make a second revolution.[9]

This list of opinions, of course, does not prove that there was no such thing as 'Soviet patriotism', since that is a quality defined in deeds, not words. Now for deeds: on 15 February 1927 the Information Department (Informotdel) of the OGPU reported to the party Central Committee:

> After publication of the speeches of comrades Voroshilov and Bukharin at the XV Moscow *guberniia* party conference in the press, rumours of an imminent war have spread amongst the urban and rural population in many regions of the Union. This has been the basis for development of a mood of panic in some localities amongst a section of the urban and rural population. In places people have tried to hoard basic necessities – salt, kerosene, flour etc. Sometimes particular shortages of some of the most common goods have been interpreted by the population as a sign of approaching war. Peasants in the border regions are trying to exchange Soviet money for gold. In places the gold 5–ruble coin is changing hands for 10 to 12 chervonets rubles. Cases are being noted where peasants refuse to sell grain and cattle for Soviet currency, as a result of which the supply of these goods to the market is being reduced.[10]

At the end of 1927 the position in the consumer market was increasingly difficult. Bundles of telegrams and reports came in to the centre from various regions of the country to the effect that 'residents have literally gone crazy and begun to clear not just bread products but everything – pasta, flour, salt, sugar, and so on – from the shelves of cooperative stores'.[11] 'The preparation of the population for war' coincided with the next twist in the inflationary spiral. The chervonets ruble, worth 55 prewar kopecks at the time of the currency reform in early 1924, had fallen to 40 kopecks on 1 January 1927 in terms of the Narkomfin Conjuncture Institute retail price index, and at the end of 1927...who knows, since the Conjuncture Institute was closed in 1928 as no longer necessary.[12]

In October–November 1927 informal rationing of some primary necessities was introduced in the country's industrial centres, which embittered the population still more. An OGPU Informotdel summary dated 29 October 1927 reported in particular:

> On grounds of the shortage of bread, persons of an anti-Soviet disposition are spreading rumours among the workers about the approach of war and the export of grain to repay debts, kindling discontent with the work of cooperative and Soviet organs, alleging that 'there is no flour because the communists don't know how to run the economy' (Iaroslavl' *guberniia*), that 'Soviet power and the party will drive the workers to revolt by their policies', and agitating for declaration of a general strike (Proletarka factory, Tver' *guberniia*). Great discontent among the workers is caused by the need to queue for bread. At the TsKR stall (Sormovo, Nizhegorod *guberniia*) queues form from the evening onwards. Because of the shortage of bread there have been cases of people not coming to work (Lugansk okrug), and cases of threats directed at the administration have been noted.[13]

In addition to the speculative demand, the shortage of bread products on the market in autumn and winter 1927 was also caused by poor supply from the countryside in comparison with previous years. The peasants evidently were also 'preparing for war', but to a still greater extent their refusal to sell grain reflected their dissatisfaction with low procurement prices and the high prices and shortage of industrial goods. From the point of view of the population's behaviour, the country was in a peculiar state of simulation of an external war, although not in fact at war. Moreover, by the spring of 1928 the growing bitterness of the struggle for grain in the countryside was damaging the morale of the Red Army, largely composed of recruits who were of rural origin and sympathy and who maintained correspondence with their families in the countryside.[14]

In the light of the obvious military and economic backwardness of the USSR, the growing economic crisis, and the social and political fragility of the ruling regime described above, the party–state leadership's alarm about the deteriorating international position of the country during 1927, the apotheosis of which was the breach in diplomatic relations with Great Britain, is understandable. 'War is inevitable', Zinov'ev declared on behalf of the United Opposition in July 1927; 'the probability of war was clear three years ago, but now one has to say *inevitability*'.[15]

These two words, 'probability' and 'inevitability', bandied about in various ways in both public and party circles in discussing the international situation, reflected the alarm of some at the USSR's lack of military and economic preparation to defend itself, and others' hope that war would resolve the contradictions of socialist construction in one country once and for all (i.e. that it would lead to world revolution and put an end to the remnants of capitalism within the country). The official party leadership headed by Stalin, however, resolutely rejected both defeatism and communist militarism. 'War is inevitable', Stalin said in July 1927, 'of that there can be no doubt. But does that mean that it cannot be put off even for a few years? No, it does not. Hence the task is to put off war against the USSR either to the time when the revolution is ripe in the West or until imperialism suffers more powerful blows from the colonial countries (China, India)'.[16]

'THE PREPARATORY PERIOD FOR WAR'

With hindsight, Stalin, Zinov'ev, and others like them could be criticised for lack of perspicacity (there was no war against the USSR at the end of the 1920s) or even accused of using the 'war alarm' factor in the political interests of their own struggle for power. But that is not important. What is important is what the people invested with power did to 'strengthen the defence of the land of Soviets'. There is every reason to maintain that, in fact, from 1928 the party and government led the country into 'a period of preparation for war'. What this means had been explained clearly enough to the Politburo by Frunze in May 1925:

> Preparation for rapid and planned transition by the country and its armed forces from a state of peace to war is one of the most complicated and responsible tasks facing the guiding apparatus of the country and the army. Whichever of the warring sides deals with this task better will gain enormous advantages over the side which lags behind. This explains the efforts of general staffs in all countries to reduce the time needed for mobilisation and deployment of the armed forces in war readiness as much as possible.
>
> Before World War I, in a number of European states these efforts took the form of carrying out a number of highly significant mobilisation measures even before the factual announcement of mobilisation.

> The idea of establishing a special preparatory period has proved fully justified.
>
> Timely and gradual conduct of preparatory measures for war facilitates the maintenance of secrecy while carrying out mobilisation work, and does not disrupt the normal work of the state apparatus. A sudden transition to work on preparation for war, on the other hand, as there was in the autumn of 1923, has results of only dubious value, giving the likely adversary a clear picture of what is going on.
>
> Everything said above applies not only to the armed forces but also the country as a whole.[17]

Also in 1925, the NKVM had drawn up a draft 'law on the preparatory period for war' dividing the period into two stages: first, from the time when international relations began to become more complicated to the time when the possibility of armed conflict became clear; and second, from the time when the possibility of armed conflict became clear to the announcement of mobilisation.[18] On the basis that the first stage of the preparatory period for war had already started, the Politburo, in a decree of 27 June 1927, charged A.I. Rykov with

> raising the question at closed sessions of USSR and RSFSR Sovnarkom of immediate preparation within the people's commissariats (each in its own sphere) of measures to reinforce the country's defence and of measures to accelerate the pace of all work and to eliminate the most serious shortcomings, especially intolerable in present circumstances.[19]

The state organ directing and co-ordinating mobilisation work was the Council for Labour and Defence (STO) and its 'business sessions' (*Raspor-iaditel'nye Zasedaniia* – RZ STO). The basic working apparatus of RZ STO, according to a decree of 25 June 1927, was provided by Revvoensovet (RVS) and USSR Gosplan.[20]

These organs were given extraordinary tasks as well as their usual ones. Thus RVS was responsible for drawing up a plan for the conduct of war, preparing assignments for all people's commissariats to ensure mobilisation of the Red Army, and co-ordinating and collating the mobilisation plans of commissariats responsible for both administration (internal affairs, justice, foreign affairs, health, and education) and the economy (industry, transport, trade, finance, postal and telegraphic services, labour, and agriculture). USSR Gosplan was responsible for co-ordinating perspective plans for development of the Soviet armed forces with the general perspective plan for economic development, for working out control figures for the evolution of the economy in the event of war, and for co-ordinating and collating (jointly with RVS and NKVM) the mobilisation plans of individual commissariats into a unified mobilisation plan for the whole USSR.[21]

At the end of 1927 the people's commissariats were ordered to set up mobilisation departments or mobilisation bureaux as part of their structure. Personal responsibility for this work was placed directly on the people's commissars. In republics, *kraia* (territories), and *oblasti* (regions), mobilisation administrations and departments were created in the government apparatus of Union republics, and in krai, oblast', and even some *raion* (neighbourhood) authorities. By 1931 the total number of staff employed in mobilisation organs at the centre and locally was 31 858.[22]

In July–August 1927 the commissariat leaderships reported to RZ STO on their plans for carrying out the mobilisation work. In transport it meant increasing the carrying capacity of the railways, preparing designs for construction of strategic main lines, and checking personnel (jointly with the OGPU security agency) and dismissing politically unreliable staff.[23] In trade it meant creation of a state food fund to guarantee the mobilisation requirements of the Red Army and supplies for major urban centres, as well as stocks of agricultural raw materials and imported goods 'to cover the needs of industry as a whole during a year of war'.[24] For postal and telegraphic services it meant drawing up plans for transmission of telegrams reporting on mobilisation, the construction of strategic telephone and telegraph lines and operational communications centres, organisation of a field postal service, and creation of stocks of line equipment.[25] In finance it meant taking financial and organisational measures to ensure that systems of state defence could be put into operation without interruption.[26] For foreign trade it meant the organisation of underground channels for foreign communications.[27] The necessity and expediency of mobilisation work were recognised even in such parts of the state apparatus as the trusts and administrations for edible fats, flax, cattle, sheep, and seeds under the commissariat of agriculture, furs and exportable fruits under the commissariat of foreign trade, and the dairy, edible fat, and fishery cooperatives under the commissariat of supply.

DEFENCE INTERESTS IN THE FIRST FIVE-YEAR PLAN

In 1928–9, despite the improvement in the international situation, mobilisation work did not slacken. NKVM completed preparation of a five-year plan for building up the armed forces and a five-year programme of orders for armaments and peacetime supplies. The final version of the latter is shown in table 2.1.

This programme proved unrealistic and in practice was scarcely half fulfilled by Soviet industry.[28] However, the rush to try to fulfill it meant loss of the planning perspective that seemed to have been found at the end of 1927 after the colossal labours of compiling the first five-year plan for economic development. It would be wrong to think that defence requirements were not

Table 2.1. NKVM five-year programme of orders, 1929/30–33

	1929/30	*1930/31*	*1932*	*1933*
Artillery (units)	999	3577	8017	4870
of which, small calibre	–	1546	5375	2720
medium calibre (76–152mm)	987	1965	2492	2074
large calibre (over 152mm)	12	66	150	76
Mortars	–	500	–	–
Artillery shells (thousands)	2365	1690	7297	5016
Aerial bombs (thousands)	220	460	300	314
Rifles (thousands)	150	305	385	375
Machine guns	26500	49500	75800	61650
Rifle rounds (million)	251	410	666	800
Aircraft	1232	2024	3496	3332
Tanks	340	1288	3400	7000

Source: GARF, 8418/25/14, 2–3 (28 April 1941).

adequately taken into account in the first five-year economic development plan confirmed by the government. The total expenditure on defence in the plan, allocated to maintenance of the army and development of defence industry, amounted to 6415 million rubles.[29] The share of defence industry's requirements in the total volume of industrial production in the final year of the five-year plan was to be 36.2 per cent for rolled metals and 52.4 per cent for sulphuric acid, although only 12 per cent for cotton. Proportions were much less favourable to defence requirements, however, if we consider potential mobilisation needs rather than planned peacetime production. The plan guaranteed only half the mobilisation requirement for high-grade and alloy steels, and one third that of non-ferrous metals.[30] The NKVM leadership saw such discrepancies as undermining the country's defence capacity, because there were not just one but two plans for building up the armed forces, the peacetime plan and the mobilisation plan; it continually substituted the latter for the former in an attempt to get VSNKh to develop capacity in accordance with the mobilisation plan rather than the peacetime plan. VSNKh found itself in a ridiculous position. It had to plan a capacity reserve for potential war production at the expense of capacity for the actual production consumer goods, while it also bore responsibility for the quantity and quality of the latter.

The apogee of the bureaucratic struggle between NKVM (for the army) and VSNKh (for industry) was the preparation and confirmation of the S30 mobilisation plan. VSNKh proposed the following figures for deliveries: 2.2 billion rifle rounds, and 11 million artillery shells of all calibres. NKVM angrily objected that the quantity of military production planned by VSNKh was even lower than had been received from the factories of tsarist Russia in

1915. As the basis of the S30 mobilisation plan NKVM proposed the following figures: 'to give the army, during the first year of war, 19 million shells, 3 billion rifle rounds, and 53 500 machine guns'.[31] The presidium of VSNKh had to give way and thus recognise unwillingly that a decisive condition for fulfilment of the first five-year plan was not going to be balanced development of the various sectors of the economy, but complete disregard of its original parameters for the sake of satisfying the ambitions of the nascent Soviet military-bureaucratic imperialism. Later, in 1932, in order to conceal this general bias of the country's industry towards military production, the Politburo issued a top-secret decree to the effect that information on all the basic indicators relating to military industry should be hidden in the general totals for all Soviet industry (the role of secrecy is discussed further in Chapter 1).[32]

On 15 July 1929 the Politburo adopted a most portentous decree 'On the condition of defence of the USSR' which, first, summed up two years of work by the state apparatus in conditions of *de facto* (if officially unannounced) preparation for war; and, secondly, set out the prospects for further development of the armed forces and defence industry (see also Chapter 3). The Politburo noted (a) that the technical basis of the armed forces was still very weak and far behind that of contemporary 'bourgeois' armies, (b) that material provision for mobilising the army was still far from satisfactory under the current mobilisation plan, (c) that material reserves for defence were completely inadequate, and (d) that the level of readiness of industry as a whole, including military industry, to meet the requirements of a military confrontation was completely unsatisfactory. The presidium of VSNKh was accused of deficiencies in its work as follows:

> There are still no plans for the mobilisation of industry for war. The deadlines which do exist for deployment of some production lines are exceedingly long and in no way satisfy the army's requirements. There is no plan for supplying industry when mobilised with equipment and labour. Within industry a series of sharp discrepancies remains between defence requirements and production capacities. The existing technical personnel in all industry, and especially in defence industry, are completely failing to ensure that the Red Army's requirements for equipment are satisfied in the design and implementation of new types of weapons. These negative phenomena in defence industry in the recent period have been aggravated by long-term and systematic wrecking on the part of the old specialists.[33]

The Politburo approved the five-year plan for building up the armed forces drawn up by NKVM and recognised as correct its basic principles: to have no fewer men than the likely adversary in the main theatre of war, and to be superior to the enemy in the two or three decisive types of weapon – artillery, aircraft, and tanks. In accordance with this doctrine the Politburo set the size of the fully mobilised army at the end of the five-year plan at 3 million men.

The number of combat aircraft for the army was to be 3000, with 3000 tanks, 3579 light cannon, 798 heavy cannon, 1218 medium-calibre anti-aircraft guns, 712 small-calibre anti-aircraft guns, and 120 big guns. The RKKA was also to have no less than 150 000–180 000 motor vehicles and the necessary quantity of tractors.[34]

The Politburo allowed RZ STO to set the size of allocations for the country's defence not lower than the level of the optimal variant of the first five-year plan, and in case of necessity in excess of these levels. Beside this, the Politburo proposed that the government should speed up the pace of construction in the first three years of the five-year plan in all sectors of military significance. The decree also especially noted the necessity of creating material reserves for defence: a two months' food stock for the Red Army 'for the mobilisation period and the first period of war', reserves of fuel, regularly renewed stocks of agricultural raw materials, and stocks of imported goods.[35]

INDUSTRIAL MOBILISATION AND 'BUILDING SOCIALISM'

Such urgent and extensive preparations for war by the Soviet party-state leadership (which naturally were kept as secret as possible and the full extent of which was known only at the very top) cannot fail to prompt the thought that there is a direct link between them and the mass collectivisation which started in the countryside at the end of 1929. The collectivisation of peasant agriculture, in terms of its compressed timescale and cruel methods, fits exactly into the framework of the 'preparatory period for war'. It is no accident that, in a note of 5 April 1929 analysing the degree to which defence interests were being taken into account in the five-year economic development plan, the defence sector of USSR Gosplan observed:

> In the plan for the development of agriculture the major factor of importance for defence is significant growth in the socialised sector. There can be no doubt that in wartime conditions, when it is especially important to retain the capacity for control, the socialised sector will be of paramount importance. No less important is the existence of large production units, which are more easily subject to planned influence than many millions of small scattered farms. The proportion of marketed production of grain supplied by the socialised sector at the end of the five-year plan will amount to 39 per cent, which is equivalent to the full annual requirements of the Red Army in time of war.[36]

Thus the 1927 war alarm was far from in vain. It demonstrated the weakness of the party-state *nomenklatura* regime ruling the USSR from both a military and a social and political point of view. From this weakness, which it fully recognised, the ruling regime drew the appropriate conclusions for itself, namely, that the country's military and economic backwardness were liable to undermine the regime's authority through international complications, that with the slightest threat of growing into a major war these international complications would reveal serious internal problems, and that the latter would arise above all in the area of relations between the authorities and the peasantry, which made up the backbone of the mobilized army. On the basis of these conclusions the Soviet party-state leadership took a fundamental decision to eliminate the country's military and economic backwardness in the shortest possible time, and for this purpose to switch the administrative apparatus to the conditions of the 'preparatory period for war'. This meant special discipline and responsibility, and absolute loyalty and devotion to higher levels on the part of lower ones, and, finally, made it possible to use methods of military mobilisation to direct the redistribution of the human, material, and financial resources required at every stage, even at the cost of disrupting balanced planning.

NOTES

1 Nezhinskii (1990).
2 The possibility of a renewed commercial blockade inspired by Britain was, however, taken seriously in Berlin as well as in Moscow. See Carr (1976), vol. 3, 9n. But this was far from an immediate military threat.
3 Tucker (1977), 566–7, 568; see also Sontag (1975).
4 GARF, 8418/16/1, 24–33. Frunze's request was only met in part, actual nominal outlays on defence rising to 638 million rubles (Davies 1958: 83).
5 GARF, 8418/16/3, 434.
6 GARF, 8418/16/3, 435.
7 GARF, 8418/16/3, 432.
8 GARF, 8418/1/13, 71.
9 RTsKhIDNI, 17/85/213, 10–11.
10 RTsKhIDNI, 17/85/159, 158–159.
11 RTsKhIDNI, 17/2/317 (v–11), 8.
12 For nominal and real values of chervonets rubles in circulation in 1923–4 see Davies (1958), 53.
13 RTsKhIDNI, 17/85/147, 2.
14 See reports of that time in *Krasnaia zvezda*, cited by Carr (1971), vol. 2, 349.
15 RTsKhIDNI, 17/2/317 (v–1), 45.
16 RTsKhIDNI, 17/2/317 (v–1), 123.
17 GARF, 8418/16/1, 82–84.
18 GARF, 8418/16/1, 82–84.
19 RTsKhIDNI, 17/162/5, 52–53.
20 GARF, 8418/8/157, 95–96.
21 GARF, 8418/5/86, 43.

22 GARF, 8418/1/76, 3–4.
23 GARF, 8418/1/76, 6–9.
24 GARF, 8418/1/76, 22–29.
25 GARF, 8418/1/76, 10–18.
26 GARF, 8418/1/76, 2.
27 GARF, 8418/5/86, 43.
28 GARF, 8418/25/14, 2–3.
29 GARF, 8418/3/52, 20.
30 GARF, 8418/3/52, 9–12.
31 RGVA, 40442/1/38, 73–74.
32 RGAE, 1562/329/120, 37. In a 1935 memorandum to a Sovnarkom committee, Osinskii referred to this decree, adopted on 8 January 1932, and explained that, in accordance with it, 'all data on the work of industry, both in information published by Narkomtiazhprom and by TsUNKhU, will contain information on military industry'.
33 RTsKhIDNI, 17/162/7, 102–103.
34 RTsKhIDNI, 17/162/7, 107–109.
35 RTsKhIDNI, 17/162/7, 111–112.
36 GARF, 8418/3/52, 17–19.

3 The Red Army and economic planning, 1925–40

Lennart Samuelson

INTRODUCTION

From the early 1930s a central goal of Soviet forced industrialisation was to create the foundations of a modern armaments industry. Thanks to its new heavy industry and machine-building sectors, by 1941 the Soviet leadership could withstand armed attack even by the much more industrialised Germany. The general framework of Soviet economic planning in the 1930s has been analysed, as well as its war economy in 1941–5.[1] There also exists a specialised literature on the Soviet art of war in the interwar period.[2] However, until the archives opened in the 1990s it was impossible for western (and most Soviet) scholars to do empirical research on related themes.[3] Now that it is possible to study Soviet defence industry plans and programmes at least for the period up to the Second World War, how does this evidence add to our knowledge of the driving forces behind the rearmament and different phases of the Soviet military build-up? What patterns of interaction between the military and political leadership can be discerned in the planning process? How did external threat assessments influence economic planning for war?

A wide range of plans for every year between 1926 and 1941 has been mentioned in Soviet military histories, which tend to present an image of smooth co-ordination between the start of the plan era and the technological reconstruction of the armed forces.[4] However, none of the defence plans were published at the time. Until recently it was a matter of speculation whether there existed a special defence-industry five-year plan, since the published five-year plan for 1928/29 to 1932/33 did not contain any precise figures for weapons production. Thanks to pathbreaking research there is now a better understanding of the structure, size, and development of the defence budget during the initial five-year plans.[5]

In this chapter I will describe how the outlook, threat perceptions, and doctrines of the Soviet military changed from the mid-1920s to the late 1930s. By 1925 the military leadership had initiated a reform of the armed forces and the central apparatus. At the same time, the economy was coming to the end of its postwar recovery period, and the fourteenth party congress in December 1925 proclaimed industrialisation as a priority goal. Further, the military's call for a central agency responsible for the complex of military and civilian planning is analysed. Finally, I introduce as an important parameter the long-term goals of the military – their requirement of essential armaments in case of war (*mobilizatsionnaia zaiavka*, or *mobzaiavka* for short). The aspirations of the Soviet military are exemplified by Mikhail Tukhachevskii (1893–1937), one of the most energetic and farsighted thinkers of the time. Tukhachevskii, Chief of the General Staff (1925–8) and Chief of Armaments (1931–6), was as concerned for the current performance of Soviet industry as he was for its ability to fulfil targets for wartime capacity.[6]

ECONOMIC MOBILISATION: THE HISTORICAL CONTEXT

Historians have tended to neglect the 'paper planning' for war carried out in the 1920s and 1930s, on the grounds that in most if not all cases the actual wartime industrial mobilisation bore little resemblance to the prewar plans. Thus the defeat of France in 1940 was attributed in part to deficient economic preparations. The same holds true to a certain extent for the United States, where the actual industrial mobilisation after Pearl Harbor made only partial use of the plans drafted by the military in the preceding years.[7]

World War I had also evolved quite differently from the war plans drawn up beforehand. The main cause of the failure of the prewar mobilisation and military plans, not only Tsarist but also German, Austrian, and French, was incorrect assumptions by the General Staffs concerning the duration and intensity of a modern great war. The ammunition supply norms and mobilisation calculations of the period from 1890 to World War I, as well as the demands placed on defence industry in general, were designed to maintain only the mobilisation reserves required for short wars. During the decades preceding World War I, the Russian military had developed a system of mobilisation reserves. These reserves were exhausted by early 1915, while the current production of existing armaments factories proved insufficient. As in other belligerent countries, Tsarist Russia had to mobilise the machine-building and other sectors to supply its armed forces. After World War I, it was accepted that future wars would depend on industry in a much more profound sense than was understood before 1914.

Lenin's admiration of the German war economy of 1914–18 is well known. However, among military economists of the 1920s the contemporary French and American efforts to create a permanent mobilisation organisation were perhaps even more influential. Soviet ideas about preparing the economy for war were not specific to or even originated by the Bolsheviks. They were very much an attempt to 'catch up' with French, British, and American progress in the 1920s. In the mid-1920s, Soviet military periodicals devoted special sections to issues of what was called 'industrial mobilisation', 'state defence', or 'economic preparedness for war'. There were many references to western experience. Already in the late 1920s, before the Nazi takeover in Germany, contemporary Soviet observers pointed to the 'militarisation' of western societies and economies, meaning both traditional rearmament and the involvement of new types of paramilitary troops.[8] The evolution of industrial and economic mobilisation in the West was regularly followed by the Soviet periodical press, notably in the open journals *Voina i revoliutsiia* and *Voina i tekhnika*, as well as in secret bulletins like *Mobilizatsionnyi sbornik* which was circulated by Military Intelligence.[9] During 1930–2, the responsible Soviet officials would even follow courses in Germany, where the techniques of secretly mobilising the industrial resources of the nation were most highly developed.[10]

The Soviet practice of mobilisation evolved swiftly from 1927 onwards. Mobilisation departments were set up in most of the people's commissariats (industry, agriculture, foreign and internal trade, labour, etc.). Conferences were held regularly on the division of tasks between the commissariats, the planning organs and the military. Subsequently, the mobilisation network was extended to mobilisation departments in enterprises. Already in the early 1930s, the mobilisation network in administrative and production units comprised tens of thousands of workers. From 1929 onwards, the central authority called for trial mobilisations at factory level. By ordering a certain number of plants in a town or region to switch to three-shift and full capacity working, the administration could more easily determine which bottlenecks would arise when a whole region or sector worked at the planned mobilisation levels.

WAR PLANS AND DOCTRINES IN THE LATE 1920S

The decisions of the fourteenth party congress in December 1925 stressed industrialisation. This was heralded by Mikhail Tukhachevskii, then Chief of Staff of the Red Army, as a new starting point for considering the forms of future wars. In 1926–7, the Staff formulated its first war plans since the Civil War. Tukhachevskii's 'Report on defence' summed up the pessimistic conclusions:

> At present, neither the USSR nor the Red Army is ready for war.... A successful defence of our country is possible only if we disrupt the force concentration (*rasstanovka sil*) of our enemies during the initial period... Only after several years of successful industrialisation will our capacity for a protracted war increase.[11]

Tukhachevskii commissioned economists like S.G. Strumilin and L. Kritsman to analyse the interdependence of military and economic plans. He further commissioned several Army Staff Directorates to investigate the probable forms of future conflicts.

A bulky report under the title 'The future war' was presented in 1928. The authors included Tukhachevskii himself and three prominent military intelligence officers. This report essentially provided a platform for the further modernisation of the Red Army. Through an analysis of demographic and economic development in the neighbour states of Soviet Russia, as well as surveys of major technical changes in general, the report outlined a series of possible particular applications of new weapons and probable new forms of battle. In subsequent years the Soviet military would incorporate these new perspectives in their doctrines of 'deep battle' (*glubokii boi*) and 'deep operations' (*glubokaia operatsiia*).

In essence, Tukhachevskii aimed to avoid a static war of position in the future. He argued against those in the Red Army who tended to rely on Russian Civil War experiences, expecting a future war to be won by swift cavalry operations thanks to 'revolutionary spirit'. The coming war would most likely be protracted, with both mobile and more stationary phases. While not denying the factor of morale, Tukhachevskii opted for a consecutive mechanisation, motorisation and general modernisation of the armed forces.[12]

The conclusions of 'The future war' of 1928 were more comforting than of the first war plans two years earlier. With regard to the actual capability of the neighbouring states, estimates showed their organisation and mobilisation strength to be lower than their theoretical potential. Their industries and economies would probably be able to supply less than fifty per cent of the items necessary in wartime. The USSR would have superiority in manpower and economic resources; however, the armed strengths of the opposed forces would be approximately equal during the first month of war. This 'excludes the chance of speedily crushing all our western neighbours'.[13]

'The future war' concluded that the most decisive results of an operation could be achieved by action on the enemy's flank and rear by encirclement. The Intelligence experts of the Red Army concluded: 'The existing means and organisation of our western neighbouring armies, as well as the resources of the Red Army, can by no means guarantee our success in such operations.'[14] Therefore, if the Red Army was to be able to undertake decisive operations, it must receive appropriate equipment and education. For the probable theatres of war, the Red Army would need:

1 motorised infantry machine-gun units, reinforced with large tank units equipped with fast moving tanks and motorised artillery
2 large cavalry units, which must be strengthened with armoured forces (armoured cars, fast-moving tanks) and firepower (the greatest possible saturation with automatic weapons)
3 large-scale air assault units.[15]

However, the authors of 'The future war' did not specify any numbers for the required strength of these forces. This was perhaps logical given that in

1927/28 no Soviet industry yet existed that could handle large-scale tank-building. Furthermore, tank forces were seen largely as reinforcing the infantry and cavalry.

As the Soviet economy approached prewar production levels, that is, by 1927/28, plans for future expansion were successively revised. Tukhachevskii expected that industrialisation would soon permit the Red Army to wage a war with huge amounts of artillery, chemical weapons and motorised troops. V.K. Triandafillov, I.A. Khalepskii, Ia.A. Alksnis, and others produced a series of books and articles on high speed operations with mechanised forces, airborne assaults, and infantry movements supported by tanks. Consequently strategic, organisational and mobilisation concepts for a new kind of warfare had to be elaborated.

The Red Army's perception of the likely scale of a war in the late 1920s is shown in table 3.1. The opposing coalition was perceived as the Soviet Union's immediate neighbours – Poland, Romania, the Baltic States and Finland. The unknown factor was eventual support from major European states like France or Britain. While the balance of military equipment was updated regularly, the number of divisions (approximately 100) was a relatively stable factor in Soviet war plans until 1933. Through concentrated actions of the Red Army, small countries such as Estonia and Latvia could be crushed and sovietised within the first few months of war. Even under the most favourable conditions, however, assuming no west European assistance, it would still take half a year to subdue Poland. A protracted war against Poland would eventually drain the latter country's limited human resources, but that could take up to three years. The sovietisation of Romania was to be undertaken only after victory over Poland.

Tukhachevskii and the other authors of 'The future war' expected five to ten years to pass before the Soviet Union would have enough resources to equip

Table 3.1. A Soviet estimate of the military balance: the Soviet Union versus a coalition of likely adversaries, 1928 (units)

	Likely adversary coalition	*Red Army*
	(1)	(2)
Infantry divisions	109	100
Aircraft	1 190	1 046
Tanks	401	90
Guns	5 620	7 034
Military personnel	3 100 000	2 660 000

Source: RGAE, 4372/91/213, 109 (report by a Government commission chaired by Defence Commissar Voroshilov on the five-year plan, April–May 1928). The coalition of likely adversaries was defined as Poland, Romania, the Baltic States, and Finland.

its army and air force for a mobile campaign against a country like Poland. In 1927, therefore, the Red Army had to plan for a war of exhaustion (*istoshchenie*), a protracted war with some highly mobile periods of manoeuvre combined with trench warfare on parts of the front and stationary intervals between operations. RKKA training had to include offensive as well as defensive operations. In this respect, the advocates of 'deep operations' came close to the reasoning of General Alexander Svechin (1878–1938) and others who advocated a strictly defensive doctrine for the Soviet armed forces. Svechin expressed deep scepticism about plans for Soviet industry to catch up with western technology even over a period of 15 years. After a series of sharp debates in 1930–1, Svechin was manoeuvred out of influential positions. Thereafter, Soviet industry would provide the material basis for a mass army with armour, chemical weapons and aircraft step by step and on a grand scale.

While the international tensions of 1927 (the 'war scare') produced a crisis situation in Soviet society at large, the military authorities did not have an immediate war danger to cope with.[16] On several occasions in 1927 Tukhachevskii explicitly rejected the idea that a conflict was imminent. For example, in a letter to Trade Commissar Anastas Mikoian in June 1927 he stated:

> The Red Army proceeds precisely from the assumption that war is unlikely during the next five years. If we assumed conversely that war was likely before that date, it would not make sense to work on a five-year plan which the war would in any case interrupt.[17]

But it was still central to their Bolshevik ideology that the capitalist world would eventually launch a war to liquidate the socialist state. Most military documents from these years do indeed refer to a forthcoming war between capitalism and the Soviet Union as 'inevitable'. An Army Staff review of Gosplan's drafts for 1927/28 likewise referred to an 'inevitable military collision' (*neizbezhnoe voennoe stolknovenie*), and therefore emphasised:

> The five-year plan must become a plan for the economy in the circumstances of a prewar situation (*predvoennaia kon"iunktura*).[18]

The time horizon outlined by the military for the planners is captured well in another report by NKVM on a Gosplan proposal from 1927. The military criticised the lack of adequate defence considerations and necessary structural changes in the economy with respect to the 'inevitable armed confrontation between the USSR and the capitalist world'. In this report to Gosplan NKVM stated, however, that they assumed the Soviet Union would not have to fight a war before 1931/32.

> It is obvious that we can hardly . . . count on a second five-year period of peace, and, consequently, if a war erupts in 1932–4 the following reflections will turn out to be true.[19]

Long-term planning thus relied explicitly on the assumption that at least five years of uninterrupted economic development lay ahead. Military resources had to be accumulated until industrialisation had been completed. The backward economic situation called for huge mobilisation reserves to withstand an (as yet unlikely) coalition attack. They should be sufficient eventually to allow the crushing of states such as Poland in a more distant future. The goal of operations was to establish Soviet regimes in the defeated countries. A technically backward Soviet Union could not successfully launch such a war. The Soviet war plans and discussion in 'The future war' of 1928 already implied a 'Blitzkrieg' concept, although differing in several key elements from the later German doctrine. This overall task was a long-term underlying preoccupation of the Red Army. The new strategic thinking involved, first, new equipment and increased mobilisation capacity from a brand new defence industry, and, second, the formulation of new doctrines for offensive action.

THE DEFENCE SECTOR OF USSR GOSPLAN

Military theoreticians and military economists argued that, just as Gosplan handled plans for peacetime construction, a distinct organisation should draw up plans for a war economy.[20] A major problem for the military authorities during the 1920s in formulating defence considerations for a five-year plan was uncertainty. It was impossible to 'plan the war' or even to predict when it would most probably break out. Consequently the planners should take the five-year plan as their framework and determine the best use of newly created production facilities for armament production. Since the war would be protracted, the maximum level of war production and the minimum necessary level of civilian production must be calculated simultaneously; to avoid a collapse of machine-building and metallurgy for essential productive and transport needs, alternative plans for the overall wartime allocation of resources were required. The combined requirements of defence could best be understood, if an 'economic plan of the war' (*khoziastvennyi plan voiny*) and a special plan for the first year of war (*plan na pervyi god voiny*) were developed together.

Organisational problems of the defence industries were a major concern for Chief of Staff Tukhachevskii. Defence policy was being discussed in various bodies – first, in the military organs and the Politburo; second, in the Interdepartmental Mobilisation Committee (*Mezhduvedomstvennaia Mobilizatsionnaia Komissia*); finally, in the government, the Council of Labour and Defence (*STO*).[21] On 20 February 1927, Tukhachevskii called for the formation of a new supreme defence authority, which would replace some of the above-mentioned organisations.

In a subsequent report, Tukhachevskii stated that strictly centralised control through Gosplan's defence sector was necessary because of the isolation in which the Soviet Union would most likely find itself in case of war. 'Bourgeois states' supposedly could switch their heavy and machine-building industry to military production. Foreign trade could contribute to the supply of consumer goods. The Soviet Union, however, would have few foreign states to rely on. Since a war would probably come swiftly, this eventuality must be planned for in advance. Because there would be no time for 'improvisations', Tukhachevskii proposed that the defence sector should be divided into four sections according to their tasks: [22]

1st section	Formulation of wartime alternatives to general economic plans
2nd bureau	Operational section: preparation for regulation of the economy during mobilisation and its organisation according to mobilisation plans
3rd section	Peacetime economic development (*rekonstruktsiia*) taking into account defence considerations
4th section	Scientific secretariat: research on preparation of the economy for war and on the wartime economy

The main task of an authority responsible for defence-economic preparations would be to study current economic processes, as well as operational plans and their fulfilment. The contingency plan for war should be so flexible that it could come into operation at any time of the year, and be capable of adjustment in the light of changing military demands. Tukhachevskii argued that a special planning organ was necessary to account for defence needs in peacetime, and to prepare the direction of the economy in wartime:

> [Any] significant peacetime disproportion in our economy will inevitably increase in wartime. This requires us to influence the development of the economy so that 'bottlenecks' which weaken our defence capability disappear in the process of economic restructuring and thus create a favourable economic environment for waging war.[23]

Gosplan's Military Commission was guided by a RZ STO resolution of 4 May 1927 (RZ were the *Rasporiaditel'nye Zasedaniia* or 'business sessions' of STO, the Council for Labour and Defence). VSNKh had responsibility for the mobilisation of Soviet industry as a whole. All appointments to mobilisation organs in the people's commissariats were to be made in agreement with the military, and were to be selected from the officers corps of the Red Army.[24] RZ STO had left open whether the Military Commission was to become a permanent body of Gosplan or not. Tukhachevskii proposed, as mentioned, that a defence sector be established within the Gosplan framework.[25] He then went on to plead for a central role for the military in this planning authority:

> Since Gosplan's defence sector determines the general direction and development of the economy in regard to defence interests, *the leadership of this sector must obviously be carried out by the Red Army Chief of Staff*, who shall also be a member of the Gosplan Presidium.[26]

This paved the way to the establishment of a specialised defence sector with Gosplan on 25 June 1927, although not under Tukachevskii's leadership.[27]

Gosplan as a whole, with the participation of all of its sectors and subsectors, drafted long-term plans for the economy. Gosplan's defence sector prepared plans for defence industry, military transport and other defence-related activities. The Defence Commissariat and the operational administration of the RKKA Staff formulated the war plan (*plan voiny)*, the armed forces' operational plan in case of war. The pre-1941 war plans have been available to Soviet historians, so their general character is known.

The economic defence plan (*khoziaistvennyi plan oborony*) was formulated jointly by the RKKA Staff and Gosplan's defence sector. In May 1928, the first 'control figures for the economy during the first period of war' were finally transmitted to just five persons in key positions, under instruction to be kept as secret as the military war plan.[28] In 1928 and 1929, 'plans for the first year of war' were elaborated. These documents were sent to a few commanders of military districts and to a few leading officials. They were to be opened only in case of war, as was the case with the mobilisation plan for the troops.[29] The first such plans, however, were unsatisfactory and were not approved by the government. In explanation, Gosplan officials complained that the wartime economic plans had been drafted simultaneously with other pressing matters such as the annual and five-year economic plans. The practical results during this period could thus best be characterised as a series of preparatory steps, in organisation as well as in the formulation of plans.[30]

THE DEFENCE INDUSTRY TARGETS

While the military authorities and planning agencies thus elaborated the main directions for defence plans, the party intervened in the formulation of defence policy at certain critical stages. The empirical evidence from Politburo minutes and ultra-secret 'special files' (*osobye papki*) indicates that the Politburo, as the highest decision-making party organ, tended to step in to finalise propositions made by the Red Army Staff, the Defence Commissariat, or Gosplan.

During the spring of 1927, the Politburo held special sessions devoted to the reorganisation and planning of the defence industry. Reports were received from Defence Commissar K.E. Voroshilov, and appointed commissions would thereafter draft resolutions for the Politburo. The Politburo commissions could include other military representatives. The resolutions themselves were classified 'top secret' (*sovershenno sekretno*) and distributed on a 'need-to-know' basis. Those resolutions which were published would stress the growing importance being attached to military strength. The fifteenth party congress of December 1927 stressed the defence aspect in its resolution on the five-year plan:

> Taking into account a possible military attack by capitalist states against the proletarian state, the five-year plan should be worked out devoting *maximum attention* to the fastest possible development of those sectors of the economy in general, and of industry in particular, which play the main role in securing the country's defence and economic stability in wartime. [31]

'Maximum attention' to defence-related sectors of the economy was still only a vague slogan. None the less it permeated the atmosphere of planning. This was the case during the whole of 1928 and well into 1929. On one hand the defence sector (with other Gosplan sectors), and on the other the military authorities, had engaged in several rounds of sessions, conferences, and meetings to discuss various aspects of defence industry. As will be demonstrated below, the military had reason to reiterate its position on defence preparedness in the face of the seemingly more complacent civilian planners.

The first five-year plan was adopted by the Congress of Soviets in April 1929, and by the party conference in May. However, the defence industry section of that plan had not yet been finally agreed. The Red Army Staff had formed several commissions in order to reconsider the figures for rearmament between 1928/29 and 1932/33. When even these sessions could not come up with a definite version of the defence industry plan, the issue was referred to the Politburo. The highest decision-making circles decided to devote a series of special Politburo meetings to the defence industry. These sessions were held in July 1929. At Politburo sessions on 1 and 8 July 1929, the state of the country's defence was discussed.[32] The Politburo listened to reports on the defence industry from I.P. Pavlunovskii, and others of VSNKh, from Defence Commissar Voroshilov, and from several leading military officers. It then appointed two commissions to draft resolutions 'On the condition of defence of the USSR' (*O sostoianii oborony SSSR*) and 'On the defence industry' (*O voennoi promyshlennosti*). The final resolutions from the Politburo would prompt revisions in the plan for 1929/30 by demanding higher targets than those recently adopted by the Congress of Soviets.[33]

The resolution of 1929 'On the condition of defence of the USSR' strongly emphasised that it was 'appropriate to apply foreign experience, to receive technical assistance and to acquire crucial experimental models from abroad' (this resolution is also discussed above in Chapter 2). Already during the first five-year plan, the Soviet extractive and processing industries had hundreds of contracts with western firms.[34] Although some general framework for foreign technical assistance may have been included in the original five-year plan, each grand new project undertaken in the course for the plan period would require adjustments in all related sectors.

The Politburo also approved a Red Army plan for expansion over the period 1929–34. The basic guiding principles of the plan were to be:

> in quantity not to lag behind the probable enemy in the main theatre of war,
>
> in quality to be stronger than the enemy in two or three decisive types of weapons, namely in aviation, artillery, and tanks.[35]

It was planned that the army should deploy 3 million men at mobilisation. In the Politburo's opinion, the Soviet air force was outdated in quality and in fighting capability. Especially troublesome was the lack of Soviet aeroengine manufacture as well as the lack of serial production. The Council for Labour and Defence (STO) was therefore to undertake a revision of plans for the aircraft industry, to propose concrete measures, and to make new budget appropriations. The air force should have a peacetime strength of 2000 active aircraft plus 500 in the first echelon reserves, and up to 1000 in other reserves. The artillery goal was to have a total of 9350 light, heavy and antiaircraft guns, and 3400 small-calibre artillery systems.[36]

The tank program was likewise revised. It now aimed at a peacetime force of 1500 front-line tanks, with 1500 to 2000 in reserve for the first period of war, and a further supply of 1500 to 2000 tanks. The tank models and the organisational structure of Red Army tank units were determined by a Politburo decision of 25 November 1929 which prescribed the introduction of tanks, basically for use in the tactical zone of combat, as a means for strengthening the infantry and cavalry in breakthrough operations.

The established Soviet historiographical view of the first five-year plan was that threats from abroad, specifically the Japanese invasion of Manchuria in 1931, forced a redirection of resources to the defence sector. This argument was used by Stalin to explain why several plan targets had not been fulfilled. It is true that in 1932 the budget assignments to defence were sharply increased.[37] But the change in priority towards defence had been initiated by the Politburo already in the summer of 1929, only a few months after the five-year plan had been approved by the Congress of Soviets. The resolution stated that:

> Approving the measures taken by the government to guarantee defence interests in the five-year plan, the Politburo proposes *an acceleration in the rate of construction of branches of defence significance during the first three years of the five-year plan*, in order to eliminate as rapidly as possible

weak points and disproportions, and in particular, in order to strengthen the domestic production of nonferrous metals, chemicals, and machine-building.[38]

From the military's point of view, such targets corresponded to the war plans already mentioned. The war plans were based on a wartime strength of 3 million men and 100 or more divisions. This force structure was considered sufficient for repelling any coalition of border states in the scenarios most often envisaged. However, during the first years of the five-year plan period, military officials such as Tukhachevskii and Triandafillov came step by step to advocate the buildup of a motorised mass army more rapid even than that authorised by the Politburo. Some reflections on these proposals will highlight the width of divergence between different currents within the Soviet military.

First, table 3.2 summarises the various targets set for wartime capacity by the various mobilisation plans authorised up to 1930 in order to give a rough notion of the magnitudes intended, were war to erupt in the early 1930s. This table confirms a colossal increase in Soviet military-economic aspirations from the few hundreds and thousands of aircraft, tanks, and guns envisaged for annual wartime production in 1927 to the tens of thousands proposed in 1930. (Indeed, as comparison with table 5.1 will confirm, the figures for aircraft and tank units written into the revised version of MV-10 in 1930 were of an order of magnitude comparable to annual wartime production a decade later in World War II; however, the aircraft and tank units of World War II were far more complex and expensive than in 1930; annual wartime artillery production would also exceed MV-10 by many times.)

The current output of armaments was set by the level of defence orders (*voennye zakazy*) for weapons and combat equipment, which in turn were determined by military requirements for training, basic equipment, and reserves. The main categories in the annual defence orders evolved during 1930–2 as shown in table 3.3. Again, they reveal striking growth in the main

Table 3.2. Production requirements of NKVM for one year of war in mobilisation plans, 1927–30 (units)

	1927	*1928*	*1930*	
		S-30	*MV-10*	*MV-10 revised*
Aircraft	2 905	4 267	7 098	12 500
Tanks	150	1 055	20 000	40 000
Guns	3 763	4 562	12 610	18 467
Shells (mn)	37.9	51.2	40.0	–

Source: RGAE, 4372/91/1268, 32 (Gosplan report on the first five-year plan, 1933).

Table 3.3. NKVM procurement of weapons, 1930–2 (units)

	1930	*1931*	*1932*
Aircraft	899	860	1 734
fighters, bombers	378	220	144
reconnaissance	328	389	659
other	193	251	931
Tanks	170	740	3 038
Guns	952	1 966	2 574
Shells (thousands)	790	750	1 200

Source: GARF, 8418/25/14, 2–3 (Komitet Oborony), cited by Harrison and Davies (1997), tables A.1–A.6.

categories (though not in all the subcomponents, e.g. fighter aircraft). In each case current procurement was, however, only a small fraction of procurement under the mobilisation plan for the event of war in force at the time.

How did military and economic planners evaluate what had been accomplished through the first five-year plan? By 1933, the leadership counted on a wartime army of 150 infantry divisions, equipped with modern weapons and technical equipment. Some of the more apparent changes are illustrated in table 3.4, which expresses vividly the extent of modernisation achieved since 1927.

When Voroshilov summed up the achievements of 1932, he proudly asserted:

> According to all the main indicators (quantities, armament, and training) at the end of the first five-year plan, the Red Army is capable of victoriously taking on the army of any capitalist country.[39]

Nonetheless, he also noted deficiencies such as the lack of reserves of all the principal types of arms, and particularly of shells and cartridges. Mechanisation was still limited, and most artillery was horse-drawn. The number and types of tanks did not allow for deep breakthrough operations.[40] Voroshilov's judgement of the industrial prerequisites is of particular interest:

> The most serious factor is the obvious, systematic lag in the mobilisation- and defence-preparedness of our industry. Its procurement possibilities are almost two years behind the requirements of the Red Army.[41]

When Gosplan's defence sector compiled a report on the results of the first five-year plan in late 1932, it emphasised, as did the Defence Commissar's report, a whole range of new weapons being produced in the country for the first time.[42] At the same time, the Gosplan report used the potential

Table 3.4. The Red Army stock of armament in 1927 and 1933

	1927	*1933*
Aviation	Less than 1 000 old bombers	Almost 5 000 aircraft
Tanks	73 old tanks[a]	10 000 tanks, pocket tanks, and armoured vehicles
Trucks	1 000	12 000–14 000
Artillery	7 000 guns at deployment (1929)	17 000 guns at deployment
	26 000 heavy machine guns	51 000 heavy machine guns
	48 000 light machine guns	67 000 light machine guns
Chemical weapons	1.5 million old gas masks	Modern antigas equipment, *plus* 3 000 aviation and 300 truck gas projectors 500 gas mortars

Note:
[a] On January 1, 1929, the Soviet Army had 90 tanks, 3 500 lorries and cars and 180 caterpillar tractors. The tanks consisted of 45 Ricardo, 12 Taylor, 28 Renault and 5 others of obsolete type, and in general had low combat value. The lorries were mostly old, foreign types (FIAT, White), and only 680 lorries were Russian-built (RGVA, 40432/1/475, 41)

Source: RGVA, 33988/3/301, 196–197.(Report by Voroshilov to Sovnarkom chairman Molotov, Gosplan chairman Kuibyshev and NKTP chairman Ordzhonikidze, June 1932).

satisfaction of military requirements as the most appropriate success indicator.[43] The report defined the significance of this indicator as follows:

> The NKVM requirement (*zaiavka NKVM*) is that connecting link, by means of which the preparedness of industry, and all other sectors of the economy, are led in a common direction. It is not just a departmental document; in the system of a planned socialist economy, the requirement is based on the total production capacity of the economy. The requirement, in turn, reflects the levels of technical and economic development achieved by the country... The NKVM requirement contains in concentrated form an indicator of the exertions that the country must undertake to secure its defence capability in peacetime, and to guarantee victory in war.[44]

The mobilisation request had risen many times in quantity over the five-year plan. However, Gosplan noted that the level of Soviet mobilisation requirements still lagged not only behind the level achieved by the great powers during the First World War, but even more behind the contemporary goals of the western powers. Gosplan's defence sector assumed that the mobilisation capacities of the advanced capitalist countries would be approximately 40 000 to 50 000 tanks and aircraft, and that their wartime artillery shell production would be around 100 million rounds. Consequently, the backwardness of these branches of defence industry occupied a large portion of the planners' analysis and recommendations.[45]

CHANGING PERSPECTIVES IN THE MID-1930S

During much of the 1920s and the early 1930s, the military's war plans were based on the threat assessment of a possible coalition of border states such as Poland and Romania, supported by France or Britain. From 1933 onwards, the Red Army would instead have to reckon with a possible war on its western front with Germany, or with Germany in coalition with Poland, and also a Japanese attack against the Soviet Far East. From 1935, with the Anti-Comintern Pact threatening a concerted two-front attack led by Nazi Germany and Japan, the Red Army's mobilisation requirements were once again recalculated.

It is important to point out that the long-term threat assessment which provided the framework for the second five-year plan was made in 1932. When the plan was implemented, the threat structure had changed radically because of the Nazi takeover in Germany. The quantitative targets of the second five-year plan, however, were not drastically changed until the last years of the plan. Until then, it seems that the capacity buildup and mobilisation possibilities of Soviet industry were deemed sufficient to repulse the German armed forces which were not yet at full strength.

On its western frontiers the Soviet military still saw a Polish-Romanian coalition, supported by France, as the most likely enemy. From this perspective, the Army Staff in 1932 defined the overall purpose of the army development plan (*plan stroitelstva vooruzhennykh sil*) to be that:

> The Red Army should be technically as well equipped as the most advanced armies of the capitalist world (the USA and France). It must be capable of waging war simultaneously in the west and in the east... The Soviet Union must achieve weapons superiority over France, the strongest enemy of the USSR in Europe, and her allies on the western borders, Poland and Romania, especially in aviation, tanks, and chemical weapons.[46]

Much of the Soviet rearmament potential during the second five-year plan was intended to come from civilian enterprises working in cooperation with the defence industry. Table 3.5 shows the scale of armaments production to be achieved in case of war which was envisaged for 1933 (the first of the second five-year plan) in June of that year and also for 1938 (the first of the future third five-year plan). While in 1932 some targets had been temporarily

Table 3.5. The NKVM mobilisation request for 1932, 1933 and 1938 (production for one year of war), June 1933

	1932 mobilisation plan for supply of one year of war	*1933 MR 15*	*1938 M-18*
Aircraft	7 490	14 500	30 000
Tanks	19 800	32 200	45 000
Guns	18 000	28 615	41 600
Shells (million)	46.4	84.2	160
Chemical weapons (tons)	63 000	150 000	250 000

Source: RGVA, 40438/1/184, 7–8 (request by Defence Commissar Voroshilov, sent to Gosplan Chairman Kuibyshev, June 1933.

reduced below the extreme ambitions of 1930 (table 3.2), the figures once again indicate rapidly rising military-industrial aspirations.

Two distinctive traits of the Soviet military's industrial requirement in the 1930s deserve extra comment. First, the seemingly staggering figure for annual wartime production of 45 000 tanks refers to the light and medium tanks which formed the core of the mechanised corps and armoured support for infantry divisions in the 1930s. Most of these tanks were to be produced at the Stalingrad, Khar'kov, and Cheliabinsk tractor factories and the Nizhnii Novgorod automobile factory. At these plants, separate shops were working continuously on tank production while the main production lines were turning out caterpillar tractors for collective farmers. By the time of World War II, however, technical requirements had shifted to heavier tanks. When the prototypes for the much more expensive T-34 and KV-1 were designed in the late 1930s, mobilisation requirements were fixed in units at a correspondingly lower level.

The second feature of the mobilisation request which deserves emphasis is the fourfold increase in wartime targets for chemical weapons. The Soviet Union had signed the convention of 1926 against the use of chemical weapons, renouncing their first use while reserving the right to retaliate in kind if attacked by chemical means. During the second and third five-year plans (1933–7 and 1938–42), production facilities were not only expanded, but every possible measure was taken to defend against airborne chemical agents. The relocation of new factories to the east of the Urals was undertaken basically in order to avoid strategic bombing by chemical as well as by conventional means (that the Red Army would ever retreat beyond the Dnepr river seems not to have featured in the imagined scenarios of military and economic planners). Factories in Russia and the Ukraine trained their employees to work while wearing gas masks.[47]

In early 1935, following a number of articles in the German press critical of the allegedly threatening Soviet rearmament, Tukhachevskii was to write a rejoinder. This article was carefully prepared, and was checked by Stalin himself. In a *Pravda* article entitled 'The war plans of present-day Germany' Tukhachevskii warned against German plans of aggression. He sketched the assumed size of each branch of the German army. He referred for example to Germany's intention to set up 12 corps and 36 infantry divisions. He quoted data on aircraft production in Germany as 15 units per day, with over 4000 expected to be produced in 1935 alone. Although Tukhachevskii saw the implications of Germany's huge stock of lorries and cars for military motor transport, the production of tanks in Germany had not yet reached a level commensurate with that of Soviet industry. Naturally, the mobilisation capacity of Soviet industry was a well-concealed trump card for the Red Army.

Tukhachevskii's conclusions (duly corrected by Stalin) bear little relation to the actual quantitative balance between the USSR and Germany in 1935. Rather, they project a worst-case scenario based on failure of the attempts to create collective security arrangements. Tukhachevskii emphasised Hitler's expansionist ambitions and the character of the German 'Blitzkrieg' doctrine. Against those western practitioners of appeasement who might have hoped to divert Hitler eastwards, the article stated:

> Germany's imperialist plans are not only anti-Soviet. This direction is just a suitable cover to hide its revanchist plans in the west (Belgium and France) and south (Poznan, Czecho-Slovakia, and Anschluss [with Austria]). In addition to this, Germany will no doubt need French ores. It must also expand its naval bases.[48]

At this time both I.P. Uborevich, Commander of the Belorussian Military District, and deputy Defence Commissar Tukhachevskii proposed changes in Soviet war plans. Tukhachevskii noted that the threat situation had changed drastically, since the Soviet Union now faced a combined German-Polish alliance as the main organised enemy force. The Soviet Union would in all likelihood face a two-front war since Japan would probably join such an anti-Soviet coalition. After a detailed survey of the likely attack scenarios in the west, Tukhachevskii concluded with sharp criticism of the Army Staff for 'substantially underestimating defence needs'. Whereas the Staff proposed a strength of 112 divisions in the areas close to the country's western borders, the appropriate superiority ratios, in Tukhachevskii's estimate, required 160 infantry divisions.[49]

In Uborevich's proposal for a new war plan in the west, the anti-Soviet coalition of Germany, Poland, and Japan would also include Finnish participation. Finland was expected to attack the Leningrad region with the support of a German expeditionary force. Twenty-five to thirty infantry divisions and motorised corps would attack from Lithuania and Latvia. The German army was expected to be highly mobile, thanks to its estimated 150 000 trucks. Of particular concern for the Soviet side was the report of new chemical weapons in the German arsenal against which there was no effective protection as yet. Despite the 'gigantic production possibilities' of German industry, Uborevich saw a chance of victory if the hostile forces could be crushed separately, before their full mobilisation. He proposed that a two- or three-fold Soviet superiority in air power would be the key to crushing the military and economic power of Poland and Germany. This victory could be achieved if Poland was attacked immediately, in the initial period. [50]

In 1936, leading military officers took part in a strategic wargame based on a conflict between Germany and the USSR. The results of this simulation tended to indicate that the Red Army's war plans had failed to take due account of Germany's potential.[51] From then on, the USSR was entrenched in a classical arms race with the more industrialised Germany. Consequently, when Gosplan started to draft the defence industry targets for the third five-year plan, it was essential for them to gauge approximately the enemy's maximum likely strength. In 1937, Gosplan's defence sector used the Red Army's Military Intelligence estimates shown in table 3.6 (parts (A) and (B)). These figures are obviously only one of many Intelligence estimates made in the prewar period. When compared with actual wartime production (part (C)), the German figures especially appear somewhat overstated; moreover, by 1937 any unanticipated increase in the quality and complexity of wartime weaponry units was already not such an important factor.

As a consequence of such estimates, the mobilisation targets projected in these drafts were raised substantially for the third five-year plan (1938–42). The total capacity for aircraft production was to increase from 20 600 in 1938 to 50 000 aircraft by 1942, for tank production from 35 400 to 60 775 units (evidently still assuming an important role for light tanks) and for artillery shell production from 101 to 489 million rounds.[52] A detailed analysis of the defence components of the third five-year plan in its definite form would require more data than has yet been made available. Although the conditions of production for the defence industry turned out to be drastically different from what the planners had assumed, a note on the actual Soviet production after evacuation and a transition to wartime plans in 1942 may illustrate the changes. As may be seen from table 5.1 below, the Soviet output of armaments in 1942 was 21 700 combat aircraft, 24 400 tanks and self-propelled guns, and 133.3 million shells. However, as already noted above, the numbers of tanks planned beforehand are not comparable with the numbers actually produced in 1942, since in the interim the character of the tanks themselves had changed, and much of the capacity from the factories in Cheliabinsk, Sverdlovsk and Nizhnii Tagil had been turned over to production of the medium T-34 and heavy KV-1 and their later successors.

Table 3.6. Soviet estimates of the military capacity of Germany, Poland, and Japan, 1937 (units)

	Combat aircraft	*Armoured combat vehicles*	*Shells (mn)*
	(1)	(2)	(3)
(A) In operation in 1937			
Germany	4 500	5 000	–
Poland	1 600	2 000	–
Japan	3 000	900	–
Total	9 100	7 900	–
(B) Expected wartime production			
Germany	42 000	48 000	228
Poland	4 800	4 800	21.6
Japan	12 000	2 500	60–80
Total	58 800	55 300	309–329
(C) Actual production, 1942–4 (annual average)			
Germany	21 700	11 700	–
Poland	–	–	–
Japan	13 600	800	–
Total	35 300	12 500	–

Source: (A) and (B) are from RGAE, 4372/91/3002, 139 (Gosplan defence sector, 1937); (C) is from Harrison (1998a), 15–16.

CONCLUSION

In the prewar years, a specific system for defence planning was established in the USSR. During the initial phase (approximately 1925–9), comparable systems for achieving military-economic preparedness in France, Germany and the United States were studied. By the time the Soviet leadership adopted the first five-year plan in April–May 1929, Gosplan and VSNKh had established their respective subsectors for defence planning and mobilisation preparedness. The military were heavily represented in these bodies both for the sake of expertise and as a pressure group. While the first five-year plan (1928/29 to 1932/33) included specific targets to modernise the Red Army, the more secret plan for mobilisation preparedness was based on a reckoning of what could be produced in the case of war by specialised defence industry *plus* other sectors after mobilisation. This pattern was repeated for the second and third five-year plans. However, the annual production plan targets for 1931 and 1932 were less determined by the five-year plan. Other factors, such as technical assistance from the west in tank and aircraft production, called forth repeated revisions. When an external threat, such as that of Japan in 1931 or of Germany in 1933, appeared to take on a more distinct character, the annual plans for current production were shifted upwards. In other words, to the extent that mobilisation targets were realistic, threat-induced changes can be said to have created a semi-mobilised state in the economy.

How realistic were the mobilisation targets aimed for by the Red Army, and adopted by the government? This complex question may be divided into several separate issues, of which only three will be summarised here. First, were the targets technically feasible – would it have been possible for producers to switch from peacetime to wartime levels of production by following their blueprints at any given point in time? Second, were the wartime mobilisation plans drafted with due regard to their repercussions throughout the economy? Third, did the mobilisation targets correspond to what turned out to be the real demands of an actual war? As far as the third question is concerned, the war followed a quite different course from that envisaged. In the summer and autumn of 1941, instead of smoothly switching to war production, more than a thousand engineering and chemical factories were hastily evacuated from the western borders, and countless others were destroyed. Therefore, only preliminary answers to the first and second questions can be offered, since the plans' technical feasibility and interrelatedness were never tested under *ceteris paribus* conditions. Therefore, they must be judged by some other criterion than historical experience.

It would be easy to criticise the mobilisation planning process on the basis of contemporary reports of the OGPU economic department which, after raids on a number of factories, accused managers of neglecting to update their mobilisation plans. Similar accusations by the Red Army tended to depict the actual state of economic preparedness in the mid-1930s in somewhat gloomy colours. These reports were, of course, partial and tendentious. At the same time it is true that Gosplan and VSNKh not infrequently lacked the initiative to go beyond summing up deficiencies – concerning which they were well informed – to practical steps for the improvement of production and mobilisation plans at the enterprise levels.

During the early and mid-1930s, the authorities opted for a solution where most reserves for potential wartime production should be laid down in civilian factories, especially in the machinebuilding, automotive, chemical, and aircraft industries, in order to keep down the cost of defence industry construction. There was probably some wishful thinking here; for example, Soviet managers certainly understated the skills required in order to shift from assembling caterpillar tractors to producing light or medium tanks. On the other hand, the alternative seemed to be investing huge sums in a specialised defence industry at the outset, not knowing whether or when these capacities would ever be used. It is easy to understand the attraction to Gosplan of a solution that promised to give the best of both worlds: first, producing tractors and other equipment for agriculture, then taking on the burden of the war against capitalism, and finally, after the expected victory for socialism, returning to civilian production.

Within this framework of dual military and civilian designations of industry, the military authorities could likewise argue for higher targets. The archival data now show the precise mobilisation objectives. In the actual combat of 1941–5, it became evident to German intelligence officers and other western military observers that their prewar estimates had fallen far below what the Soviet industry was actually capable of producing.[53]

However, it is still difficult to assess the real prewar preparedness and actual mobilisation status of Soviet industry on strict *ceteris paribus* assumptions, since the loss of Soviet territory in 1941–2 meant that the war followed a course completely unforeseen by prewar mobilisation plans. Since the late 1920s, the authorities had evacuation plans for the immediate border areas. The Red Army's war plans of that time included the possibility of falling back in the west, for example retiring towards the Dnepr before launching a counter-offensive to crush the enemy. Later war plans were calculated, erroneously as it now seems, on holding the border and directly launching a counter-offensive. Therefore, even during the intensive phase of constructing new defence factories in 1938–40, the authorities did not hesitate to locate them in central Russia and the Ukraine. Stalin's miscalculations with regard to 'Operation Barbarossa' and the Soviet military disaster of 1941 deprive us of an economic standard by which to judge the actual performance of the Soviet industry after the crash evacuation. At best, one might simulate what the industry might have produced, provided that the Red Army had been allowed to go into full alert in May 1941, instead of waiting for most of the air force to be wiped out on the field airstrips at dawn of Sunday 22 June.

NOTES

1 Carr and Davies (1969); Zaleski (1971); Zaleski (1980); Harrison (1985); Sapir (1997).
2 Fedotoff-White (1944); Erickson (1962); Glantz (1991); Schneider (1994).
3 For historiographical discussion see Davies (1993).
4 For an interesting discussion of such plans see Tupper (1982), 9–12. A number of plans were known from Soviet works and legal documentaries. A chronological listing of plans can be found in the appendix to Cooper (1976).
5 Davies (1993); see further Chapter 4.
6 For a more complex analysis of the principles and practice of Soviet military and economic planning, see Samuelson (1998).
7 Cf. Crmieux-Brilhac (1981).
8 Zhigur (1930), 46–47.
9 See surveys by Vishnev (1928), Vishnev (1930), and Ogorodnikov (1931).
10 The Politburo approved one study visit on 10 February 1932 (RTsKhIDNI, 17/3/872, item 28/8). For a report on the visit to Germany see RGVA, 33988/3/218, 48.

11 RGVA, 33988/2/671, 140 (report on the war plan by Tukhachevskii, 1926).
12 RGVA, 33988/2/682, 8 (Tukhachevskii's 1926 guidelines for investigation of 'The future war').
13 RGVA, 33988/2/682, 22
14 RGVA, 33988/2/688, 18.
15 RGVA, 33988/2/688, 18.
16 For an analysis of events and major speeches by party leaders, see Meyer (1978).
17 RGVA, 7/10/303, 104ob (Tukhachevskii to A. Mikoian, July 1927).
18 RGVA, 7/10/303, 123ob (NKVM report, no exact date, 1927).
19 RGVA, 7/10/303, 137 (NKVM report, note before 15 May 1927).
20 Volpe (1926), 11–13.
21 RGVA, 4/14/91, 3–9 (memo by Tukhachevskii).
22 RGAE, 4372/91/43, 24–22 (Tukhachevskii's memo on a defence sector in Gosplan, 18 June 1927).
23 RGAE, 4372/91/43, 23ob.
24 RGVA, 7/10/100, 278 ('Postanovlenie RZ STO o sisteme organizatsii mobilizatsionnykh appparatov').
25 RGAE, 4372/91/43, 23ob.
26 RGAE, 4372/91/43, 24 (emphasis added).
27 RGAE, 4372/91/43, 61, 72 (resolution of RZ STO, 25 June 1927).
28 RGVA, 7/10/499, 168–169.
29 RGVA, 4/1/921 (resolution on plan for the first period of war).
30 For the RZ STO directives of the third version of 'control figures for the first period of war' and for measures in case of war erupting in the second half of 1928/29, see RGAE, 4372/91/345.
31 KPSS (1970), vol. 4, 33 (emphasis added).
32 RTsKhIDNI, 17/3/748 (Politburo minute no. 89, item 22, 8 July 1929). The minute refers to earlier Politburo sessions on defence questions on 23 March and 20 August 1928.
33 RTsKhIDNI, 17/162/7, 101–12, 113–21, special file (osobaia papka) to Politburo minute no. 89, items 11 and 22, 8 and 11 July 1929.
34 RGVA, 33987/3/250, 74. For a survey of many defence-related industries developed with the help of Western experts, see Sutton (1971), Chapters 11–15.
35 RGVA, 33987/3/250, 75.
36 RGVA, 33987/3/250, 75–6.
37 See Davies (1993).
38 RGVA, 33987/3/250, 81. This passage is not in the published version of the resolution (KPSS (1970), vol. 4, 281–3.
39 RGVA, 33988/3/301, 195 (Voroshilov to Sovnarkom chairman Molotov, Gosplan chairman Kuibyshev and heavy industry commissar Ordzhonikidze, June 1932).
40 RGVA, 33988/3/301, 196. Voroshilov has often been depicted as a lukewarm proponent of modernisation and a long-time defender of the role of cavalry (e.g. Rapoport and Geller (1995), 189–190). The internal reports at hand, however, show that Voroshilov supported both the upgrading of infantry divisions with tank battalions and the expansion of tank forces.
41 RGVA, 33988/3/301, 195 (Voroshilov to Molotov, Kuibyshev, and Ordzhonikidze, June 1932)
42 RGAE, 4372/91/312, 95–94 ('Itogi oboronnoi podgotovki promyshlennosti v 1-i piatiletke', 31 October 1932).
43 RGAE, 4372/91/312, 95–94, 102ob.
44 RGAE, 4372/91/312, 95–94, 102–102ob.
45 RGAE, 4372/91/312, 99–96.

46 RGVA, 4372/91/1097, 158.
47 For a fascinating example of these trials, see '12 000 Elektrozavod employees worked in gas masks', *Krasnaia zvezda*, 23 February 1936.
48 RGVA, 33987/3/400, 13–28; Tukhachevskii's article 'Hitler's war plans' appeared in *Pravda* on 29 March 1935. The original manuscript, showing Stalin's annotations, has been published in *Izvestiia TsK KPSS*, no. 1 (1990), 169. The sentence quoted was actually proposed by Stalin in place of Tukhachevskii's more purple formulation.
49 RGVA, 33987/3/400, 226–236 (Tukhachevskii to Voroshilov, 5 February 1935).
50 RGVA, 33987/3/279, 124–149 (Uborevich's report on the war plan, 19 February 1935).
51 Isserson (1963); Zakharov (1989).
52 RGAE, 4372/91/3002, 137–133 (Report of the chairman of Gosplan).
53 Kahn (1978), Chs. 19 and 24 (373–9 and 445–61); Herndon and Baylen (1975), 493–7.

4 Defence spending and defence industry in the 1930s

R.W. Davies and Mark Harrison

INTRODUCTION

In this chapter we aim to show the changing economic significance of defence outlays in the 1930s. This was a decade of rapid rearmament, but its pace and character were highly variable. Phases of rapid progress for the defence sector were interrupted by episodes of difficulty and setback. These phases were not at all synchronised with overall developments in the economy.

Between 1928 and 1940 Soviet real incomes per head of the population rose by roughly 60 per cent. There was also substantial change in the structure of production, and the share of industry, construction, and transport rose over the same period from 28 to 46 per cent of net value added.[1] These were turbulent years in which little went smoothly. Until 1928 the Soviet economy was still recovering from World War I and the Civil War. Under the first five-year plan (1928–32) there was rapid industrialisation but real GNP per head rose little because of setbacks in agriculture. Nearly all the interwar growth of average incomes took place under the second five-year plan (1933–7), and especially in what Naum Jasny called the 'three good years' of 1934–6, which were years of good harvests, rapidly rising production, de-rationing of consumer markets, and rising wages and farm incomes.[2] Under the third five-year plan (1938–42), there was renewed stagnation of incomes until it was interrupted by war in mid-1941.

The defence sector grew rapidly in most of these years, but the evidence advanced below is that real outlays (especially on munitions) grew most rapidly in the early and late 1930s. The 'three good years' on the other hand, were for defence industry years of struggle and tribulation.

WHAT THE BUDGET FIGURES SHOW

Reliability of defence data

Between 1931 and 1934, the published Soviet figures for defence expenditure were considerably underestimated. In 1933, the first year of the second five-year plan, the published figure for expenditure of the People's Commissariat for Military and Naval Affairs (NKVM, renamed People's Commissariat for Defence or NKO in 1934) was 1421 million rubles but the true figure was 4299 millions.[3]

In the 1934 budget the deception continued. The published estimate was 1665 million rubles while the true estimate was 5800 millions.[4] But in September 1934 the Soviet Union joined the League of Nations; and in November of that year the Permanent Commission on Disarmament at Geneva prepared to adopt a far-reaching document on the publication of military budgets. In November and December Litvinov, the People's Commissar for Foreign Affairs, sent memoranda to Voroshilov asking for new instructions about the data to be submitted to the League; Voroshilov was head of the People's Commissariat for Defence (NKO), into which the People's Commissariat for Military and Naval Affairs (NKVM) had been reorganised in the previous June. In Litvinov's memorandum of 21 December, having received no instructions from Moscow, he pointed out that eight countries, including Britain and France, had already submitted budget documents to the League. Litvinov emphasised that the new procedures would involve 'the publication and submission of far more detailed and full information than we submitted in 1932–3 and require a fundamental change of all our system of publishing data on military expenditure'.[5]

On 4 January 1935, a laconic Politburo decision ruled that in the published report on the 1934 budget 'expenditure on the NKO shall be shown in the sum of 5 billion rubles' and that the estimate for NKO in the 1935 budget should be given as 6.5 billions. This decision was formally confirmed three days later by the Sovnarkom.[6] The Politburo evidently decided that no useful purpose would be served by continuing the gross concealment of defence expenditure practised in the previous three years. Soviet fears of Japanese aggression in the Far East, with which the United States strongly sympathised, and the victory of Hitler and the National Socialists in Germany, provided adequate justification for the substantial military expenditure, and made it necessary to portray the Soviet Union as a formidable military power.

But this was not yet the full truth. The Soviet authorities were anxious to cover up the fact that they had falsified past published figures for defence expenditure. In a memorandum to Litvinov on 11 March 1935, Voroshilov rejected the proposal from the League that expenditure for the previous three years should be recorded.[7] Moreover, the data now published for 1934 and 1935 were not the whole truth. A memorandum sent to Molotov from the secret department of Narkomfin, the People's Commissariat for Finance, in January 1935 revealed that the actual expenditure in 1934 amounted to 5355 million rubles not 5000 millions, and that the estimate for NKO for 1935 was 7492 not 6500 million rubles.[8]

Publication and reality finally coincided in the 1936 budget. On 15 December 1935, the Politburo resolved that 'expenditure for NKO shall be shown in the budget in full'.[9] The same figure for 1936 appears both in the published budget and in the archives – 14 800 million rubles.[10]

A separate issue is the coverage of the defence budget administered by NKVM-NKO. The NKO budget figure, even when truthfully published, did not cover all defence-related expenditure. In all years, separate allocations in the budget covered expenditures on special, convoy and NKVD armies, on strategic stockpiles, and defence-related expenditures in civilian commissariats and in local soviets (for example, on mobilisation planning, civil defence, and military R&D). And the substantial expenditure on investment, working capital and subsidies in the armaments industries continued to appear under the 'national economy' heading in the state budget. On 25 March 1935, a Politburo resolution on 'openness in military expenditure' (the Russian word was *glasnost'*) agreed that the military expenditures of the civilian people's commissariats and local agencies could be reported to the League. But it also insisted that information on investment in the armaments industries should not be provided, except in the case of subsidies to armaments factories in the narrow sense. This was on the plausible grounds that in western countries private investment in the private armaments industry was not reported.[11] Thus investment in armaments industries (table 4.10 below) does not form part of the expenditure of the NKO.

So far only patchy information has been traced on defence expenditure under other budget headings. In the 1933 budget, the NKVM appropriation amounted to 4.7 billion rubles, but to this figure may be added other outlays on defence-related items as follows: internal and frontier troops – 560 million rubles, defence industry investment and subsidies – 630 million rubles, and defence-related outlays by civilian agencies – 720 million rubles. Thus the broader defence-related total of 6.6 billion rubles was 40 per cent more than the NKVM subtotal.[12]

Too much should not be made of this point. Except in the years 1931–5, Soviet interwar defence budgets corresponded roughly with a modern western definition of 'defence consumption', and with the measures of defence outlays used in other countries. Other outlays in the broader 'defence-related' category either contributed more to other goals than to defence (for example, the maintenance of large internal security forces the primary task of which was defence of the regime against its internal enemies), or else added to society's ability to sustain a larger military burden in the future through accumulation of fixed assets and the stock of knowledge, rather than contributing to defence in the present. Therefore both consistency and comparability direct our attention first and foremost to the defence budget itself, and only secondarily to wider concepts of defence-related expenditure.

The long-run context

Table 4.1 shows the evolution of defence budget outlays from 1928/29 to 1940. In the first five-year plan period, nominal outlays on defence rose from 880 million rubles in 1928/29 to 4034 million rubles in 1932. At the same time total government spending rose roughly in proportion, so that the defence share, which fell at first, had returned to about 10 per cent by the end of the period. The low point marked in 1931 should not neglected – the 7 per cent which our table shows for that year, although much higher than the false figure given out in public, was still the lowest percentage of the whole interwar period. Still, the relative decline of 1930–1 was only temporary, and says more about the growth of government administration and public investment than any absolute decline in the defence sector.

In the early years of the second five-year plan, the proportion of one tenth was maintained. In 1936, however, there was a very sharp increase in the budget share of defence, which rose in one year from 11 to 16 per cent; by 1940, almost one third of the state budget was being allocated to defence, which was now consuming more rubles than the entire state budget of 1934.

The nominal value of defence outlays at currently prevailing ruble prices is not, on its own, particularly interesting (on the other hand, as students of

Table 4.1. Budget outlays, total and on defence, 1928/29–40 (million rubles and per cent)

	Budget total, million rubles	*Defence outlays*	
		million rubles	*% of budget*
	(1)	(2)	(3)
1928/29	8 784	880	10.0
1929/30	13 322	1 046	7.9
1930(4)	5 038	434	8.6
1931	25 097	1 790	7.1
1932	37 995	4 034	10.6
1933	42 081	4 299	10.2
1934	55 445	5 393	9.7
1935	73 572	8 174	11.1
1936	92 480	14 858	16.1
1937	106 238	17 481	16.5
1938	124 039	23 200	18.7
1939	153 299	39 200	25.6
1940	174 350	56 752	32.6

Sources: Plotnikov (1955), 92, 132, 206, 215, 255, 261, 324, 423, 433, except 1931 from Davies (1993), 593, and 1932–6 for which see archival figures in table 4.7 (col. 4). Differences between archival and published figures are trivial for 1935 and 1936, and for 1937 the two coincide.

Soviet defence outlays in the 1960s and 1970s are all too well aware, it is certainly a useful start). Knowing how many millions of rubles were expended on defence merely invites the question 'how much is a lot?' The ruble figures give us little impression of underlying change in the scale and cost of defence activity. Nominal values were affected by abrupt changes in the price of goods and services in general and of defence goods in particular. There are various ways of standardising the ruble figures, each of which has its own advantages and difficulties. One obvious method commonly adopted in official documents, already shown in table 4.1, is to compute the defence share of the state budget. But the defence share of the budget requires much interpretation, given the profound changes affecting the role of state finance in the economy as a whole. The share of the state budget in overall economic activity was changing from year to year, and was expanding violently in the first five-year plan period. There are various alternative approaches to the measurement of defence activity in its wider context, each with its own advantages and difficulties.

REAL OUTLAYS ON DEFENCE AND MUNITIONS

Physical indicators

An impressionistic overview of the growth of real resources commanded by the defence budget is provided by tables 4.2 and 4.3. In the 1920s the Soviet Union maintained a regular army and navy of 586 000 (table 4.2). This was a small army, being less than one in a hundred of the potential labour force (the demographic cohort of working age).[13] There may be some under-counting in so far as these figures do not include the internal security troops of the OGPU-NKVD. Nor do they count the part-time personnel of the territorial army, conscripts engaged in non-military service, or those undergoing military training prior to call-up. In 1926/27 these together would have added 842 000 to the published figure.[14] Of course the military value of these additional numbers was far less than that of the 586 000 regular soldiers. As far as later years are concerned, it is important also to bear in mind that the territorial army units were absorbed into the regular army in 1939. In the case of series A it is not clear whether established or actual strength is intended; the shortfall of series A in 1937 below the census figure of that year shown in series B may reflect recruitment above establishment (it is unlikely to be due to the date of the census, which took place at the beginning of the year).

As table 4.2 shows, the size of the regular armed forces began to grow rapidly after 1931, and numbers more than doubled under the second five-year plan. By 1937 up to 1.7 million men and women were in the ranks (col. 2), almost one in 50 of the labour force. Even so, the rate of growth was about

Table 4.2. Personnel of the Soviet regular armed forces (thousands)

	Series A	*Series B*
	(1)	(2)
1926/27	586	–
1928	–	–
1929	–	–
1930	–	–
1931	562	–
1932	638	–
1933	885	–
1934	940	–
1935	1 067	–
1936	1 300	–
1937	1 433	1 683
1938	1 513	–
1939	–	2 099
1940	4 207	–

Sources:
(1) Hunter, Szyrmer (1992), 138.
(2) AN SSSR (1991), 164; 1939: RAN (1992), 241, 244.

to accelerate again; between 1937 and 1940, the number of regular forces personnel trebled, reaching 4.2 million and one in 25 of the labour force. However, part of the exceptional growth of 1939 and 1940 is explained by absorption of the territorial units into the regular army.

What matters from an economic standpoint is not just the number of soldiers, but the value of the military services which they supplied. This question is usually answered with reference to their opportunity cost, i.e. the wage incomes which armed forces personnel would have attracted in a civilian occupation. In other words, the real value of military services provided by a given number of soldiers tended to rise through time.

At the same time as numbers of service personnel expanded, so too did the supply of weapons and other military stores with which they were equipped. Figures for annual NKO procurement of ground and air weapons from 1930 onwards are now available in somewhat more detail than previously published series, in 18 separate lines of defence products.[15] These figures are combined into an index of the number of weapons supplied to the armed forces, valued at 1937 unit prices, which suggests an increase of more than twenty-fold between 1930 and 1940 (table 4.3, col. 1).

It is important to understand the peculiarities of this measure. First, it is an index of defence procurement, not production. The two could differ significantly. Defence procurement was usually less than production by the value of

Table 4.3. Alternative measures of the real growth of munitions procurement, 1928–1940 (1937 prices and per cent of 1937)

	Number of weapons procured (present estimate)	*Munitions procurement from Moorsteen and Powell*
	(1)	(2)
1928	–	4.5
1929	–	5
1930	13.7	7
1931	25.0	7
1932	53.5	7
1933	80.5	7
1934	80.8	30
1935	58.0	50
1936	94.2	90
1937	100.0	100
1938	171.4	135
1939	246.0	200
1940	287.8	282

Sources:
(1) Table A-7, appendix to Davies, Harrison (1997).
(2) Moorsteen, Powell (1966), 629.

deliveries to industrial stocks of work in progress and finished goods, to industrial testing and experimentation facilities, to the armed forces of the NKVD, and to net exports (e.g. supplies of weapons to Spain in the civil war there, less supplies of warships and other weapons acquired from foreign firms). Because of these factors the relative levels of production and procurement could vary from year to year. However, their long-run trends were unlikely to diverge by much.

Second, as a measure of procurement our index is a short cut at best. It is based on crude numbers more than real values. It combines numbers of fighters, bombers, heavy and light tanks, large- and small-calibre guns, and so on, weighted roughly by relative 1937 unit values. This short cut takes no account of the changing technical level and performance of a fighter aircraft, medium tank, or large-calibre gun (in precisely the same sense as numbers of soldiers tell us nothing about their skills and training). Given that these things generally improved during the period, a number-of-weapons index puts a *lower bound* on our estimate of real growth in munitions procurement. It also omits warships, and so neglects the shipbuilding dimension of interwar rearmament altogether.

Warship construction presents many problems. Available series (gathered from published sources) are reported in table 4.4. They show a more than 40-fold increase in crude tonnage of ships entering service in 1940 compared with 1930 (col. 8). But the series are severely affected by qualitative change,

Table 4.4. Ships entering service with the Soviet Navy, 1930–41 (units and tons)

	Surface ships			*Submarines*			*Combined tonnage*	
	units	*tons total*	*per ship*	*units*	*tons total*	*per ship*	*total*	*% of 1937*
	(1)	(2)	(3)	(4)	(5)	(6)	(7)	(8)
1930	1	600	600	1	934	934	1 534	22
1931	1	600	600	5	4 690	938	5 290	75
1932	5	3 000	600	–	–	–	3 000	43
1933	1	600	600	15	10 845	723	11 445	163
1934	3	1 452	484	34	7 828	230	9 280	132
1935	3	1 463	488	32	13 777	431	15 240	217
1936	13	7 360	566	46	25 110	546	32 470	462
1937	6	2 156	359	9	4 869	541	7 025	100
1938	16	40 474	2 530	14	8 800	629	49 274	701
1939	14	32 048	2 289	14	8 845	632	40 893	582
1940	8	45 058	5 632	21	16 390	683	61 448	875
1941 (Jan.–Jun.)	2	23 230	11 615	7	3 980	569	27 210	387

Sources: Calculated from Korabli (1988), Dmitriev (1990) (figures supplied to the authors by Julian Cooper). Surface ships were light cruisers, battleships, destroyers, patrol boats, minesweepers, and gunboats.

especially the shift in favour of capital warship construction under the third five-year plan, as the striking change in average tonnage of surface ships entering service from 1938 onwards reveals (col. 2). Tonnage entering service was generally highly volatile; for example, more than 40 per cent of deliveries under the whole second five-year plan entered service in a single year, 1936. This reflected in part the construction period required for finished warships, which was both long and variable, resulting in year-to-year fluctuations in work in progress which were large relative to annual value added. A measure of naval shipyard production or value added in shipbuilding would presumably rise much more smoothly. For these reasons we do not try to incorporate shipbuilding into our aggregate measure of munitions procurement.

The number-of-weapons index shown in table 4.3 (col. 1) suggests that the real procurement of munitions nearly doubled from the end of the first to the end of the second five-year plan (1932–7). The pace of change was slow, however, compared with the rates of expansion recorded before and after, when munitions output measured in this way quadrupled in two years (1930–2), and nearly trebled in three (1937–40).

The usefulness of the number-of-weapons index can be pursued in two confrontations. One is a with an index of defence procurements originally computed by Moorsteen and Powell using a variety of indirect evidence to fill the gaps in Bergson's series; the other comparison is with available budget series for defence procurements at currently prevailing prices. In table 4.3 our present estimate (col. 1) is contrasted with the index of Moorsteen and Powell (col. 2). The Moorsteen/Powell index suggests that munitions procurement grew 14 times over the period from 1930–2 to 1937, and 40 times over the decade. It contains a lot of interpolation, so its precise year-to-year movement is not particularly significant, but its level in the early 1930s is very clearly understated because its authors did not know about the official concealment of weapon procurements in those years. Our index shows more modest growth comparing 1937 with 1930, with a far higher proportion of this growth taking place in the early 1930s under the cloak of secrecy. On the other hand, it should be born in mind that our own figures certainly understate the long-run growth of real procurements. Comparing 1940 with 1937 the two indexes are roughly in agreement.

The second confrontation is between volumes and values. In table 4.5 the number-of-weapons index (col. 1) is compared with an index of defence procurements (col. 2) at currently prevailing prices. When real outlays are divided by nominal outlays, an implicit unit price deflator is the product (col 3). The comparison suggests that from 1930 through to 1933 the unit price of a typical weapon was probably falling; this is consistent with the available evidence of official estimates, and also of heavy downward administrative pressure on industry. After 1933 unit prices began to rise, a trend which persisted until the outbreak of the second world war.[16] Again, we know of

Table 4.5. Nominal NKO outlays on military equipment compared with the number of weapons procured, 1930–40 (per cent of 1937)

	Number of weapons procured (present estimate)	*Nominal NKO outlays on military equipment*	*'Typical unit' price index (col. 2 divided by col. 1)*
	(1)	(2)	(3)
1930	14	6–9	44–66
1931	25	15	60
1932	53	27	51
1933	80	27	33
1934	81	34	43
1935	58	39	68
1936	94	81	86
1937	100	100	100
1940	288	345	120

Sources:
(1) table A-7, appendix to Davies, Harrison (1997).
(2) as Davies (1993), 594; 1932–7: table 4.7; 1940: Harrison (1996), 284.
(3) col. 2 divided by col. 1.

particular cases where the prices of existing weapons rose markedly in the mid-1930s, and we can also presume that the price of the typical weapon was rising because the assortment of weapons was shifting rapidly towards much more complicated, costly items. If we take into account the improvement in product technology and complexity over this period, however, the quality-adjusted price level may have been rising more slowly, stable, or even falling.

However it is measured, defence production grew far more rapidly than either GNP or civilian industry. Between 1930 and 1940, the supply of munitions grew many times – 20-fold or more. Over a slightly longer period, 1928–40, civilian industry value added grew by two and a half times, and GNP doubled.[17] If we confine our attention to the second five-year plan (i.e. comparing 1937 with 1932), the development of these different branches was somewhat more in proportion. The number of weapons supplied doubled, while civilian industry value added, and GNP as a whole, both grew by roughly two thirds.

Official documents also reveal that the main increase in the number of the defence industry's plants and innovation facilities took place between 1927/28 and 1936. At the end of the 1920s a mere 45 establishments were counted in the secret core of the defence industry complex.[18] At the moment of handover from Narkomtiazhprom to the new Narkomoboronprom in December 1936 their number had grown to 183 – a fourfold increase. There was little further increase in their numbers before the second world war; when Narkomoboronprom was broken up in 1939, 218 factories were transferred to the specialised defence industry commissariats.[19]

This picture, too, may be somewhat understated. First, the typical defence establishment of 1936 was certainly much larger and better equipped than its equivalent from the end of the 1920s. What pointed in this direction was not only the normal processes of industrial growth, but also the changing composition of the defence industry, and especially the rise of huge, vertically integrated aircraft production complexes. Second, the growth of the defence industry after 1936 may be understated by the number of factories because the increase of defence orders for weapons and military equipment was so rapid that it could not be met by existing specialised defence producers and resulted in a great increase in subcontracting of defence orders to civilian industry.[20]

All such figures neglect the great qualitative transformation of the defence industry in the period. But they do tend to confirm the idea of a break in the pace of defence mobilisation in 1935, when the numbers produced of many important types of weapons fell, e.g. rifles, medium and large-calibre artillery, medium tanks, and all aircraft other than fighters. The two issues – the qualitative transformation of the mid-1930s, and the production break in 1935 – are closely related. The assortment of weapons and the techniques of production were both in a state of flux.

As far as the product assortment is concerned, fighter aircraft can serve as an example. According to the chief of the aircraft industry, thirteen new types of aircraft were being introduced in 1934 and 1935.[21] What this meant can be illustrated in the case of fighter aircraft. In 1933 the number of fighter aircraft ordered was 360, of which 321 (90 per cent) were I-5s. By 1935 fighter production had risen to 839, but I-5s had been completely phased out, and now 800 (95 per cent) of the 839 ordered were I-15s and I-16s, none of which were being produced in 1933.[22] The I-5 was a biplane with a maximum airspeed of 286 kph. The I-15, also a biplane, could attain a maximum of 360 kph, while the top speed of the I-16, a monoplane, was faster still at 454 kph.[23] The introduction of newer, more sophisticated models of aircraft and tanks with more demanding production requirements goes a long way towards explaining the sudden dip in the number of weapons being produced in 1935 – partly because of the sharp increase in the value of each weapon, partly because of the disruptive influence of widespread technological restructuring of the production process. To give a single but not untypical example, in 1935 and 1936, when the old TB-3 bomber was being replaced by the new SB and DB-3, planned procurement of bombers was fulfilled by just 26 and 36 per cent in each year respectively.[24]

In other branches of defence industry the pace of product modernisation was less hectic, but attempts were made to bring about rapid change in process technologies. In 1933 a broad subsector of the defence industry comprising artillery, small arms, ammunition, tank armament, and optical equipment began a changeover to 'production according to Type "B" specifications' (*chertezhi lit. 'B'*), with the aim of setting higher standards of adherence to specifications, uniformity of measures and materials across the range of producers of identical or related products, and interchangeability of parts. Two main benefits were expected to flow from widespread adoption of Type 'B' specifications. One was a great reduction in unit costs. The other was much easier enforcement of product quality standards. The changeover was supposed to be completed in 1935, but in practice was accompanied by much disruption, footdragging from the side of industry, and delay.[25]

Deflating the value of outlays

Table 4.6 shows alternative estimates of real defence outlays provided by Abram Bergson. He estimated that, if defence outlays are deflated to constant prices of 1937 (col. 1), then by 1937 the real volume of defence activity was 10 times the level of 1928, and that between 1937 and 1940 there was a 2.7-fold further increase. This estimate confirms striking real growth, although not on the scale of the nominal budget figures – over the same subperiods, the ruble value of defence outlays at current prices rose 20 times and 3 times respectively. However, a Gerschenkron effect is present. Bergson also calculated the

Table 4.6. Real defence outlays according to Bergson, 1928–40 (billion rubles and per cent of 1937)

	At 1937 prices:		*At 1928 prices:*	
	billion rubles	*% of 1937*	*billion rubles*	*% of 1937*
	(1)	(2)	(3)	(4)
1928	1.7	10	0.74	7
1937	17.0	100	10.60	100
1940	45.2	266	–	–

Source: Bergson (1961), 128, 153.

series up to 1937 in 1928 prices (col. 3). In 1928, capital was scarce and capital-intensive machinery expensive relative to later years. Since machinery was substituted for labour-intensive goods and services as it became relatively cheaper during the 1930s, series for real outlays based on early-year weights grow more rapidly than the same weighted by late-year prices.

The principles of Bergson's methodology were sound. He attempted to break down nominal defence outlays into their separate components (maintenance of personnel and facilities, the purchase of weapons and military equipment, defence construction costs, and so on), and compiled separate price deflators for each component in order to reevaluate them in prices or costs of a given year. From our point of view one significant disadvantage of Bergson's series is that it was computed only for periodic benchmark years, with no figure for the early 1930s, and did not capture the turning points which would be revealed by annual series.[26] It used fruitfully the data available at the time, but has not proved particularly robust in the light of the archival evidence. This point is best illustrated by the example of defence orders for weapons and military equipment.

Table 4.7 presents the series now available for budget defence outlays over the second five-year plan, distributed among military equipment (weapons and other military stores), construction (barracks and other troop facilities, fortifications, airfields and so on), and maintenance (the running costs of the armed forces: the pay and subsistence of troops, their personal kit, the costs of military transport, operations, and equipment repairs). This table confirms a near fourfold increase in ruble outlays on the procurement of weaponry between 1932 and 1937, the final years of the first and second five-year plan periods. The figures also show that military equipment was a sizeable proportion of the defence total, usually around one third, but less in particular years such as 1935, and tending to fall towards the end of the period as the demands of modernisation began to yield to the growing urgency of numerical expansion of military personnel.

Table 4.7. State budget appropriations to the NKVM/NKO (the defence budget), 1932–7 (million rubles at current prices and per cent)

	Military equipment	*Construction*	*Maintenance*	*Total*	*of which, % on equipment*
	(1)	(2)	(3)	(4)	(5)
1932					
Actual	1 532	900	1 602	4 034	38
1933					
Budget	–	–	–	–	
amended	1 753	678	2 307	4 738	
Actual	1 506	620	2 173	4 299	35
1934					
Budget	2 494	812	2 494	5 800	
amended	2 292	745	2 764	5 801	
Actual	1 948	717	2 729	5 393	36
1935					
Budget	2 662	628	4 202	7 492	
amended	3 194	1 108	4 983	9 285	
Actual	2 226	1 186	4 762	8 174	27
1936					
Budget	5 420	2 036	7 349	14 805	
amended	5 914	2 428	8 180	16 522	
Actual	4 558	2 518	7 782	14 858	31
1937					
Budget	7 594	1 875	10 569	20 038	
amended	8 108	1 925	10 588	20 621	
Actual	5 658	1 936	10 472	18 066	31

Note: construction expenditure is given as credits opened for construction. Credits utilised were lower (from RGAE, 4372/91/3217, 3) (million rubles):
1933 532; 1934 704;
1935 1 086; 1936 2 323

Sources:

1932 Military equipment is from RGVA, 4/14/1667, 20 (dated 10 January 1936). For construction see Davies (1993), 593 – this is probably a planned figure, and therefore too high. The total figure is from GARF, 8418/10/148, 5 (report from the secret department of Narkomfin to Molotov, January 1935).

1933–5 For the amended budget and actual figures see RGAE, 4372/91/3217, 4 (report from the defence sector of Gosplan, dated 11 May 1937).

1934 The budget figure is from RGAE, 4372/91/1824, 56 (Gosplan report, dated 31 January 1934); ruble sums for separate items are calculated by us from percentages given in the source.

1935 The budget figure is from RGVA, 4/14/1667, 16 (report dated 26 December 1935). Another report in this file dated 3 January 1936 (ibid., 17) gives the final budget as 9635 million rubles.

1936 RGVA, 51/2/444, 2–12 (report of the financial department of NKO, dated 26 February 1937); we have estimated actual outlays as credits opened less those unutilised. These figures *exclude* foreign currency outlays (11 million rubles in the original budget; 43 million as amended, and 24 million actually spent).

1937 For the original and amended budgets, see RGVA, 51/2/445, 1, 11, and for actual outlays ibid., 13–14 (report of the financial department of NKO, dated 13 June 1938). These figures *include* foreign currency outlays (17 million in the original and revised budgets, and 11 million actually spent).

The deflators which Bergson applied to his estimate of munitions outlays were based on what he thought was happening to input costs and the prices of comparable goods. He used a freehand average of prices for civilian machinery and related material inputs (high-grade steel, rolled nonferrous metal products, and inorganic chemicals), and wages of public sector industrial workers. On this basis, Bergson suggested, munitions prices must have risen by roughly two-thirds between 1928 and 1937, and by another one-fifth up to 1940.

The evidence of official documents suggests that price trends affecting munitions were at best highly volatile, and at worst virtually impossible to pin down into a quantitative overall measure. Superficial indications are that they fell from the late 1920s through to 1932 or 1933, and thereafter rose. Thus, for their own purposes defence officials often calculated the cost of the current year's procurements at prices of the previous year to illustrate how much of the change was attributable to price inflation or deflation. The price changes taken into account probably only covered the subset of products procured in both years, and therefore could either overstate or (more likely) understate the underlying change. These calculations suggested a price level which fell continuously from 1928/29 through to 1933.[27]

For the mid-1930s we depend on available documentation of the changing prices of individual weapons, which is necessarily anecdotal in character. Thus between 1932 and 1935 there is fragmentary evidence of substantial inflation in the prices of particular weapons.[28] The same kind of incomplete evidence may suggest some reversal of the upward trend in 1936 and 1937.[29] However, more general indications are that the inflation continued. In November 1936 the chief of the General Staff complained that 'there is no military item for which we have not had a price increase by 10, 20, 30 or more per cent' during the year.[30] A Gosplan document, however, put the increase in armament prices at 8.6 per cent in 1936 compared with 1935.[31]

All these indications suffer from a common defect. To what extent may the prices of goods which remained in serial production from one year to another be thought of as proxies for the prices of all goods? They were only a part of the overall product assortment, a highly variable part, sometimes only a small part. New products ought to be incorporated into any measure of overall price change at prices 'comparable' with existing products, but what comparability means in practice may be difficult if not impossible to determine. For overall price stability, the same proportionality between price and user quality for new as for existing products is required; products introduced at higher price/quality ratios may have contributed to price inflation even if the prices of defence products already in serial production were being held stable from year to year or forced down.

Above, we gave the example of the wholesale conversion of the aircraft industry in 1933–5 from I-5 fighters to a new generation of I-15s and I-16s. As it happens, the factory price of an I-16 in 1936 was 86 000 rubles, whereas the price of an I-5 in 1934 had been 56 400 rubles.[32] Thus, in two years the price of a 'typical' fighter aircraft rose by one half. However, what matters to us is not the increase in the ruble price, but the proportion between the prices of the two aircraft and their real production requirements in plywood and metallic sheets and spars, instruments and controls, machining, assembly, spares, and so forth. Whether this proportion rose or fell cannot be judged on present information.

1935: setback and transition

What was happening in the mid-1930s? The year 1935 was intended to be one of sweeping modernisation in defence industry. Modernisation was to have been reflected in both the product assortment and in the techniques of production. Revolutionary change in the product assortment was foreshadowed in the planned turnover to new models of tanks and aircraft. The revolutionisation of production itself was blueprinted in the wholesale transfer to Type 'B' specifications already noted, which was intended to shake Soviet war production out of its craft traditions and bring it into a new era of standardised mass production.

This vast programme soon got into trouble. By September 5 only 29 out of 139 items in the artillery and ammunition industries had been transferred to Type 'B' specifications, and these not completely.[33] The industry urgently demanded that the transfer should be delayed; otherwise factories would temporarily have to cease production.[34] The military objected. On behalf of NKO, Gamarnik triumphantly sent Molotov a copy of a telegram he had acquired in which Pavlunovskii, then head of the defence industry, ordered a factory director to abandon the planned transfer to Type 'B' specifications for the sake of fulfilling the current output quota:

> The main programme must be fulfilled... If you don't prepare Type 'B', use drawings of current production.[35]

The difficulties were compounded by the switch to new types of armaments. In the aircraft industry, as late as October 1935 some factories were still struggling with the orders for 1934. Then in November, Voroshilov complained to Molotov and Stalin that only 859 of the 1334 aircraft planned for January–October had been delivered; and this included only a single aircraft out of the three key new types scheduled to be produced in 1935.[36] In 1935 NKO outlays on orders from the aviation industry was actually lower than in 1934 (table 4.8). The Commission for Defence, on Stalin's proposal, replaced the head of the aircraft industry by M.M. Kaganovich, with Tupolev as chief engineer.[37]

Armaments production as a whole was also unsatisfactory. The production of the armaments industries as a whole, measured in 1926/27 prices, including

Table 4.8. Military equipment orders of NKVM-NKO, 1932–7 (million rubles at current prices)

	Aircraft	*Vehicles and tanks*	*Artillery stores*	*Chemical stores*	*Shipbuilding and naval aviation*	*Railways*	*Experimental*	*Communications, technical stores*	*Engineering stores*	*Total*
	(1)	(2)	(3)	(4)	(5)	(6)	(7)	(8)	(9)	(10)
1932										
plan	312	428	791	74	322	4	–	88	37	2 056
actual	246	229	580	58	316	3	–	64	35	1 531
1933										
plan	417	341	500	48	351	6	–	67	55	1 785
actual	347	279	448	39	275	5	–	62	43	1 498
1934										
plan	510	345	568	49	565	15	–	92	49	2 193
actual	440	354	470	30	544	7	–	56	46	1 947
1935										
plan	611	475	956	62	881	14	–	77+26	55	3 157
actual	427	448	563	44	591	13	–	73+12	56	2 227
1936										
plan	1 608	1 085	1 391	87	1 332	46	119	116+32	96	5 912
actual	1 104	937	1 102	49	1 000	39	88	112+33	92	4 556
1937										
plan	2 740	1 037	2 093	106	2 194	38	136	149+23	118	8 634
actual	1 816	871	1 403	75	1 114	30	67	134+30	92	5 632

Sources:
1932–5 RGVA, 4/14/1667, 20 (report of the financial department of NKO, dated 1(January 1936).
RGVA: 51/2/444, 2ob-4 (report of the financial department of NKO, dated 26 February 1937).
1937 RGVA, 51/2/445, 66ob-68 (report of the financial department of NKO, dated 13 June 1938); includes small sums received for 'restoration of credits'. In addition to sums listed, 41 million rubles was allocated to 'packing for fuel', and 27 million rubles spent. The plan was cut by 400 million rubles (from 8674 to 8274 million) on account of planned price reductions.

Table 4.9. Gross production of armament industries, 1932–7 (million rubles at 'unchanged' 1926/27 prices)

	Series A		*Series B*		*Series C*	
	armament	*total*	*armament*	*total*	*armament*	*total*
	(1)	(2)	(3)	(4)	(5)	(6)
1932	1 500	2 900	–	–	–	–
1932	–	–	1 094	2 084	–	2 795
1933	–	–	1 265	2 083	–	2 387
1934	–	–	1 414	2 742	–	3 015
1935	–	–	–	–	–	4 319
1936	–	–	–	–	3 846	6 620
1937 plan	6 550	9 140	–	–	6 558	9 054

Sources:
Series A RGAE, 4372/91/ 3217, 113–14 (report from the defence sector of Gosplan to the head of Gosplan, dated 20 May 1937).
Series B GARF, 8418/10/148, 13 (report to Molotov, dated 11 January 1935); 1934 is preliminary.
Series C RGAE, 4372/91/3217, 116–18 (20 May 1937).

civilian production, greatly increased (table 4.9), but this was largely a result of the expansion of civilian production by these industries, not of armaments. Even shipbuilding, a success story in 1934, increased production by only 12 per cent.[38] Total military equipment orders measured in current prices increased by only 14 per cent (table 4.7); and the number-of-weapons index (table 4.3) shows a substantial decline in the number of weapons purchased by NKO.

While the armaments modernisation programme largely failed in 1935, defence investments reflect the intensification of the defence effort (table 4.10). The initial plan for the national economy as a whole proposed an absolute decline in investment; within this total the allocation to construction in NKO (628 million rubles) was also lower than actual expenditure in 1934. But during 1935 the allocation was increased to 1174 million;[39] and credits of 1186 million were eventually provided, of which 1086 were eventually utilised (table 4.7). Similarly the initial plan for investment in the armaments industries envisaged a sharp decline;[40] eventually, however, they received 19 per cent more than in 1934. Total investment in NKO and the armaments industries increased from 6.5 per cent of all investment in 1934 to 8.1 per cent in 1935 (table 4.11).

The programme of modernisation already designated for implementation in 1935 became all the more urgent in so far as this was also a year of change for the worse in Soviet threat perceptions. In the course of 1935 Nazi Germany adopted an increasingly aggressive stance, introducing conscription in

Table 4.10. Capital investment in armament industries, 1932–7 (million rubles at current prices)

	Plan	*Fulfilment*
	(1)	(2)
1932	702	778
1933	560	604
1934	874	761
1935	–	905
1936	1 918	1 467
1937	2 972	–

Note: on 17 January 1937, the Politburo approved 3015 million rubles for the 1937 plan (see text).

Sources:
1932 plan: GARF, 5446/57/16, 157 ('other', Sovnarkom decree dated 13 December 1931).
1932–6 fulfilment, 1937 plan: RGAE, 4372/91/3217, 115 (report of defence sector of Gosplan to head of Gosplan, dated 20 May 1937).
1933 plan: GARF, 5446/1/71, 63 ('other', Sovnarkom decree dated 5 January 1933).
1934 plan: GARF, 8418/9/200, 1–2 (appendix, dated 16 February 1934, to Sovnarkom decree, dated 2 January 1934).
1936 plan: GARF, 5446/57/40, 139–41 (Sovnarkom decree, dated 8 February 1936).

March; Italy invaded Abyssinia in October; a Berlin–Tokyo axis loomed on the horizon. On 31 March *Pravda* reported on the state of German rearmament in alarming detail.[41] In December Litvinov warned Stalin that Hjalmar Schacht, President of the Reichsbank and supreme Economics Minister, had privately told a French banker that Germany intended to divide up the Soviet Ukraine with Poland.[42] The armed forces' establishment strength was raised and the conscription age lowered.[43]

In the economy, the practical effect of these heightened fears were reflected practically in 1936 and the subsequent years remaining before World War II. In 1936 alone capital construction by NKO, measured in current prices, increased by as much as 114 per cent, and investment in the armaments industries by 62 per cent (tables 4.7 and 4.10). NKO and armaments investment taken together increased from 8.1 to 11.9 per cent of all investment (table 4.11). Moreover, in 1936, in contrast to 1935, a large increase in armaments production was achieved. Military equipment orders in current prices increased by 105 per cent (table 4.7); the orders achieved amounted to 77 per cent of the revised planned figure, as compared with only

Table 4.11. The share of defence in investment, 1932–7 (per cent)

	% of total investment			*% of industrial investment*
	by NKO	*by armament industries*	*by both*	*by armament industries*
	(1)	(2)	(3)	(4)
1932				
plan	–	–	–	–
fulfilment	4.4	3.8	8.2	7.5
1933				
plan	3.8	3.1	6.9	5.5
fulfilment	3.0	3.4	6.4	6.0
1934				
plan	3.2	3.5	6.7	6.8
fulfilment	3.1	3.4	6.5	6.5
1935				
plan	3.0	–	–	–
fulfilment	4.4	3.7	8.1	7.2
1936				
plan	6.3	8.4	14.7	13.7
fulfilment	7.3	4.6	11.9	10.3
1937				
plan	5.6	9.1	14.8	21.3
fulfilment	6.4	–	–	–

Sources: Defence construction: table 4.7 (credits actually utilised).
Defence industry investment: table 4.10.
Total and industrial investment, 1932: Davies (1996), 506; 1933–7: Zaleski (1980), 647–58.

70 per cent in the previous year. The real increase in defence production in 1936 was certainly less than 105 per cent. But even our number-of-weapons index, which does not allow for technical improvements, shows a rise in production of 62 per cent (table 4.3).

Thus in 1935 the stage was being set for recovery and sustained rapid growth of war production on a new technological basis in the following years. However, such qualitative changes make purely quantitative comparisons of production and capacity in the late 1930s very difficult in relationship to the earlier years of the same decade, and in some respects not very meaningful.

TRENDS IN THE DEFENCE BURDEN

If the size of the armed forces grew more rapidly than overall labour resources, and if defence production grew more rapidly than total output, it follows that defence outlays as a whole probably grew more rapidly than national resources. From this an increase in the defence burden is inferred. Here we touch on another approach to measuring the economic impact of defence activities – a direct comparison of defence outlays with national income. This can be done using either the Soviet net material product (NMP) concept or a western gross national product (GNP) measure. It can also be done at either current or constant prices.

When budget defence spending is compared with NMP, it tells us something about the burden of defence upon the material production sphere. NMP measures the total value of final goods, including intermediate services (such as freight transport) but not final services (such as passenger transport). Part of the defence budget is expended on final services such as the military services provided by armed forces personnel, but servicemen are enabled to supply their services because they are supported by the material production sphere. On the other hand budget spending can also be compared with GNP, and shows how society allocates its total of resources available among civilian and defence tasks, without making arbitrary judgements as to whether services are more or less basic to economic life than goods.

The defence burden can be measured in current or constant prices, and a different meaning is implied in each case. When both defence spending and national income are valued at constant prices, their changing proportion shows the changing relative scales of defence production and total output. However, a rising defence share of GNP at constant prices need not necessarily mean rising civilian sacrifice. For example, if defence goods became relatively cheaper, then more of defence goods could be supplied without detracting from resources allocated to civilian objectives; on the other hand, if they became relatively more expensive, then the same volume of defence goods would involve a rising opportunity cost in terms of other goals. This is revealed when the defence burden is calculated at currently prevailing prices. In short, the defence burden at constant prices shows changing relative volumes of production, but the same ratio at current prices suggests the welfare implications.

Defence and national income

It is much harder to compare defence spending with national resources than with the resources in the hands of government, as was done in table 4.1. One reason is that our national income measures for the mid-1930s are highly imperfect. National income at prevailing prices may be readily compared with budget totals and subtotals, but the figures available contain huge gaps. The official (or at least, officially accepted) series for net material product at prevailing prices is broken for 1931 and 1933–6. Abram Bergson calculated GNP at prevailing prices, but only for the benchmark years 1928 and 1937. The feasible comparisons are presented in table 4.12. Official figures based

Table 4.12. The defence burden, from TsSU and Bergson, 1928–40 (per cent)

	TsSU, % of NMP at prevailing prices	*Bergson, % of GNP:*	
		at prevailing prices	*at factor costs of 1937*
	(1)	(2)	(3)
1913	4.5	–	–
1928	3.0	2.4	1.3
1929	3.1	–	–
1930	3.2	–	–
1931	–	–	–
1932	4.5–4.8	–	–
1933	–	–	–
1934	–	–	–
1935	–	–	–
1936	–	–	–
1937	7.2	6.2	7.9
1938	9.0	–	–
1939	11.9	–	–
1940	14.7	13.0	17.3

Sources:

(1) The defence share in 1913, calculated from Davies (1993), 602 (outlays of the War Ministry only). NMP in 1928–30 from Wheatcroft, Davies (1985), 127; in 1932 from Davies (1996), 505; in 1937–45 from RGAE, 4372/95/168, 79–80. Defence outlays in 1913 from Davies (1958), 65; other years from table 4.1, cols 2, 3, adjusted to calendar year.

(2, 3) Calculated from Bergson (1961), 46, 128.

on an NMP accountancy (col. 1) make possible the following observations: in the late 1920s the defence burden on welfare was relatively low at 3 per cent or so, by comparison with the pre-revolutionary benchmark of 1913, but the latter had been exceeded by 1932, and in 1937–40 the burden climbed to a level unprecedented in peacetime. If it had taken 7 years to double the defence share of the budget between 1930 and 1937, it took only 3 years to double it again between 1937 and 1940, when almost 15 per cent of national income was being consumed by defence. The recasting of national income at prevailing prices to a GNP basis by Bergson (col. 2) does not significantly alter this view; since the ruble value of GNP was a little larger than NMP, the level of the defence burden appears slightly lower, and its dynamic is the same.

Comparisons may also be carried out in real terms (i.e. at constant prices or costs), but again there are fundamental difficulties. Official figures of NMP expressed in the 'unchanged' prices of 1926/27 are generally considered unreliable and are not considered here. Western estimates of real Soviet

Table 4.13. The defence burden in proportion to labour incomes, 1928–40

	Public sector annual earnings, rubles	*Total employment, thousands*	*Defence outlays per person in employment, full-time equivalent*	
			rubles	*% of earnings*
	(1)	(2)	(3)	(4)
1929	800	51 100	19.66	2.5%
1930	936	51 500	23.65	2.5%
1931	1 127	52 800	33.90	3.0%
1932	1 427	53 400	75.54	5.3%
1933	1 566	54 200	79.32	5.1%
1934	1 858	57 700	93.47	5.0%
1935	2 274	62 800	130.35	5.7%
1936	2 770	62 300	238.89	8.6%
1937	3 047	66 000	264.86	8.7%
1938	3 467	69 100	335.75	9.7%
1939	3 867	71 600	–	–
1940	3 972	79 100	717.47	18.1%

Sources:
(1) Zaleski (1971), 344–5; Zaleski (1980), 562–3, 592–3.
(2) Total employment (full time equivalents) from Moorsteen, Powell (1966), 643.
(3) Defence outlays from table 4.1, cols 2, 3, adjusted to calendar year, divided by col. 2.
(4) Col. 3, divided by col. 1.

GNP are preferable on this and other grounds. However, for our purposes defence outlays must first be computed in the same prices or costs as GNP. Bergson estimated GNP by end-use (including defence outlays) at adjusted factor costs of both 1928 and 1937, but only for those years. Moorsteen and Powell estimated GNP by sector of origin for every year after 1928, but there was no annual series for overall real defence outlays (as distinct from the procurement of weapons) to be compared with GNP.

Bergson's figures for GNP and defence outlays at constant 1937 factor costs are shown in table 4.12 (col. 3). In comparison with the defence share at prevailing prices (col. 2), these suggest a lower defence burden (1.3 per cent) in 1928, and a greater subsequent increase in the real volume of defence goods and services relative to total real output. The comparison shows that the welfare impact of the increase in the relative volume of defence activity was softened by the relative cheapening of defence items.

Defence and wage incomes

In order to find annual series which will throw at least some light on the dynamic of the defence burden during the second five-year plan period, we make use of a compromise measure of the defence burden on welfare: the total defence budget, divided by total employment, expressed relative to public sector wage earnings. The advantage of these figures is that they are available in annual series, and each series is relatively robust, but their drawback is that they do not give a full picture, since overall economic welfare is only imperfectly associated with wage incomes, and besides not all employees received the public sector wage (collective farmers were the most numerous exception). The percentages which are computed do not mean that defence outlays were paid out of wages, only that the ratio between them can be expressed numerically.

The results of this comparison are shown in table 4.13 (col. 3). They show clearly a doubling of the defence burden – but from a low level – in the course of the first five-year plan. In 1932–5 this burden remained roughly flat at 5 per cent or so. In 1936 a sharp increase was marked, and the level of the burden now rose continuously, if unsteadily, to the unprecedented 'peacetime' level of 18 per cent in 1940.

CONCLUSION

The evolution of Soviet interwar defence spending can be divided into three phases. The first phase was one of economic demobilisation after the Civil War. After the immediate post-Civil-War cutbacks defence outlays tended to drift upwards, but with economic recovery and the growth of the public sector the burden of defence on both national income and fiscal revenues tended to go on falling. This phase lasted until 1930.

In the second phase, which began in 1931, there was rapid rearmament and the real burden of defence outlays on national resources shifted to a higher level. The burden on government resources did not grow, because the government's share in national resources was now far larger than before. At the same time the change in pace of defence activity was greater than might appear on the surface from purely quantitative measures. There was an increased rate of military-technical innovation, and obsolete weaponry was phased out, so that rearmament in the third phase would be based on new weapons of a much higher technical level.

Thus the second phase was no more than a brief transition to the third phase which began in 1936. In the third phase the growth of real defence spending accelerated sharply. Its relative burden also grew markedly and became unprecedentedly heavy by peacetime standards. Rapid rearmament gave way to intense mobilisation.

The period of the second five-year plan must therefore be seen in its context. It began with rapid rearmament already under way. Before it was over, it also witnessed the transition from rapid rearmament to intense mobilisation, which came in 1936. This transition was one of considerable difficulty for the defence sector. The years 1934–6 were 'three good years' for production and living standards generally, but the armed forces struggled to achieve their programmes, lurching from setback to crisis before successfully forcing defence activity to a higher level in both quantity and quality.

NOTES

1 Davies, Harrison, and Wheatcroft, eds (1994), 269, 272.
2 Jasny (1961), 14.
3 See Cooper (1976), 35 and table 1 below. The figure given for 1933 as the actual expenditure in Davies (1993), 593, was evidently the planned estimate, though this was not stated in the archival source.
4 See Cooper (1976), 35, and table 1 below.
5 For these memoranda see *Vestnik MID*, no. 3 (61), 1990, 70 1.
6 RTsKhIDNI, 17/162/17, 119; GARF, 5446/57/35, art. 23/6ss. The Politburo decision was taken by correspondence. A further Politburo decision by correspondence on February 19 resolved that NKO should prepare data on military expenditure for the League of Nations Yearbook and submit it to the Politburo for approval (RTsKhIDNI, 17/162/17, 104). These documents were not available for the account in Davies (1993), 581–2.
7 *Vestnik MID*, no. 3 (61), 1990, 76, and the further memorandum from NKO of 4 April (ibid., 79 – clause 6).
8 GARF, 8418/10/148, 5.
9 RTsKhIDNI, 17/162/19, 16 (decision by correspondence); the same decision was adopted as a Sovnarkom decree on the following day (GARF 5446/57/38, 183 – art. 2673/441s).
10 See Cooper (1976), 35 and table 1 below.
11 RTsKhIDNI, 17/162/17, 159–60 (decision by correspondence).
12 GARF, 8418/8/137, 11–12 (appendix to Sovnarkom decree dated 5 January 1933). Figures cited by Davies (1993), 593, similarly showed that in January-March 1933 the total allocation to defence purposes was 39.8 per cent greater than the allocation to NKVM. The 1935 budget showed an even higher proportion of non-NKO defence expenditure: GARF, 8418/10/129, 1–2 (decree of Commission of Defence dated 2 April 1935, which does not, however reveal a figure for internal and security troops).
13 For numbers in the labour force (1926/27 – 83.7 m, 1932 – 88.6 m, 1937 – 89.6 m, 1940 – 100.8 m), see Eason (1963), 77.
14 RGVA, 33988/3/81, 39 (Red Army staff memorandum, 5 August 1927); the authors are grateful to Lennart Samuelson for this reference.
15 For these figures see the appendix to Davies, Harrison (1997).
16 The result is notably in agreement with the index of munitions procurement prices computed independently by Bergson (1961), 72, which showed 1928 as 60 per cent of 1937, and 1940 as 120 per cent.
17 Moorsteen, Powell (1966), 622–3.
18 RGAE, 2097/1/1051, 17–18 (15 November 1929).
19 For further detail see Simonov (1996), 38–41.

20 Tupper (1982).
21 GARF, 8418/10/31, 52 (14 October 1935).
22 Kostyrchenko (1992), 432–3.
23 Iakovlev (1979), 24, 32.
24 Simonov (1996), 91–2.
25 These difficulties are attested by a variety of reports and memoranda in RGVA, 4/14/1298, 140–44 (Efimov to Voroshilov, 9 September 1935), 145 (Voroshilov to Piatakov, 2 December 1935), 147 (Kaganovich to Molotov), 150 (Gamarnik to Molotov, October 1935), 151–2 (Efimov to Tukhachevskii and Pavlunovskii, 31 January 1935); RGVA, 4/14/1315, 198–201 (Pavlunovskii to Voroshilov, 4 November 1935).
26 Holland Hunter and Janusz M. Szyrmer have recently produced a new estimate of real defence outlays estimate in annual series between 1928 and 1940 (Hunter, Szyrmer (1992), 41). This estimate therefore fills in the gaps between benchmark years left by Bergson, but contains several disadvantages. Calculated in 'balanced' 1928 prices, it generally confirms a picture of rapid growth (the prices are described as 'balanced' because they are derived from an input/output table after balancing). It shows somewhat less real growth than either of Bergson's (an 8-fold increase over 1928–37, and a 2.3-fold further increase to 1940). This reverse Gerschenkron effect is surprising and implausible. Unlike Bergson, Hunter and Szyrmer did not disaggregate defence outlays and deflate the components independently. Instead, they simply deflated total nominal defence outlays by an index of wages of engineering workers, with the intention 'to capture at least most of the inflation in the cost of military equipment' (Hunter, Szyrmer (1992), 299). The wage index used ended in 1934 and Hunter and Szyrmer extended it to 1940 by guesswork. Regardless of the reliability of the wage index, this meant assuming in addition that wage earnings in engineering and the defence industry moved together, that unit total costs in the defence industry moved in proportion to wage earnings, and that the costs of maintenance and operation of the armed forces moved in line with weapon costs. It appears likely that Hunter and Szyrmer under-estimated the true change in the volume of defence activity by understating productivity growth and cost reductions in the defence industry, if for no other reason. For the early 1930s the Hunter/Szyrmer series also suffers from the official concealment of rearmament: there is therefore a false break in the series in 1934, when official distortion ended. It appears, however, to confirm a true break in 1936, with a 60 per cent estimated increase in real defence spending in a single year.
27 RGAE, 4372/91/2196, 1–2 (report from the head of the special sector of TsUNKhU to the head of the defence sector of Gosplan, 4 January 1934).
28 This arises from a comparison of prices given in RGVA, 4/14/880, 13–14 (Khrulev to Voroshilov, 17 January 1933) with prices listed by sources given in note 27.
29 RGVA, 4/14/1626, 9 (Red Army General Staff memorandum dated 25 August 1936); RGAE, 7733/36/40, 109 (appendix to Sovnarkom decree dated 17 December 1936); RGVA, 51/2/441, 62–3 (decree no. 108 of the Sovnarkom defence committee of 3 September 1937).
30 RGVA, 4/14/1626, 15 (Egorov to Voroshilov, 3 November 1936).
31 RGAE, 4372/91/3106, 94–3 (dated 12 December 1936) (510 million rubles out of a total of 5912 million was attributed to price increases).
32 For the I-16 in 1936 see Simonov (1996), 104, and for the I-5 in 1934, RGVA, 4/14/1287, 132–4 (undated memorandum) (according to RGVA, 4/14/880, 14, the 1932 price of an I-5 had been only 24 500 rubles).
33 RGVA, 4/14/1298, 142 (memorandum by Efimov to Voroshilov, 9 September 1935).

34 RGVA, 4/14/1298, 147 (M. Kaganovich, deputy people's commissar for heavy industry, to Molotov, 9 September 1935).

35 RGVA, 4/14/1298, 149 (Pavlunovskii to Premudrov in Molotovo, 12–13 August 1935); for Gamarnik's letters of October 1935 see ibid. 148, 150.

36 GARF, 8418/10/31, 65, 65ob, 66 (dated November 11).

37 GARF, 8418/10/31, 9 (decision dated 2 December 1935).

38 RGVA, 4/14/1883, 25 (report dated 7 January 1937).

39 See RGVA, 4/14/1667, 11 (report to Voroshilov from the financial department of NKO, dated 14 December 1935).

40 According to a decree of the Defence Committee dated 2 April 1935, it was planned at only 494 million rubles, a cut of 35 per cent (GARF, 8418/10/129, 1–2).

41 The article was written by Tukhachevskii and personally edited by Stalin. For Stalin's corrections, see *Izvestiia TsK*, 1 (1990), 160–70.

42 *Izvestiia TsK*, no. 2, 1990, pp. 211–12; in his letter Litvinov criticised the Soviet press for its 'Tolstoian position of non-resistance to evil' in relation to Germany.

43 RTsKhIDNI, 17/162/18, 24 and 35–7 (dated May 10), and 123 (dated August 28).

Part III
The war and the postwar period

5 Wartime mobilisation: a German comparison

Mark Harrison

INTRODUCTION

In World War II, the Soviet mobilisation of industry appears to have been more successful than the German. Yet in terms of prewar resources and *ex ante* mobilisation potential there is no obvious reason why this should have been the case. In production, resources, and mobilisation preparations there were many similarities. The obvious differences were mostly to the Soviet disadvantage. Yet the Soviet economy produced weapons on a larger scale than Germany, and more of Soviet war production came earlier in the war. How can this be explained?

By a process of elimination, I arrive at the factor of mass production. In *Why the Allies Won*, Richard Overy emphasised the role played by 'American and Soviet productionism' in contrast to 'Germany's bureaucratised economy'. Drawing on the copious evidence of memoirs, official reports, and war production statistics, he wrote:

> No war was more industrialised than the Second World War. Factory for factory, the Allies made better use of their industry than their enemy.[1]

German failure was to be explained, Overy argued, by a lack of commitment to mass production. The purpose of this chapter is to try to isolate more precisely the significance of Soviet mass production. The origins and consequences of production systems are a multi-faceted topic, the dimensions of which are gradually becoming clearer with new research. Some additional historical factors can be explored, if not yet definitively.

THE SOVIET ADVANTAGE IN WAR PRODUCTION

To begin with, in what sense was Soviet war production more successful? I have in mind that Soviet industry was mobilised more rapidly than German industry, showed a different time profile of output, with a higher proportion of cumulative output earlier in the war, and secured higher flows of weapons at all stages. Both the overall volume and the phasing of output were significant in their own right, but I do not mean to imply that either was decisive on its own. The Soviet Union was not Germany's only enemy; had German

Table 5.1. German and Soviet war production, 1940–5 (physical units)

	1940	*1941*	*1942*	*1943*	*1944*	*1945*	*Total*
Germany							
Ground and air munitions, thousands							
Rifles, carbines	1 352	1 359	1 370	2 275	2 856	665	9 877
Machine pistols	119	325	232	234	229	78	1 217
Machine guns	59	96	117	263	509	111	1 155
Guns	6	22	41	74	148	27	318
Mortars	4.4	4.2	9.8	23.0	33.2	2.8	77.4
Tanks and SPG	2.2	3.8	6.2	10.7	18.3	4.4	45.6
Combat aircraft	6.6	8.4	11.6	19.3	34.1	7.2	87.2
Warships, units							
Submarines	40	196	244	270	189	0	939
USSR							
Ground and air munitions, thousands							
Rifles, carbines	1 462	2 421	4 049	3 438	2 451	703	14 524
Machine pistols	92	95	570	643	555	272	2 227
Machine guns	96	149	356	458	439	109	1 607
Guns	15	41	128	130	122	77	513
Mortars	38	42	230	69	7	3	390.1
Tanks and SPG	2.8	6.6	24.7	24.0	29.0	22.6	109.7
Combat aircraft	8.3	12.4	21.7	29.9	33.2	20.9	126.4
Warships, units							
Major naval vessels	33	62	19	13	23	11	161
USSR/Germany							
Rifles, carbines	1.1	1.8	3.0	1.5	0.9	1.1	1.5
Machine pistols	0.8	0.3	2.5	2.7	2.4	3.5	1.8
Machine guns	1.6	1.5	3.0	1.7	0.9	1.0	1.4
Guns	2.4	1.8	3.2	1.8	0.8	2.9	1.6
Mortars	8.7	10.1	23.5	3.0	0.2	1.1	5.0
Tanks and SPG	1.3	1.7	4.0	2.2	1.6	5.1	2.4
Combat aircraft	1.3	1.5	1.9	1.5	1.0	2.9	1.4
Warships	0.8	0.3	0.1	0.0	0.1	–	0.2

Sources: Ground and air munitions (SPG are self-propelled guns): Germany (within contemporary frontiers, so Greater Germany, but excluding occupied territories, in particular Czechoslovakia) is from IVMV, vol. 12 (1982), 200 (tanks in 1940 include armoured cars); USSR (also within contemporary frontiers) is from RTsKhIDNI, 71/25/7882, 4–20, except mortars from Harrison (1985), 250. Major naval vessels (excluding landing craft, torpedo boats, and other auxiliary craft) and submarines: Overy (1995b), 1060.

war production accelerated faster, or achieved a higher overall volume, Germany might still have been defeated, whether by the Soviet Union or by a combination of other powers. None the less it is true that the struggle on the eastern front was very evenly balanced for a period of some 21 months from the autumn of 1941 to the summer of 1943. For most of this time the Soviet

Union was being defeated, and there was several points at which outright military and economic collapse could not be ruled out. Therefore the comparative mobilisation of industry was certainly of very great importance.

Annual figures and cumulative totals of war production of the two powers in physical units are shown in table 5.1. It is notable that overall Soviet production outweighed that of Germany in virtually every item listed; only in shipbuilding did Soviet industry fail to compete. More remarkable is the fact that the Soviet advantage was at its greatest in 1942; just when its struggle against the Wehrmacht for the military advantage was at the most intense, the Red Army was receiving combat aircraft at twice the rate of delivery to the enemy, and 3 or 4 times the flow of most other types of ground forces' armament. After 1942 the pace of German war production accelerated, but Germany's context had already changed to one of commitments multiplying out of control and an inexorable unfolding of defeat.

This Soviet-German contrast could be set in a more general comparison. Good serial data for overall war production is available for five cases of great powers in modern great wars: the Soviet Union, the United States, and Germany in World War II, and Britain in both World Wars. The acceleration of war production is a tricky thing to capture objectively since obvious measures such as growth rates and percentages of cumulative output are heavily dependent on the degree of prewar mobilisation and the frequency of sampling relative to the duration of the war. The most appropriate general model seems to be that of the logistic curve, the parameters of which will reflect the rapidity with which the mobilisation potential is saturated. In each of the five cases indicated the war production measure may be indexed as percentages of peak output. I then look for the logistic curve which best describes the path of war production prior to the wartime peak.

Results are shown in table 5.2 and graphed in figure 5.1. For four cases the logistic model is found to be robust. The estimated b parameter of the logistic curve allows us to rank the four in order of diminishing 'steepness' of the war production curve as follows: the United States, the United Kingdom in World War I, the Soviet Union, and the United Kingdom in World War II. The differences among them, however, are not great as a visual check with figure 5.1 confirms. The truly exceptional case is that of Germany, where a match to the logistic curve is found only with some difficulty, and two of the three parameters are not statistically significant. A fit can be found only on the implausible basis that, at its wartime peak, German war production was just beginning the slow ascent of a logistic curve of immense height.

One might more simply conclude that, on this evidence, Germany's industrial mobilisation was a comparative failure. The approach to the peak was too gradual. A logarithmic scale would show little change in growth rates in 1942 with the supposed transition from Göring's regime of 'incompetence, arrogance, and egotism' to the 'production miracle' stemming from Speer's

Table 5.2. Logistic curves fitted to war production series: five cases

	USSR	USA	United Kingdom		Germany
$t = 0$	1944 (Q3)	1943 (Dec.)	1944 (Q1)	1918	1944 (July)
k	1.0322**	1.0763**	1.0771**	1.0657**	569.09
a	−3.6564**	−2.3103**	−2.5527**	−2.8906*	6.4055
b	−1.3153**	−1.7974**	−1.0075**	−1.5592*	−0.34359**
n	19	42	16	5	58

Notes:
k, a, b, and t are parameters of the logistic curve of war production y, where:

$$y = \frac{k}{1 + e^{a+bt}}$$

Here t is time scaled in years set to zero at the measured peak of war production, k estimates the war production asymptote on which the logistic curve converges, a fixes the displacement of the curve's inflection point relative to $t = 0$, and b is a measure (with negative sign) of the rate at which saturation is progressively achieved. The number of observations is given by n.
* Significant at the 5 per cent level.
** Significant at the 1 per cent level.

Sources: Soviet Union: Harrison (1996), 190 (output of ground and air munitions). Series are annual for 1940 (which counts four observations), then quarterly.

Britain, World War I: Hardach (1977), 87. Annual series, 1914–18, in physical units (rifles, guns, machine guns, tanks, aircraft) converted to index numbers and given equal weights in 1918.

Britain, World War II: Harrison (1990), 665; quarterly observations from the last quarter of 1939, with the first half of 1940 missing.

Germany: 1939 (Q4) to 1941: quarterly index numbers for armament and ammunition from USSBS (1945), 283, each quarter counting three observations; 1942 onwards: all munitions, monthly index numbers from Wagenführ (1954), 178–81.

USA: *Survey of current business*, February 1945, 24 (July 1940–December 1943), and table S-2 in subsequent issues. Thanks to Hugh Rockoff for this source. Series are half-yearly from July 1940 through 1941 (counting six observations each time), then monthly from 1942 onwards.

policies of rationalisation; if anything, after the relative stagnation of 1941, the Speer reforms simply pushed German war production back onto the gradually rising trend already established in the period from late 1939 to late 1940.

In summary, the Soviet Union outproduced Germany in all branches of war production other than shipbuilding in World War II. Soviet production superiority was especially marked in 1942. Despite the fact that this was a war which German leaders had planned, and which took Soviet leaders by surprise, and despite the burdens imposed by Germany's deep penetration of Soviet territory, Soviet industry was mobilised more rapidly than German industry. The Soviet Union's war production was already within 5 per cent of its peak in the last quarter of 1942, a full 18 months before Germany's began to crest.

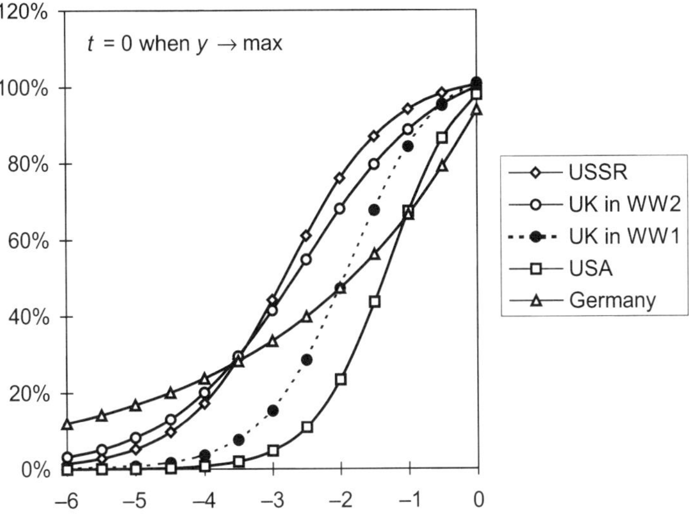

Fig. 5.1. Fitted logistic curves of war production: five cases
Source: as table 5.2.

It used to be argued that this was simply Hitler's clever plan; the slow growth of German war production in the period 1939–41 was chiefly attributable to a self-imposed limitation of demand. Nazi leaders intended to win Germany's wars quickly and without major expenditure of munitions, which would have required cutbacks in civilian consumption and an early imposition of strict discipline on the mechanisms for resource allocation.[2] This view is now recognised to be defective. Richard Overy has shown that in the period 1939–41 German civilian consumption was significantly repressed; Hitler allocated major resources to war production and investment in autarky, and demanded a strong acceleration in the pace of war production. The only thing that went wrong with this programme is that the increase in war production did not materialise. Instead, productivity fell.[3]

Thus the main difference between Soviet and German industry in terms of wartime outcomes is that in the period 1941–3 Stalin's programme for the procurement of munitions was more successful than Hitler's. Below I investigate various hypotheses as to why this should have been the case. Taking them in order, I rule out various possibilities – that Soviet industry had a greater mobilisation potential arising from superior prewar productive capacity or productivity, a more advantageous resource environment, and prewar mobilisation plans and procedures. The answer lies by default in wartime economic management of both demand and supply side factors.

OVERALL PRODUCTION AND PRODUCTIVITY

On the eve of World War II the Soviet and German industrial sectors were of comparable size in terms of workforce, Of course, in overall employment terms the Soviet Union was much larger. As table 5.3 shows, Germany's employed population was just less than half the size of the USSR's. Almost all the difference, however, is accounted for by the agricultural sector. In fact, the non-agricultural workforces of the two countries were very similar in size: 29.2 million in Germany, 32.5 million in the USSR. The table also shows that numbers employed in each country in industry, construction, and transport were quite similar (18.6 million in Germany, 20 million in the USSR). However, the Soviet Union had substantially larger numbers engaged in transport, which no doubt reflected the country's greater territorial extent; and substantially fewer engaged in artisan production. The latter imbalance is explained in part by the suppression of small rural industries in the course of collectivising agriculture ten years previously.

The levels of development of the two countries' industrial sectors (and therefore the volumes of output) were probably very different, although the computation is complicated and must use a chain of binary comparisons in which the Soviet relativity is the weakest link. According to Stephen Broadberry, output per worker in German manufacturing in 1937 was at virtually the same level as in the UK, while US manufacturing output per worker was just over twice the British level.[4] At the beginning of the 1950s Walter

Table 5.3. Employment in the German and Soviet economies, 1939/40 (thousands)

	Germany, 1939	*USSR, 1940*
(A) The employed population		
Total	39 416	81 850
agriculture	11 224	49 317
nonagriculture	29 192	32 533
(B) Industry, construction, transport		
Total	18 638	20 064
industry[a]	15 115	13 755
large-scale industry	9 779	11 643
artisan industry	5 336	2 112
construction	1 399	2 355
transport	2 124	3 954

Note:
[a] Including electricity supply, but excluding construction.

Sources: Germany from Abelshauser (1998), table 4.17 (A); USSR from Harrison (1996), 258, 272. Figures for both countries include forced and foreign labour.

Galenson carried out a binary comparison of Soviet/US gross industrial output per worker in 1936–9 and arrived at a figure of 40 per cent; combined with Broadberry's figures, this would suggest a prewar Soviet/German productivity ratio of roughly 80 per cent or a little less.[5] A similar ratio is implied for total output of industry since the workforces in the two countries were of similar size. But a more recent study by Remco Kouwenhoven (which involves backward extrapolation from a binary Soviet /US comparison of gross industrial output per hour worked for 1987) is much more pessimistic, giving 21 per cent in 1937 falling to 10 per cent in 1940.[6] The Soviet/US ratio fell towards World War II because US productivity gains coincided (as we shall see) with a Soviet productivity setback. But the Soviet/German ratio probably did not deteriorate so sharply. Still, Kouwenhoven's figures combined with Broadberry's point to a prewar Soviet/German productivity ratio of at most 40 per cent.

When synthetic comparisons are difficult, it is commonplace to turn to indirect, usually physical indicators. A few are collected in table 5.4. From a Soviet source (although not, originally, intended for wide circulation), they present a relatively favourable picture, suggesting that Soviet prewar industrial production was much more than 40 per cent of Germany's; but they also indicate (as one would expect) that the Soviet advantage was greater in basic materials, fuels, and energy, than in more highly fabricated products. However, such comparisons are almost always biased by missing products in ways which are not always immediately apparent. The source cited in the table draws our attention to one which would be counted to the Soviet advantage – the fact that the Soviet Union produced oil, where Germany did not. On the other hand, the table entirely ignores fabricated products other than industrial machinery, especially those important for transport, communications, information, and consumption, in which Germany certainly had the advantage. Thus no firm conclusions may be drawn from the table. Certainly it does not justify any greater optimism about the production potential of Soviet industry than the measures suggested by Kouwenhoven.

Table 5.4. The relative volume of industrial production in physical units, 1940 (Germany, per cent of USSR)

Iron ore	203
Pig iron	107
Crude steel	96
Electric power	77
Coal	61
Cement	52
Metal-cutting machine tools	47

Source: TsSU (1959), 60–1.

It is worth adding that the impact of the first years of conflict would swing the overall balance further in Germany's favour. Territorial expansion would add the industrial assets of much of continental Europe to Germany's side. Enemy occupation would subtract significantly from Soviet production capacities. The occupation of industrialised Europe (but probably not of the agrarian territories of eastern Europe and the western USSR) would be a real gain for Germany, outweighing the costs of aggression.[7] On the other hand, Allied bombing later in the war would force German production below its maximum potential.

THE RESOURCE ENVIRONMENT

To evaluate the potential of industry for further mobilisation it is necessary to consider not only its initial stocks and their utilisation, but also its wider context. Did the larger Soviet non-industrial population and territory constitute a superior mobilisation reserve for Soviet industry?

In some obvious sense the answer is yes. The Soviet territorial expanse, blessed by rich deposits of minerals and materials, was nearly 50 times Germany's. The German density of settlement was 16 times that of the USSR.[8] Thus the Soviet balance of natural resources to population, and still more so to industrial workers, was relatively advantageous. In the same spirit there was some obvious sense in which the 49 million Soviet agricultural labourers constituted a much larger reserve for industry than the 11 million German farm workers.

However, the real mobilisation value of these Soviet human and material reserves was much less than the mobilisation value of the quantitatively more restricted numbers of Germans and more limited German territory. This was because of low levels of non-industrial productivity and economic integration. The mineral resources were inaccessible or otherwise difficult to exploit without major investments in transportation and complementary services. The agricultural workers were locked into low-productivity employment from which they could not be easily extricated in case of need.

Table 5.5 shows some significant differences between prewar Germany and the Soviet Union in regard to agriculture. In Germany agricultural achieved half the productivity of non-agricultural workers (when calculated at German domestic prices). In the USSR farm workers' productivity was only one third (in Soviet prices) of the level achieved by non-agricultural workers, which was itself only a small fraction of the productivity standard set by German non-agricultural workers. Therefore it took nearly three-fifths of the Soviet workforce to feed Soviet citizens to rather lower dietary norms than were achieved in Germany by one-quarter of the German workforce (aided, it is true, by limited food imports).

Table 5.5. Agricultural employment and productivity in Germany and the Soviet Union, 1938/40

	Germany, 1938/39	*USSR, 1940*
Agricultural workers, % of working population	26	57
Net output per worker in agriculture, % of non-agriculture	50	33

Source: Gatrell, Harrison (1993), table 8.

Superficially this could appear to the Soviet mobilisation advantage. Suppose (as was probably the case) that not only the average but also the marginal product of labour was higher in prewar industry than in agriculture.Then, if wartime output is measured at constant prewar prices, a redistribution of labour from agriculture to industry will result in a small loss of real agricultural output more than compensated by a large increase in the real output of industry. Food supplies do not deteriorate by much, there is substantial growth of war production, and total output and productivity improve. The problem here is that prewar priccs do not correspond to wartime utilities. The prewar Soviet Union was a low-income country where the marginal utility of food was relatively high and would rise steeply with wartime deprivation. There was much less scope for belt-tightening than in Germany. Therefore, wartime labour shortages were soon felt just as acutely in agriculture as in industry, and the mobilisation of labour out of agriculture was quickly followed by reverse movements.

One further possibility which might be mentioned is that Soviet industry was better placed than German industry in wartime because of supplies of forced labour. However, the evidence does not support this view. By 1944 3.5 million foreign labourers and prisoners of war were employed in German war production (one third of the munitions workforce) compared with half a million in 1941.[9] In contrast, in 1942 when Soviet war production was already near its peak, of 853 000 workers mobilised into the defence industry only 68 000 were forced labourers of the 'NKVD special contingent'.[10] This is not to say that the Stalinist regime did not possess and utilise sweeping powers of coercion over the working population, and it is clear that the defence industry workforce was strictly regimented.[11] However, forced labourers were more likely to be engaged in construction, logging, mining, and farming than in industrial production, and their total (counting prisoners in GULAG camps and colonies and 'special settlers' in internal exile) was less than 2 million in 1944 and did not exceed 3 million at any point in this period.[12]

In summary, from the point of view of resources and productivity Soviet industry was generally worse placed than German industry for war mobilisation. The obstacles facing it were twofold. One was the legacy of relatively low productivity in industry itself, stemming partly from an historical capital accumulation deficiency, partly from inefficient utilisation of capital assets and technological lag. The other lay in a poorly integrated, low-productivity non-industrial environment.

MOBILISATION PREPARATIONS

The scope for wartime mobilisation depended not only on existing overall resources but also on specific preparations. The extent of prewar mobilisation and contingency planning would prove very important in preparing industry for war production and more far-reaching mobilisation tasks. Here there are notable similarities between German and Soviet industry in the degree of preparation.

First, by 1940 both countries were producing munitions on a comparable scale. According to my own previous estimate, in 1940 the Soviet Union was slightly ahead in overall terms. This assessment looks to be confirmed by the figures shown in table 5.1, which shows Germany to have been lagging somewhat in all areas except naval armament; when qualitative differences (especially for aircraft) are taken into account, however, the extent of the German lag was probably less than would appear.

Second, it is apparent that in the prewar years both countries had made major investments not only in specialised munitions capacities but also in the supporting facilities which would guarantee domestic supplies of industrial materials for war. In Germany the core tasks of the second four-year plan of 1936–40 administered by Hermann Göring were the substitution of domestic for imported iron ore, of hydrogenated coal for imported oil, and of synthetic for imported natural rubber. These programmes took up 60 per cent of Germany's industrial investment in 1937–9; if aircraft and shipbuilding are included, the proportion rises to 70 per cent.[13]

The common stress on heavy industrialisation and a military-industrial build-up in Soviet interwar economic development is almost too well known to require documentation. Between 1928 and 1940 the fixed capital stock in Soviet machine-building and metallurgy grew by more than eight times, in contrast to relative stagnation for consumer goods, agriculture, and housing.[14] By the mid-1930s producer goods (including defence industry) were taking 85 per cent of industrial investment.[15] The share of the defence industry itself in industrial investment rose slowly at first from 3.3 per cent in 1928/29 to 7.8 per cent in 1932, and eventually to more than 30 per cent in the national economic plan for 1941.[16]

Third, German and Soviet industrial leaders had made significant commitments to further mobilisation planning. Here quantitative comparisons are hardly possible. Serious mobilisation planning began in Soviet industry in the early 1930s (see Chapters 2 and 3); soon it was stimulated by incoming intelligence of the progress in mobilisation planning being made in Germany. Through the 1930s a series of industry-wide mobilisation plans was adopted, and was reflected in a ceaseless cascade of lower-level mobilisation plans and assignments which flowed down the ministerial hierarchies to industrial establishments. Of course there were defects of commission and omission, and it was hard to maintain a sense of reality.

On the other hand, the quality of German mobilisation planning was probably lower than appeared to easily-impressed Russians (see Chapter 11). As late as August 1939 the high command of the Wehrmacht was complaining that mobilisation plans were complete only for the steel, chemical, and synthetic oil industries (essentially those covered by the four-year plan). In coal mining and machine tools they were in preparation, and in the rest of manufacturing industry they simply did not exist.[17] It seems likely that the leaders of both countries, from Stalin and Hitler down, consistently believed themselves to have more time to complete their war preparations than would actually be available, and this belief was common and shared.

Fourth, as of 1940 both countries' industries contained a significant slack of poorly utilised resources in reserve. There was no visible unemployment of either labour or fixed capacity. Instead, the reserve was being formed by declining productivity. Table 5.6 shows that in the period 1939–41 productivity in the German munitions industry fell by one-quarter. Richard Overy has commented that 'the large increase in the proportion of the industrial workforce involved in military production did not produce a proportionate increase in military output'; in the aircraft industry the workforce increased by 50 per cent, but the output of finished aircraft by only 15 per cent.[18]

No such indicators are available for the Soviet defence industry before the war; industry as a whole, however, certainly suffered a serious negative shock

Table 5.6. Output per worker in German industry, 1940–4 (per cent of 1939)

	Basic industry	*Munitions production*	*Consumer industry*	*Industry, total*
1940	104.1	87.6	115.9	106.6
1941	114.6	75.9	133.3	104.2
1942	113.5	99.6	121.1	109.9
1943	108.7	131.6	124.7	115.5
1944	87.6	160.0[a]	132.3	111.0

Note:
[a] Lower bound.

Source: Abelshauser (1998), table 4.14.

Table 5.7. Labour productivity in Soviet industry, 1928–50 (per cent of 1937)

	Industry value added	
	per worker	*per hour worked*
1928	100	94
1929	109	102
1930	110	107
1931	95	94
1932	71	71
1933	77	74
1934	84	80
1935	92	89
1936	101	99
1937	100	100
1938	101	101
1939	104	104
1940	102	91
1941	110	85
1942	143	100
1943	159	107
1944	156	106
1945	116	89
1946	84	69
1947	91	75
1948	103	85
1949	116	96
1950	113	100

Source: Calculated as figures compiled for Harrison (1998b), appendix A. Industry value added is measured at 1937 factor cost.

to productivity at this time. Table 5.7 shows that output per hour worked in Soviet industry fell by 20 per cent between 1939 and 1941. Output per worker was maintained only by the imposition of a longer working week with severe controls on timekeeping and absenteeism. Unfortunately, in the absence of prewar employment series for defence industry we cannot investigate the distribution of the Soviet shock between civilian and defence industry.

Nor, despite their tantalising coincidence of scale and timing, can we really be sure whether the underlying causes of the Soviet and German shocks were the same or different. The historiography of the German case appears to concur with Albert Speer in blaming Göring's regime ('incompetence, arrogance, and egotism', and so on). As for the Soviet case, the most likely cause was the overstraining of industrial and consumer supplies and labour motivation by the preceding wave of investment mobilisation, purges, now accelerating rearmament, and military operations in Poland, the Baltic, and against Finland on top. But in a broad and general sense the national context was the same in each case – rapid rearmament, with an impatient government dominated by a sense of growing urgency, squeezing the civilian sector and throwing both material and financial resources at industry in order to get quick results, regardless of rising shortages and pressure on supplies.

In summary, German and Soviet industry both approached total war in 1940 with experience of rising military production, underpinned by several years of large-scale investment in *Tiefrüstung* (armament in depth), mobilisation plans which were unrealistic and incomplete in hindsight (but how could these ever be otherwise?), and a considerable reserve of poorly utilised capital and labour.

THE PRODUCTION SYSTEM

If Soviet wartime industrial achievements cannot be attributed to superior industrial resources, or nonindustrial resources, or a superior mobilisation capacity laid down before the war, then the production system must be considered as an independent factor. German failure and Soviet success in establishing mass production appear to have been decisive in determining comparative outcomes.

Documenting the comparative transitions is not easy. The accounts of the participants composed after the event speak eloquently in support of the mass-production hypothesis, but are self-interested. On the Soviet side, postwar planners and engineers were keen to claim wartime success in simultaneously cutting costs and achieving long runs of output of standardised weapons produced to the exacting standards required for interchangeability of parts, partly in a triumphalist spirit, partly because this was the lesson sanctified by high-level leaders to be marked and learned by postwar military-industrial managers at lower levels. On the German side the most vocal memoirists among the organisers of war production such as Albert Speer needed to emphasise the scale of the obstacles against which they had struggled, in order to promote their place in history.

German evidence from the time is more compelling, being less tainted with hindsight, and has been painstakingly assembled by Richard Overy. This evidence shows that German leaders concerned with the overall balance of national resources were painfully aware of the excessive cost of maintaining a wide assortment of specialised weaponry continually redesigned to changing military requirements and finished according to the exacting craft traditions of German industry.[19]

Table 5.8. Labour productivity in Soviet engineering and metalworking, 1941–5 (value added, per cent of 1940)

	Per worker	*Per hour worked*
1941	126	104
1942	247	182
1943	273	198
1944	290	213
1945	207	184

Source: calculated from Harrison (1996), 216.

Quantitative evidence which would enable a proper German-Soviet comparison is harder to come by. Wartime productivity series for Germany and the Soviet Union can be compared from tables 5.6 and 5.8. Table 5.8 shows that value added per hour worked in Soviet engineering and metalworking more than doubled during the war, and, with the increase in hours worked, value added per worker more than trebled. Table 5.6 showed that in Germany output per worker in war production more than doubled. In the German case, making up for the prewar loss of productivity explains part of the wartime gain, and the same factor may perhaps have been at work in the Soviet Union. Thus the scale of wartime productivity gains should not be surprising since it is clear that the scope for rationalising and cost-cutting in both countries was very great as the scale of war production rose. Value added per worker in Soviet industry increased by more than gross output per worker in German industry, but the share of value added in gross output probably rose in both countries.[20] The wartime gain was clearly faster and came sooner (most of it by 1942) in the Soviet Union than in Germany (not until 1944). These measures of productivity are certainly important, but they are not decisive since they tend only to confirm what we already knew.

Of more significance in illustrating different approaches to mass production is table 5.9, documented more fully in the case of Soviet aircraft in table 5.10. Table 5.9 shows that as late as the beginning of 1944 German industry was attempting to build several times the number of types of ground and air weaponry being built in the Soviet Union. While this sort of table is always vulnerable to international differences of definition, it seems likely that the variation revealed is too large to attribute to nuances of meaning.[21] Only after the reforms imposed upon industry and the army by Albert Speer in the early months of 1944 did the German assortment contract to Soviet dimensions or (in the case of aircraft) even less.

Table 5.9. Numbers of weapon types in production in Germany and the Soviet Union, 1944

	Germany		*USSR*
	(A)	*(B)*	
Artillery	26	8	5
Antitank guns	12	1	2
Antiaircraft guns	10	2	3
Tanks, armoured vehicles	18	7	6
Aircraft	42	5	18

Sources: For Germany see Overy (1994), 363; (A) is for January, and (B) shows post-Speer reform figures. For USSR, ground forces armament figures are derived from first quarter serial production data in RTsKhIDNI, except aircraft based on annual series in Kostyrchenko (1994), 235–7.

Table 5.10 illustrates the scale of mass production of Soviet aircraft, and also the underlying difficulties of evaluation. In the years 1941–5, 34 factories built 23 aircraft models. However, several models were built in more than one factory, and many of these factories built more than one model. The number of integrated production runs, therefore, was neither 23 nor 34 but 70. More than 140 000 aircraft were built in total, on average roughly 6000 per model, 4000 per factory, and 2000 per run. Around these averages there was marked variation. Eight 'numbered' factories built three-quarters of this total (an average of nearly 14 000 aircraft each), while 26 factories built the remainder (1250 each).[22] The longest single run was 15 000 Il-2 fighters at factory no. 18 – more than one tenth of total Soviet wartime aircraft production by numbers. The eight largest runs accounted for three-fifths of the total (11 000 aircraft per run). But the remaining 62 runs were on average of only 900 aircraft each. Thus there was certainly an impressive core of largescale mass production, but also a diffuse periphery of much smaller runs of a more variegated model assortment.

THE CHARACTER OF DEMAND AND SUPPLY

In this differentiation of German from Soviet experience, both demand and supply factors were apparently at work. On the demand side we find soldiers of the different armies making different tradeoffs between quantity, quality, and variety. In Germany, the army and air force continued to insist upon a diversified assortment of weaponry specialised to different tasks and frequently adjusted to outward movements of the technological frontier, despite the ballooning cost in terms of national resources. Military inspectors and procurement agencies were unwilling to sacrifice qualitative improvement

Table 5.10. Production runs of Soviet aircraft, 1941–5

(A) Totals and averages	
Models	23
Factories	34
Runs	70
Aircraft	142 756
per model	6 207
per factory	4 199
per run	2 039

(B) By factory

Factory no.	*Number of aircraft produced*	*Per cent of total aircraft produced*
21	17 511	12
18	16 933	12
153	16 878	12
1	16 236	11
292	12 134	8
387	11 403	8
22	10 202	7
30	8 865	6
subtotal	110 162	77
Other factories	32 594	23
Total	142 756	100

(C) By model

Model	*Factory no.*	*Period of production*	*Number of aircraft produced*	*Per cent of total aircraft numbers*
Il-2	18	1941–5	15 099	11
Il-2	1	1941–5	11 929	8
Il-2	30	1941–5	8 865	6
U-2	387	1942–5	11 403	8
Iak-9	153	1941–5	11 237	8
Pe-2	22	1942–4	10 058	7
La-5, La-5fn	21	1942–5	9 229	6
Iak-1	292	1941–4	8 534	6
subtotal	–	–	86 354	60
Other aircraft	–	–	56 402	40
Total	–	–	142 756	100

Source: calculated from Kostyrchenko (1994), 235–7.

and assortment for the sake of long production runs and low cost; Hitler and Speer had to fight this tradition in order to impose full-scale mobilisation upon industry in 1943 and 1944.[23]

In contrast, in the interwar period Soviet munitions procurement agencies had evolved a rigid and coercive system for the enforcement of qualitative specifications and the rejection of substandard products, and also of standardisation and limitation of unit costs (see Chapter 12). In the Soviet case the control of costs proved not to be the enemy of quality, so long as quality was interpreted as robustness and effectiveness in the hands of Soviet Army conscripts and the rough conditions of combat on the eastern front, rather than technological sophistication and finish for their own sake.

Thus it seems doubtful that Germany's relative lack of success should be ascribed to 'overbred organisation' (in Speer's words), or the 'ponderous inflexibility' of a 'heavily bureaucratic command economy'.[24] Both countries operated a bureaucratic system of military procurement in which chiefs of staff were influential as consumers and were able to enforce their preferences. However, German and Soviet preferences differed. Soviet military chiefs were willing to trade off a certain degree of variety, specialisation to tasks, and frequent adjustment of weapons to the technological frontier for the sake of volume, uniform robustness, and low unit cost. The German military placed a higher value on variety, specialisation, and continual technological improvement, and continued to accept a sacrifice in volume, standardisation, and financial cost well into the war period. Thus the differentiating factor on the demand side lay in policy, not system.

As for the supply side, the enemy of mass production in both countries was the old-established artisan tradition of continental industrialisation. The leaders of Soviet industry had apparently been more successful in killing off the Russian pre-revolutionary artisan tradition than their German counterparts who proved to be too heavily indebted to it to combat it when necessary. In the Russian case the suppression of craft resistance to mass production was certainly not achieved in a day. If we go back to the 1920s we can identify at least five historical phases of the process:

- the destruction of rural handicrafts in 1929–30; compare prewar artisan employment in Germany and the Soviet Union (table 5.3 above);
- the promotion of 'class-war' industrialisation during the first Five-Year Plan (1928–32), of which a key aspect was the revolt of young workers in large-scale industry against craft traditions; simultaneously, a drive for mass production of standardised machinery products;[25]
- the Stakhanov movement of 1935–6, including a renewed assault on restrictive craft traditions; simultaneously, a drive in defence industry for standardisation and interchangeability of parts in the teeth of perceived opposition from lingering artisan resistance;[26]

- the purges of 1937–8;
- the war itself, which finally entrenched the perceived virtues of mass production long into the postwar decades.

German experience was quite different. In prewar Germany the Nazi regime made a determined appeal to both industrial interests generally and the skilled worker in particular through comprehensive vocational training and apprenticeship programmes in industry. Superficially this course was driven by the needs of rearmament. Werner Abelshauser argues, however, that in practice it went far beyond such needs. At the beginning of the war traineeships represented something like 5 per cent of the total workforce. This 'oversupply' of skilled workers persisted right through the labour shortages of the war period; towards the end of the war there were still half a million apprentices in engineering. Indeed, Abelshauser picks out wartime investment in the human capital of the industrial workforce as one of the key factors in the German postwar economic recovery.[27]

It would be wrong to give the impression that the Soviet regime neglected vocational training either before or during World War II.[28] A quantitative comparison with Germany is not possible; however, it seems likely that Soviet policy was differently motivated and gave more restricted results compared with Germany's.

CONCLUSION

In this chapter I have attempted to isolate the role of mass production in the production superiority of Soviet war industry compared with its German counterpart in World War II. In Germany the predilection of the armed forces for the latest novelty and the widest possible variety of weapons conspired with industry's artisan traditions to limit the scope for wartime rationalisation and cost reduction. In the Soviet Union, in contrast, both industry and the armed forces were committed to a mass production strategy, regardless of its disadvantages of restricted variety and the difficulty of interrupting production runs to upgrade weapons. This is not just the assertion of a stereotype but can be documented, although very imperfectly; more research, especially the development of better comparative quantitative indicators, would certainly be revealing. As a result, Soviet war production was able to accelerate faster when it was needed in 1942, and the Soviet Union outproduced Germany in overall volumes despite an industrial base inferior to Germany's in both scale and development level. However, it is not ruled out that the survival of a craft tradition paid off for Germany in its postwar economic recovery and development.

NOTES

1. Overy (1995a), 207.
2. For examples, see Klein (1959); Milward (1965).
3. Overy (1994), 250–4, 344–9.
4. Broadberry (1995), 83.
5. Galenson (1953), 207.
6. Kouwenhoven (1996).
7. Liberman (1996), 36–68.
8. Harrison (1996), 10.
9. USSBS (1945), 214
10. RGAE, f. 4372, op. 42, d. 986, l. 118.
11. Barber and Harrison (1991), 163–7.
12. Harrison (1996), 269.
13. Overy (1994), 263.
14. Hunter and Szyrmer (1992), 44–5.
15. This was the average figure for the outcome of the second Five-Year Plan (1933–7), cited by Zaleski (1980), 232.
16. Davies (1994), 145.
17. Overy (1994), 199.
18. Overy (1994), 346.
19. Overy (1994), 347–8, 352.
20. Harrison (1996), 231–2.
21. Overy (1995a), 201, remarks: 'At one point in the war there were no fewer than 425 different aircraft models and variants in production. By the middle of the war the German army was equipped with 151 different makes of lorry, and 150 different motor-cycles'.
22. In the same spirit Overy (1995), 186, notes that two thirds of all Soviet wartime tanks were built in three giant factories in western Siberia. But we do not know how the residual was distributed.
23. Overy (1994); Abelshauser (1997).
24. This is the view advanced by Overy (1995a), 206–7, who also supplies the citation from Speer.
25. Cooper (1977); Kuromiya (1988).
26. Siegelbaum (1988); see also Chapter 4.
27. Abelshauser (1998).
28. Harrison (1985), 139–40.

6 New postwar branches (1): rocketry

Mark Harrison

INTRODUCTION

Before World War II the Soviet Union was a regional military power but certainly not a world player. Within a few years after the war, as a result of the rapid development and deployment of new weapons, the USSR had become one of the two global superpowers. Its defence industry, and especially the creation of new production branches for atomic weapons and missiles, jet aviation, and radar, played a fundamental part in this process.

The development of these branches was therefore a success story in Soviet terms. Sometimes it is claimed that this was the *only* success story. Hence the stereotype of the Soviet Union as 'Upper Volta with rockets'. But quite apart from demeaning both the USSR and Upper Volta (a country no doubt rich in history, if poor in GNP), this cliché begs the question of how the Soviet Union, itself a relatively poor, newly industrialising country, had the capacity to become a strategic missile superpower.

In this chapter I explore the effort which was required of the Soviet Union for such rapid progress in the case of rocketry. This progress depended partly on the Soviet Union's own scientific and technological (resources, and partly on advances made in other countries; it was Germany where many of the most important wartime advances had been made. At the end of the Second World War the Red Army was in occupation of a sizeable fraction of the German scientific and industrial potential for new weapons, and both the occupation authorities and the Kremlin leadership made determined efforts to exploit this fact. Thus it is of very great interest to establish what were the respective contributions of Soviet and German prewar and wartime rocketry to creating the new postwar strategic missile industry in the Soviet Union.

Much of this investigation can be carried out on the basis of sources available in the west for many years, especially the official accounts of the development of Soviet missile technology, US government evaluations, the memoirs of German scientists, and so on. Other sources have become available only comparatively recently: a few documents in Moscow, secondary accounts written by Russian historians with access to ministerial archives, and the memoirs of Soviet participants. These throw further light on the facts previously established.

SOVIET ROCKETRY: SOME ISSUES

A short history

Soviet rocketry was already militarised in the 1920s. There were two main agencies for such research, the Gas Dynamics Laboratory (GDL) of NKVM (the commissariat for the armed forces), and the Jet Propulsion Research Group (GIRD) of Osoaviakhim (the civil defence society). In 1933, largely on the initative of the Red Army's chief of armament Army Commander (later Marshal) M.N. Tukhachevskii, rocketry was centralised in a new Jet Propulsion Research Institute (RNII) under Narkomtiazhprom (the heavy industry commissariat, responsible for defence industry). Its main lines of development were rocket artillery and aviation.[1]

Rocket artillery involved small solid-fuelled rockets, launched from tubes mounted on trucks or aircraft, which could be fired in salvoes at the ground forces of the enemy. The aviation uses of rocketry included booster rockets, which could be either solid- or liquid-fuelled, to assist piston-engined aircraft in take-off and combat manoeuvres. Rocket aircraft, for which the rocket was the main motor, were usually powered by larger liquid-fuelled rockets.

By the beginning of World War II the Soviet Union possessed a commanding lead in solid-fuelled rocket artillery. The first military use of rockets was against the Japanese in 1938 at Khalkin-Gol as an air-launched weapon. In the years before 1941, rocket mortar shells launched from truck and tank platforms were also successfully developed. Most famous of these weapons was the BM-13 *Katiusha* designed by G.E. Langemak, a solid-fuelled barrage missile which delivered a 22kg warhead over a 5km range; its terrifying salvoes gave the Red Army a decisive edge in rocket artillery in the Second World War.

If we speak of a German lead in rocketry, therefore, we must immediately qualify it by adding that it was not in artillery, but in rocket aviation and long-range rocketry based on larger, more complex liquid-fuelled rocket motors. This lead is illustrated in table 6.1. By the end of World War II the piston-engined aircraft had reached its limits of speed and altitude. Liquid-fuelled rockets were tested first in Germany in 1931; Tikhonravov's GIRD-09 was tested two years later in 1933. The first German rocket aircraft, the Heinkel He-176, was flight-tested in 1937; the Soviet Union's RP-218 designed by S.P. Korolev, was ready for flight testing in 1938, but for reasons to be explained the programme was cancelled. A modified aircraft, the RP-318, slower and less powerful than the He-176, was test-flown in 1940. In wartime the Soviet lag persisted. The BI-1, tested in the Soviet Union in 1942, was technically the world's first rocket fighter; the German Messerschmitt Me-163a, which preceded it, lacked armament. But the BI-1 never got beyond the experimental

Table 6.1. Innovation in liquid-fuelled rocketry, Germany and USSR, 1931–49

	Germany		*USSR*	
First liquid-fuelled rocket	1931	Various experimental rockets of the amateur *Verein für Raumschiffart.*	1933	The experimental GIRD-09, designed by M.K. Tikhonravov, reached a height of 6000 m.
First rocket aircraft	1937	The experimental Heinkel He-176, powered by a Walter motor developing 600 kgf of thrust.	1940	The RP-318–1, designed by S.P. Korolev, powered by a 140 kgf motor, could fly for 110 seconds at 140 kph. The motor was based on an original design by V.P. Glushko, but both Korolev and Glushko were in prison at the time.
First rocket fighter	1943	The delta-wing Messerschmidt Me-163b, powered by a 1600 kgf Walter motor, could fly for 7–8 minutes at 880 kph, and saw action in aerial combat in 1944.	1942	The BI-1 (BI stood for the designers, A.Ia. Berezniak and A.M. Isaev), powered by a 1100 kgf motor designed by L.M. Dushkin, could fly for 7 minutes at 800 kph. The BI-1 was intended to be an operational combat aircraft, but the test programme was halted after a fatal crash in 1943.
First long-range missile	1942	The A-4 (V-2), with a 25 000kgf motor and a 1000 kg warhead, had a range of 240 km; in 1944–5 some 6000 were produced, of which just over half were successfully launched at Allied targets.	1949	Although the Soviets successfully tested the R-1 (a somewhat improved copy of the V-2) in 1948, the first such Soviet-designed missile was Korolev's 600 km-range R-2, eventually deployed in Germany in 1951.

Sources: Ordway and Sharpe (1979), 15 (the *VfR* rockets), GARF, 8418/6/23, 42 (GIRD-09), von Braun and Ordway (1975), 108 (the He-176), and 109 (the Me-163b); Shavrov (1988), 130–3, and Egorov (1994), 402–4 (the RP-318–1); Shavrov (1988), 285–90, and Egorov (1994), 405–9 (the BI-1); von Braun and Ordway (1975), 106, and RTsKhIDNI, 17/127/1296, 10–11 (the V-2); Ivkin (1994), 74 (the R-2).

stage; the Me-163b of 1943 was, in contrast, an operational aircraft and was used in action. The BI-1 was jerry-built, and suffered from a fundamental design flaw – its straight leading-edge wing, which caused it to lose aerodynamic stability at trans-sonic speeds. The Me-163 was not only more powerful, but also had a revolutionary delta wing.

None of these bore comparison with the German V-2. The first long-range missile, with a range of 240km and a rocket motor developing 25 *tons* of thrust, the V-2 was in a class of its own. Conceived in 1936, the V-2 would have been ready for testing in 1940 but for Hitler's premature judgement (in 1939) that the war would be over before it was ready for use. Tested in 1942, by the end of 1944 it was being mass-produced; immune to air defence, it was used to bomb London as well as cities in liberated northwestern Europe. It was the single most important technological prize for the invading Allied armies in 1945.

The Soviet rocket specialist G.A. Tokaty, who defected to Britain in 1948, later cited from his own introduction to a Soviet official report prepared in postwar Germany:

> Point by point comparisons disprove the somewhat rooted opinion that we are, scientifically and technologically, inferior to the Germans, French, British and Americans... M.K. Tikhonravov's rocket No. 09 was launched long before V-2 appeared on paper;... L.S. Dushkin's engine ORM-65 was designed, built and test-fired before anybody knew about the German HWK-109–509;... our B-1 was designed, constructed, and flight-tested before the German Me-163B... But the historic fact is that they, the Germans, produced thousands of V-2s and many Me-163Bs, while we failed to have operational rockets of the V-2 calibre and rocket fighters.[2]

But even these words understated the German achievement, which was not just a production success. The German Messerschmitt Me-163a (though not the Me-163b) flew *before* the Soviet BI-1, and the Soviet ORM-65 (designed by V.P. Glushko, not Dushkin, for the abortive RP-218) never flew at all, although Dushkin's derivative RDA-1–150 powered the first rocket flight of the RP-318 in 1940. And Tikhonravov's GIRD-09 was not remotely comparable with von Braun's far larger and more powerful German V-2.

After World War II, the Soviet Union quickly caught up with German wartime standards and surpassed them. By 1947 Soviet rocket designers had built a rocket plane, the I-270, more powerful than the Me-163b.[3] The I-270 probably took German designs as a starting point, but it was soon recognised that these held little of importance for the future.[4] More significant was the fact that by 1948 they had built an improved version of the V-2 which they called the R-1 (its NATO designation became SS-1 *Scud*), and by 1949 a longer-range missile based on a different concept, the R-2 (SS-2 *Sibling*).

Within a few more years they would have intercontinental ballistic missiles, space rockets, and the *sputnik*.[5]

Leads and lags

Traditional accounts of Soviet rocketry are mainly concerned with establishing technological leadership, that is, with answering the question 'who was first?' in relation to invention (the creation of a working concept), and then innovation (its application to production).

To begin with there are two extremes. In Soviet accounts the postwar development of Soviet rocketry was represented in such a way as not to acknowledge German technological leadership, or at least any German priority of invention. Instead, Soviet writers (including Tokaty, who, having defected, was entirely free from official restraints) emphasised the home-grown antecedents of postwar Soviet technological developments. The memoirs of even the frankest participants limited the German contribution to priority in establishing a missile industry based on mass production.[6] At the other extreme were western historians such as Antony Sutton, who wrote a multivolume work on the history of Soviet technology in the 1960s and 1970s.[7] Sutton's essential message was that western capitalism exercised technological leadership almost exclusively; the great majority of Soviet machinery products had western origins. It was the Soviet capacity to import and copy western products, and the willingness of western countries to make their technologies available, that gave the Soviet Union the technology of a superpower.

In between the two extremes are those who found that, like the Soviet dogmas against which it reacted, Sutton's approach failed to provide a satisfying account of the Soviet technological development process. By concentrating on identifying western antecedents for Soviet machinery products, it neglected those less numerous fields where technological leadership belonged to the Soviet Union, and exaggerated the relative contribution of western inventiveness. In the 1970s and 1980s specialists associated with the Centre for Russian and East European Studies at the University of Birmingham developed an intermediate approach. They criticised both Soviet orthodoxy and the dogmas of western Cold Warriors. While accepting that in an aggregate sense the Soviet Union was a technological laggard, they identified a more differentiated pattern of sectoral leads and lags which varied across branches of industry and shifted through time.[8] This more realistic approach was an advance, although it was still within the limits of an inquiry into technological leads and lags.

One such limitation is that the traditional leads-and-lags approach, no matter how objectively pursued, tacitly assumes all countries to be converging on the same predetermined path of technological development unless prevented by unsuitable institutions. If this was the case, then certainly the only interesting research task is to establish who first identified the path to be followed, and the delay after which others followed. But what if the path wasn't given in advance, but was worked out as part of a conditional, path-dependent process?

Whether and how laggards catch up with leaders is a major concern for modern growth economics. Empirical investigation usually shows that catching up is a conditional, not automatic process. Catching up appears to require societies to display a 'social capability' for taking up technological opportunities.[9] The overcoming of a lag is as remarkable as the establishment of leadership. Success in imitation needs to be explained just as much as invention. According to David Landes,

> Th[e] readiness and even eagerness to learn from others, including other Europeans – industrial espionage is a theme running through all modern European history – was testimony to an already thriving indigenous technology; good innovators make good imitators.[10]

Echoing Landes, Joel Mokyr has called the gain from imitation an 'exposure effect' arising from 'openness to new information', and points out that 'not all societies were capable of taking full advantage of exposure effects'.[11] Imitation was not necessarily an easy option. According to Ulrich Albrecht, the 'Russification' of imported technologies usually involved a major R & D effort for adaptation to local conditions; copying without adaptation usually resulted in failure. Albrecht therefore proposes 'add-on' engineering as more accurate than the more usual term 'reverse engineering' to describe what really happened.[12]

The technological frontier

Talk of catching up presupposes that we can identify the technological frontier. The idea of a frontier always presents us with three problems: (a) where is it? (b) in which directions is it expanding? (c) where is the optimum? In rocketry in the 1940s these questions were made particularly difficult to answer by increasing returns and technological interdependence. To answer them fully required readiness to finance an expensive, pluralistic, open-ended process of technological exploration. On the part of inventors it also demanded an obsessional drive hard to distinguish from selfishness and wrong-headedness.

Increasing returns

Increasing returns were present in the trilateral trade-off between three attributes of missile technology together making up its military value: *mass* (the number of rockets to be built from given resources), the *destructive power* of each rocket (let us say, the product of range and payload), and *control in*

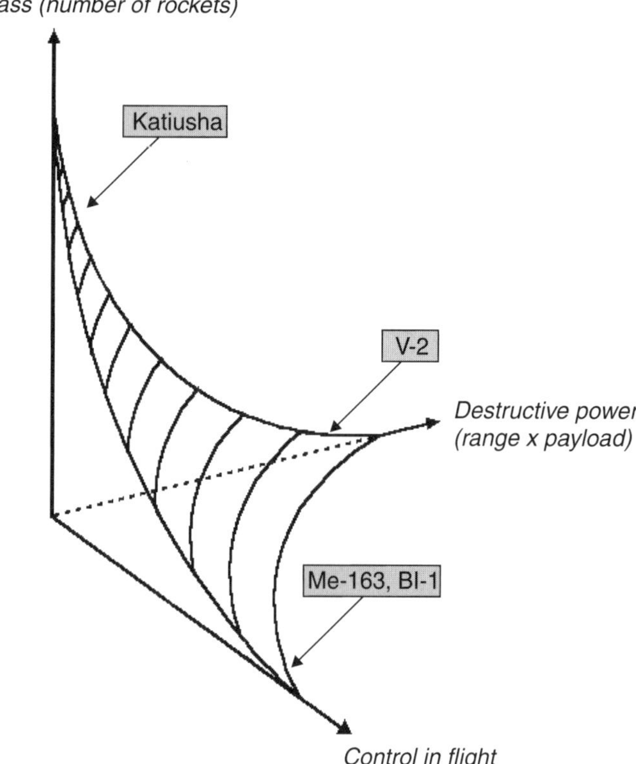

Fig. 6.1. The technological frontier of jet propulsion in the 1940s: a hypothesis

flight (the capacity to manoeuvre, select a target, and return for reuse). Each of these attributes was embodied to an extreme in one or another of the outstanding products of the time. The Soviet *Katiusha* rocket represented the principle of mass – a barrage weapon, solid-fuelled for one-time use, small and expendable, more terrifying than accurate or destructive, fired in salvoes. The German Be-163 and Soviet BI-1 were built for control in flight by a pilot; their rocket motors used more powerful liquid propellants, requiring greater technological sophistication, capable of throttling in flight and of refuelling on the ground for repeated use. For its time the German V-2 represented the ultimate in destructive power.

In between these three extremes there was very little of interest to the military user. As small solid-fuelled rockets were made larger or of longer range, the destructiveness of their shotgun effect on the enemy's front line diminished rapidly. Only a very large, very long-range missile could be matched with a target of commensurate value and a guaranteed destructive effect – a city, say. Similarly, there was little point in making small liquid-fuelled rockets either for aviation (not powerful enough to propel a piloted aircraft) or for bombardment (too expensive to justify single use against tactical targets). Only large ones made sense for piloted flight, or very large ones for strategic use.

Figure 6.1 illustrates the technological frontier under increasing returns. Increasing returns made it easy for designers to become locked into one specialised aspect or another or rocketry, and to 'miss' developments which were technologically available but required leaps of imagination. Varying the mix of attributes in the direction of the average brought few or even negative returns. Wherever the optimum was, it did not lie in compromise.

Technological interdependence

The uses of rocketry depended to a high degree on the parallel development of complementary technologies, especially the turbojet and the atomic bomb.

The paths of rocket and jet technology were interwoven as scientists addressed the possible application of rocketry to aviation. How was jet propulsion to be applied most effectively to solving the problem of high-speed, high-altitude flight? In the 1930s, most saw it in rocketry. Only a visionary few saw it in the air-breathing jet engine, which obtained its supply of oxidiser from the atmosphere and did not have to carry its own oxidiser supply. The concept of the turbojet was developed simultaneously in Britain, Germany, and the Soviet Union at the end of the 1920s.[13] In the 1930s, practical work proceeded in parallel in Germany and Britain, but the first jet aircraft did not fly there until 1939 and 1941 respectively. By the end of World War II jet aircraft operated under combat conditions in small numbers on both sides, but the real shift out of piston engine technology would come after 1945.

In the meantime the stress and temperature requirements of an operating turbojet required great advances in metallurgy and fuel science; these were beyond the reach of many countries such as the Soviet Union where the first indigenous turbojet design was built only in 1945, and then only for experimental use in ground testing.[14] Even in western Europe and the United States the future pre-eminence of turbojet aviation continued to be widely contested. Many experts regarded Frank Whittle as an obsessed crank, and for much of the 1930s it would have been hard to find the evidence to prove them wrong. This is why rocket aviation remained on the R&D agenda for so long, not only in wartime Germany but also for a few postwar years in the Soviet Union and the United States. There was not yet any guarantee that other means would be found in the foreseeable future to make aircraft fly higher and faster than before.

Thus, because air jet technology did not develop in a predetermined way, the path of rocketry was also unpredictable, and was dominated by uncertainty. The application of rocketry to aviation was conditioned by the difficulty of solving the problems of the turbojet, which in turn depended on advances in fuel science and metallurgy. In much the same way, the evolution of the ballistic missile depended on finding something worthwhile to put in the warhead, and this turned out to rest upon advances in nuclear science and technology of which few rocket scientists could have had even a glimmering of suspicion before 1945. The development of large, reliable, liquid-fuelled rockets was hugely expensive; justifying the expense required correspondingly valuable targets which could be attacked with sufficient accuracy and a weapon of sufficient destructive power (accuracy and destructive power could be traded off against each other, of course) to damage or destroy them.

Would the atomic bomb prove practicable? If so, then could it be delivered against targets of intercontinental range, and how large a rocket would be required? The first atomic weapons were too bulky to go in anything but relatively slow, vulnerable aircraft.[15] In the subsequent search for an efficient combination of bombs and missiles, the evolution of national technologies diverged; the Soviets took the quicker road of building very powerful rockets to carry very bulky bombs, whereas the Americans took the slower road to miniaturisation of weapons which could be carried by smaller, cheaper rockets.[16] In this it could be said that each country initially followed its comparative advantage, but the result was optimal for each only in a very short term sense. In the long run, each country found itself locked into a disadvantageous path with heavy switching costs; the Americans struggled to lift heavy payloads into space, while the Russians lost the race in nuclear weapon technology.

In summary, in the interwar period, Soviet rocketry specialised in solid-fuelled rocket artillery and liquid-fuelled rocket aviation. Soviet designers did not see the opportunity seized by von Braun and the Germans in long-range strategic bombardment; instead they built the *Katiusha*. They invested few resources in turbojet development, and concentrated significantly on rocket aviation, but here too they lagged both in propulsion technology and airframe design. Rocket artillery was the only area in which they established world leadership. But this acquires greater significance when we reflect that the Soviets were therefore laggards in everything *except that which actually counted* on the battlefield in World War II. None of the areas in which others led were sufficiently developed by 1945 to make a difference to the war. The V-2 was too inaccurate, too unstable, too limited in range, and too expensive to be really worth firing off in large numbers at Allied cities with a merely conventional warhead. Turbojet aviation was still in its infancy, and German turbojets were tricky and unstable.

Still, Soviet designers did not explore the whole surface of jet propulsion technology before 1945. The special German achievement was to show where a significant section of the frontier actually lay; they showed that the concept of a big, long-range ballistic missile was realisable. If it had been realised once in Germany, it could be realised again by others.

EXPLAINING THE SOVIET LAG

There were several possible factors in the Soviet pattern of leads and lags. I classify them below under overall resources, institutions (the military R&D system), and the influence of a conservative technology policy.

The shortage of overall resources

A shortage of overall national resources certainly limited the Soviet innovation process relative to Germany's. Soviet prewar real GDP was of a magnitude similar to Germany's, but the ratio of GDP per head was only about two fifths. The two countries had industrial workforces of similar size, but in the Soviet Union industrial productivity was much lower. Thus the USSR certainly had fewer and lower-grade resources available to spend on military R&D. This must be regarded as an important conditioning factor, given the very high cost of the kind of open-ended exploration of all aspects of the technological frontier in rocketry which was required if the chances of missing a technological opportunity were to be minimised.

Overall resources, however, were not the decisive factor. The UK, with an economy the same size as Germany's and richer in per capita terms, was behind Germany in rocketry if not also in jet technology; the USA, with its far larger and wealthier economy, was well behind Britain and Germany in both respects.

The military R&D system

Institutional factors peculiar to the Soviet economy might be construed as inimical to a pluralistic, experimental approach to military technology. The general principles underlying Soviet economic organisation included a hostility to the duplication of facilities involved in competition. The economy of resources associated with centralisation of effort was commonly regarded as more important than the danger of missing out on successful applications. Uniquely, however, these constraints were not applied to military R&D.

The record of Soviet military-technical innovation before, during, and after World War II was outstanding in many fields. Without doubt this reflected effective military R&D institutions. The Soviet R&D system in the aircraft, tank, and armament industries was characterised by pluralism and competition among rival design bureaux. There was only one real client, the defence ministry, but there were several arenas in which to plead for threatened causes. The Army, as the final consumer of new weapons and equipment, encouraged innovation and enforced high standards. This setup provided a quasi-market test for Soviet weapon designers and defence suppliers at least as effective as the quasi-markets for military goods in Germany, France, Britain, or the United States. Soviet designers were able to produce at least some first-class guns, tanks, and aircraft in the course of preparation for World War II. In rocketry itself, lack of resources did not stop the pioneering development of the *Katiusha*.

But it was probably significant that the rocket mortar had an obvious and immediate military application. On the other hand, the advocates of large liquid-fuelled rockets for use in aviation were widely suspected of being dreamers with a hidden agenda of space exploration decades in the future – 'space fanatics' – and in this there was more than a grain of truth.[17]

Soviet military R&D institutions were effective under most but not all circumstances. They appeared to fail under two conditions, (a) if the project was too big for rivalry to be financially feasible, or (b) if rivalry was resolved by political coercion. In the case of liquid-fuelled rocketry both were undoubtedly present and interacted with each other. Liquid-fuelled rocketry was very expensive, so that scientists' demands continually outran the resources available. The security organs were suspicious of scientists who wanted to spend so much government money on projects of doubtful immediate utility.

Technological conservatism

A tradition of conservatism in Soviet policy for military R & D was noted by the Soviet atomic scientist P.L. Kapitsa in the following terms:

> ... suspicion of scientists and engineers was a major reason for the Soviet Union's poor record in developing technologies that were new in principle ... Soviet ideas did not receive full support until and unless they had been proved by Western experience.[18]

Rocket aviation was often regarded as a diversion from the real task of developing weapons for the coming war.[19] When rocketry was centralised in 1933 in the RNII, rocket aviation was omitted from its terms of reference. Korolev's work was only adopted by the RNII in 1935, after a campaign fought within the Red Army and Academy of Sciences.[20] Even this victory was short-lived. Soon the country was swept by the Ezhov purges. In 1937 Tukhachevskii, the Red Army's leading proponent of rocketry in all its applications, was arrested and executed as a traitor. The purge of RNII began in October with the arrest of the institute's director I.T. Kleimenov and the *Katiusha*'s designer Langemak.[21] In June 1938 work on Korolev's rocket plane was suspended, the apparent grounds being the need to concentrate resources for rearmament on projects of more immediate military application.[22] A few days later Korelev was arrested, accused of being a Trotskyist saboteur, and sentenced to ten years' forced labour.[23]

Official hostility to Korolev's work on rocket aviation was clearly a factor (according to one source he was accused of 'criminal lack of results').[24] It is true that the NKVD showed little bias towards *individuals* engaged in different lines of work. Korolev and his chief collaborator, the liquid-fuel propulsion expert Glushko, were both imprisoned, but Langemak perished, credit for his work being redirected to his assistant A.G. Kostikov, who survived.[25] But impartiality towards individuals did not mean indifference to alternative projects. The rocket artillery and air jet programmes were continued, while the testing of liquid-fuelled rocket aircraft was cast temporarily into limbo.

Thus several of the Soviet Union's rocket specialists were executed or dispersed to forced labour camps, and began the war in prison. The lucky ones were eventually re-employed in the NKVD's special design bureau (*sharashka*) no. 29 under the aircraft designer A.N. Tupolev, where they designed jet and rocket boosters for piston-engined aircraft and other auxiliary projects of immediate application, but they were no longer in a position to follow the path dictated by their own inventiveness. The RNII itself was disbanded, and rocketry was reorganised under NII-3 of the Commissariat for Ammunition; under wartime pressures the latter was renamed the State Institute for jet propulsion technology (GIRT) in 1942.

It hardly needs stressing that imprisonment and execution were not appropriate arguments in the incentive structure facing Soviet defence designers. On the other hand there may have been a grain of truth in the accusation levelled against the rocketeers that they were diverting state funds for defence into private projects for space exploration. The ultimate goal of stepping off the earth into the cosmos was clearly a powerful motive among the Soviet rocketeers. In the postwar years this motive would be openly acknowledged, but only after space exploration had been legitimated by virtue of its military applications and contribution to Soviet prestige. Ironically, exactly the same accusation was levelled against von Braun and his German colleagues by Himmler in 1944, and again there was some semblance of truth to it.[26]

The evidence of these developments is therefore that in respect of liquid-fuelled rocketry before World War II the Soviet model of pluralism and rivalry in military R&D failed. Many obstacles were placed before Soviet designers, and they were prevented from undertaking the open-ended experimentation which the technological environment called for. Without these obstacles the Soviet lag behind Germany in rocket aviation would have been significantly shortened. Whether Soviet designers would, could, or should also have moved in the same direction as the Germans towards long-range ballistic missiles seems much less likely, even improbable.

We cannot identify unambiguously the reasons for official conservatism. There were both good and bad reasons why Soviet government policy might have emphasised the virtues of conservatism. One explanation is that centralised control over technological exploration was fostered by vested interests resistant to change and distrustful of any kind of heterodox thinking. It is consistent with the latter argument that the normal model of pluralism and rivalry in military R&D was prevented from working by the coercive intervention of the NKVD.

Another, equally plausible explanation, however, is that the Soviet Union, a relatively poor country, could aim to avoid the costs of exploring uncharted technological territory by leaving the task to more industrially developed countries; Soviet technology could rely on the spillover benefits arising from others' R&D spending. The expense and long time horizon required for effective development of liquid-fuelled rocketry may simply have been too great for normal arrangements to work in a poor country faced with a growing war emergency. Even for Germany the missile programme was appallingly expensive and produced only limited returns. The V-2 had many drawbacks; in some ways it would make more sense to describe it as the ultimate achievement of *prewar* rocketry – the end of that road, not the beginning of a new one. Among its defects was a high failure rate, of which the most important cause was instability in flight arising from a badly designed tail assembly. Its range suffered from the limitations inherent in an integral, one-piece design (the rocket casing had to accompany the warhead to the target). Its unit cost, inclusive of R&D overheads, was high both in terms of badly needed submarines and night fighters foregone, and relative to the value of the target.[27] The whole V-2 programme may have cost the German economy half as much again as the atomic bomb project cost the the much larger US economy.[28] Later Speer would come to see his support for the V-2 programme as 'probably one of my most serious mistakes'.[29]

When we attempt to explain the Soviet wartime lag in long-range rocketry, we may thus consider the factors of resources, system, and policy. In each case we find influences at work, but we cannot easily assign weights to them. These were unique events, with a big role for chance variation in initial conditions, resulting in prolonged divergence of the German and Soviet technological development paths.

THE IMPACT OF GERMAN ROCKETRY, 1944–5

Soviet liquid-fuelled rocketry lagged behind German benchmarks before 1945. Behind this lay a defective exploration of the technological space. The problem was not that Soviet resources had been used up in the search, but that the Soviet search was insufficiently thorough. It was limited by several factors including the overall shortage of resources, a coercive political regime, and wartime emergencies. This failure might be designated rational (the Soviet Union being a poor country with limited resources and other priorities), or the result of institutional conservatism and myopia. Whichever is the case, Soviet rocket scientists certainly felt it as a failure.

It is not clear when Moscow first became aware of the scale of German wartime rocketry developments. The western Allies knew enough about Peenemünde to bomb it in 1943. According to Chertok it was Churchill's letter to Stalin of 13 July 1944 which renewed Soviet interest in rocketry.[30] However, already on 18 February 1944 Stalin's war cabinet, the GKO, had resolved to reestablish a jet propulsion research unit as NII-1 of Narkomaviaprom. This gave new priority to jet propulsion technology, and 1944 saw the accelerated flight-testing of several rocket- and ramjet-assisted aircraft.[31] Also in the summer of 1944, the rocket specialists were released from captivity; Korolev's release was dated 13 July, too soon to be in reponse to Churchill's letter.[32]

Hitler finally launched the V-2 campaign in September. In the same month, Soviet forces overran the V-2 proving ground near Debica in southeastern Poland. The objects which they found – fuel tanks, combustion chambers, elements of the guidance system – were crated up and sent back to Moscow for investigation in NII-1. There they were examined with slack-jawed incredulity.[33] The V-2 was 15 or 20 times more powerful than the largest liquid-fuelled rocket yet constructed in the Soviet Union. The very measurements of the V-2, incidentally, reflect the empirical, path-dependent character of its development. Its performance had been specified in 1936 by Gen. Walter Dornberger in multiples of the famous Paris Gun of World War I – twice the range, and ten times the payload – and its dimensions in terms of the maximum limits imposed by German railway transport.[34] Soviet rocketry specialists began immediately to think about developing long-range missiles along lines which were inevitably defined in relation to the new baseline established by the V-2; this transpired without any stimulus arising from foreknowledge of atomic weaponry and the advantages of a missile delivery system.

The occupation of Germany set the stage for inter-Allied competition over German technological assets. The Americans quickly secured the services of the main group of leading German specialists from Peenemünde, who brought with them a large number of V-2s and tons of technical documentation; they were thereby protected against de-Nazification and flown to America to work for the US government on short-term contracts, leaving their families in Germany. Helmut Gröttrup, a guidance systems expert, alone of the top personnel from Peenemünde chose not to leave Germany. The German specialists of the second rank also stayed behind.

Initially, Soviet use of German specialists in rocketry followed a form of collaboration. In the autumn of 1946, however, it was switched to a predatory model.

The Russians in Germany: collaboration

Soviet rocket specialists began to arrive in Germany in April 1945; they formed the first echelon of what became known as the 'inter-departmental' commission sent from the USSR to inspect and evaluate German rocketry. Represented on the commission were the Red Army's chief artillery administration in addition to the ministries of armament and mortar armament, the aircraft, chemical, and electrical industries, and shipbuilding.[35] It was 'inter-departmental' also in the sense that at this time no one in Moscow was in overall charge of Soviet rocketry; responsibility was slipping out of the hands of Narkomaviaprom (the ministry for the aircraft industry) and would soon fall into the lap of Narkomvooruzheniia (the ministry for armament under D.M. Ustinov). Other members of the 'inter-departmental' commission arrived in the summer and late autumn; by the end of the year 30 or more of the top names in Soviet rocket science would be at work in Germany. Listed with their specialised experience and affiliations (where known) in table 6.2, these were experts who knew fairly precisely what they were looking for. According to G.A. Tokaty, they arrived prepared with detailed lists of all the main German aerospace research and production establishments, considerable information about the leading German personnel, and knowledge of the history and development of German rocketry and aviation.[36]

The Soviet acquisition programme had to overcome numerous obstacles. Peenemünde itself had been bombed by the Allies in March 1943; the bombing itself had not been especially effective, but had initiated a policy of dispersal of auxiliary establishments into the German interior.[37] In February 1945, the bulk of its remaining facilities and personnel had been transferred to the neighbourhood of the V-2 underground production facility at Nordhausen in Thuringia (ironically, Nordhausen would turn out to be no more than a dozen kilometres to the east of the demarcation between the Soviet and western occupation zones). Before surrender, the Germans had destroyed or concealed the majority of 'objects, test beds, models and materials'; in going over to the British and Americans, the principal German scientists had taken with them virtually all the main technical documents.[38] Before handing over the Mittelwerk factory at Nordhausen to the Red Army on 1 June 1945, the Americans shipped out roughly 100 V-2 missiles; they also took possession of 14 tons of technical documentation which von Braun and his colleagues had concealed in a tunnel in the Harz mountains.[39]

Table 6.2. Soviet rocket specialists and officials sent to Germany, 1945–6

Specialists	
Barmin, V.P. (Minselmash)	rocket artillery specialist; sent to Germany, August 1945; chief engineer, Institute 'Berlin' (SAM missiles); Institute 'Nordhausen', responsible for documentation of the V-2 launch system; afterwards, NII-88 (Minvooruzheniia) responsible for launch assemblies
Berezniak, A.I., NII-1 (Minaviaprom)	liquid-fuelled rocket motor specialist; co-designer with Isaev of the wartime experimental BI-1 rocket fighter; worked on first V-2 fragments received in Moscow, 1944; sent to Germany, 1945; worked in Institutes 'Rabe' and 'Nordhausen'
Boguslavskii, E.Ia.	guidance systems specialist; worked under Riazanskii in Institute 'Nordhausen'
Budnik, V.S., NII-1 (Minaviaprom)	sent to Germany, 24 May 1945; first chief, joint CKB at Sommerd (Erfurt), Institute 'Nordhausen' (V-2 documentation); after Germany, Korolev's deputy, NII-88 (Minvooruzheniia), responsible for design work
Chertok, B.E., NII-1 (Minaviaprom)	guidance systems specialist, liquid-fuelled rockets; worked on first V-2 fragments received in Moscow, 1944; sent to Germany on 23 April 1945; organised Institute 'Rabe' (Nordhausen); chief of sector for guidance systems, Institute 'Nordhausen'; after Germany, liaison with the Germans in Gorodomlia for Minvooruzheniia
Chizhikov, S.G. (Minaviaprom)	worked in Institute 'Rabe' (Nordhausen)
Gaidukov, L.M., Gen.	rocket artillery specialist; chief of party central committtee department; head of 'inter-departmental' commission sent to Germany, 24 April 1945; chief of Institute 'Nordhausen'; after Germany, chief of NII-88 (Minvooruzheniia); assistant to Nosovskii, chief representative of the special committee for jet propulsion technology in Germany, 1946
Glushko, V.P., NII-1 (Minaviaprom)	liquid-fuelled rocket motor specialist; imprisoned 1938–44; sent to Germany, August 1945; Institute 'Nordhausen', responsible for documentation of the V-2 rocket motor, and in charge of production of rocket motors; after Germany, chief designer of rocket motors, NII-88 (Minvooruzheniia), and chief of NII-456 (Minaviaprom)

Table 6.2. (Contd.)

Isaev, A.M., NII-1 (Minaviaprom)	liquid-fuelled rocket motor specialist; co-designer with Berezniak of the wartime experimental BI-1 rocket fighter; worked on first V-2 fragments received in Moscow, 1944; sent to Germany, 1945; organised Institute 'Rabe' (Nordhausen) under Chertok; Institute 'Nordhausen', responsible for test firing at Leesten
Kerimov, K.A.,	rocket artillery specialist; sent to Germany, 1945; head of joint Soviet-German OKB for telemetry, responsible for redeveloping the V-2 'Messina' guidance system
Korolev, S.P.	liquid-fuelled rocket designer; prominent in GIRD, then RNII; imprisoned 1938–44, employed in TsKB-29 (NKVD); sent to Germany, August or late October 1945; technical leader of 'Vystrel' group, responsible for test-firing V-2s; deputy chief and chief engineer, Institute 'Nordhausen'; designated chief rocket designer, 1946; after Germany, chief designer of long-range ballistic missiles, NII-88 (Minvooruzheniia)
Kuznetsov, N.N., Gen.	artillery commander; assistant to Nosovskii, chief representative of the special committee for jet propulsion technology in Germany, 1946
Kuznetsov, V.I.	sent to Germany, 9 August 1945; Institute 'Nordhausen', responsible for V-2 guidance system; after Germany, chief of NII-10 (Ministry of the Shipbuilding Industry), responsible for gyroscopic guidance mechanisms
Mishin, V.P., NII-1 (Minaviaprom)	ballistics specialist; worked on first V-2 fragments received in Moscow, 1944; sent to Germany, 9 August 1945; chief of successful mission to Prague in pursuit of V-2 documentation archive; Institute 'Nordhausen', in charge of ballistics bureau; recruited by Korolev, took over from Budnik as chief, joint Soviet-German OKB at Sommerd (Erfurt), Institute 'Nordhausen' (V-2 documentation); after Germany, Korolev's first deputy as chief designer, NII-88 (Minvooruzheniia), responsible for ballistics and V-2 redevelopment
Mrykin, A.G.	Gaidukov's deputy as head of 'inter-departmental' commission, sent to Germany, 24 April 1945
Pallo, A.V.	liquid-fuelled rocket motor designer; sent to Germany, December 1945; Institute 'Nordhausen', in charge of test firing under Isaev at Leesten

Pashkov, G.N. (Gosplan)	chief, Gosplan defence sector; sent to Germany, 1945, after Germany, chief of Gosplan missile department
Piliugin, N.A., NII-1 (Minaviaprom)	worked on first V-2 fragments received in Moscow, 1944; sent to Germany, 9 August 1945; worked on V-2 documentation, Institute 'Nordhausen', responsible for guidance system; after Germany, Riazanskii's deputy responsible for guidance systems, NII-885 (Minvooruzheniia)
Pobedonostsev, Iu.A. NII-1 (Minaviaprom)	specialist on pulsejets; worked on first V-2 fragments received in Moscow, 1944; sent to Germany, 24 August 1945; Institutes 'Berlin' and 'Nordhausen'; after Germany, chief engineer of NII-88 (Minvooruzheniia)
Raikov, I.O. (Minaviaprom)	sent to Germany, 1945; worked in Institutes 'Rabe' and 'Nordhausen'
Riazanskii, M.S. (Minprom sredstv sviazi)	sent to Germany, 9 August 1945; worked on V-2 documentation, Institute 'Nordhausen', responsible for guidance system; after Germany, responsible for guidance systems, NII-885 (Minvooruzheniia)
Rudnitskii, V.A. (Minselmash)	rocket artillery specialist; sent to Germany on 9 August 1945; Institute 'Nordhausen', responsible for redeveloping V-2 ground equipment
Semenov, A.I.	deputy chief of 'inter-departmental' commission sent to Germany, 24 April 1945
Smirnov, S.S. (Minaviaprom)	sent to Germany, 1945; worked in Institutes 'Rabe' and 'Nordhausen'
Sokolov, V.L. (Minaviaprom)	sent to Germany, May 1945; defected to the United States, October 1946
Tiulin, G.A.	sent to Germany, 1945; Institute 'Nordhausen', following Mishin as chief of ballistics bureau
Tokaty (Tokaev), G.A., Col. TsAGI (Minaviaprom)	rocketry specialist; sent to Germany, June 1945; chief rocket scientist of the Soviet air force; member, special commission on the Sänger project, 1947; defected to the United Kingdom, 1948
Voskresenskii, L.A., NII-1 (Minaviaprom)	worked on first V-2 fragments to be received in Moscow, 1944; sent to Germany, 1945; worked in Institutes 'Rabe' and 'Nordhausen'; headed the 'Vystrel' group after Korolev

Table 6.2. (Contd.)

Officials	
Iakovlev, N.D., Gen.	artillery commander; member, Council of Ministers special committee for jet propulsion technology, 1946; visited Germany with Ustinov, 1946
Malenkov, G.M.	Central Committee secretary from 1939; member, GKO, 1941–5, responsible for aircraft production; deputy chairman, Council of Ministers, since 1946, responsible for industry; Politburo member from 1946; chairman, Council of Ministers special committee for jet propulsion technology, 1946
Nosovskii, N.E.	member, Council of Ministers special committee for jet propulsion technology, 1946; chief representative of the special committee in Germany
Riabikov, V.M., deputy minister of armament (Minvooruzheniia)	naval artillery specialist; Ustinov's deputy; sent by Ustinov to Germany in 1945–6 to evaluate German-Soviet missile development
Serov, I.A., Gen. (MGB)	member, Council of Ministers special committee for jet propulsion technology, 1946; organised deportation of German scientists to USSR ('Osoaviakhim'), 1946; head of State Commission for long-range missiles, 1947; member, special commission on the Sänger project, 1947; attended first V-2 launching, 1947
Stalin, V.I., Gen.	air force commander; instigated arrest of Shakhurin (minister, Minaviaprom) and Novikov (chief of air force), 1946; member, special commission on the Sänger project, 1947
Ustinov, D.F., minister of armament (Minvooruzheniia)	took over main responsibility for missile development from Minaviaprom in 1946; deputy chairman, Council of Ministers special committee for jet propulsion technology, 1946; visited Germany, 1946; head of state commission for study and generalisation of the experience of rocket building in Germany, 1946

Sources: compiled from Budnik (1991), Chertok (1992a–e), Danilov, (1981), Egorov (1994), Golovanov (1994), Ivkin (1994), Kerimov (1994); Konovalov (1991), Pashkov (1989), Rebrov (1995).

The Soviet group found 10 complete V-2s, of which 5 were shipped back to the Soviet Union.[40] The loss of the all-important V-2 documentation was made partially good from a consignment of German government papers stranded in Prague at the end of the war in the course of transshipment to Austria; a Soviet mission led by V.P. Mishin spirited them back to the Soviet Union under the noses of the Czechoslovak authorities.[41] Another mission to Vienna secured the documentation of the V-2 guidance system.[42] The booty was not limited to the V-2, as table 6.3 indicates. Soviet acquisitions included not only strategic weapons but also anti-aircraft and anti-tank missiles, and air-to-air, air-to-sea, and air-to-surface missiles. The summary statistics reported in table 6.4 number Soviet acquisitions in literally dozens of different kinds of missiles, rocket motors, guidance systems, and fuels.[43] These tables illustrate well the thoroughness which which German rocket science had mapped out the accessible technological territory. But there is no doubt that the V-2 was understood by everyone to be the most important prize.

The utilisation process followed two phases, of which the first proceeded in the Soviet occupation zone of Germany. It began with location of available materials and personnel (mostly of the middle rank), and recruitment of the latter to their former employment under new masters. The German specialists were driven to collaborate by a variety of motives, including the promise of food rations, the protection offered from de-Nazification, and the professional desire to continue in their chosen field of work; the top German specialists could get these things from the Americans, but only the Russians were offering them to the lower rank personnel. What none of them could get, not even Wernher von Braun, even from the Americans, was the promise of being able to carry on without leaving Germany – a decisive factor behind Gröttrup's decision to work for the Russians.

At Nordhausen the Russians secured the services of some 200 specialists who had remained in the neighbourhood, and set up work in an informal research institute, which Chertok christened 'Rabe' (in English 'Raven', shortened from *Raketenbau*) in nearby Bleicherode. Reinforced by subsequent arrivals from Moscow, Institute 'Rabe' was soon engaged in a variety of tasks, including reverse engineering and copying of German rocketry products, filling gaps in their technical documentation, and completing and testing unfinished German design work.[44] At the same time, all over the Soviet occupation zone, similar joint Soviet-German enterprises, institutes, and other establishments were being created wherever rocketry and aviation technology had been formerly practised. By the spring of 1946 the total number of German rocket specialists involved had risen to 1200.[45]

Such joint endeavours did not proceed without difficulty. Nordhausen and Bleicherode were right on the western edge of the eastern occupation zone; the German employees lived on both sides of the border, and were as

Table 6.3. Main items of German rocketry captured by Soviet forces, 1945

Surface-to-surface missiles	
V-2 (A-4)	guided liquid-fuelled rocket (height 14 m, weight 12 500 kg, propellant turbopump-fed liquid oxygen and ethyl spirit, thrust 25 000 kg, warhead 1000 kg, range 300 km)
Rheinbote[a]	solid-fuelled multi-stage rocket (height 11 m, weight 1540 kg, first-stage thrust 38 000 kgf, warhead 32 kg, range 150 km)
Rocket and anti-tank artillery	
320 mm	incendiary shell (range 4 km)
210 mm	demolition shell (range 5 km), 5-tube launcher
200 mm	demolition shell (range 6 km), 6-tube launcher
158 mm	fragmentation, smoke, and chemical shells (range 5.5 km)
150 mm	artillery rocket shell
105 mm, 75 mm	recoilless cannon
88 mm *Panzerschreck*	anti-tank shell and launcher
80 mm	fragmentation shell (range 5.8 km), 48-tube launcher
Panzerfaust	anti-tank shell (range 60–100 m)
Surface-to-air missiles	
Enzian[a]	radio-controlled liquid-fuelled rocket (weight 2000 kg, range 15 km)[b]
Hs-117 *Schmetterling*[a]	liquid-fuelled rocket (weight 450 kg, range 10 km)[b]
Rheintochter[a]	liquid or solid-fuelled rocket (self-guided or radio guided, two solid-fuel launch boosters, weight 1500 kg, range 15 km)[b]
Taifun[a]	liquid or solid-fuelled barrage missile (weight 30 kg, range 12 km)
Wasserfall[a]	liquid-fuelled rocket (height 8m, weight 4000 kg, thrust 8000 kg, warhead 100–150 kg, range 15 km)[b]

Air-to-surface missiles	
RS-1000	solid-fuelled armour-piercing rocket (weight 1000 kg)
RS-1800	solid-fuelled armour-piercing rocket (weight 1800 kg)
Air-to-ship missiles	
Henschel	guided cruise missile (length 3–4 m, wingspan 3 m, weight 1000 kg, warhead 250 kg)
Hs-293	radio-guided liquid-fuelled torpedo (weight 1000 kg, range 16 km)
Hs-294[a]	liquid-fuelled torpedo (weight 2200 kg, range 14 km)
SB-800[a]	solid-fuelled rocket
Air-to-air missiles	
Drache	heat-seeking rocket
R-100[a]	solid-fuelled rocket
SS-500[a]	solid-fuelled rocket
X-4[a]	wire-guided rocket shell (weight 50 kg, range 3–5 km)
Piloted aircraft and rocket motors	
DFS-346[a]	supersonic rocket aircraft
Messerschmitt Me-163B *Komet*	rocket fighter
Walter HWK-109-509	liquid-fuelled rocket motor (thrust 600 kgf)

Notes:
[a] Prototype or experimental.
[b] Von Braun and Ordway (1975), 111–12, give alternative figures for range as follows: *Enzian* – 30km, *Schmetterling* – 16 km, *Rheintochter* 1 and 2 – 12 km and 35 km respectively, *Wasserfall* – 27 km.

Source: compiled from RTsKhIDNI, 17/127/1296.

Table 6.4. Summary of German jet propulsion technology captured by Soviet forces, 1945 (number of types in each category)

Category	*Number of types*
Liquid-fuelled rockets	8
Solid-fuelled rockets	41
[Rocket and jet] engines	32
Guidance systems	186
Liquid fuels	32
Solid fuels	80

Source: RTsKhIDNI, 17/127/1296, 15.

vulnerable to western as to Soviet pressure. Various agencies competed for their loyalty. Elsewhere, amid general suffering and deprivation the local population was jealous of the privileged life accorded to the German specialists, regardless of their wartime responsibilities. Moreover, the German specialists themselves tended to adopt a proprietary attitude to their own knowledge, which they became reluctant to share with their Soviet colleagues, and tried to monopolise it, since it was the only source of their bargaining power *vis-à-vis* their new employers and of their privilege relative to their compatriots.[46]

The transition to a predatory model

The transition to the second, predatory phase of the utilisation process began with Ustinov's bid for control over the development of long-range rocketry, and finished with the wholesale transfer of German assets and specialists to Soviet territory.

To begin with, rocketry lacked a patron. The 'inter-departmental' commission had no parent ministry in Moscow. According to Iaroslav Golovanov, Korolev's biographer, Gaidukov had offered his children to more than one potential foster-carer. At Narkomaviaprom, Shakhurin lacked interest. As far as he was concerned, rocketry was an artillery matter. Reporting to Malenkov on the installations remaining at Peenemünde in June 1945, he had recommended their transfer to the Commissariat for Ammunition.[47] Subsequently he tried to recall his aviation specialists from Nordhausen, an order which Gaidukov had politely ignored.[48] But Vannikov of the Ammunition Commissariat (later Minselmash) was absorbed in the atomic bomb project. Ustinov, People's Commissar for Armament, held his counsel, and sent his deputy V.M. Riabikov to Germany to review the situation. Armed with Riabikov's report, and supported by a powerful coalition (Beriia, Malenkov, Bulganin, Vannikov, and Iakovlev), Ustinov went to Stalin. The result was that Stalin gave rocketry to Ustinov.[49]

By a Council of Ministers decree of 13 May 1946, signed by Stalin and Ia.E. Chadaev, a 'special committee for jet propulsion technology' was formed under the leadership of G.M. Malenkov, with Ustinov as one of his two deputies.[50] The committee was given inclusive powers and exclusive responsibilities for oversight of developments in its field. The decree fixed core priorities (the copying of the German V-2 and *Wasserfall* missiles), lead organisations (Ustinov's Minvooruzheniia for liquid-fuelled missiles, Minselmash for powder rockets, and Minaviaprom for aviation), a further list of supply ministries for subcontract work, and new and revised organisational structures for ministries, enterprises, and research outfits including the conversion to missile production of armament factory no. 88, the attachment to it of a new research institute NII-88, and establishment of a new central firing range for missiles tests. It ordered Minaviaprom to transfer 20 rocket specialists to Minvooruzhenia, and prohibited any agency from seeking to recall its personnel from work on jet propulsion (as Shakhurin had previously tried to recall his aviation specialists from Nordhausen).

As for the work in Germany, the decree confirmed what had become the official model of knowledge transfer. The German research installations and personnel concerned with the V-2, *Wasserfall*, *Rheintochter*, *Schmetterling*, and other missiles, were to be reassembled and put back to work. Alongside each German were to work Soviet specialists sent by Moscow to acquire German skills and knowledge. Privileged rations and other conditions were assigned to German and Soviet personnel alike; MGB General Serov was commissioned to ensure the supply of consumer goods, accommodation, and vehicles adequate for the conditions of 'normal work', and the defence ministry in Moscow and occupation headquarters in Germany were ordered to help him as required. The procurement of supplies in Germany and equipment from the United States were to be financed partly under reparations, partly from 70 million German marks and $2 million from Soviet currency reserves. Ustinov, Iakovlev, and Kabanov were ordered to Germany for a fortnight with a team of specialists to set this work up on a proper footing; Nosovskii, assisted by Kuznetsov and Gaidukov, was sent to head up the work in Germany for as long as it continued.

But the decree also foreshadowed the end of the German phase. It required the Malenkov committee 'to resolve the question of the transfer of design bureaux and German specialists from Germany to the USSR by the end of 1946', and ordered the lead ministries in Moscow and designated subcontract organisations to prepare the ground for their relocation, including the provision of accommodation for several hundred Germans 'by 15 October 1946'.

Arriving in Nordhausen in the second half of May 1946, Ustinov saw that the scale of work required was clearly greater than could be done under Chertok's Institute 'Rabe'.[51] He put the Nordhausen operation on a new, more regular and elaborate footing. An Institute 'Nordhausen' was formed, with Korolev as deputy director and chief engineer. The Nordhausen Institute became the lead organisation for a complex of more specialised joint establishments in the district, working on V-2 technical documentation, the rocket motor, the guidance system (the former Institute 'Rabe'), the launch system, test-firing, and telemetry. In August, Ustinov set up (and headed) a state commission for study and generalisation of the experience of rocket building in Germany.[52] His visit to Germany was also the occasion for Ustinov to name Korolev chief designer of long-range missiles.[53] The collaborative work in Germany moved to a climax.

The exact motivation of the decision to relocate the entire German operation to Soviet territory is not known. It was probably prompted by the difficulties of operating in Germany already outlined above, especially the difficulty of maintaining secrecy. Other factors may have included the increasing permanence of the German partition, and the rising importance attached in Moscow to securing a demilitarisation of Germany's western zone, which made the maintenance of joint military R&D establishments in the eastern zone an embarrassment. The timing of the decision's execution, at the end of October 1946, may also have been influenced by the simultaneous breakdown of the Paris peace talks. [54] However, greater foresight is suggested by the fact that the mid-October deadline for availability of the deportees' living accommodation had already been fixed in mid-May.

The deportation, codenamed 'Osoaviakhim', was carried out suddenly and without warning, between 3000 and 3500 German specialists being shipped off to the Soviet Union at the end of October, accompanied by their family members, personal property and household effects, and office and research facilities. Among them the 2800 rocketry and aviation specialists were the largest single contingent; most of these were probably from the aircraft industry, since von Braun later put the number of rocket specialists alone at no more than 200. There were also nuclear, electronic, optical, radio, and chemical specialists.[55] The first rank of German rocket science was largely missing, represented only by Gröttrup.

'Osoaviakhim' was in fact the second wave of such deportations, the first wave, mainly of atomic scientists, having been spread over the months from May to September 1945. By 1948 some 200 000 German scientific workers (including family members) were living and working on Soviet territory.[56] In quantity if not in quality, this was 'probably one of the largest mass movements of 'brains' in the recent history of the civilized world'.[57]

Back in the USSR

In Moscow, meanwhile, a framework had been established for absorption of the German resources. Overall responsibility for strategic rocketry was assumed by Ustinov, with Minvooruzheniia as the coordinating centre of a broad network of collaborating and subcontract organisations. As laid down in the May decree, a new research institute for long-range rocketry was attached to the former artillery factory no. 88 (so the institute became NII-88; an auxiliary institute for guidance systems became NII-885). These institutes brought together the main members of the Soviet team in Germany with the German specialists.[58]

Their initial brief was to test-fly the German V-2, then copy it from components of Soviet manufacture. These terms of reference were significantly extended in March 1947 when a meeting at the Kremlin took a decision, if only in principle, to find an intercontinental means of delivering an atomic weapon. Two alternatives were under consideration, both of them speculative – either to develop ballistic rocketry significantly beyond the V-2 concept, or the so-called Sänger project for a skip-glide orbital rocket-plane (the 'antipodal bomber').[59] The Sänger project had already been under investigation by a group at NII-1 under M.V. Keldysh.[60] The Kremlin meeting set up a special subcommittee, including Vasilii Stalin, Serov, Tokaty, and Keldysh. The Russian specialists were divided; Keldysh thought the project was feasible, whereas Tokaty had reservations. Stalin then referred the matter to the German specialists (against Tokaty's more self-reliant inclination), who tended also to scepticism.[61] At this point the Sänger project was abandoned in favour of ballistic rocketry, which meant that the future fell into the hands of the new chief designer of long-range missiles Korolev.

Here can be seen starting to re-emerge the prewar tensions between officials and scientists. It was the officials – Stalin himself, his son Vasilii Stalin (now an air force general, and a fierce critic of Soviet aviation technology), and Ustinov – who insisted on starting from German technological foundations, where the specialists, whose professional pride was at stake, usually wanted to diverge sooner and more radically from German starting points.[62]

The results of the combined efforts of the German and Soviet specialists over the following years can be stated briefly. One year after the return to Soviet territory, in October-November 1947, 11 German V-2s were launched from the new testing site at Kapustin Iar near Astrakhan; five reached the target, roughly equalling the Germans' own wartime success rate. A year later, the Soviet version of the V-2, but with an improved tail section and guidance system, was ready for testing; 12 were launched in October-November 1948, of which 7 reached the target.

At the same time both the Soviet and German teams had been working on new, longer-range missiles which departed from the V-2 concept in a detachable warhead. Korolev had unveiled his concept, which would eventually become the R-2, in March 1947.[63] When the R-2 was tested successfully, in

May–June 1949, the Soviet specialists could be said to have significantly exceeded the German 1945 benchmark.[64]

THE GERMANS IN RUSSIA

What part was played by the Germans? There were 150 of them, headed by Gröttrup, attached to NII-88. Probably the initial model for their utilisation was the traditional one of independent Soviet and German design bureaux independently pursing projects on competitive lines. But it did not work out this way, for reasons of security, motivation, the difficulty of teamwork, scientific nationalism, and finance.

Security

Basically the Soviet officials did not know what to do with them. To use them effectively would have meant placing them at the heart of the Soviet missile programme. Instead they were systematically isolated and kept in the dark. At first they were located in a Moscow suburb, but over a few months they were reassembled in a more remote location – Gorodomlia, an island in the upper Volga, the site of a former medical research institute.[65] The reasons for this were doubtless related to security, although not necessarily in a straightforward way. Security in the obvious sense had already been guaranteed by relocating the German specialists on Soviet territory, restricting their movement and controlling their correspondence. Keeping them away from the Soviet missile programme must have reflected more complex motivations. If the Germans might eventually return home, for example, the less they knew the better. One could imagine the Russians in the position of the interrogator who knows less than the witness; under such circumstances a question may give the witness more information than the answer gives to the interrogator. Another factor may have been the secretiveness encouraged for its own sake throughout the Soviet system in defence of official privilege.

Motivation

Under the circumstances German motivation and morale were always fragile. These men and women thought at first that they would be called on as key players in the Soviet space programme; what they wanted was to get into space and they didn't much care who they had to work for to do it – Hitler one year, Stalin the next. 'War has to serve science!' Gröttrup declared in 1947 just as he had in 1944.[66] At first Ustinov encouraged the Germans' self-important attitudes; 'You're to give the orders! *You* are C-in-C of rocket construction!' he told Gröttrup.[67] The truth of the predatory model, when it dawned on them, had to be a devastating blow – they were there only to transmit their knowledge and experience to others, and would not be given any independent role. On top of this the Germans were given no assurances or hints as to when or whether they would ever go home. At the same time, although materially privileged by comparison with Soviet employees, and not held under penal conditions, they were subjected to intense surveillance and control over movement.

The difficulty of teamwork

The V-2 had been built by teamwork – a systems engineering approach. In Russia Gröttrup struggled vainly to maintain the collective spirit developed in Peenemünde and Nordhausen, first against the demands of competing ministries for personnel and equipment, then against the internal tensions in the group. The collective spirit depended upon leadership and trust. The possibilities of leadership were undermined by erosion of the Germans' goals and motivation, and their arbitrary reallocation to tasks, while the suspiciousness of the watchers and the divisive allocation of privileges destroyed trust. 'How different it was at Peenemünde!', wrote Irmgard Gröttrup in a fit of nostalgia: 'There, we were like one big family'.[68] Under these conditions teamwork soon became impossible.[69]

Scientific nationalism

To make matters worse, the Russians themselves were divided over the potential role of the Germans. The officials were more committed to making use of them than the specialists. Once the V-2 had been successfully tested, the Germans were commissioned to design rockets of longer and longer range, the key to which was detaching the warhead in flight, for example the R-10 which was the Gorodomlia analogue to the R-2 being developed simultaneously by Korolev. Not knowing anything about Korolev's activities, the Germans thought that with this concept they had stolen a march on the Soviet specialists; at the same time, they worried that Korolev would try to steal their ideas and key personnel.[70] The fact was that Korolev was indeed developing a similar missile, but had no intention of either acknowledging a German contribution, or of letting any of the Germans anywhere near it. The proprietary, defensive attitudes of the Soviet specialists (as distinct from the officials) were by now well established; having lost six years of work on liquid-fuelled rocketry in prison, emerging to find the Germans already realising ideas of which he had only dreamed, Korolev had no intention of spending the rest of his career working under German instruction to German designs.[71] In the same spirit Glushko ignored the Germans allocated to him to work on propulsion and soon allowed them to go to Gröttrup.[72] Probably the campaign of scientific and cultural nationalism initiated in 1946 by A.A. Zhdanov also played into the Russian specialists' hands.

Finance

All this made an inescapable dilemma for Ustinov. Long-range missiles cost far more to build than guns, tanks, or aircraft. The German aircraft specialists held under similar conditions worked on many designs, several of which reached the stage of experimental prototypes and were test-flown.[73] In rocketry real pluralism and rivalry were too expensive; Ustinov could not afford to carry through competing projects beyond the design stage. He could not realise the German and Soviet designs simultaneously. Nor could he merge them; for national reasons he could not place Korolev under Gröttrup, but nor could he place the Germans under Korolev since Korolev would refuse their unwanted assistance. The Germans were left without a role. At first Ustinov strung them along with promises of approval and funding; eventually he had no alternative but to switch the Germans to low grade tasks, and eventually out of secret work altogether.[74] He began to send them home; by the end of 1953 they had all gone back to Germany.

CONCLUSIONS

In 1945–7 the Soviet Union gained from Germany three things relevant to the tasks of reaching the technological frontier mapped out locally by Germany, and then going beyond. These were, first, the practical concept of what was already possible in long-range rocketry; second, the physical assets represented by the German trophy material – working models and parts, documents, and research and production facilities; and third, the human assets and embodied technological knowledge of the German specialists themselves.

I rank these in diminishing order of importance. Most important was just for the Soviet authorities to know that the frontier of rocketry already lay further out that anyone in the Soviet Union had previously imagined. Next most important was to have access to the German weapons, design documents and facilities; these told them most about the range of the frontier which Germany had explored, and how to get there. Of least value were the German personnel.[75]

One might expect it to be the other way around. Modern ideas about the factor of human capital in economic growth and catch-up processes lead us to place greatest emphasis on human development and embodied knowledge, then on physical capital, and least on disembodied conceptual knowledge. Why do such ideas mislead us here? The assets which the Soviet Union gained from Germany must been assessed in relation to those Soviet assets already accumulated. Thus the Soviets already had their own rocket specialists to match the specialists found in Germany. They had their own working models of rocketry and design and production facilities, but across a much narrower range of the spectrum than in Germany. They lacked altogether, until the Germans gave it to them, the concept of a V-2. Thus the concept was more critical than the trophy assets, and both were more important than the German specialists themselves.

There is another reason for arguing that the German specialists were less important than may appear at first sight. The Russians *also* failed to make the most of them because they applied a predatory model of embodied knowledge transfer which proved unworkable. Its acquisition was handled in a very wasteful way. Embodied knowledge was the most difficult aspect of technology to transfer, as the experience of the Gorodomlia Germans confirmed, because it existed primarily in the collective mentality. The predatory model destroyed the Germans' teamwork approach. This also implies that Soviet science and industry successfully absorbed German missile technology largely on the basis of its own human resources. Moreover, the destruction of the Germans' teamwork did not prevent the Russians from evolving their own teamwork under Korolev.

Thus Soviet postwar successes were built partly on German foundations, but it was easy to do this given that there was already a previous accumulation of Soviet experience and expertise. Some of this experience was not directly useful, but was useful experience in searching the technological frontier and in learning by trial and error, so was not just technological failure or economic waste. The problem was not that resources had been used up in the search, but that the Soviet search had been incomplete; it was limited by several factors including overall shortage of resources, a coercive political regime, and wartime emergencies. As a result the prewar development process had slowed down, and some of the accumulated resources had been dispersed, but they were reassembled once a sufficiently high priority had been attached to their further development in 1944. Thus Soviet science and technology were able to build on German achievements and soon to surpass them.

NOTES

1 GARF, 8418/6/243, 35–7.
2 Tokaty (1968), 343.
3 Egorov (1994), 419–20.
4 Albrecht (1993), 41–2.
5 The R-1/SS-1 *Scud* was fired in anger 43 years later by Iraq in the war for Kuwait (Albrecht (1993), 90).

6 In addition to Tokaty, cited above, see also the interview with V.P. Mishin conducted by Konovalov (1991). Similar statements, one by Glushko, another attributed to Korolev, are cited by Albrecht (1993), 80.

7 Sutton (1968, 1971, 1973).

8 See Amann, Cooper, and Davies (1977) (see especially chapters by Holloway (1977), Kocourek (1977)); Amann and Cooper (1982, 1986) (especially chapter by Holloway (1982a)). For a more recent work in this worthy tradition, by a German historian in English translation, see Albrecht (1993).

9 Abramovitz (1986).

10 Landes (1969), 28.

11 Mokyr (1990), 188.

12 Albrecht (1993), 97–100.

13 B.S. Stechkin's article outlining the concept of the turbojet appeared in Russian in 1929; the priority of invention is usually accorded to Frank Whittle, whose first UK patents were registered in 1930; and it was in Germany that the first turbojet-powered aircraft, the Heinkel He-178 (based on a design independent of Whittle's) flew in August 1939. See Egorov (1994), 424; Gibbs-Smith (1970), 196.

14 Egorov (1994), 435.

15 Holloway (1982b), 393.

16 Von Braun and Ordway (1975), 140.

17 See for example Albrecht (1993), 87.

18 Cited by Holloway (1994), 147.

19 Kerimov (1994).

20 Egorov (1994), 398–9.

21 Albrecht (1993), 76.

22 Romanov (1990), 133.

23 Romanov (1990), 136–8.

24 Kerimov (1994).

25 Medvedev (1978), 36–7.

26 Ordway and Sharpe (1979), 46–8.

27 Milward (1977), 106.

28 Ordway and Sharpe (1979), 242.

29 Cited by Ordway and Sharpe (1979), 249.

30 Chertok (1992a).

31 Egorov (1995), 413–24, 431–6.

32 Romanov (1990), 174.

33 A graphic account is given by one of the participants, Chertok (1992a).

34 Ordway and Sharpe (1979), 28.

35 Ivkin (1997), 34 (report of Beriia and others to Stalin, 17 April 1946).

36 Tokaty (1968), 342.

37 Ordway and Sharpe (1979), 111–29.

38 RTsKhIDNI, 17/127/1296, 5.

39 Von Braun and Ordway (1975), 118.

40 RTsKhIDNI, 17/127/1296, 15–16.

41 Budnik (1991); Konovalov (1991).

42 Kerimov (1994).

43 RTsKhIDNI, 17/127/1296, 18.

44 Budnik (1991), Konovalov (1991), Chertok (1992b, 1992c).

45 Ivkin (1997), 34 (report of Beriia and others to Stalin, 17 April 1946).

46 Sokolov (1955), 20–6, gives an account of the working of joint Soviet–German aviation design bureaux.

47 Dated 8 June 1945, this document was published by Ivkin (1997), 32.
48 Golovanov (1994), 358–9.
49 For the joint recommendation of this group, dated 17 April 1946, see Ivkin (1997), 33–4. The decisive meeting with Stalin followed on 29 April, with Riabikov also in attendance (ibid., 41n). For other detail see Golovanov (1994), 362–4.
50 The text of this decree was published in *Nezavisimaia gazeta* (Moscow), 24 February 1995. Malenkov's other deputy was I.G. Zubovich, detached from the Ministry of the Electrical Industry for this purpose. Other members of the committee were the artillery commander N.D. Iakovlev, P.I. Kirpichnikov, A.I. Berg, P.N. Goremykin, I.A. Serov, and N.E. Nosovskii.
51 Chertok (1992b).
52 Konovalov (1991), Chertok (1992c). Other details of the Nordhausen Institute, based on Tokaty's and Gröttrup's memoirs, can be found in Ordway and Sharpe (1979), 320–2.
53 Konovalov (1991); Rebrov (1995).
54 Thanks to Naomi Azraeli for these suggestions. See also Kuvshinov, Sobolev (1995), 105.
55 Kuvshinov and Sobolev (1995), 105; von Braun and Ordway (1975), 118.
56 Semiriaga (1995), 142–3.
57 Schroder (1955), 27.
58 Chertok (1992d, 1992e); Ivkin (1994), 74.
59 The meetings were described by Tokaty (1964), 280–1, (1968), 345–6.
60 Holloway (1994), 247.
61 Tokaty (1968), 346; Ordway and Sharpe (1979), 329.
62 For the scientists' viewpoint see Tokaty (1968), 343, 345–6; Chertok (1992d).
63 Ishlinskii (1986), 298–300 (G.S. Vetrov). For an account of the contemporaneous German work see Ordway and Sharpe (1979), 329–30.
64 Budnik (1991), Chertok (1992d), Ivkin (1994), 74.
65 For accounts of the Germans' work and life in Gorodomlia, see Gröttrup (1959), Ordway and Sharpe (1979), 325–6, 335–43.
66 Gröttrup (1959), 56.
67 Gröttrup (1959), 30.
68 Gröttrup (1959), 52.
69 Ordway and Sharpe (1979), 342.
70 Gröttrup (1959), 107.
71 Chertok (1923d).
72 Ordway and Sharpe (1979), 327.
73 Kuvshinov and Sobolev (1995).
74 Chertok (1992d).
75 German personnel were probably more important to the Americans, and von Braun and others played a leading role in the United States missile and space exploration programme for a quarter of a century after the war. See Ordway and Sharpe (1979).

7 New postwar branches (2): the nuclear industry

N.S. Simonov

INTRODUCTION

Recently many articles and a few books have been devoted to the history of creation of the Soviet atom bomb. Most, however, have not been able to rely on original documents.[1] A rare exception from this point of view was a collection of articles by original participants in the Soviet 'uranium project' entitled 'The Creation of the First Soviet Nuclear Bomb', published by Energoatomizdat in Moscow in 1995.[2]

Relating 'how it really was', the authors of this collection have unearthed previously unknown facts and have overturned presumptions, referring to original documents such as decrees of the Soviet government, official papers and reports, and entries in log books, as well as reports in the Soviet and foreign press, the specialist scientific and technical literature on atomic energy, and so on. In many cases the documents themselves remain classified to the present day. However, their existence and general tenor has entered the public domain. So there is no need for the historiography of the Soviet defence-industry complex still to be written as if these documents did not exist or were completely inaccessible.

The existing historical literature is also silent concerning the economic consequences for the Soviet Union of assimilating the production of nuclear and thermonuclear weapons as a permanent military-industrial activity. All that was known hitherto was that this activity gave rise to a closed branch of the Soviet economy – 'medium engineering'.

THE ORIGINS OF THE 'URANIUM PROJECT'

It was undoubtedly reports of intelligence agents to the effect that the major powers had brought atomic weapons research and development to the stage of practical results which drove the Soviet leadership to organise such work itself. On 10 March 1942 People's Commissar for Internal Affairs L.P. Beriia presented to the State Defence Committee a wide-ranging report on the activity of the British uranium subcommittee (the 'Maud Committee') led by the world-famous physicist, Professor G.P. Thomson of Imperial College. His report stated specifically that:

In a number of capitalist countries, in connection with research being carried out on nuclear fission with the aim of obtaining a new energy source, study of the question of utilising atomic energy for military purposes has begun.

In 1939 intensive scientific research work on developing techniques for applying uranium to new explosive substances was initiated in France, Britain, the USA and Germany. Such work is being carried out in conditions of great secrecy.

The activities of the British Uranium Committtee on atomic energy issues are characterised in materials obtained by the NKVD from Britain in the form of intelligence... This research is based on using one of the uranium isotopes (uranium-235) which possesses the properties of effective fission. For this uranium ore is used, the most significant reserves of which are found in Canada, the Belgian Congo, the Sudetenland, and Portugal.... The British scholar [Rudolf] Peierls and the physicist Dr Bays have worked out a technique for separating out the uranium-235 isotope with the aid of a diffusion apparatus designed by Dr [Francis] Simon, which is also recommended for practical use in the business of deriving uranium for preparation of a uranium bomb...

The applied side of development is based on a few central propositions underpinned by theoretical calculation and experimental work as follows.

Professor Peierls of the University of Birmingham has determined theoretically that a 10-kilogram mass of uranium-235 is the critical amount. A quantity of this substance of less than critical signficance is stable and entirely safe, whereas in uranium-235 with a mass greater than 10 kilograms a progressive fission reaction arises which produces a colossal explosive force. In designing bombs the active component should consist of two separate halves, the combined mass of which exceeds the critical amount. For producing the maximum force of explosion of these uranium-235 components... their rate of displacement is worked out at about 6000 feet per second. At lower speeds the chain reaction is attenuated.

Professor [Geoffrey] Taylor considers that the destruction power of 10 kilograms of uranium-235 will correspond to 1600 tons of TNT. The main complexity in the production of uranium bombs consists in the difficulty of separation of the active uranium-235 component from other isotopes, the preparation of the bomb casing, and getting the necessary speed of displacement of the constituent masses.

According to data of the firm Imperial Chemical Industries (ICI)... the cost of the whole project amounts to £4.5 million to £5 million, and the likely cost of a single bomb to £326 000.[3]

In this way the higher Soviet leadership became convinced not only that the practical use of the atomic energy of uranium-235 for military purposes was a realistic proposition, but also obtained an impression, two years before the first American atomic bomb test, not only of the operating principles of a nuclear bomb, but also of the technical specificities of its manufacture, and of the approximate cost of the whole project.

The USSR's Allies in the anti-Hitler coalition supposed, wrongly, that Soviet scholars would penetrate the secrets of atomic weapons manufacture only with some delay, and that the Soviet economy, exhausted by warfare, would be in no condition to grapple with solving such a complex productive and technological task before 1955. In this connection one may take for illustration an event (amusing in the light of Beriia's report of 10 March 1942 on the work of the British Uranium Committee) which transpired at the international conference at Potsdam (17 July–2 August 1945) during a meeting of the leaders of the 'Big Three' – Stalin, Truman, and Churchill. The first American atomic weapon test had taken place at Alamogordo on the day before the beginning of the meeting. Subsequently the Soviet Marshal G.K. Zhukov reported as follows in his memoirs:

> I do not recall exactly the date, but following a session of the heads of governments Truman told Stalin of the existence in the USA of a bomb of unusual force (he did not call it an atomic weapon). At the moment of this communication, as has been written abroad, Churchill directed his gaze to Stalin's face to see his reaction. But the latter gave away nothing of his feelings, creating the appearance that he found no significance in Truman's words. As did Churchill, so too many other Anglo-American authors considered as a result that probably Stalin did not actually understand the significance of the communication he had received.[4]

The implementation of the Soviet 'uranium project' can be dated from 20 September 1942. On this day the State Defence Committee (GKO) issued a decree 'On the organisation of work on uranium', in which it charged the USSR Academy of Sciences

> to resume work on investigation of the realisation of use of atomic energy through fission of the uranium nucleus and to present to GKO by 1 April 1943 a report on the possibilities of creating a uranium bomb or uranium fuel.[5]

It remains the case, however, that it was only after the Potsdam conference, and the immediately following atomic bombing of Hiroshima and Nagasaki that the decision was taken actually to produce a Soviet weapon.

THE THREE COMPONENTS OF THE 'URANIUM PROJECT'

On 27 November 1942, at the height of the battle of Stalingrad, the GKO adopted a resolution 'On the mining of uranium', in which it charged Narkomtsvetmet (the People's Commissariat of Nonferrous Metallurgy):

> (a) by 1 May 1943 to organise the mining and processing of uranium ores and the derivation of uranium salts in the quantity of 4 tons at the Taboshary 'V' factory of Glavredmet [the chief administration of rare metals]; (b) in the first quarter of 1943 to compile a composite design for a uranium factory with a productive capacity of 10 tons of uranium salts per year.[6]

In this way was determined the first two basic directions of the Soviet 'uranium project': first, the organisation and execution of scientific research, and second, the organisation of extraction and processing of uranium ore.

At a meeting with V.M. Molotov at the beginning of 1943 leading Soviet physicists confirmed the reliability of the theoretical computations and experimental designs derived by intelligence agents from top secret information about the American 'uranium project' (the Manhattan project).[7] On 15 February 1943 the Soviet government issued a decree concerning the establishment of a secret Laboratory no. 2 under the USSR Academy of Sciences (from the second half of 1949 the USSR Academy of Sciences Laboratory for Measurement Instruments). The 40-year old Professor of Physics Igor' Vasil'evich Kurchatov was designated its chief.[8]

With the establishment of a specialised laboratory the third basic thrust of the 'uranium project' was determined – the creation of an experimental (subsequently industrial) reactor for the production of plutonium-239 from naturally occuring uranium-238, and of an industrial apparatus for extracting enriched uranium-235 – the fissile materials from which atomic weapons are manufactured. These two paths, leading respectively to a plutonium bomb and a uranium bomb, were both adopted because each looked exceptionally uncertain and difficult.

To start up the experimental reactor required about 50 tons of pure natural uranium in the form of metal blocks of 32- and 35-millimetre diameter amounting to 36 tons, 9 tons of uranium dioxide pellets of 80 mm diameter, and 400 tons of absolutely pure graphite as the neutron decelerator. A uranium-graphite reactor was chosen over a heavy-water reactor (which would have required less uranium), because graphite was easier to obtain than heavy water (not until 1950 was heavy water first used in a Soviet nuclear reactor). However, uranium was also very difficult to obtain; almost all deposits known at that time were far beyond Soviet frontiers. At Kurchatov's request on 8 December 1944 the GKO adopted a decision to establish a largescale uranium mining enterprise, Combine no. 6, in Central Asia on the basis of the few known Soviet deposits. The organisation and leadership of this enterprise was handed over to the USSR NKVD and its Ninth Administration headed by A.P. Zaveniagin. During 1946–7 Combine no. 6 extracted and processed more than 290 tons of uranium ore and supplied 86 tons of uranium in 40 per cent concentrate.

The technology for obtaining metallic uranium which had been commissioned for Laboratory no. 2 was developed in the chief administration for rare metals of Narkomtsvetmet. The first pure metallic uranium ingot, with a mass of more than one kilogram, was cast at factory no. 12 of the People's Commissariat for Ammunition in the town of Elektrostal' in December 1944.

The Moscow Electrode Factory was commissioned with processing and supplying pure graphite for the experimental reactor. Oil coke was used as the basic raw material, the first batch of which was prepared at the Moscow Neftegaz factory.

In August 1945 the world was shaken by news of the colossal destruction and numerous civilian casualties of the Japanese cities which the United States Air Force, under the orders of President Truman, subjected to bombardment with an uranium weapon (Hiroshima on 6 August) and a plutonium weapon (Nagasaki on 9 August).

Thanks to the German physicist Klaus Fuchs, who participated in the British and American nuclear programmes, as well as to other intelligence, Soviet physicists and military leaders already knew the detailed plans of the American plutonium bomb tested on 16 July 1945 in the desert at Alamogordo. They knew its size and general mass, its ten designated principal components, the detailed description of the design of its polonium-beryllium neutron source (the 'trigger') and so on. However, to use this information, it was necessary to repeat step by step the path already traversed by American scholars to create a theory of neutron diffusion, calculate critical mass, and so on.[9] Otherwise mistakes would be unavoidable, each of which might conceal a deadly threat to the participants in the experimental and design work both in a direct and in an indirect sense; thus Commissar Beriia somtimes threatened to send the atomic scientists 'where Makar never drove the calves' [i.e. beyond the limits of the community, therefore by implication to the Gulag].[10] At that time experimental work in the Soviet Union as in the United States not infrequently resulted in nuclear accidents because of the lack of experience in controlling the spontaneous atomic fission which comes about in the presence of a critical mass of 510 grammes of plutonium-239 or 800 grammes of uranium-235.

From another point of view, the development of an experimental and design base was constrained by the lack of a production base in the economy; to establish the latter, given that this was in the middle of World War II, required mobilising the economic potential of the whole country.

Following the US detonation of three nuclear bombs the necessity of intensifying work on the 'uranium project' in the USSR became obvious.

Alarmed in all seriousness by the unforeseeable consequences of retention of its nuclear weapons monopoly by the United States, the Soviet leadership took a decision to make the realisation of the 'uranium project' (now designated 'Programme no. 1') a national priority.

THE SPECIAL COMMITTEE

On 20 August 1945 the GKO adopted Resolution no. 9887 'On the Special Committee of the GKO' for general oversight and leadership of the realisation of the 'uranium project'. The committee was composed of L.P. Beriia (chairman), Central Committee secretary G.M. Malenkov, Gosplan chairman N.A. Voznesenskii, deputy prime minister M.G. Pervukhin, Commissar for Ammunition B.L. Vannikov, deputy Commissar of Internal Affairs A.P. Zaveniagin, the physicists I.V. Kurchatov and P.L. Kapitsa, and NKVD General V.A. Makhnev, chief of its secretariat. Kapitsa, however, was allowed to resign in December after a far-reaching disagreement with Beriia. He objected to Beriia's unqualified interference (as he saw it) in scientific decisions, and also argued that the Soviet scientists should be allowed to find a less costly path to the bomb, rather than being ordered to copy that chosen by the Manhattan project. On the latter he was overruled, but it may be that in more general terms his defence of the atomic physicists' autonomy had some effect.[11]

It is understandable if Beriia, as People's Commissar of Internal Affairs, was designated chief administrator of the 'uranium project' (in fact there were three NKVD representatives on the special committee, the other two being Makhnev and Zaveniagin). Within Beriia's sphere of authority were deployed thousands of convict labourers, dozens of industrial enterprises of varied assortment (including for the mining of uranium), several military-industrial research institutes and design bureaux, and so on. Moreover, it was also through Beriia that the stream of intelligence had flowed from abroad concerning work on the atom bomb in other countries. In addition to these major considerations it may be added that, as Academician A.M. Petros'iants has written, of all the Politburo members and other high leaders of the country Beriia was most qualified in matters of technology policy. 'All this', Petros'iants indicates:

> I know not from second hand but from personal contact with him on many technical problems involved in tank building and atomic issues... he assigned to all work on the nuclear problem the necessary scale and scope of activity and dynamism. He possessed enormous energy and capacity for work, and was an organiser capable of carrying everything he began through to a conclusion.[12]

The Special Committee was to bear responsibility for developing atomic energy R&D; expanding the scope of geological prospecting and establishing the Soviet Union's raw material base for uranium extraction; the exploitation of uranium deposits beyond Soviet frontiers in Bulgaria and Czechoslovakia; the organisation of industry for uranium processing and the production of specialised equipment and materials, the construction of atomic-energy installations; and the development and production of the atom bomb.

A First Chief Administration (PGU) of the USSR Sovnarkom was established as the leading organisation for the above-mentioned activities, itself subordinate to the GKO Special Committee. The GKO Special Committee was charged with determining and confirming the scale of budgetary allocations to the PGU, and the allocation of labour and material-technical resources. These requirements were included by USSR Gosplan in utilisation balances as 'GKO special outlays'.

Vannikov, released from his duties as People's Commissar for Ammunition, was made chief of the PGU and deputy chairman of the GKO Special Committee. His first deputy was Zaveniagin; others were N.A. Borisov, P.Ia. Meshik, P.Ia. Antropov, and A.G. Kasatkin. Subsequently PGU membership was extended to V.S. Emel'ianov (deputy minister for the iron and steel industry), E.P. Slavskii (deputy minister for non-ferrous metallurgy), and A.N. Komarovskii (chief of the NKVD chief administration for industrial construction).

No organisation had the right to interfere in the administration, business organisation, and operational activities of the PGU, without the specific permission of the GKO. The PGU reported solely to the GKO Special Committee.

In a direct line of subordination to the PGU were placed several largescale production organisations. Among them may be distinguished in particular Factory no. 48, a producer of mining and chemical equipment for uranium extracting enterprises; Combine no. 6, for mining and processing of ores and concentrates of uranium; Factory no. 12, a producer of metallic uranium; Combine no. 817 (PO Box Cheliabinsk-40), a radiochemical producer of plutonium-239; and Combine no. 813 (PO Box Sverdlovsk-44), a gas-diffusion plant producing enriched uranium-235.

The leading research and design organisations of the PGU were Laboratory no. 1; Laboratory no. 2 with its filial, the future KB-11; and Laboratory no. 3. NII-9 was transferred to the PGU from the NKVD; NII-13 and NII-26 from the Ministry for the Chemical Industry; design work was carried out by GSPI-11 and GSPI-12 (the Moscow Design Office).

Contiguous issues were tackled by drawing in institutes and design bureaux of various agencies including the Radium Institute, Institute of Chemical Physics, Institute of Physical Problems, and P.N. Lebedev Institute of Physics, all of the USSR Academy of Sciences; the Leningrad Physical-Technical Institute; NII-6, GSKB-47, and NII-504 of the Ministry of Agricultural

Engineering; NII-88 of the Ministry of Armament; NIIKhimMash (the chemical engineering research institute) amd NII-42 of the Ministry of the Chemical Industry; TsKB-326 of the Ministry of Communications Equipment; the design bureau of Factory no. 92 (Gor'kii); the special design bureaux of the Kirov factory (Leningrad), the Ordzhonikidze Gidropress heavy engineering factory (Podol'sk), the Gork'ii engineering factory, and so on.

Enlisting the services of scientific institutions and design organisations for the 'uranium project' was carried out by the GKO Special Committee's Technical Council, of which the scientific secretary was Academician A.I. Alikhanov. In December 1945 the Technical Council was recast as the Engineering-Technical Council and, in April 1946, as the Scientific-Technical Council (NTS) of the USSR Council of Ministers PGU. Its membership now comprised B.L. Vannikov (chairman), M.G. Pervukhin and I.V. Kurchatov (his deputies), V.A. Malyshev, A.P. Zaveniagin, A.F. Ioffe, V.G. Khlopin, A.I. Alikhanov, N.N. Semenov, D.B. Skobel'tsin, Iu.B. Khariton, A.I. Leipunskii, and B.S. Pozdniakov.

THE MEANS OF PRODUCTION

It was possible to significantly accelerate the commissioning of the experimental reactor at the expense of defeated Nazi Germany. A special commission led by Zaveniagin uncovered in Germany's eastern zone (where it abutted the American zone) 100 tons of uranium concentrate. At the end of 1945 this was delivered to Factory no. 12 (Elektrostal') where it was turned into uranium brickettes and blocks of the quantity required to load the reactor. Factory no. 12 was equipped from dismantled facilities at Oranienburg in Germany and directed by Nikolaus Riehl, a Russian-speaking German scientist; this was one of the principal German contributions to the Soviet uranium project.[13]

F-1, the first experimental uranium-graphite reactor in Europe, was commissioned in Moscow on 25 December 1946, delivering a self-sustaining, controlled uranium fission reaction. (In the United States a uranium-graphite reactor had been started up by Enrico Fermi on 2 December 1942.) The full-capacity operation of F-1 gave rise to maximal accumulation (1–2 mg) of plutonium in the uranium blocks loaded into the reaction chamber. With the help of the experimental reactor a technique was worked out for quantitative control of the physical properties of uranium and graphite used to check their quality when loading and unloading the industrial reactor of Combine no. 817 at Kyshtym (PO Box Cheliabinsk-40), which had been built at furious pace. In January 1947 the foundations of the industrial reactor were laid, and all the equipment had been installed and the reaction chamber prepared by the beginning of 1948.

KB-11: the bomb factory

On 8 April 1946 the USSR Council of Ministers adopted decree No. 806–327 under which was organised KB-11 (PO Box Arzamas-16), headed by P.M. Zernov, a former deputy minister for the tank industry, and the physicist Iu.B. Khariton, and based on the filial of PGU Laboratory no. 2. The task of this new organisation was defined with extreme precision: to produce a device, i.e. a nuclear bomb.

For the location of the nuclear centre was chosen the town of Sarovo on the border of the Mordovian ASSR with Gor'kii oblast'. This was the location of the *Katiusha* Factory no. 550 of the former People's Commissariat of Ammunition, handed over in 1946 to the People's Commissariat of Agricultural Engineering. On 21 July 1946 the USSR Council of Ministers adopted decree no. 1286–525 'On the plan of development of work of KB-11 under Laboratory no. 2 of the USSR Academy of Sciences'. Factory no. 550 was handed over to the MVD construction administration. From the beginning of 1946 right up to the 1990s not only the nuclear centre KB-11 (VNIIEF from 1 January 1967) itself but also the whole residential zone around it were strictly isolated from the outside world. The town of Sarovo was wiped off all maps of the Soviet Union and excluded from all statistical returns.

KB-11 was confronted with the task of building a nuclear bomb in two variants: a plutonium bomb using spherical implosion (RDS-1) and a uranium bomb with a gun-barrel mechanism for creating a critical mass (RDS-2). The plutonium bomb was to be tested by 1 January 1948, and the uranium bomb by 1 June of the same year. In February 1948 these deadlines were extended to March and December 1949.

Combine no. 817: plutonium

The plutonium was to be obtained from the industrial reactor of Combine no. 817 with subsequent radiochemical processing. To obtain enriched uranium-235 the method of gas-diffusion and separation required assimilation of a new type of engineering technology – atomic engineering, with exceptionally complex instruments, devices, and apparatuses never before applied in the Soviet economy.

Both the plutonium and uranium variants for manufacture of an atomic bomb were worked on and implemented in parallel, but for a number of reasons both objective and subjective the completion of a uranium device was delayed by 18 months.

At the beginning of 1945 at the instance of the PGU, the Chemical Engineering Research Institute directed by N.A. Dollezhal' began development of the industrial uranium-graphite reactor for Combine no. 817. The August deadline for handover of the project was very tight. In distinction from the F-1 experimental reactor, the industrial reactor had a cooling system using several thousand cubic metres of pressurised water which was admitted and washed over the uranium blocks via conduits manufactured out of aluminium. To load the reactor required about 150 tons of pure uranium and more than 1000 tons of graphite. When the designated quantity of plutonium had been accumulated the uranium blocks were unloaded and reloaded. The reactor was equipped with automatic control and safety systems, controls on changes in the discharge of water, temperature, and so on.

Participants in the design and experimental testing of the industrial reactor included Proektstal'konstruktsiia (director N.P. Mel'nikov), A.S. Abramov's design bureau of the Ministry of the Aircraft Industry, the All-Union Institute of Aviation Materials (VIAM, director A.V. Akimov), the Academy of Sciences Institute of Physical Chemistry (director Academician A.N. Frumkin), the All-Union Institute of Hydraulic engineering (Prof. V.V. Mishke), and KB-10 of the Podol'sk engineering factory. The reactor's unloading system was prepared by Gor'kii factory no. 92 (director A.S. El'ian).

To give an impression of the scale of construction work on the three plants of Combine no. 817 it is sufficient to state that to lay the foundations of the production structures required removal of 190 000 cubic metres of soil and rock, and the laying of 82 000 cubic metres of concrete and 6000 cubic metres of brickwork; the installation included 5000 tons of metallic construction, 230 kilometres of pipework of various diameters, 165 kilometres of electric cable, 5745 items of valve-regulating equipment, and 2800 varied instruments. Employed on the construction were 45 000 people, including convict labourers; to build the factories of Combine no. 813 (PO Box Sverdlovsk-44) there were assigned 30 000 persons of the 'NKVD special contingent'.[14]

At the 'A' factory of Combine no. 817 the loading of uranium blocks was completed, and the reactor was experimentally started up, on the evening of 7 June 1948. However, the first major accident happened already on 19 June. The supply of cooling water to the centre of the reaction chamber was cut back by a half-opened valve for surplus water. The level of radiation exceeded permissible norms by several times, and the reactor had to be shut down. The damaged uranium blocks were removed by 30 July. At the insistence of Vannikov and Kurchatov the damage had to be put right while the reactor was operating again in order not to interrupt the production of plutonium, which led to contamination of the site and excessive irradiation of the shift personnel and repair brigade. Despite this the reactor still had to be shut down on 20 January 1949 for capital repair.

Since there was a shortage of exploitable uranium, they removed the partly exposed but highly radioactive uranium blocks from the shut-down reactor without taking any special precautions, and used them subsequently for reloading.

The irradiated uranium blocks from the factory 'A' industrial reactor were then transferred to the radiochemical factory 'B', where the plutonium was extracted in concentrated solution. The latter was passed on to the chemical-metallurgical factory 'V' for manufacture of metallic plutonium parts for the atomic bomb. The recovered uranium contained a significant quantity of uranium-235 which was intended for utilisation in the gas diffusion plant of Combine no. 813 for enriched uranium-235 being built in the town of Verkhne-Neivinsk (PO Box Sverdlovsk-44).

In the first months of operation of the plutonium combine, dosimetric control was virtually nonexistent. Over a few years radiation sickness was diagnosed in 2098 workers, while 6000 people received a cumulative dose of more than 100 REM, in some cases 25 REM or more in a single year. In addition to production personnel, radiation sickness affected 124 000 people living in the floodlands of the river Tech in the Cheliabinsk and Kurgan oblasts, into which were discharged radiochemical effluents in the years 1949–52. On 29 September 1957 one of the storage containers for radioactive waste was breached. Of 20 million Curies of radionucleides held in storage, 18 million were released into the territory of the Combine's industrial site, and 2 million into 1000 square kilometres of the territory of Cheliabinsk and Sverdlovsk oblasts.

Let us compare the character of technical processes for extracting enriched uranium-235 and weapon-grade plutonium-239. To extract the plutonium formed within irradiated metallic uranium, the uranium had to be dissolved in order to obtain a concentrated solution of plutonium. In so far as this was an industrial undertaking, not a laboratory, it is understandable that the capacity of equipment of factory 'B' of Combine no. 817 was measured in hundreds or even thousands of litres, and the quantity of acids and reagents to be employed exceeded the quantity of uranium loaded for chemical processing by many times. The uranium solution was precipitated in acetate, separating the plutonium from the uranium and fission products. The plutonium concentrate was then subjected to further purification in an affinage: the uranium fell out as a precipitate, the plutonium remaining in solution. The solution was now oxidised by a bichromate with fluoric acid added; the rare metal fluorides were now precipitated, again leaving the plutonium in solution. The solution was dissolved in bisulphate, and finally the plutonium was precipated out, the quantity being one ten thousandth (0.01 per cent) of the mass of the uranium initially loaded for processing, and sometimes even less because of losses arising from the excessive superficial surface area of the equipment.

The first batch of finished output left Combine no. 817 only in February 1949. The difficulties did not finish with this, in so far as now the basic task became the derivation of metallic plutonium and of plutonium parts. Pure plutonium is a metal which melts at 640 degrees and boils at 3227 degrees

Centigrade. In its structure and properties it is very different from many metals, for example in its low plasticity, low resistance to corrosion, and high toxicity. When compacted it heats spontaneously. To work with it under normal conditions is practically impossible. Smelting and casting plutonium requires a near vacuum in the foundry, with an inert atmosphere for cooling and a special press for working the metal. The critical mass of weapon-grade plutonium has not one but several values; to achieve a critical mass accidentally because of inaccurate laboratory analysis and mistakes in meter readings was entirely possible at practically all stages of the technological process.

Combine no. 813: enriched uranium

To separate the uranium-235 isotope used in manufacture of a nuclear weapon from natural uranium the gas diffusion method was used. Natural uranium is transformed into a gaseous compound. Uranium hexafluoride is most appropriate for this purpose, since it becomes a gas under a pressure of less than one atmosphere (i.e. in a vacuum) and at a temperature of less than 56 degrees Centigrade. Passing this gas (which is chemically highly aggressive) through a cascade of porous barriers over a distance of several kilometres results in a gradual filtering out of the heavier uranium-238 and an increase in the proportional content of the lighter uranium-235. Since the uranium-235 content of naturally occurring uranium is only 0.7 per cent, the uranium hexafluoride must pass through the porous partitions several thousand times before its share rises to 90 per cent. To obtain 1 kilogram of enriched uranium requires the expenditure of between 175 and 220 kilograms of pure natural uranium, and roughly 600 000 kWh of electrical power to supply the compressors propelling the uranium hexafluoride.

To build a gas diffusion plant for enriched uranium was a most complex technical-engineering problem for that time, the accomplishment of which did not proceed without mistakes and delays in development of the technological equipment, especially the porous partitions. The PGU enlisted eminent scholars and engineers to solve this problem. The most successful designs were for porous plate manuactured from sintered nickel powder developed by the Moscow Hard Alloys Combine of Mintsvetmet, and the design for a tube filter developed by east German specialists headed by the Nobel prizewinner Gustav Hertz in institutes 'A' and 'G' in Sukhumi.

During 1948–9 the diffusion apparatuses were manufactured by the Gor'kii Engineering Factory, and promptly equipped with porous barriers by subcontracting enterprises which also assembled and installed them in cascades. Setting up and making ready this technologically unique equipment in Combine no. 813 took a whole year – longer than specified in the government assignment. The most complex problem was producing a vacuum and securing the passage of the uranium hexafluoride through tens of thousands of connectors and linkages between diffusion apparatuses. The final degree of enrichment of the first industrial batches of uranium-235 obtained by the gas diffusion method was no better than 75 per cent, when the requirement of a uranium bomb was for not less than 90 per cent – a standard achieved only in 1951.

Simultaneously with the gas diffusion method, the electromagnetic separation of uranium isotopes was tried out under the scientific guidance of Academician L.A. Artsimovich at factory no. 418 in the town of Lesnyi (PO Box Sverdlovsk-45). This factory, built in 1946–9), had the world's biggest electromagnetic apparatus with a weight of 6000 tons. Its brass vacuum chambers weighed more than 1000 tons. Although the electromagnetic method of uranium enrichment eventually proved cost-ineffective, it played an important role in the further enrichment of the uranium-235 obtained from Combine no. 813. It was this uranium which was used in the second Soviet atomic bomb tested in 1951.

THE FIRST ATOMIC TESTS

Meanwhile in the course of a year's operation of the industrial reactor at Combine no. 817 a quantity of weapon-grade plutonium had been extracted sufficient for manufacture of an atom bomb (RDS-1). On 27 June 1949 a meeting was held at the Combine in which there participated Kurchatov, Vannikov, Zaveniagin, B.G. Muzrukov, Khariton, Ia.B. Zel'dovich, D.A. Frank-Komenetskii, and G.N. Flerov. The mass of the plutonium bomb was finally decided. So as not to risk a failure, its mass was determined by analogy with the first American atom bomb test, i.e. 6.2 kg.

On 5 August 1949, two hemispheres of metallic plutonium were manufactured by hot pressing at factory 'B' for RDS-1. The technology for this was still under development, and those who carried it out had no guarantee that a spontaneous atomic fission reaction would not occur in the process. The same day the bomb was formally accepted by its purchasers. The act of acceptance was signed by Khariton, A.A. Bochvar, and V.G. Kuznetsov. On 8 August the plutonium components were transferred by a special train to KB-11 in Sarovo. Measurements carried out there confirmed that RDS-1 matched the technical requirements and was suitable for testing on the firing range.

The automated implosion detonators and high-voltage apparatuses for RDS-1 were prepared by NII-504 of the Ministry of Agricultural Engineering and by NII-6. The assembly had to set off simultaneous detonations to an accuracy of millionths of a second. Participants in developing the component connections were GSKB-46 (Ministry of Agricultural Engineering), TsKB-326 (Ministry of Communications), and the design bureau of NII-88 (Ministry of Armament). The theoretical calculations were carried out by subdivisions of the Steklov Mathematics Institute, the Institute of Physical Problems, and the Geophysics Institute, all of the Academy of Sciences.

Preparation for the testing of RDS-1 had begun three years before its culmination. It included establishing a special site for the firing range, and installing structures and specialised equipment and instruments. The full set of research and experimental work was developed by scholarly collectives of the Academy of Sciences Institute of Chemical Physics, the State Optics Institute, specialists from the military academies, and others. The firing range was set up by engineering troops of the Ministry of the Armed Forces in the steppe on the near side of the Irtysh river, roughly 170 kilometres to the west of Semipalatinsk in the Kazakh SSR. In the centre of the experimental site was installed a metal latticed tower 37.5 metres high. On the range there were installed 1300 different instruments for physical measurement of 9700 distinct indicators for investigation of the penetrating radiation.

By 26 August 1949 all participants in the test, headed by Beriia as chief administrator of the 'uranium project' and under the chairmanship of Pervukhin, had been assembled on the Semipalatinsk firing range. The final installation of the atomic bomb was completed at 4 a.m. on the 29th. At this moment the weather worsened sharply; the wind strengthened to 12–15 metres per second, and rain fell. To avoid any surprises the time of the test was brought forward by one hour. Exactly at 7 a.m. the test of the first Soviet atom bomb was initiated. After the nuclear detonation on the firing range, comprehensive measures of its explosive effects and other research activities were undertaken.

The first serial models of the RDS-1 nuclear weapon were manufactured in the experimental plants of KB-11 in 1950. They were never deployed by the military as armament, but were stored disassembled in special warehouses.

An atomic bomb based on enriched uranium-235 was tested at the Semipalatinsk firing range in 1951. It was half the weight of the first plutonium bomb, but twice as powerful. The 6-year lag behind the United States in this respect was offset by more rapid establishment of additional production facilities at Combines nos 813 and 817, and also in the building of more powerful uranium-graphite reactors in the new enterprises of Combines nos 816 (Tomsk-7) and 815 (Krasnoiarsk-26).

THE SUPPLY OF RAW MATERIALS

On 17 November 1951 a heavy-water (deuterium oxide) reactor for producing weapon-grade plutonium was started up at Combine no. 817. In distinction from the uranium-graphite reactors, heavy water in the reaction chamber allowed the formation of a given quantity of plutonium from one tenth or one fifteenth of the initial quantity of uranium and one fiftieth or one sixtieth of the previous requirement for graphite.

Obtaining heavy water proved a highly complex task in which the USSR Ministry for the Chemical Industry only succeeded three years after its receipt of the GKO assignment of 4 September 1945. Apart from institutes of the Ministry for the Chemical Industry, and especially the L.Ia. Karpov Physical Chemistry Institute, Laboratories nos 2 and 3, the Academy of Sciences Institute of Physical Problems, the laboratory of the German Professor M. Volmer in NII-9, and other organisations all took part in establishing techniques for obtaining heavy water and studying its properties. The Soviet government was compelled in the direction of building heavy water reactors – despite the greater risks arising from the formation of an explosive mixture inside, and the resulting chance of a spontaneous fission reaction – by the inadequate development of the nuclear industry's raw material base.

In August 1945 a First Administration (led by P.Ia. Antropov) was established under the PGU of the GKO Special Committee, responsible for building the ore-mining enterprises and hydro-metallurgical factories of Combine no. 6, and for organisation of their mining and processing of uranium ores. Upon the First Administration was also laid responsibility for establishing uranium-ore mining and processing enterprises in East Germany, Bulgaria, and Czechoslovakia.

A number of organisations were transferred from Mintsvetmet to the PGU – ore administrations nos 11 (Taboshary), 12 (Adrasman), 13, 14, 15 (Tiuiamuiun), factory 'V', and so on. From these enterprises was established the first national uranium mining Combine no. 6, the territorial administration of which was located in Leninabad (Tadjikstan SSR). In 1946 the industrial mining of uranium was begun (alongside the mining of iron and other ores) in the Krivoi Rog deposits of the Ukraine, where Combine no. 9 was established.

Geological exploration and prospecting for uranium on Soviet territory was carried out by the First Chief Geological Exploration Administration of the USSR Sovnarkom Committee for Geological Affairs from October 1945. A number of organisations were enlisted to carry out this work: from 1943 the All-Union Institute for Mineral Raw Materials (VIMS), from 1945 the All-Union Institute for Exploratory Geophysics (VIRG), from 1946 with its expedition no. 1 the USSR Academy of Sciences Institute for the Geology of Ore Deposits (IGEM), and from 1947 the All-Union Geology Institute (VSEGEI).

In the initial period of creating a raw material supply for the uranium industry the opening of quarry workings was accomplished with hand drills [drifters]; they loaded the mined material into trolleys by hand, rolled them by hand or horse power on wooden rails to the unloading point and then conveyed the ore by mule or camel to the processing works where it was broken up into pebbles and treated with alkaline solutions; after sedimentation of the solids in concrete basins the solution of uranium salts was dried out on racks over an open fire. This heavy manual labour was performed mainly by prisoners and special settlers. The quarry workings were continually liable to landslips and flooding, resulting in lost seams; because the character of oil and gas discharges had been insufficiently studied, there were several significant accidents in the quarries of the Combine in 1945–9.

During the period 1946–9 roads and power lines were brought to the enterprises of Combine no. 6, and a thermal power station was built on local coal supplies, along with workers' settlements, repair shops, compressor stations, and so on. The level of mechanisation of basic productive processes in the quarries rose by 50 per cent; the labour productivity of a cutter rose nearly threefold. The processing works were redesigned; the fragmentation and crushing of uranium ore began to be carried out with the aid of up-to-date equipment, for the alkalisation and sedimentation of ores they used a completely mechanised chemical technology, and the drying of the concentrate was done in special ovens with mechanical loading. These measures permitted an increase in the extraction of uranium in the concentrate from 40 per cent in 1945 to 60 per cent in 1947 and 74 per cent in 1950.

On 27 December 1949 the USSR Council of Ministers adopted resolution no. 5744–2162 on establishment under itself of a Second Chief Administration, and, under the latter, a First Administration (headed by N.B. Karpov) to guide the development of the uranium industry's raw material base, and a Department for Foreign Sites (headed by V.I. Trofimov) 'to guide the development of the raw material base for uranium in the People's Democracies'. In addition to Combines nos 6 and 9, the Second Chief Administration (VGU) was given charge of the Kuznets mines (Poland), the Jachymov mines (Czechoslovakia), the Soviet-Bulgarian Mining Association (SBGO), and the Wismuth joint-stock company (East Germany). The uranium ore mined abroad was transferred to the USSR for subsequent hydrometallurgical processing.

In 1951 the VGU acquired two new mining enterprises: Combine no. 11 in Kirgiziia and Mining Administration no. 10 in the North Caucasus. The establishment of mining enterprises came as the last phase of exploration, when sufficient reserves of uranium ore had been determined for industrial development. As of 1 January 1950 compared with the beginning of 1945 the national uranium raw material base had expanded by a factor of 16, providing for an increase in mined uranium by 8 times. In 1951 on Antropov's initiative a special industrial-branch institute, NII-10 (VNIIKhT), later PromNII-Proekt, was created under the VGU. In addition to uranium, VGU mined other materials widely used in the nuclear industry such as beryllium, lithium, niobium, zirconium, boron, hafnium, and so on. Prospecting for these materials was done by the N.M. Fedorovskii All-Union Institute for Raw Materials (VIMS) on assignment for the VGU.

Table 7.1. Uranium ore mined in the USSR and allied or occupied territory, 1945–50 (tons)

	Ore mined:			Metal mined in ore	Metal extracted in chemical concentrate at Combine no. 6
	total	*in USSR*	*in East Germany, Czechoslovakia, Poland, and Bulgaria*		
	(1)	(2)	(3)	(4)	(5)
1945	18.0	18.0	–	14.6	7.0
1946	110.3	50.0	60.3	50.0	20.0
1947	338.2	129.3	208.9	129.3	65.8
1948	634.4	182.5	451.9	182.5	103.3
1949	1267.3	278.6	988.7	278.7	170.3
1950	2056.8	416.9	1639.9	416.9	236.9

Source: Sozdanie (1995), 197.

According to data for 1945–50 which has been published, but not verified from other sources, the mining of uranium ore and its processing into chemical concentrate by PGU and VGU enterprises grew at the rates shown in table 7.1. Thus from 1945–50 the mining of uranium ore increased more than 100 times, while the production of pure (metallic) uranium rose over the same period by a factor of 28.5. The Soviet Union depended for three quarters of its supply of uranium on ores imported from eastern Europe.[15]

From the 1072 tons of metallic uranium obtained it was possible to build seven industrial reactors, sufficient to obtain up to 100 kilogrammes of plutonium-239 per year under optimal technical conditions. If this quantity were divided into bombs of 6.2 kilograms each, the result would be 16 devices of the RDS-1 type. From the same quantity of natural uranium it would be possible over a period of years, and depending on factory capacities, to extract not less than 7.6 tons of highly enriched uranium-235, from which not less than 7000 devices of the RDS-2 type could have been prepared.

The significance of these calculations should not be overstated, since they concern the Soviet Union's military-economic potential rather than the much smaller number of nuclear devices which was actually manufactured and deployed in the Soviet Army's armament at the beginning of 1950s. In the early years, however, the supply of uranium was the binding constraint on Soviet progress towards the bomb. In the words of David Holloway, '[t]he length of time the Soviet Union needed to develop the atomic bomb was determined more by the availability of uranium than by any other factor'.[16]

THE COST OF THE 'URANIUM PROJECT'

A key issue in the implementation of the Soviet 'uranium project' is its cost. According to official returns the American Manhattan Project cost the American taxpayer more than two billion dollars between 1941 and 1945. It is unclear whether this sum comprises only outlays on research and development, or extends to outlays on the building of industrial reactors and enterprises for uranium enrichment, the mining and processing of uranium ore and pure graphite, the production of heavy water and creation of metallic uranium, not to mention the cost of a firing range for nuclear weapon tests. If the two billion dollars included the latter outlays in addition to research and development, then it would evoke some scepticism.

Prior to the Manhattan Project the United States had no facilities to mine or process uranium, graphite, heavy water, and so on. Underlying the process of building an atomic weapon was the creation within an extraordinarily compressed timetable of a new branch of the economy, that is, the nuclear industry, to establish which involved creating specialised supply facilities in the engineering, instrument-making, electrical and vacuum, chemical, and metallurgical industries. A successful atomic weapon test was the clearest evidence that a nuclear industry had been created in the country, and that the atomic weapon was being assimilated into serial and mass production. For this reason the Soviet government declined to confirm the fact of the successful RDS-1 test for two years, in order within this period to accumulate a quantity of weapon-grade plutonium and enriched uranium sufficient to deter a likely aggressor, and to create types of aviation and missile technology for delivery of nuclear weapons.

The total cost of the Soviet 'uranium project' will probably never be known if, in addition to outlays on research and development, we look to take into account the real expenditures on the creation of the Soviet nuclear industry. In the annual accounts of fulfilment of the USSR State budget, figures for outlays of the First and Second Chief Administrations were not shown separately. Nor were they identified in the annual cash-flows reported by the USSR State Bank. In some official reports of the USSR Ministry of Finance there are disaggregated 'special outlays' of the Ministry of the Armed Forces and the Ministries of the Navy, Internal Affairs, and State Security, but these bear no direct relation to the nuclear industry; nor do the headings for 'other outlays'.[17] Only in connection with a single memorandum of the Ministry of Finance for 1952, found by the author in the Russian State Economics Archive, is it possible to say that the figures directly bear upon the question under consideration. The figures, authenticated by the chief of the Ministry of Finance special group M. Dubnikov, are shown in table 7.2. Under the secret heading of 'special works', in addition to PGU and VGU outlays were entered outlays of the Third and Fourth Administrations responsible for work on vacuum-tube, infrared, and radar technologies. Therefore it

Table 7.2. Plan of finance of 'special works' for 1951–5 (million rubles at current prices)

	Current outlays on 'special works'	*Capital outlays on 'special works'*	*Outlays on 'special works'*		
			total	*% of spending on defence*	*% of total government spending*
	(1)	(2)	(3)	(4)	(5)
1950 report	4361	4251	8612	8.3	2.1
1951 report	5804	6115	11919	10.4	2.7
1952 confirmed	7515	5558	13073	10.1	2.8
1953 plan	6012	7914	13926	11.2	2.7
1954 plan	7700	5940	13640	12.4	2.5
1955 plan	8277	4018	12295	10.4	2.3
subtotal, 1951–5	35308	29546	64854	10.9	2.6

Sources:
(1–3) RGAE, 7733/36/3924-e, 74.
(4–5) Col. 3 divided by figures for government spending on defence and total government spending (results, not plans) for 1950 in RGAE, 7733/36/3958, 36, and 1951–5 in RGAE, 7733/36/5745, 6.

is not possible to confirm categorically that the figures in table 7.2 relate only to the nuclear industry. The figures shown are equivalent to roughly one tenth of the outlays on defence recorded in Soviet state budgets in the first half of the 1950s. It may be added, however, that in 1950 a CIA report estimated total employment on the Soviet 'uranium project' throughout the Soviet Union and eastern Europe at between 330000 and 460000 workers, with up to two-thirds of that number engaged in mining, and smaller numbers in research, production, and construction.[18]

Whatever the precise ruble value of the Soviet 'uranium project', one of the participants, A.P. Aleksandrov (later President of the USSR Academy of Sciences) wrote the following on this score in 1980:

> Today one can say openly and directly that a significant part of the difficulties experienced by our people in the first postwar years was associated with the need to mobilise huge human and material resources in order to do everything possible within the most compressed timetable for successful completion of the scientific research and technical designs for producing a nuclear weapon.[19]

THE NUCLEAR INDUSTRY IS BORN

After the successful test of the first Soviet atom bomb, perspectives for applying its basic product of fissile materials to non-military goals opened up before the Soviet nuclear industry. Already at the end of 1946 on the initiative of USSR Academy of Sciences President Academician S.I. Vavilov the USSR Council of Ministers adopted a resolution 'On the development of research on study of the atomic nucleus and the use of nuclear energy in technology, chemistry, medicine, and biology'. This resolution also confirmed a corresponding list of projects to develop the theory of nuclear reaction and radioactivity, the geology and geography of radioactive elements, the chemistry of uranium and its compounds, the metallurgy of uranium and its alloys, techniques for separating isotopes, the effect of radiation on living organisms, and economic uses (in power generation, transport, etc.) of nuclear energy. To co-ordinate this work a Scientific Council was set up under the Academy of Sciences President, comprising Academicians Vavilov (chairman), Skobel'tsin, Frumkin, A.N. Nesmeianov, L.A. Orbelli, corresponding Academy of Sciences member I.K. Kikoin, and Professor G.M. Frank.

In 1950 the reactor physicists of Laboratory no. 2 and designers of NII-KhimMash began to develop a reactor for an atomic power station. Their design was realised in 1954 when the world's first atomic power station was commissioned in Obninsk (Kaluga oblast'). In 1953 there began the building of submarines based on a miniaturised two-chamber reactor with a capacity of tens of thousands of horse power. In 1960 the world's first ice-breaker was launched, with an atomic steam-generating apparatus, opening navigation in the ice of the Northern Arctic Ocean.

Establishing nuclear power and engineering on the basis of the nuclear industry required the creation of a unified system of scientific, engineering-technical, and production-economic guidance of the main enterprises, research institutes, and design bureaux subordinate to the First, Second, and Third Chief Administrations of the Council of Ministers and other ministries and agencies. By a decree of the Supreme Soviet presidium dated 2 April 1953 a new Union ministry was established – Minsredmash (the Ministry of Medium Engineering); V.A. Malyshev, deputy chairman of the Council of Ministers and Lieutenant-General of tank engineers, was designated minister (he died in 1957 of acute leukaemia). The Council of Ministers confirmed the staff and structure of the new ministry in a secret resolution of 1 July 1953.

NOTES

1 Ershov (1988); Goncharov (1990); Gubarev, Rebrov, and Mosin (1993); Stranitsy (1994). Holloway (1994) introduced a large quantity of interview material provided by the original participants.

2 Sozdanie (1995). For a rare earlier glimpse, see also Rol' razvedki (1992).

3 Rol' razvedki (1992), 109–11; also Sozdanie (1995). The agent responsible for supply of this information was probably the 'fifth man', John Cairncross. The Maud Committee was named after Maud Ray, the former governess of the Danish physicist Niels Bohr. For the original Maud Committee report see Gowing (1964), 394–436. The costs estimated in the original are somewhat different from those cited by Beriia: £8.5 million as the total cost of building 36 bombs each of explosive power equivalent to 1.8 kilotons of TNT, or £236 000 each; the latter sum was compared with £392 000 as the equivalent cost of 1.8 kilotons in conventional bombs, making the nuclear weapon somewhat cheaper per equivalent ton of TNT.

4 Zhukov (1970), 685. For alternative interpretations of this episode see Holloway (1994), 117.

5 RTsKhIDNI, 644/1/58, 40.

6 RTsKhIDNI, 644/1/58, 144.

7 For Kurchatov's reports see Rol' razvedki (1992), 111–16, 116–18.

8 This was therefore two months earlier than the date of 12 April suggested by Holloway (1994), 96.

9 Of the Soviet scientists who used this information, only one or two were aware of its foreign origin. For an evaluation of the role of Fuchs, see Holloway (1994), 106–8, 138.

10 The translator thanks Aleksei Vernitskii for this interpretation.

11 Holloway (1994), 139–41, 148.

12 Sozdanie (1995), 55.

13 Riehl was one of a handful of German atomic scientists who worked in the USSR after the war (see also reference to Gustav Hertz below). For an assessment of their role see Holloway (1994), 110–11.

14 Sozdanie (1995), 81, 362.

15 This was an even higher proportion than the two-thirds estimated by the CIA at the time (cited by Holloway (1994), 177).

16 Holloway (1994), 223, continues: 'As soon as uranium was available in sufficient quantity, Kurchatov was able to build and start up the experimental reactor. The first production reactor was built as soon as there was enough uranium for it. The physicists were ready to assemble and test the bomb as soon as plutonium had been extracted from uranium irradiated in the reactor and fabricated into two metal hemispheres. It was this path, rather than the design and development of the weapon itself, that determined how long it took the Soviet Union to build the bomb. Vernadskii and Khlopin had been right in 1940 when they stressed the importance of acquiring uranium; the great failure of the years 1943–5 was that more was not done to find uranium in the Soviet Union.'

17 According to Bystrova (1996), 8, the officials responsible for finance of the armed forces complained in their report for 1946–7 of the 'uncontrolled finance' of the PGU which had presented no accounts to the Ministry of Finance.

18 Cited by Holloway (1994), 172.

19 Sozdanie (1995), 65.

Part IV
The defence-industry complex and society

8 The defence-industry complex in Leningrad (1): the interwar period

Aleksandr Losik and Aleksandr Shcherba

INTRODUCTION

Before the Revolution

The elements of a defence-industry complex were beginning to emerge in Russia at the end of the nineteenth and beginning of the twentieth centuries. From the outbreak of World War I it became a force the influence of which was clearly underestimated by Tsarism – a fact which contributed to the downfall of the latter.

Thus as early as May 1915 a congress of representatives of industry and trade in Petrograd created the Central Military-Industrial Committee (TsVPK), headed by the prominent industrialist Guchkov. Nicholas II signed the decree setting up this committee.[1] It co-ordinated 34 regional and 192 local military-industrial committees.[2] It was a powerful and active force. In Moscow, for example, the TsVPK was headed by the millionaire Riabushinskii. Its representative was appointed to the Special Assembly headed by the Minister for War, which had wide-ranging powers including oversight of the entire defence industry. In wartime conditions the influence of the military-industrial committees quickly grew, and the TsVPK became particularly influential after the Provisional Government's accession to power; its head, Guchkov, became Minister for War in the Provisional Government.

In general, however, the various elements of the defence industry did not combine into a single complex during the First World War. This was for various reasons – because of the monarchical system of government, the weakness of representative constitutional forms, and the absence of a suitable mechanism for interaction between government and industry. In conditions which demanded total mobilisation, not only of defence industry, the government could not establish such a mechanism. The result was that, although Russia had sufficient industrial capacity, it imported some weapons from France. And national unity, which was sustained by patriotic enthusiasm in the initial period of the war, soon disappeared as a result of the inadequate supply of war materials to the front.

It should be noted that industrial leaders and their political representatives were similarly unprepared to take any initiative upon themselves – confirmation of the fact that a defence-industry complex as a unified, interconnected entity did not as yet exist. The elements of such a complex which existed at that time were thus necessary but not sufficient. Transport in particular was inadequately developed. Absent in general were the specific relationships among these elements which would be capable of unifying them into a single complex.

Following the October Revolution the main institutions of the old state power quickly disintegrated. This did not, however, affect the Special Conference, which was joined by representatives of the new state, and continued to operate until 16 March 1918 – effectively until the moment of transfer of the government to Moscow.[3] The new authorities immediately came up against the requirement for new institutions which would ensure the reliable operation of the defence industry. Despite the Civil War an energetic search for these took place, and by November 1918 a Council of Workers' and Peasants' Defence had been created (from March 1920 the Council of Labour and Defence, STO).[4] In 1919 a Council of Defence Industry was established with direct responsbility for the organisation of defence industry.[5] These bodies intervened actively, sometimes using extreme measures, to conserve and revive the defence industry. High-level concern for the organisation of the defence industry persisted beyond the end of the Civil War. Despite general reductions in the armed forces, on 4 April 1921 STO issued a new 'Statute on the Council of Defence Industry'.[6] Thus the formation of new institutions of the defence-industry complex began on a nationwide scale.

Civil-war Petrograd

A special place in this process was occupied by the defence industry in Petrograd (renamed Leningrad following the revolutionary leader's death), because of its very large share in the overall volume of the country's defence production. It is enough to point out that, on 1 January 1919, 264 factories were working in Petrograd, of which 90 per cent specialised exclusively in defence production.[7]

A number of historically conditioned factors had given Petrograd's defence industry an enclave-like development. Among these were:

1 a substantial industrial base;
2 an experienced industrial workforce which permitted good timekeeping and even shift-work;
3 sufficient scientific and technical potential;
4 a developed transport infrastructure of maritime, rail, and canal facilities;
5 a high level of electrification;

6 sufficient energy sources including hydro-electricity and peat fuel supplies.

For these reasons the defence industry developed particularly strongly in Petrograd and was characterised by all the elements of the defence-industry complex in the country as a whole. For this reason, the process of formation of the defence-industry complex can be seen most clearly in the case of Petrograd.

The leading role in the city's defence-industry complex was played by the party. It was the party organs which took political decisions and provided direction for the complex as a whole, linked its component parts, and allowed them to function as an integrated complex.[8]

In 1920 a military department had been established in the Petrograd party committee under M.M. Lashevich.[9] There were also military sections in the Petrograd Soviet and its executive committee, and corresponding sections at the *raion* (neighbourhood) level. Their basic function was to co-ordinate the activity of defence industry and military units. This was carried out through the party organisations in factories and units. Military organisers were appointed to the party organisations of factories producing military products; such appointments were subject to confirmation by the party raion committee, without the agreement of which their transfer to other work was forbidden.

In consequence of its great significance for national economics and politics, as well as of its frontier position, civil-war Petrograd saw the formation of a Council (or Committee) of Defence under the Petrograd party leader and future left-oppositionist G.E. Zinov'ev. This body had unlimited powers, including powers to manage the city's defence industry, co-ordinating the work of all the institutions of government authority in the interests of defence. It was abolished after the Kronshtadt mutiny, its main functions being transferred to party organisations. The latter were not fully convinced of the need to conserve defence industry at this time of huge reduction in the size of the army and of the military budget as a whole.[10]

The transition to peace

In 1921 a sharp reduction in defence orders began. Some of the largest defence factories were temporarily shut down, while others were obliged to transfer to products for which there was a market demand, which naturally meant that they lost their defence profile. Specialised defence producers, including the Torpedo, Vul'kan, Franko-Russkii and other works, were closed for a time. The Krasnogvardeets plant began to manufacture primus stoves, the Krasnyi Arsenal plant textile equipment and the Bol'shevik plant tractors.[11] In contemporary documents the city's defence industry is characterised as 'an embalmed corpse'. At first party and state organs shut their eyes to this, putting their trust in the inevitable world revolution, and also in the belief that since Leningrad had become a border city it could not at the same time be a centre of the defence industry.

The realisation gradually dawned, however, that the role of Leningrad in defence industry could not be carried out anywhere else and that the process of converting defence plants to civilian products would have an inevitable and highly negative impact on mobilisation planning. A rapid mobilisation of defence output in the event of war would become impossible without huge new expenses which would vastly exceed the peacetime returns to civilian production. The excess was large enough that virtually all European states were now subsidising the peacetime losses of the defence industry in order to compensate them for maintaining mobilisation reserves.

It should be recognised that in the whole period between 1921 to 1926 the city's political leadership was engaged in an attempt to design a comprehensive system of defence production, and to determine on what scale and through which institutions defence production could be realised. Evidence of this is found in the unchanging structure of party, state, and production agencies of the city connected with the defence industry through the transitions from war to peace, and from relative peace to insecurity and accelerated rearmament. Naval rearmament began in 1926 with adoption of a six-year shipbuilding programme. It envisaged the building of 36 torpedo boats, 18 escort vessels, and 12 submarines.[12] The modernisation of the ground forces was accelerated in 1929 with a decision to create a tank industry.[13] The main emphasis of both these programmes was on the defence industry of Leningrad.

THE ACCELERATION OF DEFENCE-INDUSTRY DEVELOPMENT

From 1927 intensive work began on reconstructing defence industry in accordance with new needs. Naturally, new institutions appeared both in the city's political organs and in the economic system all levels. In 1926 Zinov'ev's successor as Leningrad party leader S.M. Kirov had ordered the development of a comprehensive design for the defence industry both in peacetime and for the event of mobilisation. This design amounted basically to the following. A first group of factories producing defence products was separated out from the city's other industry. Group I was placed under the unified leadership of a chief administration of the shipbuilding industry and an administration of the defence industry. Its basic tasks were:

1 in peacetime, to produce weapons and military equipment for the armed forces, and also to stockpile the reserves necessary for the initial period of war;

2 to develop and assimilate into production new models of weapons and military equipment;
3 to accumulate and conserve technical experience in defence production;
4 to take responsibility for the training and quantitative and qualitative enhancement of the industrial and scientific and technical workforce;
5 in the event of war, to act as a nucleus around which the conversion of civilian industry to war production could be organised.

A second group of enterprises included those specialised chiefly in civilian production, but with a continuing commitment to sideline military products. The enterprises of Group II were allocated among various industrial trusts; however, according to the mobilisation plan, in the event of war they would be first in line to be attached to Group I (the specialised defence producers).

The third group of enterprises was the most numerous. They produced goods for mass consumption, but were also given mobilisation assignments which were strictly binding, on paper at least. In the event of mobilisation the enterprises of Group III would also join Group I as a second tier of defence producers.

What all these enterprises had in common was a mobilisation assignment – a detailed, concise plan for conversion to military production and its further expansion. Every plant with a mobilisation assignment was required:

- to maintain its equipment in constant readiness
- to maintain a designated stockpile of materials for military production
- to maintain precise authorised mobilisation plans
- to maintain a minimal staff of personnel capable of immediate transfer to war production
- not to permit the diversion of workshops from mobilisation assignments.

Over a relatively short period of time those Leningrad plants were identified which would be assigned to Group I, along with a precise list of enterprises with mobilisation assignments. The composition of the latter broadened with the growth of military production, but its general structure remained as already indicated. The organisation of enterprises into industrial trusts had been completed in Leningrad in 1922, and this included the establishment of the shipbuilding and defence-industry trusts which were directly responsible for defence plants under the chief administration of the shipbuilding industry and the administration of the defence industry already mentioned. The two defence industry administrations were also in charge of defence research establishments and the recruitment of skilled personnel for the defence industry, and additionally they represented its interests in higher government organs.

As the structure of the defence industry evolved, the political bodies charged with its co-ordination and leadership also changed. The city party committee was generally in charge. It provided political leadership, directing and co-ordinating the activity of the city Soviet, the city executive, trade unions, and Komsomol, for the most rapid accomplishment of their assigned tasks. At city committee meetings reports were received from time to time from the heads of the defence-industry administrations and trusts and the largest defence factories.

In addition there was a hierarchy of party organisations to mirror the hierarchy of defence-industry organisation at every level from top to bottom. This enabled continuous monitoring of the situation in all parts of the defence industry and effective intervention where necessary. A military section had been previously formed in the Petrograd Soviet, the secretariat of the provincial (later *oblast'*) committee confirming a corresponding resolution on 14 November 1921.[14] In 1924 a military commission was established in the city Komsomol committee headed by the first secretary of the provincial committee.[15] On 18 August 1925 the bureau of the Leningrad provincial party committee created a Defence Commission to take responsibility for current work. This included a representative of the defence industry.[16] In the spring of 1927 the provincial government executive committee created a military group, its composition being confirmed by the bureau of the provincial committee on 13 March. Military sections were formed in the *raion* party committees, soviets, and soviet executive committees.

Having set out the chief component parts of a defence-industry complex, the city party committee began the development of an effective mechanism for their interaction. Mobilisation plans were the distinctive driving element in this. A list of those enterprises subject to mobilisation assignments was confirmed, and and it was made compulsory for them to compile mobilisation plans. Similarly, a small circle of people was designated who had the right of access to mobilisation plans. Full responsibility for compiling and executing plans was laid on the individual shoulders of enterprise directors.

MOBILISATION PLANNING

The scope of mobilisation planning

'Mobilisation preparedness' had very wide scope and potentially affected every institution and production establishment in the city, whether military or civilian (see further Chapter 11). Particular attention in questions of mobilisation was paid to the specialised defence factories producing weapons and military equipment. But it also extended to all kinds of civilian producers and service agencies, which could be expected to support the rapidly growing needs of the defence industry, as well as to maintain peacetime stocks and reserves for the contingency of war.

Thus the city authorities gave constant and considerable attention to the provision of an experienced workforce for the defence-industry complex. Schools, technical colleges, and institutes all trained personnel for the defence plants. In 1932 higher educational establishments also began to formulate their own mobilisation plans. In each college a special mobilisation officer was appointed for this purpose with the status of assistant rector.[17] New faculties, and sometimes entire educational establishments, were created solely for the purpose of training skilled workers for the defence industry.

In the field of science, mention should also be made of the research institutes, design bureaux, laboratories, and other scientific establishments specifically created for defence work, including a Central Design Bureau for naval shipbuilding established under the Shipbuilding Trust, and a Tank Bureau under the administration of the defence industry.[18] The twin administrations of the shipbuilding and defence industries directed their work, co-ordinated scientific activity, organised the accumulation of and diffusion of experience, and oversaw the introduction of new weapons and military equipment into production. Leading scholars were attracted into scientific research, while major research institutes became involved in these problems. In addition the major defence plants had their own science units, concern for which was exercised not only by factory managers but also by party, local government, and production agencies at all levels.

The construction industry was also central to the defence industry and its mobilisation preparations. In July 1938 another link appeared in the local network of the defence-industry complex – the Leningrad defence-construction administration of USSR Glavvoenstroi, established to improve the local organisation of defence construction. By a decision of Sovnarkom of 15 July 1938, the local administration was subordinated directly to Glavvoenstroi in Moscow, but responsibility for the intensity of construction work, its political leadership, and so on, was laid on the shoulders of the city authorities.[19] The oblast' and city party committees guided this aspect of its activity.

Public organisations and the media also played an important part. It would be wrong to omit the significant role of trade union organisations and Osoaviakhim, the mass association for civil defence. These had their own branches at every level of the system, and were involved in issues of mobilisation preparedness, training the workforce, and political agitation among the masses. The latter was given high priority. In view of both the importance of defence production and its secret character, military departments were created in the mass media as early as May 1927.[20]

The mobilisation hierarchy

At all levels of the vertical system of power in the city, the leading role in deciding any issue always belonged to party agencies. In this connection it must be remembered that party agencies relied in turn on the NKVD organs, which were accountable exclusively to the party and which were effectively part of its structure. The defence industry was the object of the closest attention on the part of the NKVD, and party agencies constantly used it to monitor the situation in the defence industry and to take punitive measures where necessary. This made the party apparatus highly effective at every level, and it was precisely on this that the leadership relied in those exceptional circumstances when all other instruments proved powerless.

By a decision of the secretariat of the oblast' and city party committees dated 23 January 1929, secretaries of party organisations in the factories and chairmen of factory committees were allocated a role in formulating mobilisation plans. Additionally, a list of party organisations was confirmed for factories entitled to draw up their mobilisation plans independently.[21] The combined committee of the oblast' and city parties designed model plans and carried out detailed checks on this work both at the *raion* level and directly in the factories.

The tasks of mobilisation planning were being executed for the first time. Naturally they experienced considerable difficulties. Plans were often composed in an unrealistic framework, without the necessary material foundations. Trial mobilisations exposed the incomprehension of their core tasks felt by leading personnel at all levels. On 14 January 1931 the combined secretariat of the oblast' and city party committees adopted a resolution 'On eliminating the mobilisation illiteracy of party activists'.[22] A special 40-hour programme of study was organised for party secretaries from the largest enterprises of the city subject to mobilisation assignments. All this work was guided by the oblast' party committee's 'mobilisation troika' (committee of three). Headed by oblast' party committee secretary B.P. Pozern, and meeting at 1 p.m. on the 24th of each month, the mobilisation troika assembled a city-wide mobilisation plan and checked the progress of all work at lower levels.[23] Mobilisation troiki were also formed in every party *raion* committee. A mobilisation bureau was created in the oblast' government executive committee, while mobilisation officers (*mobrabotniki*) were added to the staffs of *raion* executive committees.[24]

Between its inception in 1927 and the early 1930s mobilisation activity expanded tremendously in parallel with the growth of defence industry. The result was to create an urgent need for a single agency with wide powers to co-ordinate all mobilisation activity. For this purpose in February 1932 a decision of the secretariat created a Special Group (one of its leaders being oblast' party committee secretary Pozern) for mobilisation and defence activity in the city and oblast'. All documents dealing with mobilisation and defence questions and signed by these two individuals had the force of decrees of the oblast' and city party secretariat. The Special Group included in its staff a special sector for mobilisation preparedness.[25] With its wide powers, the Special Group carried out considerable work on raising the mobilisation preparedness of Leningrad's industry generally and defence industry in particular.

It should be added that all these measures, in contrast to others of the time, were not just transient political campaigns, but were implemented with precision and consistency. Mobilisation tasks were continually adjusted as the defence industry expanded, and weapons and military equipment were modified and developed. Party, municipal, and production agencies continually monitored enterprises' mobilisation preparedness. Such checks were carried out in compliance with plans of the oblast' and city party committees. Party and state organs also checked closely that mobilisation reserves were maintained at strictly defined levels. In May 1937, acting on party orders, NKVD organs checked mobilisation preparedness at 8 defence plants. As a result the combined oblast' and city party committee bureau adopted a resolution 'On the state of mobilisation in Leningrad industry'.[26] The latter pointed to many faults, especially as regards maintaining mobilisation reserves at the designated level. To raise mobilisation work to a higher level and carry out current work effectively, mobilisation officers were attached to enterprise staffs. The mobilisation apparatus at specialised defence plants was especially strong; for example at the Kirov works it comprised 8 people.[27]

A major role in the organisation of defence industry was played by such institutions as the Military Department and the Petrograd Council of the National Economy (PSNKh), the latter having the rights of a department of the party committee. When PSNKh was wound up in 1922 its functions were transferred to the Northwestern Industrial Bureau. In 1928 a Leningrad Council of the National Economy (LSNKh) was reestablished. In 1932 the latter was replaced by a local administration (from 1934, the local inspectorate) of Narkomtiazhprom, the Commissariat for Heavy Industry. These were the agencies working within the general hierarchy of the city and raion government executives on day-to-day management of the city's defence industry.

The *raion* executives also played a significant role through their military sections. In this complex and multifaceted activity, the city authorities on the whole communicated with associations of defence factories rather than with individual producers. It was specialised personnel at the *raion* level of local government who worked directly with individual factories. For example, on 30 November 1938 the oblast' party committee bureau adopted a resolution 'On supervision of the production of shells and explosive powder'. In this it was decided 'to order the first secretaries of *raion* committees, where there is production of shells and explosive powder, to take fulfilment of the production plan under their personal supervision'.[28] In accordance with a decision of the Leningrad city committee secretariat of 22 December 1932 the first secretaries of raion party committees were given full responsibility for all aspects of the mobilisation preparedness of defence enterprises located on their territories.[29] Thus mobilisation preparedness was supervised from the city level down to the individual plant. The factory link was weakest in this chain, but was reinforced by the introduction of party organisers from the Central Committee at defence factories.

In summary, the institutional components of the defence-industry complex had been formed by the beginning of World War I and began to be rapidly re-established immediately after the Civil War. At the end of the 1920s these elements began to be linked up into a unified complex by means of particular economic interconnections. By the end of the 1930s Leningrad's defence-industry complex was fundamentally complete. By virtue of its scale and influence it was a most powerful force, which in a variety of ways defined the character of Leningrad's social and economic development.

NOTES

1 Iurii (1981), 14. For a western treatment of this issue see Siegelbaum (1983).
2 Borisov (1948).
3 Osoboe Soveshchanie (1980).
4 Nessen (1977), 43.
5 Trudy (1922), 33.
6 Mal'tsev (1990), 17.
7 Ocherki (1980), 485.
8 Duplication was inevitable in such a complex structure. This was, above all, reflected in the existence of the Northwestern Bureau of the Central Committee and the Northwestern Industrial Bureau, which both began to operate in Petrograd in October 1921. See Ocherki (1980), 490.
9 TsGA IPD, 16/9/8907, 1.
10 Thus in the 1926/27 financial year defence outlays were only 40 per cent of the prewar level. See Girshfel'd and Mikheev (1928), 21.
11 TsGA IPD, 16/1/618, 197.
12 SVE (1977), vol. 4, 345 ('Korablestroitel 'naia programma').
13 SVE (1979), vol. 7, 662 ('Tankovaia promyshlennost'').
14 TsGA IPD, 16/1/433, 67.
15 TsGA IPD, 16/1/521a, 159.
16 TsGA IPD, 16/1/155, 11.
17 TsGA IPD, 24/1/382, 97.
18 TsGA IPD, 24/2a/12, 14 and 24/1a/27, 76.
19 TsGA IPD, 24/2a/127, 11.
20 TsGA IPD, 16/1/640, 62.
21 TsGA IPD, 24/1a/18, 55–6.
22 TsGA IPD, 24/1/417, 37.

23 TsGA IPD, 24/1a/12, 110.
24 TsGA IPD, 24/1a/15, 65.
25 TsGA IPD, 24/1/382, 7.
26 TsGA IPD, 24/2a/86, 3.
27 TsGA IPD, 24/2a/86, 21.
28 TsGA IPD, 24/2a/111, 1.
29 TsGA IPD, 24/2a/23, 198.

9 The defence-industry complex in Leningrad (2): the postwar uranium industry

Nataliia Lebina

INTRODUCTION

The defence-industry complex is an organic part of the St Petersburg economic region. At the beginning of the 1990s, 75 per cent of the city's industrial enterprises worked in the defence sector. The defence-industry complex comprised huge material resources, and a significant share of the city's intellectual resources.

The origins of the defence-industry complex go back to the prerevolutionary period. In the nineteenth century major Russian industrialists already felt it necessary to establish close contact with representatives of the Ministry of War. With the appearance of mass armies, the issue arose of how to use the country's economic strength to meet the armed forces' needs; military expenditures comprised a significant share of the state budget.

As military technology became more complex, and the scale of armaments needed by the armed forces increased, there emerged a coalition of bureaucrats and industrialists. In Russia at the end of the nineteenth century there began to take shape early elements of a social system which can be described as a proto-complex of the defence industry, but it was in the Soviet period that the defence-industry complex became a special force. This was clearly reflected in the specific social-economic structure of Petersburg. From the mid-1920s the rate of militarisation of the city's industry accelerated. The defence-industry complex grew into a powerful social organism. In this connection it is extremely important to investigate the historical traditions of the defence-industry complex, including the particular mentality of both its leaders and workers, and their attitudes to social and economic changes of the time.

Scholarly and journalistic writing has also employed the concept of 'military-industrial complex', but in several different ways (see also Chapter 1). Most commonly it is used empirically to cover the overall network of scientific-research institutes, planning and design organisations, and industrial enterprises connected in one way or another with the needs of defence.

Recently another, more analytical definition of the 'military-industrial complex' has appeared in the research literature which can be summarised as follows.[1] The military-industrial complex is a specifically militarised relationship in the structure of modern society, involving the merger of military-industrial monopolies with state institutions – above all with the departments of central government most directly linked with the creation, development, and application of military power in foreign and domestic policy.

As a rule, in the Soviet research literature on scientific and technical progress the emergence of a military-industrial complex has been linked with the state-monopoly form of capitalism, and with the appearance and growth of monopolies. While viewing the military-industrial complex as a phenomenon characteristic of most developed countries, researchers have nonetheless argued about the stages of its emergence. Some have placed the appearance of the military-industrial complex in the 1920s and 1930s, others in the 1940s and 1950s. This reflects the fact that both the prewar and postwar periods have been characterised by an arms race and its various consequences – increased state intervention in capitalist economies, sharp increases in proportions of GNP devoted to military production, and unrestrained growth of military spending in all states regardless of social systems.

In the story told in this chapter the military forces and their representatives did not play a significant, active part. There was certainly a merging of industrial and governmental interests, but the significant interaction to be described below was between the defence industry and the agencies of state security. Therefore, without passing judgement on the broader themes of a military-industrial complex and whether it existed or not, it seems appropriate in this chapter to conform to the terminology of a 'defence-industry complex' in the sense shared by the other authors of this book (see above, Chapter 1).

The formation of a defence-industry complex in Leningrad in the 1920s rested upon a particular concept of defence-industry organisation. All enterprises were divided into three groups. The first group was solely engaged in the production of armaments. The second produced both civilian and military goods. The third, while specialised by intention in the production of civilian goods, could if necessary be transferred to one of the first two groups. Responsibility for the reorientation of Leningrad industry was exercised by the party organs.

From the mid-1930s scientific-research institutes, special design bureaux, and laboratories began to appear in the Leningrad defence-industry complex. Their work was directed by the local chief administration of the shipbuilding industry and administration of the defence industry – for example the Central Design Bureau for Naval Shipbuilding and the Tank Bureau.[2] The activity of industrial, scientific, and technical organisations involved in defence matters came under the close supervision of the NKVD. However, in the 1930s the interaction of this all-powerful commissariat with organisations in the defence-industry complex was counterproductive in terms of national security. The control and punitive functions exercised by NKVD personnel served only to undermine the military-economic strength of the country. One example is the fate of Ostekhbiuro (the 'Special Technical Bureau for special-purpose military inventions') whose personnel were eliminated in the massacre of the Great Terror (see Chapter 13).[3]

In the postwar period a new stage was reached in the formation of the defence-industry complex of the country in general and Leningrad in particular. The most characteristic features of this stage were the dominant role of the NKVD-MVD in the organisation of defence industry and the growing role of scientific establishments as an organic part of the defence-industry complex. These changes were connected with the development of nuclear weapons in the USSR. In 1945 a coordinated programme to establish an industrial base for atomic weapon technology was initiated by the GKO resolution of 20 August which created a Special Committee charged with 'the leadership of all work on the exploitation of the nuclear energy of uranium', in other words for developing the Soviet atomic bomb (see Chapters 7 and 13).

THE URANIUM PROBLEM

The Special Committee was granted special and extraordinary powers for deciding all issues connected with the uranium project.[4] At the end of 1945 the committee took the decision that, in order to accelerate work, it was necessary to engage both scientists and producers in solving the problem of creating atomic weapons. To speed up design work and the immediate establishment of experimental units, to be followed by serial production of basic technological equipment, it was decided to involve two of the largest engineering plants in the country, with great experience and highly skilled workforces of engineers and workers of all engineering trades: the Leningrad Kirov Metallurgical and Engineering Plant (LKZ) and the Gor'kii Engineering Plant. On 27 December 1945 the Soviet government took the decision to organize a Special Design Bureau at the Kirov Plant (OKB LKZ, below the 'Kirov OKB') for development of the basic technology of uranium separation equipment, producing enriched uranium for atomic weapons by means of gas diffusion.[5] The problem (also discussed in Chapter 7) was to separate out from naturally occuring uranium the small proportion of the chemically identical but atomically relatively lighter and fissile uranium-235 isotope. Veterans of the Kirov OKB remember that initially researchers focused on the method already developed in the United States, which involved passing uranium in a gaseous compound through thousands of filters, at each stage removing some of the heavier U-238 isotope so as to raise the concentration of U-235.

Information about this method had been obtained with the active help of the security organs (again, see Chapter 7). Personnel from Beriia's organisation facilitated the acquisition and immediate translation into Russian of 'Atomic energy for military purposes', the 'Official report on the development of the atomic bomb under the auspices of the United States Government'. The original, published in the United States in August 1945 immediately after the bombing of Hiroshima and Nagasaki, was written by the Princeton physicist Professor Henry D. Smyth, a consultant on the Manhattan Project.[6] It is interesting to note that in the foreword to the American edition of the Smyth Report Major-General Leslie R. Groves, chief of the Manhattan Project, wrote:

> Obviously military security prevents this story from being told in full at this time. However, there is no reason why the administrative history of the Atomic Bomb Project and the basic scientific knowledge on which the several developments were based should not be available now to the general public...
>
> All pertinent scientific information which can be released to the public at this time without violating the needs of national security is contained in this volume.[7]

None the less, in the 1940s even this information, revealed to the American public by the Americans themselves, could be made available to Soviet physicists only with the sanction of the NKVD.[8]

According to the reminiscences of Kirov OKB personnel, the Smyth Report, while incomplete in some respects (for example, the implosion method for detonating the plutonium bomb was omitted), none the less contained in unexpurgated scientific form the ideas for creating atomic weapons. The well-known specialist N.M. Sinev described the Smyth Report as no less than 'an original compass, making it possible to orient oneself in the technical taiga [wilderness], so as not to get lost and to have confidence in success'. On the other hand it is curious to note that in appraising the significance of the Smyth Report, many Soviet atomic scientists involuntarily reflected the idea (then predominant in the USSR) of a specifically Soviet scientific path.

The attempt to create a Soviet variant of the gas-diffusion apparatus, pushed at all costs by the authorities, led to failure. A month before the decision to organize the Kirov OKB, the decision was taken to build a gas-diffusion plant in the Urals, in order to achieve the separation of uranium. Those in charge of the Kirov OKB were to participate in solving the technological and production problems of the separation plant, D-1. The basic efforts of the newly created group, headed by the 37-year-old turbine engineer Z. Arkin, were directed at developing the basic separation apparatus and also designing the fittings and connectors between the thousands of stages necessary for D-1. However pressure from above, expressed in the demand not to follow blindly the method already worked out in the United States, noticeably impeded the work of the group.

For the time being the Kirov OKB itself did not work on the detailed planning of the gas diffusion apparatus. This task was given to the head of the Leningrad Polytechnical Institute's department of hydraulic engineering, I.N. Voznesenskii. The latter's intention was to exclude designers from the Kirov plant from development of the diffusion apparatus. Voznesenskii wanted to design something in Leningrad that would be different in principle from the diffusion apparatus described by Smyth. Without going into the technical detail of the question, we should note that Voznesenskii's apparatus turned out to be technically inferior, as well as too cumbersome and complex. However, pandering to the party organs which were sceptical about copying the US model, Voznesenskii persisted with his design which it was attempted to put into serial production at the Gor'kii factory.

Only by the end of 1946 did it became clear that this work had run into a dead end. Those in charge of the Kirov OKB, which had been ordered to test Voznesenskii's machine, reported to Moscow. Its 'patriotic' concept was clearly mistaken. The government's assignment had turned out to be unfeasible. In addition the construction of factory D-1 in the Urals had been delayed. The plan had been that it would come into production at the beginning of 1948. Construction work in the Urals was being directed by the MVD's chief administration for industrial construction under A.N. Komarovskii. However, in the autumn of 1946 it became clear that it would be necessary to start planning factory D-1 again from the beginning on conventional lines. Good sense had prevailed in the leadership of the Special Committee.

THE MVD AND THE *SHARASHKA* MODEL

In contrast to the 1930s above all, there was no purge of the scientists, engineers, and technicians who had taken part in the development of the diffusion apparatus. The only victim was Voznesenskii, who died of a heart attack after discussion of the situation in the Kirov OKB at a meeting of the Special Committee in the summer of 1947. In addition Soviet designers were allowed to evaluate the ideas described in the Smyth Report. Work on a heavy multi-stage apparatus was abandoned. In Leningrad it was decided to develop an apparatus with fewer stages.

In 1947 significant personnel changes took place in the Kirov OKB. Sinev was appointed chief designer in June; until then he had been the Central Committee's party organizer at the Kirov plant. During the war he had worked as deputy chief designer of the Kirov plant. Arkin was now appointed deputy chief designer. Simultaneously, the group of designers and technicians was strengthened. Veterans recall that, despite their expectations, no one was repressed at the Kirov OKB. Only the internal organisation of work was changed.

In general the work day at the Kirov OKB lasted from 9 a.m. to 6 p.m., but in the 1946–8 period the chief designer's order was that for heads of groups and senior designers the working day finished at 10 p.m. After a routine visit of Beriia to the plant some of the laboratories were transferred to a round-the-clock work regime. Camp beds were installed in the premises, and despite rationing designers were provided with good food. To some extent this was similar to the *sharashka* system of penal colonies for scientific workers, which had been fairly effective. It is true, as again veterans recall, that the introduction of a special work regime had an impact on the family life of some personnel: there was a wave of divorces in families where wives were not also working at the Kirov OKB. In general it should be noted that by the 1960s the first dynasties of atomic experts had been formed in the defence-industry complex, where husbands, wives, and children worked together. And this despite the fact that traditionally there were few women in the Kirov OKB. Already in the 1950s people were retired at 45 or 50 because of the work's health hazards.

From 1948 Beriia himself took over direction of the work of the Kirov OKB. He continually visited the enterprise. At first his visits took place with great ceremony. The OKB building was situated on the territory of the Kirov plant, one and a half kilometres from the entrance. The whole distance was covered by a carpet for the honoured guest. However Beriia's visits became so frequent that this custom was dropped. His particular concern was with the work of the Leningrad scientists on preparing the D-1 diffusion plant for production. A large group of Leningrad specialists was sent to Sverdlovsk. A special resolution of the party Central Committee and Council of Ministers was devoted to the issue of personnel in the Urals; it obliged party organisations, and above all the Leningrad organisation, to select specialists who were not only highly skilled but also politically reliable, in particular communists who had proven themselves in the war, for dispatch to the Urals factory.[9]

Those sent from Leningrad worked not only on construction of the plant, but also on building the neighbouring settlement. This was a complex matter. The extensive territory of the plant was sealed off and the entry of unauthorised persons was forbidden, which complicated building work. Food had to be brought from a distance of 30 kilometres, without access by road. For a long time drinking water was taken unpurified from the Demidov lake. There was no hospital. The need for young and at the same time experienced and educated people to work on the construction site had a clear effect on the demographic situation in the town being built. Sinev recalls that in the two schools built in 1948 there were 38 first-year classes and only one final-year class.[10]

On the territory of the future factory town a special regime was established – there were no soviets for local self-government. Administrative power was concentrated in the hands of the director of the plant under construction. Order in the town was maintained by the security organs and units of the MVD internal troops. Breaches of the criminal code were dealt with by a tribunal.

The D-1 plant was a top priority not only for the Kirov OKB, but for the whole country. And Beriia's supervision of the construction played a special role in its success. Thanks to his influence all the needs of the construction works were met more or less instantly. In cases where a government decision was needed to solve a problem, it was referred to the Special Committee and the decision was issued on the authority of the chairman of the Council of Ministers (usually with Stalin's signature) literally within days.

In 1948 in Leningrad itself there was intensive work on the planning of new diffusion machines of the OK-7 type. At the Gorkii plant experimental models were named 'LP', after Lavrentii Pavlovich (Beriia). The first line of machines came on stream in the middle of 1948, but failure struck the designers – a high level of corrosion losses was discovered. Again contrary to the conventional expectation, no one was subject to repression. Furthermore, Leningraders were still more closely drawn into the establishment of plant D-1: A. Kizima was appointed director of the plant – after the war he had been in charge of the return of the Kirov plant from evacuation to Leningrad – and Sinev was appointed head of the technical section. The transfer of the chief designer of the Kirov OKB to the Urals was seen as a temporary measure for the period of the start-up and first stage of production of the first diffusion plant in the country.

In Leningrad work continued on perfecting the construction of diffusion apparatuses. Experienced technicians of the Kirov plant were sent to the Kirov OKB, as were several graduates of the Bauman Higher Technical Institute in Moscow. Before long engineers demobilised from the army joined the group. The selection of new specialists was very strict: not only their knowledge, but also their family links and contacts, and where possible their political views, were investigated. New recruits spent the first two months in a sort of quarantine, employed on the least secret parts of the work.

Supervision of the work of the researchers grew more intense. The chief designer of the Kirov OKB informed the Special Committee of the results of experiments daily by telegram and monthly in written reports. At the same time the OKB personnel were provided with significant privileges: wages were at the same level of those in the MVD, and on the territory of the Kirov works a special canteen and dispensaries were organised.

As the date for finishing the construction works drew closer, Beriia's visits to Leningrad became more frequent, as they did to the Urals. At the end of September 1949 a special train arrived in the Urals with not only Beriia, but almost the whole membership of the Special Committee. The problem was one of corrosion losses; much of the precious uranium gas going into the diffusion cascade was simply disappearing. The Leningrad specialists working in the Urals recall that three coaches of the train were disconnected from it and stationed on the railway line opposite the building for the plant's directors. In the coaches discussions of the state of construction of the plant took place. They were conducted both in the form of the usual type of meeting, and using the method of personal cross-examination, very reminiscent of an interrogation – the influence of MVD methods was still felt. However, the result was that a sensible decision was taken – to reinforce the scientific leadership of the project. True, in conclusion Beriia said:

> Everything that you requested and demanded, the country has given despite all its difficulties. So I give you three months to solve all the problems connected with starting up the plant. I warn you: if you don't fulfil the plan, it will be dry bread for you. Expect no mercy. But if you do as you are ordered, you'll be decorated.[11]

This was probably the first real threat from the MVD; however, no repressions followed.

WHAT THE KIROV OKB ACHIEVED

By this time, in fact, in both Leningrad and the Urals the necessary means for solving the problem had already been found. Work had been pursued with great intensity. In the five years from 1946 to 1951, nine designs of diffusion apparatuses had been developed in the Kirov OKB and brought into operation with varying levels of productivity, which had allowed scientists and planners to work out the optimum technological designs for diffusion plants. In a relatively short time they had managed to solve various problems:

1 to select the concept for construction of diffusion apparatuses which would provide high reliability, technical quality, and reparability;
2 to develop unique equipment for automated gas pressure regulation in the diffusion cascades, which comprised hundreds of apparatuses;
3 to provide a sealed vacuum throughout the whole complex of equipment with its hundreds of connected units;
4 to develop reliable vacuum-tight sealing valves with various communicating sections capable of operation in a highly aggressive gas medium.

A fact which played a key role in the success of the work was that scientists were in direct contact with producers. At the Kirov plant a production base was created for the new products, a special assembly shop in which the standard of cleanliness and hygiene was that of an operating theatre. There was also established a shop for coating with nickel the internal surfaces of equipment which would come into contact with the uranium hexafluoride gas. A special technological bureau was created for solving technological questions; like the OKB, it had to find solutions for complicated tasks connected with the creation of new technical models. The intensive work of the Kirov OKB and of the Kirov plant as a whole made it possible in 1950 to create Soviet types of diffusion apparatuses which were unique at that time, and to organise the production of integrated equipment to begin serial production at the D-1 plant. A large group of employees of the OKB, including Sinev and Arkin, was awarded the Stalin Prize for this work in 1951.

The history of the Kirov OKB is revealing; it combined, as it were, all the advantages and disadvantages of the defence-industry complex, based on a tight regime of secrecy. This system was partly responsible for spreading the impression in the world scientific community that Soviet specialists were poorly trained.

An example from the work of the Kirov OKB was the centrifugal method of separating uranium isotopes. Theoretically known from the early 1940s, this method was not applied because of the lack of necessary equipment. Attempts to build centrifuges for isotope separation in the United States and United Kingdom were unsuccessful. German physicists came close to achieving the centrifugal separation of uranium, particularly Max Steenbeck, who was taken from Germany to the USSR in 1945. In the autumn of 1945 he and his colleague Konrad Zippe were transferred to Leningrad, to the Kirov OKB, which at that time had been ordered by the government to develop a Soviet industrial process for gas separation by the centrifugal method. Having studied and tested Steenbeck's system, the Kirov OKB personnel came to the conclusion that it was unfeasible and had no future in industry. Steenbeck himself wrote later in his memoirs that the Leningrad physicists 'using their own ideas in the field of technical application, lagged behind our results'.[12] Soon the German physicists were transferred to Kiev and then repatriated to Germany. The scientists and designers of the Kirov OKB by 1953 had achieved a new industrial means of centrifugal separation, the 'ultra-centrifuge'. Zippe, an enterprising scientist who had had access to the work of the Kirov OKB until 1956, on his return to westen Europe patented its system as his own invention. In effect this was just plagiarism. However the regime of secrecy did not allow either the inventors themselves or their ministerial chiefs to challenge Zippe.

From the point of view of the concept of state security then prevailing, it was probably sensible to maintain the illusion prevalent in the world that the gas diffusion method of producing enriched uranium in the USSR was of low effectiveness. But the result was that for 30 years talented Russian physicists and technicians were not recognised by the world scientific community. Moreover their work was top secret in their own country. Soviet society did not realize that people working in the defence-industry complex, and in particular in the Kirov OKB, had been awarded State and Lenin Prizes, or that many of them had been awarded the prestigious title of Hero of Socialist Labour. Although these people had favourable material conditions thanks to their relatively high pay, and enjoyed superior social welfare, none the less they lived the greater part of their lives in a closed world, the result of the demands of secrecy.

SCIENCE, PRODUCTION, AND THE SOVIET 'MIDDLE CLASS'

This short case-study of the Leningrad defence-industry complex in the postwar period makes it possible to identify significant changes in the policy of Soviet political and ideological bodies in relation to the defence industry. Above all, the repressive methods of work with defence personnel which, it is known from the evidence of the 1930s, undermined the strength of the country, became a thing of the past. The role of *sharashki* in working on important defence problems gradually lessened. Particular attention began to be devoted to social aspects and the needs of those working in the defence-industry complex. This was particularly reflected in the creation of a specific production regime, various forms of material incentives, and a special system for recruiting personnel.

As a result a specific social group was formed within the defence-industry complex, a sort of Soviet middle class – the bulwark of the state in developed capitalist countries. Another new feature was the direct contact between scientific and production units in the defence-industry complex. Of course, the future 'giants' of the defence-industry complex, the so-called NPO ('science-production associations') did not appear until the 1960s: but the Kirov OKB may be considered the prototype of such an institution.

NOTES

1 Simonov (1996).
2 TsGA IPD, 24/2-a/12, 14.
3 Shoshkov (1995).
4 Starkov (1995), 154; Kriglov (1995), 36.
5 Sinev (1991), 14. In addition to published sources, the author was able to consult historical documents of the Leningrad Kirov factory.
6 Smyth (1945).
7 Smyth (1945), v; for the equivalent passage in the Russian translation, see Smit (1946), 3. The British opposed publication of the Smyth Report which, they felt,

'would be of assistance to foreign scientists and might save them several months' work' (Gowing (1964), 364).

8 The Russian translation, Smit (1946), circulated widely to Soviet scientists and designers (but not to the Soviet public), was printed in a run of 30 000 copies.

9 Sinev (1991), 52.

10 Sinev (1991), 52.

11 Petros'iants (1993), 12.

12 Shteenbek (1988), 180.

10 Krasnoiarsk-26: a closed city of the defence-industry complex

Viktoriia Glazyrina

INTRODUCTION

A unique feature of the Soviet defence-industry complex was its 'closed cities'. These were cities in the remote regions of the Volga, the Urals, and western Siberia, not marked on any map, entirely specialised in defence production and built for no other purpose (see Chapter 1). The closed cities had their origins in the evacuation of the defence industry from the regions threatened by German occupation to the remote interior in 1941 and 1942; huge production complexes evacuated from the west and south of the country were shifted bodily with a substantial proportion of their workforce to the east where new settlements sprang up around them. The secrecy attached to these new settlements was greatly reinforced after the war as they became the focus for the development and manufacture of atomic weapons.

Krasnoiarsk-26 was one of these closed cities. No published document could tell you where it was or how many people lived there. It was certainly not the same as the city of Krasnoiarsk, although it was somewhere nearby. The numerical '26' suffix was essentially just a postcode, telling you that Krasnoiarsk was the nearest sorting office for letters and telegrams.[1] Krasnoiarsk itself lies 3300 kilometres due east of Moscow on the great Enisei river in Siberia, on the same latitude as Dundee in Scotland and Edmonton in the Canadian province of Alberta, and on the same longitude as Lhasa in Tibet.

THE PLUTONIUM INDUSTRY

The first reactors for making weapon-grade plutonium were built in the USSR in the 1940s. The very first nuclear military-industrial combine was built in the Cheliabinsk region, with a uranium-graphite reactor and a factory for the chemical separation of plutonium from irradiated fuel. Originally named Cheliabinsk-40, it was later renamed Cheliabinsk-65, and more recently Ozersk. On 29 August 1949 the first Soviet nuclear device with a plutonium charge was detonated at a test site near Semipalatinsk.

Altogether, between 1944 and 1991, 13 reactors for the production of weapon-grade plutonium were built in the USSR; of these, 5 are in Cheliabinsk-65 (Ozersk), 5 in Tomsk-7 (Seversk), and 3 in Krasnoiarsk-26 (Zheleznogorsk). According to various expert assessments, the quantity of plutonium produced in these reactors was enough to make 35–45 000 nuclear bombs. At the present time in Russia there are three such reactors; two are at Seversk and one at Zheleznogorsk. Orders from the Russian Ministry of Defence for the production of plutonium have now been curtailed. There is no national programme for the production of weapon-grade plutonium. There is one plutonium depository at factory PT-1 of the production association Maiak in the Cheliabinsk region. There are no special large-scale depositories for weapon-grade plutonium.

Until recently Krasnoiarsk-26 was a top-secret military establishment engaged in the separation of plutonium for the Russian defence-industry complex. It was here that the manufacture of nuclear devices took place, and here that calculations of their effectiveness in use were carried out, together with development and testing of the most effective means of defence against atomic weapons. The construction of this enterprise was sanctioned by a joint decision of the party Central Committee and Council of Ministers in 1950, and was continuously supervised by the Soviet Union's chief of internal security, L.P. Beriia. The construction was carried out by a workforce of 65 000 prisoners of the Gulag, and 100 000 construction troops. They built a huge underground complex where production of weapon-grade plutonium began in 1958. The production reactors, the cooling unit, and 22 workshops were located in a huge cavern at a depth of 200–250 metres beneath the earth. The whole production complex went under the name of a 'mining-chemical combine'.

Today the unfinished radio-chemical factory PT-26 is located there. PT-26 was intended for the separation of plutonium from irradiated fuel obtained from Soviet reactors of the new VVER-1000 generation. A nuclear waste depository was built with a capacity of 6000 tons of heavy metallic fuel. From the very beginning, also, the underground disposal of radioactive waste from radio-chemical production was and still is practised here. According to environmental organizations, 4 000 000 cubic metres of liquid radioactive waste have been dumped up to the present day.

Around the industrial complex a city has taken shape, with a developed infrastructure and large-scale, high-technology links to the entire country more or less. It is closely connected with the cities of St Petersburg, Moscow, Kiev, Saratov, Samara, and others. What was to all intents and purposes the cream of the theoretical and applied specialists in Russia's nuclear military-industrial resources has been concentrated in the city until now.

THE GOLDEN AGE OF KRASNOIARSK-26

The period 1958–68 was one of high achievement, and saw the sun rise and shine on Krasnoiarsk-26. In those years the city and the industrial enterprise were continually visited by the country's top political leadership, including Khrushchev and Brezhnev. After successful nuclear weapon tests, there were mass awards of state decorations to workers, scientists, and weapon designers. Under conditions of a planned economy and a centralised supply system for the city and the enterprise, Gosplan granted the city extra funds for food and manufactured goods, housing, and capital construction. Thus in 1962–4 while there was rationing of bread and other foodstuffs in virtually all Soviet cities, supplies to the residents of Krasnoiarsk-26 were maintained at three times the level of the regional capital. The city's residents were able to buy more goods of all kinds, Soviet and foreign, and this was made possible by giving them a privileged share not only of local regional products but also of supplies allocated nationally from Moscow. Average incomes were significantly higher than in other cities: 160–180 rubles per month, compared with 90 rubles for the country as a whole in 1964.

All this put the city in a special position. It was termed 'A City of the Communist Future'. By 1970 its population had reached 107 800. The structure of its population was distinctive – young and highly skilled. There was a special procedure to be followed for those either visiting it or coming to live in it. A young specialist who came here to work after graduating from college would be provided with a separate apartment within a year – an unattainable dream for young people in other cities, where housing shortages were normal. There was a wide network of pre-school creches, and kindergartens, primary, and secondary schools. The enterprise had a special quota of places in colleges in Moscow, Leningrad, and Kiev, and every year special recruitment commissions came to the city to select the best students.

In the 1970s five vocational technical colleges were opened to train highly skilled workers and technicians in the city. In 1972 the scientific-research department of the factory was effectively made an independent scientific-research institute, with its own body of research students and its own Academic Committee for awarding higher degrees independently of any higher authority. The institute supplied the factory with highly qualified cadres. Its staff included leading scholars from Moscow, Leningrad, Novosibirsk, and Krasnoiarsk; attached to it at this time were four academicians, 60 doctors of science, and 48 candidates of science (the Soviet equivalent of a Ph.D.). This was a centre for serious science, devoted to finding practical solutions to problems of atomic energy.

In the 1960s and 1970s the factory had a steady stream of orders from the Ministry of Defence and the Ministry of Power Engineering, and developed models of up-to-date technological equipment for the chemical industry. It was here that these models were tested and certified for serial production by a state committee comprising scholars and engineering and technical personnel. Some models of equipment were displayed at VDNKh, the Exhibition of Economic Achievements in Moscow, and at international exhibitions. Soviet and foreign specialists regularly remarked on the high reliability and effectiveness of the technology.

WHO RAN KRASNOIARSK-26?

In 1978 a large group of scholars and developers of new technology from Krasnoiarsk-26 were given high state decorations. At the same time they began work on a new atomic reactor. But this served to strengthen the regime of secrecy at the factory and in the city. In senior classes of the secondary school and in the vocational technical colleges, special lessons on security were introduced. A Special (First) Section was responsible for the secrecy regime at the factory, as was also a department of the corresponding section of the regional KGB administration. Personnel of the Special Sections of military units located at the factory and at other sites in the city also dealt with security questions. Employees of the factory and other organisations had to sign statements promising not to disclose state secrets.

Gradually relations between Soviet (government) and party organs in the city took on a particular character. The Soviet authorities carried out the municipal functions of local self-government. In this they were subordinate to the organs of higher Soviet government authority, both in the district and in the regional capital, and were obliged to fulfil the instructions of the latter. But real power was concentrated in the hands of the higher party organs.

The party committee of the factory reported to the department of defence industry of the Krasnoiarsk regional party committee, and also directly to the department of defence industry of the party Central Committee in Moscow. The secretary of the party committee was appointed by these two higher organs. The party organisation was one of the largest in the district and had a virtually autonomous position, having to account formally for its activities only where party-political work was concerned, and not touching on specifically production questions. The director of the factory was appointed by the secretariat of the party Central Committee and the Council of Ministers in Moscow. Each year the director of the enterprise, the secretary of the party committee, and the head of the trade union organisation sent reports on their work to the Central Committee and Council of Ministers.

In 1983, on its 25th anniversary, the factory was awarded the Order of Lenin. By this time the factory and the city were considered an ideal model for the defence-industry complex. The interests of the industrialists and of Soviet and party organs completely coincided in deciding practically all issues.

Matters of a social and cultural kind and relating to daily life were decided exclusively on the basis of the interests of the factory. The party and trade union organisations were completely dependent on the director of the factory, and he in his turn obeyed strict orders from the centre. The conflicts and frictions which arose between the factory management and the party committee were always decided by higher party organs in favour of the former. Thus in 1982 a conflict between the secretary of the party committee and the factory director was the subject of a special investigation, initially by officials of the party department of defence industry, and then by the secretariat of the party Central Committee. At the root of the conflict lay divergent bureaucratic interests. The important point is that the decision of the Central Committee secretariat supported the interests of the factory, not the interests of the Ministry of Defence which the secretary of the party committee had advocated.

In those years spy mania and suspicion flourished; so did the influence of the First Department responsible for the regime of secrecy at the factory. The heightened interest of the security service in the factory and other units was repeatedly manifested. Between 1960 and 1985 a series of individuals who had shown any unusual interest in the production of weapon-grade plutonium and in the technological development and documentation of standards for tests were arrested. On the other hand, given that order was maintained by units of the special police, the incidence of crime as a whole remained at one of the lowest levels in the country.

The city received visits from cultural celebrities such as writers, singers, and composers. Almost every year there were festivals of song and of amateur artistic activity. Scientists were able to receive newly published literature not only from within the USSR but also from abroad. In the second half of the 1970s and 1980s, both white-collar and blue-collar employees were able to go abroad on holiday for the first time. The factory had one magnificent holiday centre on the Enisei river and another in the Crimea, and in addition had a special quota of free trips to sanatoria and holiday centres in the south through the trade union organisation. Also available to its personnel besides this were holiday centres and clinics of the Ministry of Defence, the party Central Committee, and the Council of Ministers.

However, by this time elements of stagnation were already beginning to appear even in such a well-resourced branch of industry as this. In the first half of the 1980s funds earmarked for food and manufactured goods for the factory began to be cut back, and there began an outflow of highly skilled personnel to Russia's central cities. In the mid-1980s orders from the Ministry of Defence started to be sharply curtailed. As a result the level of financing of housing and capital construction was reduced, as were funds for the repair and maintenance of industrial units, housing, and the factory's social and cultural amenities. At this point the once-prosperous factory began to experience real difficulties in paying workers and employees for the first time, and to reduce the volume of production, and eventually capital and housing construction effectively ceased.

KRASNOIARSK-26 IN TRANSITION – TO WHAT?

At the present time the population of Krasnoiarsk-26 is 87 500. Of this number, 58 900 are of working age. The educational level of the population remains high. Forty-three per cent have higher education, 23 per cent specialised secondary education, 25 per cent secondary education, and 9 per cent incomplete secondary. The industrial workforce totals 42 900 people, including the private sector. The turning point of 1985 in many ways disrupted production and the previously established economic relationships on which it depended. Then the 1990s saw the *de facto* destruction of this branch of industry, since none of the proposals for conversion from military to civilian production received support from the country's leadership. In practice the factory could not adapt to changed circumstances and operate in conditions of a market economy.

The average monthly income of the population in August 1995 was 598 300 rubles, including supplements to compensate for the industry's health hazards – approximately $136 at the exchange rate ruling at the time. This was significantly lower than wages in regions of the far north, but was none the less higher than the pay of engineering and technical workers and scientists in the country as a whole. According to a sociological survey 70 per cent of the city's population spent its income entirely on food.

The breakdown of central funding by the end of the 1980s and beginning of the 1990s led to a sharp worsening of the supply of food and manufactured goods. This especially affected people who did not work at the factory. A consequence was the breakdown of the infrastructure of the city's health care, school education, and pre-school provision. The numbers of doctors, teachers, and cultural workers began to decline. At the present time the number of schools, kindergartens, cinemas, clinics, and consumer and municipal service establishments in the city have been sharply reduced.

According to statistics for July 1995, there remained in the city 12 secondary schools, 2 vocational technical colleges, 21 kindergartens, 2 cinemas, 1 palace of culture, 6 public baths, 12 hairdressers, 5 laundries and 2 consumer service centres. The holiday resorts of the factory on the Enisei and in the Crimea were in a difficult position. The former had effectively been privatised by the factory administration, while the latter was now 'abroad' – on the territory of an independent foreign state, the Ukraine. Attempts to organise its use jointly with the local Crimean administration were fruitless, and rising railway and air fares in effect made it impossible for most of those working at the factory to holiday in the south.

The large majority of the population still lives in separate apartments. Until 1985 young specialists coming to work on assignment after graduating from college would be provided with well-appointed housing within a year. From 1985 the rate of housing construction was sharply reduced and so simultaneously was the provision of housing services. By 1995 there remained in the city only a construction brigade of military conscripts which merely provided minimal support for housing already constructed and the repair of production facilities. Military conscripts comprised 21 per cent of the total population, employed on guarding business premises, building sites, and the chemical and radiation civil-defence services.

The latter units play a special role in dealing with accidents and rescue work. During the lifetime of the factory three major accidents have been recorded. The first occurred in 1956 and was connected with the escape of radioactive substances from the reactor producing weapon-grade plutonium. As a result the reactor's start-up, which had been planned for the fortieth anniversary of the October Revolution in 1957, was postponed until 1958. The second accident occurred in 1969 as a result of the nuclear waste depository becoming unsealed, leading to the mass contamination of local residents. The third accident occurred for reasons which are either still unknown or have not yet been revealed; it resulted in widespread skin diseases and blood disorders. In all cases the accidents were associated with breaches of safety rules in the production process.

From 1991 there was a sharp increase in migration of the population. In the period from 1991 to July 1995, 29 700 people left the city, in particular atomic scientists, physicists, chemists, programmers, and highly skilled engineering and technical personnel, as well as teachers, doctors, and skilled workers. Of the population which remained, 82 per cent expressed lack of confidence in the future. The average life expectancy of men is 60 (compared with 65 in the country as a whole). Among women the corresponding figure is 72 (76). There has also been a decline in the birth rate. In 1994–95 it stood at only 6 per thousand people of potentially fertile age.

The change in the life of the city has led to the spread of professional criminals. In 1993–4 there were attempts to steal weapon-grade plutonium containers as well as valuable equipment and instruments. If petty crime predominated in the statistics for the period 1950–1970, now the character of recorded crime has changed. From 1993 organised crime made its appearance, although so far no mafia organizations have been discovered in the city.

The numbers of people with higher education, academicians, doctors, and candidates of science have fallen. From 1995 the training of research students was suspended, and the work of the Academic Committee is practically at a standstill. The supply of scientific literature and journals from Russia and abroad has effectively ceased. More and more frequent delays in the payment of wages led to growing social tension and to meetings and strikes in 1995.

In 1991 the majority of the population voted for the democrats. Candidates of various democratic associations and unions were able to gain support of practically the whole population. However by 1993 the situation had changed and sympathies swung towards the communists. The results of recent elections show increased support for the Liberal Democratic (extreme nationalist) Party of Russia and the Communist Party. However, in this respect the situation in Krasnoiarsk-26 is not significantly different from that of Russia as a whole. Sociological surveys show a sharp increase in the number of those who do not trust any political leader – 28 per cent in 1995.

Today Krasnoiarsk-26 has been called 'A City without a Future'. Conversion to civilian production has had very little effect, and the reduction and then complete cessation of orders has had a fatal effect on the city and factory. Environmental problems have risen sharply, and methods of health protection at the factory and at other special units have been revealed to fall short of acceptable standards. Krasnoiarsk-26 still possesses significant scientific potential, but in practice there is no call for this in contemporary conditions. The outward migration of the population continues.

NOTES

1 There are no documentary sources for a sociological or historical study of the city of Krasnoiarsk-26. Thus this chapter is based on field research carried out by the author in Krasnoiarsk-26 in the summer of 1996, rather than on published references or archival sources. That is why it lacks the customary list of references.

Part V
Regulation and control

11 *Mobpodgotovka*: mobilisation planning in interwar industry

N.S. Simonov

INTRODUCTION: CONCEPTS, INSTRUMENTS AND INSTITUTIONS

In the 1930s economic planning for the contingency of war was a distinct activity within the Soviet military-industrial complex. It evolved a distinct terminology and set of acronyms. Its central concept was *mobpodgotovka* (*mobilizatsionnaia podgotovka*, the mobilisation preparation, or preparedness, of industry). Its chief instrument was the *mobplan* (mobilisation plan) for industry decided upon at higher levels, administered by the *mobotdel* (mobilisation department) within each chief production-branch administration of each supply ministry (commissariat), and distributed to each subordinate enterprise as its *mobzadanie* (mobilisation assignment). The implementation of the industry mobilisation plan in the event of war being realised was referred to as the *mobilizatsionnoe razvertyvanie* (mobilisation deployment) of military industry.

In this chapter we look at the evolution and results of *mobpodgotovka* in the interwar years. The basic task of mobilisation planning was to guarantee wartime supplies of the necessary weaponry and combat equipment, in the quantities laid down as mobilisation requirements for the armed service agencies and the NKVD, and confirmed by the government. For this purpose mobilisation plans were compiled for industry as a whole, for the industrial commissariats, and for individual enterprises.

The *overall mobilisation plan of industry* consisted, first, of an overall assessment of requirements and a schedule for delivery of the basic types of weaponry and combat equipment; second, of a plan of measures to secure these deliveries (the expansion of production facilities within the period of the mobilisation plan, and a scheme for inter-industry co-ordination of enterprises); and third, of an overall material-technical supply plan.

The *overall mobilisation plan for each commissariat* included, first, mobilisation assignments and delivery schedules; second, the distribution of assignments among the commissariat's enterprises along with a scheme for inter-enterprise co-ordination; third, measures to secure these deliveries; fourth, a material-technical supply plan (including balances of requirements and sources of supply of each product); and fifth, measures to impose martial law at the enterprise level.[1]

In turn, the industry mobilisation plan was broken down into detailed *mobilisation assignments* to correspond with each individual enterprise or production association existing at the given time. Mobilisation assignments included, first, measures to be implemented in the enterprise upon the announcement of mobilisation or on special instruction of the government; second, a programme of production mobilisation or other assignment; third, special instructions for the execution of the programme or assignment, e.g. which products to begin to produce, of which to curtail production and to what extent, and which to abandon altogether; and fourth, preparatory measures for the execution of mobilisation assignments.

The mobilisation assignment was given out to the director of the enterprise (or association) over the signatures of the heads of the commissariat's appropriate chief administration and mobilisation department, and was entered in the commissariat's register of mobilisation assignments after confirmation by the people's commissar. All documents connected with mobilisation assignments, e.g. drawings and design and budget documentation, were held separately from other classified documents, and could be transmitted or transferred only up or down the hierarchy of mobilisation agencies. The heads of mobilisation departments of the commissariat and its chief administrations, and the factory directors, bore personal responsibility for any breach of secrecy of the mobilisation plan, 'whether in private conversation or in reporting to sessions of party, Soviet, or any other organs'.[2]

In the period 1928–38, general guidance of the process of developing, securing conditions for, and implementing the industry mobilisation plan was in the hands of the Council of Labour and Defence (STO) (initially through the medium of its management meeting, then through its Defence Committee). In 1938–41 responsibility passed to the Sovnarkom Defence Committee.

As for the mobilisation plans themselves, in the period 1932–6 these were developed by the chief administrations of Narkomtiazhprom for defence-related branches of industry, co-ordinated within the commissariat by its chief war-mobilisation administration (*glavnoe voenno-mobilizatsionnoe upravlenie,* GVMU for short). In 1937 Narkomtiazhprom was broken up, so in 1937–8 the development of mobilisation plans was taken over by Narkomoboronprom for weaponry and combat equipment, by Narkommash for vehicles and machinery, and by Narkomtiazhmash for metals, fuels, and electric power. In 1938–40 these commissariats went through a process of further subdivision, and there was also a creation of new commissariats. Thus in 1938–40 the industry mobilisation plan required more complex interministerial linkages and reconciliations. For this purpose in the spring of 1938 a Military-Industrial Committee (the VPK, chaired by L.M. Kaganovich) was created under the Defence Committee, and under the VPK a Military-Technical Bureau.[3]

THE QUALITY OF MOBILISATION PLANNING: 1928–37

To judge from the assessments of party officials involved in industry which are reported below, the quality of the industry mobilisation plans and enterprises mobilisation assignments compiled by commissariats and other agencies in the 1930s was low. In the event of 'unforeseen complications' in the international environment and a declaration of war, these plans and instructions were liable to be shown up as unrealistic, from the point of view of providing for delivery of the quantities of weaponry and combat equipment specified by the armed forces.

Thus in a memorandum dated 26 November 1933 and addressed to V.M. Molotov, P.M. Zernov, deputy chairman of the Leningrad oblast executive committee, gauged the significance of the mobilisation plans in operation in the period 1928–33 as follows:

> From the moment of inception of mobilisation work in the USSR right up to the present day industry has never had a realistic mobilisation plan according to which enterprises could develop their activity in the event of war.
>
> In the past we have had mobilisation plans (entitled 'P', 'S', or 'S-30') on paper, not based on real capacities and assimilated production processes ... The significant volume of current military equipment orders in 1931–3 has permitted industry to master production of the majority of products entering into mobilisation plans. However the organisation of mobilisation work [was so set up that] regardless of the existence of current military equipment orders industry has to the present day not been able to create a realistic mobilisation plan and effectively does not have one.
>
> In 1931 in industry there operated simultaneously three mobilisation plans: S-30, the corrected S-30, and MV-10.
>
> In 1932 in heavy industry there operated the MV-10 mobilisation plan. The system of issuing mobilisation instructions and the defects in its methodology have led to a situation where the MV-10 supply system has turned out unrealistic.[4]

N.A. Efimov, chief of the Red Army arms and artillery administration, made analogous claims concerning mobilisation work in industry in a memorandum to I.V. Stalin dated 8 November, commenting additionally on the extreme narrowness of the military-industrial base prepared for mobilisation deployment:

> A few months ago those in charge of industrial mobilisation [presented] to the Defence Committee their report, which deals not with mobilisation but with the capacities of factories in existence and attested by peacetime military equipment orders. This is unreliable. The success of mobilisation of industry depends not only on the 'narrow base' prepared in peacetime, comprising the 'core' military factories, but also on the technical preparation of a 'broad base'. The present-day condition of mobilisation work in heavy industry will disrupt industrial mobilisation in the event of war.[5]

The issue of principle in preparation of the country's military-industrial potential arose just at the time when the system of commissariat mobilisation organs was being formed. Thus, in a memo to Red Army chief of staff M.N. Tukhachevskii dated 20 February 1928, the chief of the mobilisation department of the cartridge and barrel trust drew attention to the divergence between industrial peacetime and wartime structures; this divergence, he argued, manifested itself in the higher cost of the military products of core military-industrial establishments compared with those of other engineering and metalworking factories, which in turn reflected the fact that a significant proportion of core military factories' fixed assets was idle and decaying; in peacetime there was no sense in 'loading [these capacities] with [the production of] munitions on a scale which would allow for their full utilisation', yet it would also be a difficult task to require them to assimilate civilian production technology.[6]

On 9 September 1933 STO passed resolution no. 85ss 'On provision of the RKKA with armament for one year of waging war and on capital construction of Narkomtiazhprom'. The operation of the MV-10 mobilisation plan was thereby curtailed. In November 1933 Narkomtiazhprom embarked on the elaboration of a new plan, MP-33, which was to supply quantities of weaponry and combat equipment in the event of war in the quantities shown in table 11.1.

MP-33 became effective on 1 January 1934. But in the process of working out mobilisation assignments in Narkomtiazhprom there appeared all the same flaws and defects as in the preceding mobilisation plans.

On 7 October 1934 the Soviet Control Commission's military control group presented a wide-ranging audit of the mobilisation activity of Narkomtiazhprom. It drew attention to numerous discrepancies between mobilisation plan indicators and the production capacities designated for fulfilment of the plan. For example, 92 per cent of the requirement of MP-33 for aircraft was realistically provided for, 81 per cent for artillery systems, and only 40 per cent for explosives. For the requirements of rifles, machine guns, and tanks, Narkomtiazhprom claimed 100 per cent cover by available capacities, but these claims evoked the inspectors' grave doubts for a variety of reasons – the assortment was incompletely guaranteed, there was a lack of capacities for

Table 11.1. MP-33: the supply of weaponry and combat equipment envisaged for one year of waging war in 1933

	Units
Rifles (1891 model)	2 000 000
Machine guns (all types)	120 000
Rifle cartridges	3 000 000 000
Artillery shells	60 000 000
Aerial bombs	150 000
Torpedoes	2 500
Mines	25 000
Artillery	24 410
small calibre	15 180
medium calibre	6 220
large calibre	1 940
anti-aircraft	1 070
Tanks	15 800
Pocket tanks and armoured cars	15 000
Reconnaissance aircraft	2 650
Bombers	2 020
Fighters	2 460
Training aircraft	8 730
Aeroengines	15 150

Source: RGAE, 7297/38/1, 88–102.

auxiliary production, the technological process was imperfectly installed, and so on.[7]

The Soviet Control Commission picked out a fundamental flaw in the compilation and distribution of mobilisation assignments. This was the neglect of civilian industry, which even in wartime conditions, the report argued, must provide the economy with means of production and transportation. 'The entire mobilisation preparedness of heavy industry for the first year of war', the document declared,

> is currently expressed in the preparedness of its individual branches for supply of armament and other stores [only] to the army in the field. As far as concerns the preparedness of industry for fulfilling other economic needs – in particular, the requirements of transport (for locomotives, vehicles, tractors), agriculture (for tractors, agricultural machinery, fertiliser, etc.), and equipment for industry as a whole – neither GVMU nor other chief administrations nor Narkomtiazhprom as a whole maintain any kind of activity in this connection. There is reason to suppose that in the event of war we should have phenomena with a double-edged aspect: all kinds of national economic requirements would be roughly curtailed, which

> would in turn undermine the fulfilment of military equipment orders, or else [lead] to the underutilisation or conversely overloading of equipment of different branches of industry.[8]

The commission explained this state of affairs as follows:

> GVMU aims to concentrate the entire production of military products on a few 'military factories', in an artificially formed 'military industry', ignoring our heavy industry as a whole and not wanting to get it involved in the matter. [Military production is] done this way more easily and with less consideration. To involve industry as a whole in the production of military goods it's necessary to study and be familiar with industry [as a whole]: studying its capabilities in depth, so as to make proper use of them. This is a difficult business, but absolutely necessary.[9]

The elaboration and adjustment of the MP-33 mobilisation plan continued to the end of the second five-year plan (1933–7), until, eventually, the armed forces agencies declared it to be 'obsolete once and for all'. On 3 October 1936, in a report to V.M. Molotov, chairman of Sovnarkom, Red Army chief of staff A.I. Egorov spoke of the necessity of a new industry mobilisation plan. 'In the past three years', Egorov declared,

> mobilisation assignments have become outdated quantitatively and qualitatively. A whole range of articles of weaponry and combat equipment stipulated in MP-33 has been taken out of production, and replaced by new models; many enterprises liable to mobilisation have changed their specialisations, and production capacities have been altered.[10]

On the instructions of the Sovnarkom Defence Committee, Narkomtiazhprom presented NKO with its proposals for expanding production capacities for rifle cartridges, artillery shells, powder, optical equipment, chemical agents, antigas equipment, and so on. NKO fixed its minimum requirements for the first year of war at 100 million artillery shells and 17.5 billion rifle cartridges.[11] During 1937 NKO, for obvious reasons, was unable to clarify further its minimum requirements for the first year of war, nor were the chief administrations of Narkomtiazhprom and Narkomoboronprom able to do likewise with their plans for capacity expansion of military industry. The newly appointed officials responsible for these departments did not just have to grasp the essential issues of mobilisation planning, but also to condemn the experience of their predecessors who had just been arrested.

MP-1: 1938–40

On 17 June 1938 the Sovnarkom Defence Committee adopted its resolution no. 3 on the implementation of a heavy industry mobilisation plan for the

Table 11.2. MP-1: the supply of weaponry and industrial materials envisaged for one year of waging war in 1939

	Units
Artillery systems	51 818
Aircraft	27 260
Tanks	19 290
Armoured cars	5 700
Tractors	82 300
Rifles	2 740 800
Artillery shells	233 353 000
Rifle cartridges	16 640 400 000
	Thousand tons
Gunpowder	285
Explosives	615.7
Chemical agents	227.7
Crude steel	9 500
Rolled steel	5 800
Copper	305
Lead	154.1
Aluminium	131.1
Nickel	12.1
Tin	11.1
Zinc	88.2

Source: GARF, 8418/26/9, 4–5.

period 1 January to 31 December 1939 under the title 'MP-1'. Then on 29 July 1939 the same committee adopted a further resolution no. 267ss on the introduction of a separate mobilisation plan entitled 'MP-8' to cover civilian commissariats and agencies from 1 August 1939.[12] Within its 12-month accounting period, MP-1 stipulated supplies in the quantities shown in table 11.2.

For nonferrous metals the requirements of MP-1 were not fully covered by industrial capacity, so that in the event of war, or of a total commercial blockade, Soviet industry would have been placed in a serious position. In contrast, there was much less of a problem in the supply of basic chemicals than had been the case at the beginning of the decade. Actual production capacities for concentrated nitric acid, *oleum*, chlorine, sulphur, toluol, and aniline, all corresponded with the supplies specified in MP-1.[13]

The likely costs of mobilisation deployment

The fulfilment potential of the MP-1 mobilisation plan in the period 1938–40 raises many issues. First, according to the 1938 plan, the enterprises of Narkomoboronprom, Narkomtiazhprom, and Narkommash should have generated a gross value of output at prevailing wholesale prices amounting to 67 billion rubles; since these three commissariats were also designated the basic suppliers of military-industrial products, this sum should have included 10 570 million rubles' worth of articles of weaponry and combat equipment. But the value of the entire range of military products stipulated in MP-1 was not less than 60 billion rubles in the same prices. Thus, if the enterprises of Narkomoboronoprom, Narkomtiazhprom, and Narkommash were to be withdrawn from other production to concentrate on supply of weaponry and combat equipment at the level stipulated in MP-1, 'civilian' industrial production processes and nationwide transport would be placed in a very serious position which in turn would have a correspondingly damaging influence on military-industrial production.

Indirect requirements of mobilisation deployment

A second important question was the balancing of load factors placed upon different productive capacities – a problem which, in principle, was soluble by means of a subcontracting system thought out in advance and elaborated in practice. However, having neglected subcontracting in the past, the mobilisation organs could not put right their omissions within a very compressed time horizon. According to the situation in early spring 1939, among the items produced through reliance on subcontracting were artillery shell parts (cartridges, casings, explosives, fuse glasses for chemical shells), aircraft forgings, aerial bomb casings, and various assemblies (artillery and tank manometers, stereoscopic sights, clockwork mechanisms for mines, and so on). An inquiry of the VPK ('On the state of subcontracting for the production of means of weaponry and combat equipment', 25 April 1939), openly recognised:

> At the present time subcontracting (*proizvodstvennaia kooperatsiia*) is not thought out and is unsystematically organised. The chief administrations and commissariats give no attention to this matter. Factories [i.e. prime contractors] operate on their own initiative: they seek out enterprises [to act as subcontractors], make a deal with them to accept the [sub-]contract, and try by every means possible to hold them to it. Enterprises involved as subcontractors are designated as such without any well-founded evaluation, being motivated to improve their finances on account of these [sub-]contracts. As a result [of the uncertainties associated with the subcontractors] the prime contractor does not curtail production of the parts designated for supply through the subcontracting system.[14]

Labour requirements of mobilisation deployment

A third important issue was the provision of industry with labour in wartime conditions, including standard lists of categories of army reservists whose mobilisation could be deferred so that they could be reserved to appropriate enterprises instead. Because of lack of co-ordination with NKO the mobilisation organs of the commissariats reserved for the economy only 2.5 million army reservists – a number which turned out to be completely inadequate for provision of the requirements of the defence industry and other important branches of the economy. In 1941–5 the GKO and Sovnarkom were compelled to adopt more than one thousand supplementary resolutions on issues of reservation of skilled workers to industry.[15]

The speed of mobilisation deployment

A fourth important issue was the time horizon for mobilisation deployment of military-industrial production. According to Soviet military intelligence, within the period 1933–4 Hitler's Germany was able fully to provide for the deployment of a 1.5–million strong army with infantry armament, small calibre artillery, shells, and cartridges. The number of enterprises among which German military equipment orders were distributed was 33 in 1932, rising to 200 in 1934.[16] The rapidity of this mobilisation deployment of German industry was ensured by the fact that the high command of the Reichswehr itself carried out verification and replacement of out-of-date drawings and calibres at enterprises designated in advance and within specific dates, and, evidently, kept the condition of contractors' tool-rooms under constant direct supervision. For Soviet industry, such an attitude to auxiliary production lines and documentation of the technological process was a great rarity.[17]

The system of standards in Soviet military and civilian industry, a necessary condition for interchangeability and complementarity of military and civilian production processes, was not sufficiently developed. Real progress in this direction began only in the wake of a Central Committee-Sovnarkom joint resolution of 9 July 1940 'On state all-Union standards and the procedure for adopting them'.

THE 1939 REORGANISATION OF THE DEFENCE INDUSTRY

It is not ruled out that a main factor pushing the Soviet leadership to subdivide Narkomoboronprom into four specialised military-industrial commissariats at the beginning of 1939 was the striving to instill the principles of subcontracting and specialisation into military-industrial production, so as to set up stricter operational control over technological processes, and correspondingly over the timetable of mobilisation deployment.

In a memorandum to the Central Committee and Sovnarkom a few days after the event, on 21 January 1939, Commissar of Defence Industry M.M. Kaganovich explained the necessity for creation of a 'specialised commissariat for shell' (i.e. the new Narkomboepripasov) in terms of the requirements of 'making up an integrated assortment of shell', distributed among 400 factories of various commissariats (other factors mentioned included 'supervision of fulfilment of the programme and of planned assignments', rendering 'technical assistance', and so on). The motivation for creating an Armament Commissariat (Narkomvooruzheniia) according to Kaganovich was that 'the transition to more advanced types of weapons (self-loading rifles, automatic anti-aircraft weapons, and new divisional and heavy artillery), requires deepened technical leadership'. As for the future Commissariats of Shipbuilding (Narkomsudprom) and the Aircraft Industry (Narkomaviaprom), each, in his words, 'constitute[s] an integrated production complex'.[18]

The event itself took place on 11 January 1939 with a decree of the Supreme Soviet Presidium 'On the division of the USSR People's Commissariat of the Defence Industry'. This decree established the core military-industrial commissariats within the management structure of the Soviet economic system. It was therefore a first approximation to the developed organisational form of the Soviet defence-industry complex. However, the official title of this complex ('the defence branches of industry') was more closely related to the organisational structure of government ministries than to the structure of industry by the final use of its products for defence. There was a difference between these two – much like the compromises and blurring of distinctions which would be involved if one tried to single out, say, the production of pencils for handing over to a 'People's Commissariat of Woodworking and the Graphite Industry'.

Table 11.3. The dimensions of four specialised military-industry commissariats, January 1939

	Narkom-aviaprom (aircraft industry)	*Narkom-boepripasov (ammunition)*	*Narkom-sudprom (ship-building)*	*Narkom-vooruzheniia (armament)*
	(1)	(2)	(3)	(4)
Enterprises	86	53	41	38
Research institutes and design bureaux	9	12	10	8
Construction trusts	5	5	5	4
Manual and non-manual employees (thousands)	272.6	337.1	173.2	223.2
Gross value of output, 1939 plan (million rubles)	3 877	2 668	2 300	2 685
Capital investment, 1939 plan (million rubles)	1 427	1 525	945	1 003

Source: GARF, 8418/23/2, 12.

The dimensions of the four newly formed commissariats can be judged from table 11.3. As for tank equipment and armour, production was distributed among various industrial and military-industrial commissariats. The enterprises designated as basic producers belonged to Narkomsredmash (formed on 2 July 1939), including Khar'kov factory no. 183, Leningrad factory no. 174, and Moscow factory no. 37, formerly of Narkomoboronprom. KV heavy tanks were manufactured by enterprises of Narkomtiazhmash (reorganised 23 April 1939).[19]

The production of chemical weapons was transferred from the former sixth chief administration of Narkomoboronprom to Narkomkhimprom (formed on 28 February 1939).

The relative importance of the various commissariats in fulfilling planned orders for weaponry and combat equipment placed by NKO in 1940 can be gauged from table 11.4. For comparison, in the event of a wartime mobilisation deployment of industry, the shares of these commissariats in the gross value of military-industrial production were intended (according to the computations of the VPK) to change as shown in table 11.5.

From the point of view of the basic tasks of military-mobilisation preparedness of Soviet industry, disbanding Narkomoboronprom and replacing it with several specialised military-industrial commissariats was a step in the right direction. In case of necessity the economic potential of each of them could be reinforced by conscripting other enterprises nominally subordinate to other agencies but based on related technological processes.

True, the potential for gain was limited. On one side, in the event of a surprise attack such as came in 1941, the time period required for mobilisation

Table 11.4. The planned military equipment orders of NKO, by supply commissariat, 1940 (million rubles at prevailing wholesale prices and per cent of total)

Commissariat	*Million rubles*	*Per cent*
	(1)	(2)
Ammunition	10 004	32.3
Aircraft industry	7 285	23.5
Armament	5 032	16.2
Medium engineering	2 373	7.6
Heavy engineering	1 167	3.7
Defence	903	2.9
Chemical industry	850	2.7
General engineering	719	2.3
Shipbuilding	491	1.5
Other	–	7.3
Total	30 936	100.0

Source: GARF, 8418/23/1259, 8.

Table 11.5. The planned military equipment orders of NKO, by supply commissariat, currently and in the event of war, 1940 (per cent of total)

Commissariat	*Current orders*	*Orders in the event of war*
	(1)	(2)
Ammunition	32.3	27.9
Aircraft industry	23.5	14.5
Armament	16.2	11.1
Medium engineering	7.6	11.6
Heavy engineering	3.7	5.3
Defence	2.9	–
Chemical industry	2.7	6.6
General engineering	2.3	6.8
Shipbuilding	1.5	2.4

Source: GARF, 8418/23/1259, 8; GARF, 8418/27/65, 8–9.

deployment of the military-industrial base would not be foreshortened. On the other side, in the event of losing a significant part of the country's territory through temporary occupation and the ensuing transport and energy paralysis which 1941 would witness, concentrating military-industrial production on a few enterprises at a significant distance from the front line and the radius of action of enemy aviation would allow continuity of supply of the army with weaponry and combat equipment despite having lost the full advantages of subcontracting and specialisation on the eve of mobilisation deployment of the industrial base.

MOBILISATION PREPAREDNESS ON THE EVE OF WAR

The situation on 22 June 1941 was as follows. Work on compiling the overall MP-1 industry mobilisation plan, and on specifying enterprises' mobilisation assignments, was approximately complete, if not finished in the full sense. From the late summer of 1939 (when World War II was just beginning), a number of measures had been accomplished which had prepared for its activation stage by stage. A number of decisions testify to this, for example, resolutions of the Economic Council and Sovnarkom such as 'On balances and plans for the allocation of high-grade steel and ferroalloys' (29 August 1939), 'On the compilation of balances of production and allocation of sulphuric and nitric acid' (1 September 1939), 'On the development of the USSR's machine-tool industry' (4 September 1939). These resolutions regulated the allocation of ferrous metals, basic chemicals, and machine tools, in order to satisfy the growing needs of defence industry.

The annual growth of output of the military-industrial commissariats in 1938–40 was no less than 41.5 per cent (compared with 27.3 per cent envisaged by the third five-year plan for 1938–42).[20] According to the 1940 balance of the national economy, the share of military production (27 billion rubles at prevailing wholesale prices) in commodity output of industry (390 billion rubles) was roughly 7 per cent (at the unchanged prices of 1926/27 this share would have risen to 17.4 per cent).[21]

The reallocation of material resources in favour of military-industrial and allied production induced extreme tensions over the fulfilment enterprise and commissariat plans in 'civilian' industry. The shortage of crude and rolled steel forced a decline in the output of tractors, combines, road vehicles, and so on. The Gor'kii motor factory (GAZ) was supposed to maintain a 35-day reserve of ready stocks of metals and parts. In actual fact in 1939 the factory had nothing in reserve at all. GAZ was forced to retrogress from mass flow production to low-volume production, incurring large losses on unanticipated rejigging of equipment and replacement of dies.[22] But at the same time the Red Army was in no less need of road transport vehicles than of armoured vehicles.

The third five-year plan (1938–42) originally stipulated construction of 84 enterprises for defence industry with an overall estimated value of about 3.2 billion rubles. More than 8 billion rubles of capital investment were planned for rebuilding and expanding the existing 'core' military plants.[23] After revision of the defence construction programme (July 1939), the overall value of capital investments in defence industry (Narkomaviaprom, Narkomvooruzheniia, Narkomboepripasov, and Narkomsudprom) in the third five-year plan grew to 20.3 billion rubles.[24] In 1939, 612 million rubles were allocated to research and to outlays on experimental models of weaponry and combat equipment under 6 commissariats (NKO, NKVMF, Narkomaviaprom, Narkomvooruzheniia, Narkomboepripasov, and Narkomsudprom); this sum almost doubled to 1162 million rubles in 1940.[25]

A joint resolution of the Central Committee and Sovnarkom of 10 September 1939 obliged the Economic Council and Defence Committee to 'meet daily'.[26] Such a régime was conditioned by a belief that the resolution of many immediate issues of industry's mobilisation preparedness in 1939–41 was being affected by intolerable delays. This concerned especially decisions concerning serial production of new weapon systems, the accumulation of mobilisation reserves for deployment of the wartime army, the creation of state reserves of industrial fuels, equipment, and materials, the reservation of labour, and so forth. Thus in its planned allocation of equipment orders for 1940 the NKO vehicle, armour, and tank administration assumed the continued manufacture of obsolete fighters (the I-16, I-28, I-153, and I-207), and bombers (the DBZ, SB, and SPB).[27] In quantities of tanks and aircraft the Red Army outweighed any other army, but their quality, with rare exceptions, already failed to answer to the needs of the time.

In September 1939 the Politburo adopted further resolutions on the development of aeroengine factories, and on reconstructing existing aircraft factories and building new ones. The number of aviation design bureaux was raised to 20. The research institutes and design bureaux of Narkomaviaprom were commissioned to design and build, within a foreshortened time horizon, experimental models of combat aircraft to match the requirements of contemporary aerial combat and of action in concert with different types of ground forces. The victors in a fierce competitive struggle were the design bureaux of S.V. Il'iushin (the armoured Il-2 assault aircraft), V.M. Petliakov (the Pe-2 dive-bomber), A.N. Tupolev (the Tu-2 frontline bomber), S.A. Lavochkin (the LaGG-3 fighter), A.I. Mikoian (the MiG-3 fighter), and A.S. Iakovlev (the Iak-1 fighter). From the beginning of 1941 the aircraft industry was completely converted to manufacturing new designs – 5680 units according to the plan for the first half of the year, including 2925 fighters and 2475 bombers.[28]

It was mainly those models of weaponry and combat equipment which had been brought into mass production which featured in NKO plans for military equipment orders in 1939 and 1940. Therefore plan fulfilment percentages rose (except for artillery shell) as shown in table 11.6, but the apparent improvement does not mean that the state of the military-industrial economy was any healthier. In a report to the Defence Committee 'On work for 1940 on the production-business activity of the People's Commissariat of Ammunition' (5 February 1941), Commissar for Ammunition I. Sergeev remarked in particular that:

> The production activity of Narkomboepripasov has finished up with unsatisfactory indicators. The plan decided upon by the government has been frustrated (with 87.3 per cent fulfilment). The capital construction plan has been fulfilled by 68.3 per cent. Losses from defective output amounted to 322.7 million rubles or 4.3 per cent of production costs, compared with 4 per cent for 1939.[29]

Results of the other defence industry commissariats in terms of both physical output and financial items were also far from outstanding. For example, in a memorandum to the Defence Committee (25 May 1940), Defence Commissar S.K. Timoshenko reported that as a result of verifying production costs and revising wholesale prices for artillery orders from Narkomvooruzheniia, the Red Army chief artillery administration had secured savings in the sum of more than 1.5 billion rubles. 'However', Timoshenko added, 'this result is far from the maximum attainable, since the percentage of outlays on overheads and defective output in the wholesale prices adopted for 1940 remains very large'. Timoshenko ascribed the largest additional costs to the aircraft industry which, according to his findings, loaded onto wholesale prices a markup on wage costs for overheads of between 200 and 500 per cent

Table 11.6. Weapons and military equipment ordered and supplied, 1939–40 (units and per cent fulfilment)

	[1939]			*[1940]*		
	ordered	*supplied*	*fulfilled (%)*	*ordered*	*supplied*	*fulfilled (%)*
	(1)	(2)	(3)	(4)	(5)	(6)
Artillery	19 620	16 459	83.8	8 266	13 724	166.0
small calibre	8 965	8 965	100.0	7 397	7 063	95.4
med. calibre	10 371	7 224	69.6	10 523	6 437	61.1
large calibre	284	270	95.0	346	224	64.7
Mortars	7 900	4 457	56.4	19 875	38 349	192.9
Artillery shells (thousands)	25 095	18 099	72.1	22 195	14 921	67.2
Mortar shells (thousands)	12 500	2 741	21.9	12 209	18 285	149.7
Bombs (thousands)	2 979	2 834	95.1	9 828	7 691	78.2
Rifles (thousands)	1 920	1 497	77.9	1 986	1 461	73.5
Machine guns (thousands)	115 881	96 433	83.2	46 000	–	–
Rifle cartridges (million)	2 160	2 194	101.5	3 143	2 820	89.7
Aircraft	9 091	10 758	118.3	13 864	10 565	76.2
bombers	3 611	2 744	75.9	6 090	3 674	60.3
fighters	3 875	4 150	107.1	5 800	4 657	80.2
Tanks	3 278	2 986	91.1	3 370	2 790	82.7

Source: GARF, 8418/25/14, 2–3.

and attempted to get the purchasers to pay for not less than 105 million rubles of defective output.[30]

On 23 August 1940, with the aim of controlling costs and reducing outlays on military equipment orders, the Sovnarkom Economic Council adopted a resolution on wholesale prices for military products of six commissariats (Narkomaviaprom, Narkomvooruzheniia, Narkomboepripasov, Narkomtiazhmash, Narkomtsvetmet, and Narkomstroimat). This resolution proposed in particular 'to consider incorrect the existing practice of establishing orientation prices for military products, which leads to irresponsibility of suppliers and establishes the possibility of unbusinesslike expenditure of resources'.[31]

From the autumn of 1940 wholesale prices of military products were formed in the supplier establishments, being based on standardised outlays of materials and labour time with a planned percentage for overheads. For all products 'firm' (i.e. directive) prices confirmed by the government were established. In the case of factories fulfilling orders outside the plan, prices were to be established in agreement with all-Union price lists currently in operation, and only for experimental orders was it permitted, exceptionally, to deviate by an upper limit of 50 per cent above the preliminary wholesale price.[32]

WARTIME MOBILISATION: PLANS AND RESULTS

Evaluating the results of mobilisation preparation of Soviet industry in the last prewar years in his memoirs, Marshal G.K. Zhukov asserted 'the fact of continual and rapid', even 'forced-march' development of defence industry. He considered that 'the transition from the lines of the country's peacetime development to wartime lines would signify a still greater change of course in this direction, and would lead to alteration and regeneration of the very structure of the national economy, and its militarisation in direct detriment to the interests of working people'.[33]

I do not wish to pick an argument with so venerated a memoirist as Zhukov in relation to the need to show care towards the interests of working people. However, in my view there was a colossal imbalance between the scale of outlays of labour and capital to reinforce the country's defensive capability, and the low effectiveness of use of these resources to organise military-industrial production and create new weapon systems. As for 'militarisation' of the country's economic system, this term has a well-defined quantitative measure in the ratio of direct outlays on defence to the country's net material product. From this point of view the degree of Soviet economic militarisation on the eve of the Great Patriotic War rose rapidly from 7 per cent in 1937 to nearly 15 per cent in 1940 (see table 4.12).

In comparison with these figures, in wartime 1942 the economy's degree of militarisation rose to 55 per cent or more.[34] On one hand the latter figure testifies to the unrealised potential for higher defence outlays on the eve of the Great Patriotic War. On the other hand it may be that the 15 per cent achieved in prewar 1940 was at the limit for peacetime conditions. Certainly the opinion of Gosplan's first department, the experts of which were engaged at the end of the 1950s in generalising from the experience of prewar military-industrial deployment, was that:

> we began to carry out military mobilisation preparation of our industry too late. In essence our country did not have a composite mobilisation plan for preparation of the whole national economy for the needs of war, which was unquestionably a great defect and explained to a large extent the untimely organisation of mobilisation planning.[35]

Planning for wartime mobilisation, in my view, should not be seen as an end in itself, outside a context formed by the economy's real capabilities and the condition of its various branches. Before the war, among other things, even fulfilling peacetime military equipment orders (let alone the much higher level envisaged in mobilisation assignments for the event of war) induced extreme tension in the material-technical balances of Soviet 'military' and 'civilian' industry. Optimal economic proportions were violated, the management apparatus's activity was distorted bureaucratically, and the authorities placed extreme reliance on repressive methods of enforcement of labour. As a result, the Soviet Union had (to coin a phrase), 'neither guns nor butter' in sufficient quantity.

NOTES

1 GARF, 8418/26/9, 13–14.
2 GARF, 8418/26/9, 4–5.
3 GARF, 8418/27/97, 2.
4 GARF, 8418/8/147, 37–377.
5 GARF, 8418/8/157, 30.
6 RGVA, 40442/1/38, 209–11.
7 GARF, 8418/9/211, 9–12.
8 GARF, 8418/9/211, 13–14.
9 GARF, 8418/9/211, 15.
10 GARF, 8418/11/221, 52.
11 GARF, 8418/11/221, 55–7.
12 GARF, 8418/23/73, 62.
13 GARF, 8418/26/9, 16–25.
14 GARF, 8418/26/3, 99–100.
15 GARF, 8418/27/97, 63–4.
16 Razvedupr RKKA (1936), 56–7.
17 Gastev (1937), 45.

18 GARF, 8418/23/2, 1–7.
19 GARF, 8418/23/1262, 60.
20 Industrializatsiia (1973), 128.
21 RGAE, 4372/94/945, 7.
22 Khavin (1962), 300.
23 RGAE, 4372/91/3217, 127.
24 RGAE, 7733/36/281a, 42.
25 GARF, 8418/27/664, 4–6.
26 GARF, 5446/57/65, 51–2. The Economic Council consisted of A.I. Mikoian (chair), N.A. Bulganin (his deputy), and members S.M. Budennyi, E.A. Shchadenko, L.Z. Mekhlis; membership of the Defence Committee comprised V.M. Molotov (chair), N.A. Voznesenskii (his deputy), N.G. Kuznetsov, A.A. Zhdanov, A.I. Mikoian, L.P. Beriia, B.M. Shaposhnikov, G.I. Kulik, and I.I. Proskurov.
27 GARF, 8418/23/1260, 1–4.
28 *Izvestiia TsK KPSS* (1990), no. 2, 195.
29 GARF, 8418/24/570, 26.
30 GARF, 8418/24/1449, 49–50.
31 GARF, 8418/24/1449, 37.
32 GARF, 8418/24/1449, 353–4.
33 Zhukov (1970), 191.
34 Sorokin (1971), 87–8.
35 RGAE, 4372/77/255, 212.

12 *Voenpriemka*: prices, costs, and quality assurance in interwar defence industry

Mark Harrison and Nikolai Simonov

INTRODUCTION

In this chapter we examine the Soviet system for *voenpriemka* – the acceptance by the defence ministry of military equipment produced by industry for the armed forces. The institutions concerned were evolved in the 1930s in order to contain and manage fierce conflicts of interest between the army and industry, and their operation is therefore of interest from several points of view. The military strategist will seek illumination of the factors influencing the cost and quality of Soviet weapons. The economic historian will aim to discover the logic of the business strategies pursued by Soviet producers to defend their interests under pressure. The student of political economy will wish to probe more deeply into a significant fault line within the Soviet military-industrial complex.

The evolution of institutions in this period was shaped in part by trends in real variables. As far as the latter concern us, they may be stated briefly as follows on the basis of Chapter 4 above. After the First World War (1914–17) and the economically even more disastrous Civil War (1918–21) Soviet defence spending fell to historically low levels. Budget defence outlays in 1928 were probably no more than 2.4 per cent of GNP at prevailing prices. By 1940, their GNP share had risen to 13 per cent, despite a significant relative cheapening of defence goods and services (table 4.12). In real terms (at constant factor costs of 1937) GNP in 1940 stood at twice the level of 1928, but the number of men and women in military uniform had risen seven-fold while the real volume of defence production had risen many more times than this (tables 4.2 and 4.3). Where in 1930 Soviet industry had supplied 10 500 rifles, 80 guns, 75 aircraft, and 14 tanks in each month, by 1940 the monthly rates had risen to 120 000 rifles, 1 275 guns, 880 aircraft, and 230 tanks.[1] Moreover each tank, aircraft, gun, and rifle of 1940 was far more complex and costly than in 1930.

Over the interwar period there was also sharp discontinuity in the evolution of the economy-wide allocation system. In the 1920s there was a mixed ownership system and a market economy within which the expanding public sector was increasingly driven by non-price controls. At the end of the 1920s a violent process of confiscation and centralisation greatly expanded the role of the public sector and launched the economy onto a state-led quantitative expansion drive in which investment and defence benefited from priority allocation. At first, financial discipline was temporarily lost altogether. By 1931, however, the drive for quantitative expansion at any price was being modified by the reintroduction of controls on costs and qualitative criteria under the general heading of *khozraschet* (roughly, 'business accounting'). Targets for physical output expansion remained more important than targets for cost reduction, but the latter could no longer be regarded as negligible by industrial leaders.[2]

The present chapter is based on documents found in central archives of the former Soviet Union. It represents a view from above, and relies disproportionately upon the attempts of the Soviet military to understand and control the behaviour of defence industry enterprise. Although the documentary material is largely new, the paper is written in the traditional Sovietological manner which seeks to infer underlying trends from the study of official measures and the official rationalisations offered for them. Its main emphasis is on the period between 1930 and 1940, but evidence from both earlier and later periods is introduced where available in order to provide further documentation of continuity and change in the army–industry relationship.

THE DEFENCE PRODUCER AND THE STATE

Cost and quality in a shortage economy

The control of costs and quality in defence industry is not specifically a Soviet problem. At the root of the problem lies the fact that defence production cannot be left to the market. There is only one purchaser, the defence ministry. The defence ministry pursues goals of national security, by comparison with which the meeting of financial targets usually appears to be of secondary importance. To procure weapons, the defence ministry relies mainly – though not exclusively – on a relatively small 'charmed' circle of big industrial firms, the specialised defence contractors. Even in a market economy such firms usually exercise substantial price-making power arising from the concentrated, oligopolistic market structure, the common interest of firms and government in the maintenance of excess capacity which in turn forms one of the most important barriers facing potential entrants, and the low risk that government will punish existing firms' inefficiency by forcing their exit. Together these factors work to soften the defence producers' budget constraint and encourage discretionary behaviour. As a result, the cost of defence goods is harder to control than the quantity produced.

Quality is also hard to control, and this too encourages defence producers' discretionary behaviour. The qualities of a weapon system are given *ex ante* by the specification issued by the defence ministry, which is known to everyone. In an *ex post* sense, however, quality is determined by two things. Does the design live up to its prior specification? Did the producers adhere strictly to the design? The knowledge relevant to answering these questions is held not by the defence ministry, but elsewhere. Only the frontline soldiers and airmen have first-hand knowledge of what the weapon is like to use (and in a peace-time context this knowledge is imperfect since combat conditions can be at best simulated through exercises). As for the technical conditions under which the weapon was made (which are among the most important determinants of quality), such knowledge is held at first hand by the production workers and managers; only they know whether the materials used were of the proper standard, whether the components were reliably tested, and whether the product was finished to the requisite degree of accuracy. The defence ministry can acquire this knowledge as information, but the transfer of information is again fraught with scope for discretionary behaviour. Information can be withheld, exaggerated, or distorted in transmission by those who supply it, as well as inflated or discounted by those who receive it. In the case of the producers, there is a clear incentive to conceal defects in the production process and product alike, especially since there is a good chance that the defects will either never come to light or be discounted as soldiers' grumbling.

A specific feature of the Soviet context was that *all* public-sector firms, accounting for the overwhelming bulk of industrial production, were in the position described above, regardless of the military or civilian profile of their products. They faced a single purchaser, the state, the primary objectives of which were expressed in real security and developmental targets rather than fiscal or monetary objectives; state officials were motivated primarily towards discretionary control over firms' physical resources. As the natural correlate of submission to this regime, Soviet firms' existence was guaranteed regardless of profit or loss by means of their uncontrolled access to the fiscal and monetary resources of the state – the famous 'soft budget constraint'. As a result, firms found that they operated in a 'sellers' market', with broad scope for discretionary behaviour; so long as they barely fulfilled quotas for the quantity of output handed down from above, they could in practice allocate significant resources towards internal goals such as the maintenance of a labour reserve and other excess capacities which reduced the burden of productive tasks upon both workforce and management.

Thus it was easier for the central authorities to control quantities produced than costs. Control over quality was also a perennial issue. The Soviet state's officials, although motivated towards discretionary control over firms' physical resources, were separated by a vertical hierarchical distance from the processes of production and use of firms' products. Knowledge of product and process qualities was held at lower levels by producers and users – firms, households, and service organisations (including the military). Officials were not themselves users of the great bulk of goods and services which firms produced, which weakened their direct knowledge of and interest in quality. Their knowledge of quality was filtered and aggregated through many levels of administration. Since quantities were controlled strictly, and quantitative measures were relatively unambiguous and unavoidable, firms sought to expand their scope for discretion by manipulating quality to the detriment of the user. Every factory was subject to its 'department of technical control' (*OTK*, short for *otdel tekhnicheskogo kontrol'ia*), responsible for accepting or rejecting products and reporting violations to higher ministerial authority. But officials could be found at every level to collude in firms' transgressions for the sake of fulfilment of the ministerial plan for the physical quantity of output. Defects could be concealed at each vertical stage, and users' complaints discounted as occupational grumbling.[3]

If the Soviet defence producer was in a special position, it was not because of the absence of a well-functioning market, which by the twentieth century did not exist for defence goods in western industrial market economies or anywhere else in the world. The unusual feature of the Soviet defence producer's environment was the sustained effort made by Soviet officials to set up non-market constraints on the behaviour of defence producers and limit their discretion over weapon costs and qualities to a far greater extent than in the case of civilian products. That this was so testifies in turn to the special position of the Defence Commissariat (the NKVM until 1934, then the NKO) within government. This special position was constituted by its institutional power and its objectives.

The objective of the defence ministry was to maximise national security on the basis of the resources available. Other ministries' goals were translated into simple numerical quantities, even in the services sector – tons of steel, metres of cloth, ton-kilometres of freight, numbers of publications, arrest quotas, surgical operations carried out, films released, children taught through the pedagogical year, and so on. National security was not measured in this way, and continued to be evaluated on the basis of analytical, synthetic measures. In the event of a national security failure, it was the armed forces who would bear the first and heaviest costs. The defence ministry had a vital interest in quantity, and especially in maximising the quantity of weapons which could be purchased out of a cash-limited budget, but not in substituting quantity for quality, not in quantity at any price; only in quantities of those weapons and equipment items which really would meet the perceived needs of national security. The defence ministry had little or no interest in accepting substandard equipment, or in acquiring excessively costly equipment when cheaper alternatives were potentially available. Thus defence objectives gave special weight to the control of defence production costs and quality. The power of the defence ministry, in turn, gave it institutional means to enforce these controls.

Voenpriemka, voenpred

Not much is known in the west about the operation of the system of *voenpriemka* (*voen-* stands for *voennaia* or 'military', *priemka* for the system, apparatus, and process of 'acceptance' of industrial products by the military). Most of our prior knowledge concerns the defence ministry's 'military representatives' (*voenpredy*, short for *voennye predstaviteli*) in industry. But even on this subject little was published in the Soviet Union where, 'as is so often the case . . ., the importance of the subject [was] inversely related to its frequency of mention in the press'.[4] The limited information available in the west comes primarily from the personal accounts of emigrants and from emigrant interview data.[5]

The military representative was the key figure in the system of *voenpriemka*. According to a rare official account, the military representative was:

> an officer or employee of the armed forces, permanently engaged in industrial plant fulfilling military orders, and endowed with the right to check the quality of the output produced. The military representative of the USSR Ministry of Defence checks the observance of the technological process of manufacture of weapons and military equipment and other military products, and the calculation of their production costs; carries out the acceptance of finished products after carrying out the corresponding trials and verifications of their quality and reliability; . . . and verifies the elimination of defects revealed in the process of acceptance and utilisation . . .
>
> In the USSR checking the fulfilment of military orders is implemented according to types of weapon and military equipment. It demands high technical and specialist training of military representatives, the majority of whom are engineers . . .[6]

Thus the military representatives' place of work was in defence industry, but they answered solely to the ministry of defence. Their roles and responsibilities were defined and redefined on several occasions in the 1930s, but there was always a common core.[7] The initial specification of products and technological processes was jointly agreed between the industrial ministry and the defence ministry, and could not be altered without the consent of both. The factory management officials bore direct personal responsibility for the quality of output; the job of the military representative was therefore to verify fulfilment of defence orders in both quantity and quality, and to report on failures to the defence ministry. The military representative operated in parallel with the defence industry's own system of quality assurance, the OTK. The quality of products and processes was to be verified by means of personal observation of technological processes, access to factory records, carrying out trials of finished output, and accepting or rejecting deliveries on behalf of the defence ministry. (On the shoulders of the military representative was also laid responsibility for oversight of mobilisation planning and preparedness, a subject which does not so much concern us here.)

Pre-revolutionary origins have been claimed for this system; a system called *voennaia priemka* was first established by the Imperial artillery service in 1862, and Peter the Great is credited with imposing 'military representatives' on Russian arsenals and shipyards at the beginning of the eighteenth century. The first measures of the Soviet regime to strengthen the system it had inherited were undertaken in 1920, as the Civil War drew to a close.[8] However, to draw an inference of general historical continuity from the Tsarist regime through revolution, civil war, and the New Economic Policy, to the Stalinist five-year plans would seem misleading. It seems unlikely that anything more complex than a conventional system of checks on product quality at the point of acquisition together with periodic on-site factory inspections and trouble-shooting commissions was in operation during the 1920s. Before 1930 the official documents available to us make no mention of the later 'military representative'; on the contrary, the discussions and decisions imply the absence, as yet, of this institution.

For example, in February 1926, a decree of Revvoensovet (the Revolutionary Military Council) introduced the new post of 'military assistant' (*voennyi pomoshchnik*) to factory managers in defence industry. The army proposed to detach no more than 16 to 18 officers for these new posts in 1926 and 1927. The duties of the military assistant in the factory were to oversee the fulfilment of current defence orders, the execution of mobilisation tasks, and the workplace security regime.[9] (If the *voenpred* had already existed, these roles would have been entirely redundant.) Among the reasons for the innovation of 1926 was offered the following:

> The higher command staff of the RKKA [Red Army] until the present time has not had sufficient information concerning the production possibilities of our industry, and, in particular, of specialised defence industry (*kadrovaia voennaia promyshlennost'*).[10]

However, the 'military assistant' was conceived only as a conduit for information and advice; he had no powers of veto or consent over the delivery of finished products, as did the *voenpred* of later years, and was not considered important enough for mention in subsequent accounts and definitions of the procurement process.[11]

That the 1926 statute did not yet inaugurate the *voenpred* system of modern times is, in our view, further confirmed in a statement by Red Army chief of armament I.P. Uborevich of 17 January 1930 to the effect that:

> Until now *NKVM has not had a special apparatus for observation and control of the work of industry* with regard to fulfilment, on the stipulated dates, of annual planned orders, to organisation of initiation of production [*postanovki proizvodstv*] of new models of armament and their manufacture by the required dates; with regard to organisation and initiation of construction works and in relation to preparations for fulfilment of tasks designated for wartime...[12]

The institution of the *voenpred* in the modern sense was approved by deputy Defence Commissar and Revvoensovet chairman I.S. Unshlikht on 11 February 1930 – a few days after Uborevich's report. The 1930 statute dealt comprehensively with rights and responsibilities – the responsibilities of industry, and the rights of the military.[13] Industry was to be held responsible for the quality and serviceability of defence products supplied, this responsibility being exercised by special ministerial executives for defence orders (*upolnomochennye po voennym zakazam*) in civilian industry, and in defence industry by the factory directors themselves. At the same time the military representative was accorded sweeping rights of on-site regulation and control over production processes, product characteristics, and mobilisation readiness of factories engaged in defence-related work.

The statute also defined an elaborate apparatus and system of ranks among which the functions of the military representative were to be divided. At the apex of the system were the production-technical departments (*PTO*, short for *proizvodstvenno-tekhnicheskie otdely*) of the Red Army chief of armament's administrations for artillery, the air force, the armoured forces and so on. Below the PTO stood, in order, the senior *voenpred* (responsible perhaps for a single large factory or group of factories), the *voenpred* (responsible for a single factory or workshop), the assistant *voenpred*, and on the lower rungs the auxiliary craftsmen, technicians, testers (*brakovshchiki*), and so on.

The number of military representatives in industry in the early years is not known, but by 1940 there were more than 20 000 of them, the largest group (about two-thirds) looking after production for the ground forces. The exact numbers for 1940, together with the distribution of the remainder, were as follows:[14]

Ground forces	13 791
Navy	3 004
Rear services	990
Air defence forces	34
Total	20 281

For comparison, in 1939 there were 218 specialised defence factories among the four defence industry commissariats (for the aircraft industry, shipbuilding, armament, and ammunition).[15] However, this figure does not include the large number of nominally civilian establishments engaged in defence-related work. If some allowance is made for the latter, one might guess that the number of military representatives of all grades in a typical workplace team was somewhere in the region of 30 to 50.

It took time for the institutional underpinnings of the system of price and quality controls over defence industry to be worked out. There was an unending evolution of rights and obligations on each side. The driving force behind this process was the striving of industry to preserve its scope for discretionary behaviour against the external constraints imposed by the defence ministry, combined with the countermoves of the latter.

The fact that *voenpriemka* involved a conflict of interest between industry and the military has certainly been acknowledged.[16] However, the story so far has been told exclusively from the standpoint of the activity of the military representative who did his job, whether well or occasionally badly, and who, if he (or she, but surely these were always men) interfered in or colluded with management, did so in the main harmlessly, acting in the interests of continuity of production and safeguarding the defence ministry's investment in the producer's goodwill.[17] Thus, in the absence of evidence to the contrary we might suppose that industry was largely passive in this fraught relationship. The present paper shows that, in reality, industrial managers also pursued a variety of strategies designed to counteract (counter-act: neutralise or hinder by *contrary action*) such attempts to constrain their scope for discretionary behaviour.

Bargaining with the military: first moves

The powers of the Soviet defence ministry over industry were always limited, whether as customer or as regulator. Soldiers were outsiders, and never wore a management cap. In June 1927 NKVM submitted a proposal to STO (the Council for Labour and Defence) with regard to new charters for defence industry firms. The proposal envisaged that NKVM would be given a direct voice (jointly with VSNKh, the ministry for state industry) in the appointment of defence enterprise management and chief accountants, in the approval of defence enterprise plans, reports, and accounts, and in the confirmation of proposals for investment, innovation, and other decisions affecting defence firms' capacity. This bid was wisely rejected. Apart from the incapacity of the defence ministry to manage industry, one may suppose that it would have been greatly to the detriment of the substantial civilian production carried on in defence plants. Instead, VSNKh was reminded of its obligation to 'involve

NKVM representatives in *the part of work* of trusts concerning fulfilment of military orders'.[18]

This was as far from our modern image of a 'command economy' as it was from the military concept of command and obedience. The soldiers came to industry neither as superiors to subordinates in a hierarchy, nor as adversaries seeking outright victory over the enemy on the battlefield, but as negotiators, forced to bargain with self-interested counterparts who were not always willing to cut a deal. We are accustomed to thinking of the defence producer as privileged in terms of pay, material supplies, and honorific status within the Soviet hierarchy. But there was a price to be paid for privilege, measured in terms of freedom lost to closer supervision by external agencies, which could make the value of engaging in defence production doubtful to the producer. Consequently, even the making of agreements to engage in production for the military was itself a stony path strewn with obstacles.

The producer's first gambit was to refuse defence orders. No doubt this was often just an opening move designed to reinforce industry's negotiating position when it became necessary to come to terms, but sometimes the result was that orders remained unplaced. According to administrative statute the distribution of military orders to industry was simply a matter for joint agreement of VSNKh (later, the various industrial ministries which succeeded it) with the central agencies of the Red Army chief of armament (for the artillery, armoured forces, air force, and so on).[19] In the 1930s, however, the annual process of coming to terms was so difficult that it acquired a militarised jargon of its own, becoming known within the Defence Commissariat as the 'contracts campaign' (*dogovornaia kampaniia*). Every year this campaign dragged on through January and February, with perennial delays ascribed to disputes over prices, the difficulty of finding willing suppliers of new defence products, and the desire of industry to secure a relatively homogenous assortment plan which would allow concentration on long runs of main products without a lot of attention to spare parts and auxiliary components, no matter how essential to the customer.

That the outcome could be a refusal of industry to tender for supply of military products desired by the Defence Commissariat is also attested.[20] The inducements required and offered to bring industrial agencies to the point of signing an agreement were not always lawful; a report on the slow progress of the 'contracts campaign' for 1933 lists both unauthorised price increases and illicit advance payments among the means employed by Defence Commissariat representatives to secure deals.[21]

Once defence orders were placed, and defence producers firmly identified, it is important to understand that the control of costs and quality presented industry with different issues. The defence ministry could be excluded by industry from regulation of costs and prices through *the delay and denial of information*. However, the frustration of defence ministry controls on quality was a different matter, which required an alternative course of action, a strategy of *regulatory capture*.

THE CONTROL OF COSTS: DELAY AND DENIAL

Cost-plus pricing

According to János Kornai, the official system of producer price determination under state socialism was only 'pseudo-administrative'. In theory the supraministerial committee for prices fixed every single price, but in practice it could only do so by relying on the information supplied by ministries and enterprises. Instead of the horizontal bargaining which characterises the market, there was vertical bargaining within the bureaucratic system. In reality, the prices fixed from above 'merely endorse the prices set by the producer'.[22]

Another feature of the shortage economy seems to be that firms' interest in the prices of inputs and products was not symmetrical. On the whole, firms were only weakly interested in the price of inputs; it was important to satisfy the imposed quota for output at all costs – certainly, much more important than to satisfy any auxiliary financial profit-and-loss targets – so a change in the relative price of inputs or an increase in marginal costs would have little effect on the firm's allocation decisions.[23] As for product prices, the prevalence of the soft budget constraint meant, of course, that firms had little or nothing to fear from a revenue shortfall in terms of financial viability, or to gain from a surplus, since profits were not retained and losses were made up from the state budget. To that extent it might appear that firms would also be indifferent to own-product prices. But this misconstrues the nature of the soft budget constraint. The budget constraint was *soft*, not *non-existent*, and it was not soft *ex ante*, only *ex post*. There was a *softening process* perennially at work, in which firms were active participants, described by Kornai in the following terms:

> There is advance bargaining: the goal of the firm, branch, directorate, or ministry is to make the pricing authority 'acknowledge' the costs in the price, however low the efficiency of production. There is subsequent bargaining also. A price rise is sought if extra costs have been incurred. In some other cases a disguised price rise is made. The quality assumed when the price was set is lowered, or a good material is substituted by an inferior material, or certain finishing processes are omitted.[24]

Of course, the strategy of bargaining for higher prices was only one possibility for the firm faced with an *ex ante* financial loss. The others involved bargaining for subsidies, tax breaks, soft bank loans, and so on. However, one might predict that the strategy of seeking a higher price was always preferable in the sense that it attracted less attention *ex post* from outside trouble-shooters and whistle-blowers. Certainly, firms were always motivated to prefer more gross revenue to less, especially when physical output was highly heterogeneous and the output quota was specified partly or wholly in rubles, as was especially likely to be the case in the manufacture of defence products.

The interwar documentation of the relationship between the Soviet defence ministry and the defence producers is pervaded by industry's 'drive towards the raising of prices even for established lines of output' and the military's cash-limited struggle to contain them.[25] An essential weapon in industry's drive for higher prices was the denial of early information about costs to defence agencies, sometimes on the basis that it was too early to tell or that insufficient time was available to provide the necessary information, sometimes (as will be shown) on the basis that it was too secret to reveal. In this context the authorities were sometimes forced to set prices provisionally; these prices were therefore not fixed, even *ex ante*, but flexible in the light of results. The result was in essence a cost-plus system in the sense that whatever costs were incurred were covered *ex post* by fixing prices correspondingly. The authorities fought against this practice, but were unable to eliminate it.

Where's the ballpark?

What the authorities clearly sought was a mechanism for fixing defence product prices *ex ante* in relation to planned costs, so as to create a financial incentive for firms to achieve and, if possible, exceed *planned cost reductions*. Firms frustrated this intention by failing to provide the information necessary to plan costs in advance. They were assisted in this by the exceptional complexity and heterogeneity of defence equipment and rapid change in its specification and assortment.

According to a memorandum of A.I. Rykov, writing as chief of the VSNKh committee for military orders in July 1925, temporary rules for fixing weapon prices were first established by STO in November 1923.[26] Prices for military equipment were to be determined '*orientirovochno*' (provisionally), on the basis of unit costs. *Orientirovochno* conveyed the sense of figures which need initially be no more accurate than being got into the right ballpark. More accurate 'firm' prices would be fixed subsequently so as to guarantee industry against losses on defence production. In the meantime the provisional prices ('1.2–2.3 times the prewar level') established on this basis were then used at the end of 1923 for Narkomfin's calculation of the 1923/24 budget.

At the end of 1924 STO ordered a transition from provisional prices to 'firm' prices of defence products fixed in the usual way, that is, including taxes, levies, and a 3 per cent profit markup on planned costs. However, despite the intention that the regime of provisional prices should be temporary, in practice they persisted – not just through 1924/25, as Rykov noted, but for decades. The reason given at the time was that industry dragged its heels in providing the necessary cost information to the extent that 'firm' prices could not be fixed for the 1924/25 budget year. However, for the following year the VSNKh prices committee succeeded in fixing prices for a significant range of items (personal kit, small arms and ammunition, artillery systems, aircraft and aeroengines, optical instruments, fuels, and repairs), 314 in number. These 1925/26 budget prices were substantially lower than the 1923/24 provisional prices, the reductions being forced through in the teeth of industry opposition and complaints about loss-making. Rykov asked in conclusion whether in principle weapon prices should be determined in the usual way or by some special procedure, and noted that this question was not yet resolved.

The principle was decided by a decree of STO dated January 1926. 'Firm' weapon prices were to be based on planned costs plus a 3 per cent markup for overheads. In practice, however, the defence producers continued to supply the necessary information late, so that prices simply validated *ex post* costs, and indeed included (in the view of the defence ministry) wildly excessive markups, to such an extent that in January 1930 the exasperated minister, Marshal K.E. Voroshilov, asked unsuccessfully for defence industry pricing to be referred to Rabkrin, the Workers' and Peasants' Inspectorate.[27]

In these clashes can be seen the main lines of future conflict. The military procurement authorities were keenly interested in low, fixed prices for defence products. But the administrative burden of determining fixed prices for defence products was multiplied by the growing complexity and heterogeneity of defence products, and the rapidity of military-technical innovation which meant that the profile of defence products was constantly changing. Despite being insured against lossmaking, defence producers were reluctant to supply information necessary for the planning of costs to the authorities at the time when contracts were made for the supply of products; delaying the moment for fixing 'firm' prices until after contracts had already been agreed, and products were being delivered, gave them the upper hand, since their actual costs had now to be covered.[28]

In a speech of June 1931, amidst the chaotic mobilisation of resources for the first five-year plan, faced with rising costs and pricing and growing shortages, Stalin condemned the collapse of Soviet 'business accounting' (*khozraschet*).[29] Among the many consequences of this speech, rendered urgent by its context, was renewed attention to costs and price formation in defence industry. 'The greatest difficulty over prices,' the Red Army's chief of armament M.N. Tukhachevskii wrote to V.M. Molotov in December 1931, 'is the withholding by industry of substantiated calculations and a drive towards the raising of prices even for established lines of output, in order to charge all defective work and production difficulties to the account of NKVM.'[30]

As has been seen, the monitoring of costs was a prime function of the military representatives in industry. How hard defence producers struggled to retain their autonomy in the face of scrutiny from within by their powerful customer is suggested by a report (dated September 1935) from the chief of the military and naval group of the party Control Commission to the NKVD chief N.I. Ezhov: grounds of official secrecy are being used to exclude *voenpredy* from the process of price determination, which allows many enterprises to behave 'extremely irresponsibly, self-interestedly, against the state (*kraine bezotvetsvenno, rvacheski, antigosudarstvenno*)' and engage in 'deception of the state' to exaggerate their unit costs. The report gives a single example, the 'substance' (an explosive or chemical agent) V-10, which cost not more than 70 000 rubles a ton, but sold to the defence ministry in 1935 at 123 900 rubles; but we are told that this reflected 'a widespread phenomenon'.[31]

That such practices were indeed widespread was confirmed by the finance minister G.F. Grin'ko in a memorandum to Sovnarkom on wholesale prices for defence products dated June 1937.[32] Grin'ko also pointed to the prevalence within the People's Commissariat for Defence Industry of exclusion of Defence Commissariat representatives from basic information about unit costs on grounds of secrecy; he demanded the rights of access to and verification of cost data for military representatives.[33]

This report incidentally confirms the asymmetry of defence producers' responsiveness to prices of inputs and products, for among the chief determinants of prime contractors' costs were the prices of intermediate products. Grin'ko remarked that, given the high degree of subcontracting of defence orders, securing military representatives' access to cost records of defence industry prime contractors was not enough. There was also a lack of cost-accounting between prime contractors and subcontractors when prices of intermediate products were agreed; it was not normal either for subcontractors (who wished to secure higher intermediate product prices) to offer evidence of their own costs, or for prime contractors (who were indifferent to their own costs) to request it.

Who pays for *brak*?

Grin'ko's report defined an interactive relationship between the share of defective output (*brak*) and the formation of defence product prices. The report notes first that contracts to supply the defence ministry were still frequently agreed on the basis of provisional prices, even for items already in serial production. The 'firm' prices finally paid were determined on the basis of actually incurred costs, and so bore little or no relation to the provisional prices adopted initially. Therefore the defence producer had no incentive to minimise *brak* and other losses; any costs not anticipated when provisional prices were proposed would be automatically compensated by an increase in the 'firm' price. As a result, Grin'ko argued, the defence budget bore costs which were strictly the responsibility of industry.[34]

Second, Grin'ko drew attention to the practice of enterprises' marketing of *brak* to sideline purchasers, sometimes to the military itself (for training purposes, for example). Given shortage conditions, the equilibrium price of defective products could easily be higher than the 'firm' price for products in good condition. As long as any costs involved in producing defective products were automatically covered out of the defence budget, while revenues obtained from sideline marketing of *brak* also contributed to firms' objectives, a clear incentive was established for defence producers to produce *brak*.

In short, a higher proportion of *brak* tended to result in inflation of the 'firm' prices eventually agreed, and downward pressure on 'firm' prices tended to raise further the proportion of *brak* produced.

These considerations were reflected in twin resolutions of the Sovnarkom Defence Committee in September 1937 concerning the prices of aviation products and ground forces' equipment.[35] With regard to the former, the authorities sought to limit the application of provisional prices (based on planned unit costs) to orders for new products not included in the *preiskurant* (price-list), and even in such cases to require the establishment of a corrected price (based on records of unit costs supplied by industry, naturally), once half the order had been fulfilled, so that producers would have some regard for unplanned costs at least for the second half of the contract. In the case of products produced in 1936, according to this decree, prices for 1937 should be carried over from 1936 'without budget subsidy' (i.e. of unplanned costs). As far as ground forces' equipment are concerned, the Defence Committee made similar provision to limit the application of provisional prices to new products; it also ordered the producers (the People's Commissariats of Defence Industry and Engineering) to supply cost information on request to NKO and its representatives, and allow military representatives to verify such data from primary documents. Other provisions required contracts for sideline sales of *brak* to specify prices below those prevailing for products in good condition, or, if to NKO for training purposes, at not more than 75 per cent of the regular price.

More than 20 years later, a Gosplan review of aviation product prices for 1958 reveals great continuity with prewar patterns.[36] The report calls for an end to the 'current practice of supply of military products based on realised costs and provisional wholesale prices' – the same practice which, as we saw above, the authorities first tried to abolish in 1925; it notes that cost-plus pricing in the aircraft industry was officially sanctioned during World War II, supposedly eliminated (again) in 1949, but was still much in evidence, associated with high rates of defective output and other losses. The report gives examples not just of cost-plus prices, but of many prices far in excess of unit costs revealed by investigation. The motivation associated with this behaviour by the author of the report was the drive to increase the enterprise's profit-related incentive fund (an additional factor supplementary to those considered above).

However, despite such revelations, excessive price-cost margins of '30–40 per cent, in place of the prescribed 3 per cent' in defence industry were still being remarked in August 1961 by A.F. Zasiad'ko on behalf of the Council of Ministers State Science-Economics Council; excessive prices were attributed to exaggerated cost forecasts which were never subsequently checked.[37]

Resistance to new technology

Lastly, the military could try to influence industry by controlling its choice of technologies. During the 1930s, the defence ministry struggled to enforce on industrial suppliers higher standards of adherence to specifications, uniformity of measures and materials across the range of producers of identical or related products, and interchangeability of parts, especially with respect to artillery, small arms, ammunition, tank armament, and optical equipment. This approach became known as production according to '"B" specifications' (*chertezhi lit. 'B'* – a *chertezh* is a technical draught or drawing; a *litera* is a letter of the alphabet, and includes the sense of a printer's typeface or font). Here defence officials were largely at one with their ministerial counterparts in industry, while resistance took the form of foot-dragging and non-compliance in industry from below.

Two main benefits were expected to flow from widespread adoption of 'B' specifications. One was a great reduction in unit costs; the other was much easier enforcement of product quality standards. These were to be gained at the expense of a single enemy – the 'backward, semi-artisanal method of work' in defence industry, rooted in the entrenched bargaining power and professional autonomy of the skilled, high-wage craftsman. In the official view, it was this system which gave rise to arbitrary variation in production technologies and product specifications; prevented realisation of the economies of scale and mass production; imposed great costs on the defence budget in higher prices, larger reserve stocks of incompatible spares, and repeated trials of products of unpredictable quality and reliability; fostered very high levels of rejected output (*brak*); and even (a sign of the times) 'created conditions in which sabotage by individuals and organisations could long pass unnoticed'.[38]

Deskilling of labour, and the removal of craft workers' discretion over the production process, were therefore significant means by which such defects could be eliminated. The conversion process, begun in 1933, was to have been completed in 1935, but the process lagged continually behind the targets established by agreement between industry and the defence ministry.[39] Such delays aroused protests from the military side, while industrial officials made their excuses. 'The engineering and technical cadres in defence factories', wrote Pavlunovskii to Voroshilov in November 1935,

> trained entirely in artisan methods of work, have for a long time not understood the necessity to work to a rigidly prescribed technology. A section of engineering and technical personnel, the craftsmen and skilled workers simply oppose the implementation of [this] conversion of production, and therefore it has been necessary to carry out the conversion of production in defence factories under great pressure.[40]

The strategy of delay worked for a while, but was eventually broken. The forces of resistance on the shop floor had no allies in high places; the officials in their own ministry were against them. By 1945 three waves – Stakhanovism, the great Ezhov purges, and World War II – had washed the Russian prerevolutionary craft tradition up on the beach of history. Whether all the anticipated gains were realised is another story.[41]

QUALITY ASSURANCE: REGULATORY CAPTURE

Self-regulation?

Industry could seek to deny information about costs to the defence ministry and its representatives, but could not similarly ward off the external evaluation of product quality.

Like their civilian counterparts, each defence producer was subject to control over product quality from above, through the department of technical control (OTK) subordinate to its own parent ministry. The OTK personnel reported upwards to the ministry, and were therefore nominally independent of the defence enterprise. However, they were maintained at the expense of the enterprise, and were rewarded from enterprise wage and incentive funds. Moreover, the interests of the ministry and enterprise in fulfilment of quantitative targets ran on largely parallel lines. Therefore, OTK inspectors were generally sympathetic to the problems of the enterprise and would collude with factory managers or submit to pressure from them. In civilian industry, for example, it is reported that inspectors commonly relaxed quality standards towards the end of the month when success indicators were about to be reported, or passed defective products provisionally, on the basis that deficiencies would be made good subsequently.[42]

Useful illumination of the working of the OTK system is derived from a prewar attempt to reform it. In February 1938 M.M. Kaganovich (then Commissar for the Defence Industry) proposed to Molotov that the defence-industry OTK apparatus should be devolved from the ministerial level to the level of the enterprise. His argument was that the traditional system in which the OTK reported to the ministry shared responsibility for product quality between the ministry and the enterprise, providing an escape route for enterprise management in the case of product defects. If the OTK reported to the enterprise director, then it would at least be clear who was at fault in such cases.[43]

The proposal was supported in principle by the Defence Commissariat, as well as by the majority of its purchasing departments.[44] But two dissenting voices were raised which seem more significant, in retrospect, than the supporters. Both argued for strengthening, not devolution of the existing system. One voice belonged to the chief of the Red Army engineering administration, who argued that quality control in the engineering industry, where OTK was already organised at the factory level, was just as deficient as in defence industry. In engineering factories, managers would simply override OTK personnel in the interests of quantitative plan fulfilment; where OTK was independent of the enterprise, this was less likely to happen. Another dissenter was the chief of the vehicle and tank-armour administration, who blamed the 'huge' *brak* in defence industry partly on the enterprise's drive for quantitative plan fulfilment, partly on the low status of OTK personnel, typically lower paid and less qualified than the workers over whom they exercised control.[45]

In reality, it seems unlikely that any tinkering with the OTK system could have significantly affected outcomes. Kaganovich was right that enterprise managers would always seek to disperse the blame for negative results onto higher authority, which would collude with them to conceal and condone defective work. But this was an inherent feature of the system under which higher authority fixed output quotas and input allocations for lower levels, and depended little if at all upon the administrative level at which quality assurance was organised. Much more important than its level was its positioning with respect to the division between the supplier and the customer. For the defence supplier, control by the military user was much more to be feared than the gentler parental control of the supply ministry.

Voenpriemka – the struggle for influence

Through *voenpriemka*, the military were able to enforce higher standards of quality and cost-effectiveness than those which characterised civilian industry products, while defence industry's privileged claim to first pick of high-grade personnel and materials was a necessary condition of its differential success in quality. It has been suggested that the result was to raise the average level of quality of defence products above that of products in civilian use, so that the gap between Soviet and world standards of product quality was smaller in the defence industry than in other areas. Dual-purpose products were subjected to more rigorous acceptance criteria by the military than by civilian agencies.[46] Emigrant testimony 'generally agree[s] that the voyenpredy were competent engineers, who engaged in more than just monitoring'.[47] By the postwar years Soviet military products had 'won respect throughout the world. Soviet tanks, aircraft, and small-arms weaponry are rugged, well-constructed, and capable of doing the task assigned'.[48]

This achievement was won at high cost. It relied on 'brute force', in the words of CIA Director Admiral Stansfield Turner – a combination of 'high levels of production and equally high rejection rates'.[49] This was not how it was supposed to be. According to the defence industry leader V.S. Emel'ianov 'one frequently heard at that time that to solve the problem of quality required the use of all methods: persuasion, incentives, and compulsion'.[50] In practice, compulsion dominated.

None the less, the defence industry was often cited by Brezhnevite commentators as a model for raising the quality of civilian products and management systems.[51] Defence industry schemes for raising acceptance rates and aiming for zero defects were much touted in the 1960s and 1970s, but it is not clear how widely employed they became even in defence industry, and they certainly had little impact in the outside world of civilian producers.[52] In fact these were not the first attempts to exploit defence industry experience in the civilian sphere. A precedent was Stalin's appointment of Emel'ianov, then a leader of the tank industry, as deputy chief of a new State Committee on Standards in July 1940.[53] Much later, the system of *voenpriemka* also became a model for raising the quality of civilian products under Chernenko, while the system of *gospriemka* applied to civilian products under Gorbachev was not only based on *voenpriemka* but headed by a former leader of the aircraft industry.[54]

In practice, however, even in the defence industry quality was never automatically assured. This was because enterprises always had two ways of meeting high-quality targets. One was to allocate resources to raising product quality, as high-level policymakers intended. The other was to allocate resources to lowering the target by influencing the *voenpriemka* personnel to accept reduced product quality. Sometimes the latter was less costly to the firm.

In the years of the first five-year plan the defence industry suffered from very high levels of rejected output – for example, more than 50 per cent for shells and rifle cartridges in 1931.[55] At this time it became common for defence enterprises to establish incentive funds for military representatives engaged in quality assurance and *voenpriemka*, which divided their loyalties. In August 1933 this became the subject of a report by G.G. Iagoda, then deputy chief of OGPU. In such cases the indicator forming the incentive payment was normally the quantity of output passed or accepted, 'thanks to which, naturally, attention to its quality is weakened'.[56] This report was followed a year later (on 1 September 1934) by a new Statute on quality assurance in defence industry, which, in addition to restating existing arrangements, added: 'the control and acceptance apparatus of NKVM is an organ of NKVM and the entire personal staff of this apparatus is maintained at the expense of NKVM and *does not benefit from any kind of rewards from the organs of industry*'.[57]

This simple prohibition was evidently, however, not sufficiently specific. If defence managers were not allowed to give bonuses to *voenpredy*, they could still buy military representatives goodwill with services in kind, and by sending glowing testimonials on their behalf to the defence ministry. In April 1938 the infuriated Voroshilov had to issue an order prohibiting his representatives from utilising 'absolutely any [*kakimi by to ni bylo*] *personal services* (apartment, furniture, motor vehicle, etc.)' supplied by enterprises where they were engaged in acceptance of output, as well as any compensation or reward, including *compensation for carrying out trials of factory products*; nor would he tolerate any good-hearted requests from factory managers for the defence ministry itself to reward its own representatives.[58]

Voroshilov ended by demanding a new statute on the role of the military representative. The 'Statute on the military representatives of NKO in industry' which emerged on 15 July 1939 by decree of the Defence Committee of Sovnarkom stated correspondingly that military representatives were maintained at the expense of NKO and were to receive neither payment in cash or kind, nor any kind of favours, from the defence industry.[59]

The tendency to illicit collusion among agents is a familiar phenomenon when they are forced into continual negotiation of the conflicting interests of their principals. This collusion was not confined to the 1930s. From postwar interview data Arthur J. Alexander identified cases where military representatives covered up the supply of defective tank turrets, and welded submarine structures, as well as lesser items.[60] In all the cases reported, however, the collusion was detected and the military representatives were punished with prison sentences. We are left to speculate whether these cases were exceptional or were just the tip of an unsurveyed iceberg.

CONCLUSION

This paper shows that the military representative was the focus of a protracted conflict of interest between the Soviet defence industry and the defence ministry. The defence ministry wanted cheap, high-quality weapons. Industry was usually willing to supply high-quality weapons, but not reliably or cheaply. Consequently the defence ministry was drawn into on-site monitoring of the production process and product quality, and became the most powerful customer in the Soviet economy. However, industrial managers fought to defend their autonomy against this encroachment. They employed several stratagems in doing so. One was to refuse defence orders. Having been drawn into defence production, they sought to weaken the capability of the defence ministry to verify costs by withholding information from the ministry and its military representatives, sometimes on grounds of its unavailability, sometimes on grounds of secrecy and need-to-know. In matters of quality, where the military representative could not be excluded he could sometimes be bought, and industrial enterprises also pursued a strategy of regulatory capture.

Voenpriemka did not set up an agreed or objective standard of quality, but established a field of conflict and negotiation – a three-cornered game between the defence ministry, the defence ministry's agent (the military representative), and the defence contractor, in which the rules themselves were not fully specified *ex ante*, and part of the game was to influence the way in which the rules evolved. The evidence suggests that this system worked, but not well. The system bought good-quality weapons for the Soviet armed forces, but failed to control costs and prices. It regulated the producers by coercive means, but was vulnerable to producer-regulator collusion. When it worked, it relied on high output and high rejection rates.

The system of *voenpriemka* was designed for a high-priority sector in a shortage economy, not for the whole economy. It depended for its limited success on the privileged access to material supply and skilled personnel enjoyed by a limited circle of defence producers. This could not work for all producers simultaneously. Under the circumstances it is not surprising that *gospriemka*, Gorbachev's attempt to generalise *voenpriemka* to the civilian economy, was ineffective.

NOTES

1 See the appendix tables to Harrison and Davies (1997).

2 See further Davies (1994), 1–23.

3 From 1936 onwards most Soviet industrial construction was carried out by specialised construction agencies, and a similar set of institutions was established in to monitor their costs and results (for description see Davies (1958), 258–61). The progress of fulfilment of construction contracts and authorisation of payment for work done was governed in principle by a series of 'deeds of acquisition' (*akty priemki*) issued by the purchasing organisation or investor, and validated by the bank officials responsible for construction finance. In practice the investor and contractor tended to collude in the concealment of contract violations, inflation of costs, and bidding for additional resources. The bank officials were helpless because their resources permitted them only to audit the paperwork, not to carry out on-site inspections.

4 Almquist (1990), 57.

5 See for examples Agursky (1976), Agursky and Adomeit (1978), Alexander (1978), and Almquist (1990), 57–8.

6 SVE (1976), vol. 2, 271–2 ('Voennyi predstavitel' ').

7 Among the significant statutes and decrees were the following 'Statute on military representatives in factories of military and civilian industry' (Order of Revvoensovet, 11 February 1930); 'Statute on the obligations of enterprise directorates concerning the quality of delivered products and concerning the control and acceptance apparatus of the People's Commissariat of Heavy Industry and the People's Commissariat of Defence in factories of industry fulfilling defence orders' (Order of NKO and the people's commissariat of heavy industry no. 035/143 of 1 September 1934); 'Statute on the obligations of directors and the acceptance and defects apparatus (*priemno-brakovochnyi apparat*) of enterprises of the system of light industry and military representatives of the USSR people's commissariat of defence concerning fulfilment of orders for objects of transport and kit supply of the Red Army' (Order of NKO and the People's Commissariat of Light Industry no. 105/6 of 1937); 'Statute concerning military representatives of the People's Commissariat of Defence Industry' (Decree No. 204 of the Defence Committee of Sovnarkom, 15 July 1939).

8 SVE (1976), vol. 2, 271–2 ('Voennyi predstavitel' '), where reference is made to a 'Statute on the technical acceptance of objects of military and naval supply and on the rights of the chief purchasing administrations (*glavnykh dovol'stvuyushchikh upravlenii*) concerning control over the output of military products' (decree of the Revolutionary Military Council of the Republic, October 1920).

9 RGVA, 7/11/181, 237–9 ('Concerning introduction of the position of military assistants of factory managers in factories of the defence industry administration of VSNKh').

10 RGVA, 7/11/181, 236. On the meaning of 'cadre' defence industry see Chapter 1.

11 E.g. RGVA, 33776/1/309, 65–70 ('Basic statutes on mutual relations between the organs of VSNKh and organs of the People's Commissariat of Military and Naval Affairs concerning fulfilment of military orders for the Red Army, Navy, OGPU forces, and Escort Protection', 21 February 1927; clauses 20 and 21 dealt with the special role of product acceptance workers (*priemshchiki*) of NKVM purchasing agencies).

12 RGVA, 7/10/1434, 63 (emphasis added).

13 RGVA, 33776/1/339, 54–9.

14 RGAE, 7/1/384, 146. The discrepancy between the sum of the individual figures and the total shown in the table is as in the original.

15 Simonov (1996), 108.

16 Almquist (1990), 126–31.

17 For examples, see Holloway (1982a), 325n: 'given what we know of Soviet behaviour in organisations, it is not impossible that the enterprise director and the military representative will form a 'family group' in which the military man will use whatever influence he has to ease supply shortages, etc. so that production proceeds according to plan'; Alexander (1978), 59n: 'a decline in military production below planned output goals, followed by a surge the following month, may be juggled in the account books by the military representative to show that the plan was met in both months. In this way, the plant retains its bonuses for achieving the plan in both months, and the customer gets its output while maintaining good relations with local management.' The possibility of such collusion is rejected, however, by Agursky and Adomeit (1978), 23.

18 GARF, 8418/1/75, 10 (emphasis added). The ministerial subordination of defence industry changed several times during the period which concerns us. The underlying process was one of progressive ministerial fragmentation which affected all production branches, not only the defence industry. At first defence

industry fell under the defence-industry administration of VSNKh (the supreme council of the national economy, created on 2 December 1917), which administered all public-sector industry. VSNKh was broken up on 5 January 1932 into three people's commissariats for heavy industry (*Narkomtiazhprom* – including the defence industry), light industry, and the timber industry respectively. On 12 December 1936 the Heavy Industry Commissariat was itself subdivided, and an independent People's Commissariat of the Defence Industry (*Narkomoboronprom*) was created, but three years later, on 11 January 1939, it was the turn of Narkomoboronprom to be broken up into four distinct commissariats (for the aircraft industry, armament, ammunition, and shipbuilding). The wartime and postwar years saw further subdivisions and reorganisations and the creation of several entirely new production branch ministries responsible for new military industries such as atomic weaponry, rocketry, and radioelectronics, but these involve a degree of complexity and detail beyond our present needs.

19 RGVA, 7/10/1434, 20 ('Statute on the participation of the organs of the People's Commissariat for Military and Naval Affairs in the work of industry on compilation of the mobilisation plan of industry, on defence construction in industry, and in work on the fulfilment of peacetime orders of the People's Commissariat for Military and Naval Affairs', 1 February 1930).

20 For items omitted from the naval procurement plan for 1935, 'on one side in view of the shortage of means, on the other side *because of the refusal of industry*', see RGVA, 4/14/1315, 139 (emphasis added).

21 RGVA, 4/14/880, 5, 13.

22 Kornai (1992), 149–50.

23 Kornai (1992), 146.

24 Kornai (1992), 142.

25 The quotation is from GARF, 8418/6/3, 2–3 (M.N. Tukhachevskii to V.M. Molotov, December 1931; this passage is cited more fully below).

26 GARF, 8418/16/1, 283–95.

27 GARF, 8418/4/17, 1, 6–10. The costs-plus-3-per-cent regime, further sanctified in 1931, was maintained well into the postwar period (e.g. RGAE, 7/1/384, 139).

28 The use of provisional, not 'firm' prices was another objectionable feature of the agreements with industry signed by NKVM negotiators in the 'contracts campaign' of the winter of 1932–3, forced upon them by industry's strategy of delay in providing information and coming to terms (RGVA, 4/14/880, 5, 13).

29 Stalin (1940), 384 ('New conditions – new tasks', 23 June 1931).

30 GARF, 8418/6/3, 2–3.

31 RGAE, 7733/36/12, 137.

32 RGAE, 7733/36/40, 84–6.

33 As a result the mistaken idea was fostered that military representatives bore responsibility only for quality, not for cost. Thus Mikhail Agursky had the impression that the job of the *voenpred* was 'to check only the quality of the output, not the cost and efficiency with which this output is produced' (Agursky and Adomeit (1978), 73).

34 On 'who pays for *brak*', see also GARF, 8418/6/3, 2–3.

35 RGVA, 51/2/441, 62–7.

36 RGAE, 4372/3/4, 136–40.

37 RGAE, 7/1/384, 139.

38 RGVA, 4/14/1315, 198–9 (memorandum of Pavlunovskii to Voroshilov, November 1935).

39 RGVA, 4/14/1298, 140–52.

40 RGVA, 4/14/1315, 199.

41 According to Agursky and Adomeit (1978), 23, in the postwar period the standardisation of parts in defence production led sometimes to loss of interchangeability with civilian products. Thus, 'the chief designers of military design bureaux often do not adhere to 'state standards' and demand the use of parts which may differ from the normal ones. It may then happen that different systems of standards are operative at the same plant. Thus, for example, at the Moscow aircraft factory *Znamia truda* (Banner of Labour), two standards were used simultaneously, one of them as required by the Ilyushin Design Bureau. Nothing of that sort can be imagined in civilian industry where a product will immediately be rejected by a plant if it provides for nonstandard parts where standard ones can be used.'

42 Agursky and Adomeit (1978), 23–4.

43 RGVA, 4/14/1980, 36–47.

44 RGVA, 4/14/1980, 50, 61, 67–9.

45 RGVA, 4/14/1980, 51, 59–60.

46 According to Agursky and Adomeit (1978), 27, 'It is not at all rare that plants produce three different categories of product, with different assembly lines and different work brigades, earning different levels of pay but producing basically the same or similar items. The first, with the highest quality specifications and pay levels, is the military category; the second category of production is destined for export; the third and last category of product is for "common" domestic use.' See also Holloway (1982a), 351.

47 Almquist (1990), 58.

48 Scott and Scott (1979), 297–8.

49 Joint Economic Committee (1977), 40. On high rejection rates see also Agursky and Adomeit (1978), 25; Holloway (1982a), 325; Weickhardt (1986), 196. From the 1950s and 1960s Almquist (1990), 56, reported anecdotal evidence of rejection rates at individual defence factories ranging from 50 to 100 per cent of annual output.

50 Emel'ianov (1974), 545.

51 Weickhardt (1986), 197.

52 Campbell (1972), 590–6; Almquist (1990), 54–6. According to Agursky and Adomeit (1978), 54–5, however, new management systems in Soviet civilian industry were inspired by western civilian, not Soviet defence-industry precedents.

53 Emel'ianov (1974), 541.

54 Weickhardt (1986), 206–9; Almquist (1990), 56.

55 GARF, 8418/8/2, 37–48.

56 GARF, 8418/8/175, 34.

57 GARF, 8418/8/175, 5–9 (emphasis added).

58 RGVA, 4/14/2196, 1–2 (emphasis added).

59 RGVA, 4/14/2196, 24–6.

60 Alexander (1978), 19, 59n.

13 The security organs and the defence-industry complex

Boris Starkov

INTRODUCTION

In the history of the formation of the Soviet state a special place belonged to the security organs – in successive periods, the Cheka, OGPU, NKVD, and MVD.[1] These were sometimes also called the 'administrative-punitive' organs, because of their powers to inflict extra-judicial penalties on those whom they regarded with disfavour. In part this was the legacy of the Imperial Russian state, where the Ministry of Internal Affairs was at the heart of the executive power. However to a large extent it was also the consequence of economic and political backwardness. The death of millions of people in World War I and the Civil War was an irreplaceable loss, as was the forced emigration of tens of thousands from the scientific and technical intelligentsia and the worlds of culture and education. A new society had to be created on a material, technical, and cultural base which was much more limited than that which had existed before the revolution, and in very poor living conditions. Thus both internal and external factors led objectively to a strengthening of the security organs. This was particularly reflected in the history of the formation and functioning of the Russian defence-industry complex.

Relations between the security organs and the defence industry took shape in a way which was far from simple. In the nature of things the defence industry was always the object of heightened interest on the part of both domestic and foreign security services, since its work was subject to military and state secrecy. Its post-revolutionary restoration began in the years of NEP at the hands of talented military engineers, inventors, and scientists. The latter were an outstanding galaxy of Russian patriots representing the old prerevolutionary intelligentsia. It was these who suffered the first repressive blow from the punitive apparatus. An opportunistic campaign against sabotage, begun at the end of the 1920s, continued into the succeeding years. A campaign of 'specialist-baiting' (*spetseedstvo*) in 1928 had set about destroying the internal oppositionist attitude of the intelligentsia through terror and intimidation. But already in the 1930s a sharp deficit of trained cadres had begun to be felt. This was the consequence of the 'Great Terror', which eventually made it necessary to create special scientific research institutes and design bureaux for developing new kinds of armaments directly within the NKVD system. Finally in the postwar period the latest technology and entire new branches of the defence complex were established under the direct leadership of the MVD and its all-powerful leader, L.P. Beriia. This chapter will attempt to examine certain episodes in the developing relationship between the security organs and the defence-industry complex.

At the outset it should be noted that this chapter does not provide a complete and exhaustive study of all aspects of the relationship between the defence-industry complex and the NKVD-MVD. There are still many unsolved problems and topics which are closed to researchers. The lack of sources continues to be felt; access to these is still to a significant degree limited. Under the roof of the NKVD-MVD-KGB archives lies vast information of exceptional interest and importance which would enable the history of Russian society in the Soviet period to be substantially reinterpreted. The uncovering of new documentation in the history of military technology and equipment is also possible. This must be the concern of future historians.

This article is based on documentary materials of the ministerial and state archives of the Russian Federation. Among them a special place is occupied by the documentation of investigation and rehabilitation of defence industry personnel, of the NKVD-MVD secretariat, and of changes in the structures of the defence-industry complex and the NKVD-MVD. The majority of these are used here for the first time in a scholarly publication.

PURGING SABOTAGE

On 17 July 1929 the leadership of OGPU drew up its indictment in the case of the 'counter-revolutionary sabotage organisation in the defence industry of the USSR'. In this it was asserted that OGPU had discovered a counter-revolutionary organisation, at the centre of which were the generals and colonels of the Tsarist army who had graduated from the Mikhailov Artillery Academy. 'This counter-revolutionary organisation embraced the whole of the defence industry, beginning with the highest organs of the Central Administration of Powder and Artillery Factories and the Chief Defence-Industry Administration and finishing with almost all factories in various regions of the USSR.'[2]

The head of this organisation was said to be the former general and talented military engineer V.S. Mikhailov. A scientist and an inventor, in 1917–18 he was a member of the collegium of the chief artillery administration. In 1918 he volunteered for service in the Red Army and from then on until his arrest he was the head of the chief defence-industry administration. Together with him 78 people who were arrested were also accused of participating in this counter-revolutionary organisation. Some of those arrested were of aristocratic descent as well as being generals and officers of the former Tsarist army.

G.G. Iagoda, deputy head of OGPU, was in direct charge of this case. Leading the group of investigators was the head of the OGPU economic administration, G.E. Prokof'ev. But study of the documents and materials of the investigation reveals no authenticated facts proving, for example, disruption of the rhythm of work in defence industry, damage to buildings, or degradation of the quality of products, military equipment, or instruments. The whole indictment was based partly on contradictory confessions by those arrested and partly on 'facts' established by the OGPU's own investigation of the *Genshtabisty* (staff officers) conducted from 1924. Some 350 military specialists had gone through this investigation.[3] The only verified fact was that among the military specialists were some who were dissatisfied with the new regime's attitude to them and who attempted to demonstrate their irreplaceability by all means possible. 'The old specialists will be made redundant, so it is necessary to work in such a way that they will be needed for a long time' – such was A.Iu. Klippel's description of his 'subversive' activity.[4] Another of the accused, former general M.N. Orlov, confessed the following:

> The engineers engaged in sabotage in the defence industry did not create the usual type of counter-revolutionary organisation. The task assigned to them in 1921 was to pursue a line of slowing defence industry down. Later on, they were to be guided in all their actions by the idea of sabotage. In this way the organization lived, as it were, in the minds of its members, which made it completely impossible to detect the existence of the organisation.[5]

E.I. Shpital'skii, a professor at Moscow University, confessed to intending to use force in fighting the Bolsheviks and to use technical means for this. In his confession he mentioned the idea of poisoning the air in the Bolshoi Theatre, where congresses of the Communist Party generally took place.

> I conceived then the idea of a device which would produce an emission of gases from hidden balloons without anyone being involved and at given times with the aid of such devices conveniently and safely to carry out terrorist acts.[6]

Similar confessions were given by other people investigated. There was no court examination in this case. It was replaced by a non-judicial organ of the OGPU collegium. Some of those arrested were executed, while others were sentenced to long periods of imprisonment. The falsehood of the judgments was obvious, and in the mid-1950s some of those sentenced were rehabilitated. Among the latter were Klippel, director of the Kiev Arsenal plant, and professors A.S. Zybin of the Gor'kii Polytechnical Institute and V.F. Popov of the Leningrad Shipbuilding Institute.

In November–December 1929 the work of the artillery administration was investigated by organs of the Workers' and Peasants' Inspectorate. It was found unsatisfactory. The results of the investigation were reported to Stalin. On 25 December 1929 he wrote to Molotov:

> On the military case, in a few days we will pass a Politbureau decision in connection with the measures already taken by Narkomvoen [the People's Commissariat for Military and Naval Affairs] on eliminating the sabotage. We think that it would not be appropriate to make a noise about this case. The decision will be a secret one.[7]

On 15 January 1930 the Politbureau considered the question of the Artillery Administration and ordered Revvoensovet 'to take immediate measures for a fundamental improvement in the technical arming and rearming of the army'.[8]

The case of the 'counter-revolutionary sabotage organisation in the defence industry of the USSR' was the first in a series of repressions of the most skilled specialists of the old school employed in defence industry. It marked the beginning of a cycle of 'sabotage' and repression which continued up until the death of Stalin.[9]

THE RISE AND FALL OF OSTEKHBIURO

In the years of the 'Great Terror' repression took on a exceptional scale, and the flower of Russian engineering and inventive genius was repressed on charges of sabotage and spying for capitalist states. This was vividly manifested in the affair of Ostekhbiuro, the 'Special Technical Bureau for special-purpose military inventions', devoted to the development of new types of armament for the navy.

The Ostekhbiuro was created in Petrograd after the end of the Civil War on the initiative of a group of scientists. By resolutions of the Council of Labour and Defence of 13 and 18 July 1921, it was decided to create a new structure for the development of naval weapons. On 9 August of that year Lenin signed order O-A10197, according to which the talented inventor V.I. Bekauri was put in charge of the organisation of work on inventions of a secret military character. This gave him wide powers; all organisations and their heads were directed to 'render V.I. Bekauri every assistance in carrying out the task with which he is charged'.[10]

Initially Ostekhbiuro was composed of six sections: 'special' (with a workshop attached to it), aviation, submarine, explosives, electrotechnical, and experimental. At the head of all sections were well-known scientists and inventors. Thus at the head of the special section was a leading specialist in the field of mines and torpedoes, captain in the Russian fleet and teacher in the Naval Academy B.L. Pshenetskii. The aviation section was headed by V.P. Naidenov, professor at the Nikolaev Engineering Academy. The submarine department was headed by M.N. Beklimishev, co-designer and commander of the first Russian submarine. The explosives section was headed by a pupil of Mendeleev, S.P. Vukolov. At the head of the electro-technical section was V.F. Mitkevich, professor at the Polytechnical Institute. And the head of the experimental research section was K.P. Boklevskii, head of the shipbuilding faculty of the Polytechnical Institute.[11]

The structure of Ostekhbiuro was continually changing and developing. Thus already in 1922 the explosives section and part of the submarine section were separated from it. In March 1922 an independent radio-wave section was separated from the electrotechnical section, to be headed by V.F. Mitkevich. In June 1923 the aviation section was merged with the experimental research section to form an aviation research section headed by K.P. Boklevskii; in 1926 there were 16 people in this section. Altogether there were 60 specialists in the Ostekhbiuro alone, compared with a total of 860 personnel working in the scientific and technical department of VSNKh on the defence industry at that same time.

The work of the Ostekhbiuro employees came under OGPU supervision from the very beginning. The latter kept a vigilant watch on the observance of state and military secrecy, guaranteed security in the carrying out of research and tests, and gave special attention to the political attitudes of the heads of sections and their employees. By the beginning of the 1930s seven undercover employees of the secret political section of the Leningrad OGPU were reporting on the work of Ostekhbiuro. Overall supervision of the activity of Ostekhbiuro was provided by the head of the naval section of the special department of OGPU in Leningrad, M.P. Medvedev.

Bekauri continually supplied information about the activity of Ostekhbiuro to the top political leadership of the country and to Stalin personally. His letters to Stalin about developing new forms of armaments and the progress of work on new designs are preserved in the archives. The documents show that Stalin read these letters very carefully, and his notes in the margins and his underlinings of the text show his considerable interest in the development of the latest military technology. Annual reports on the work carried out were regularly heard at meetings of the Sovnarkom government commission, where the programme of works for the succeeding period were approved. The timetable of work was reviewed at meetings with the deputy chief of Revvoensovet, I.S. Unshlikht.

In summer 1930 a Sovnarkom resolution transferred Ostekhbiuro to the jurisdiction of NKVM. On 28 August 1930 the People's Commissar for Military and Naval Affairs signed a regulation which defined Ostekhbiuro as a scientific-experimental-invention establishment within NKVM, directly subordinated to the People's Commissar himself. It was to develop and implement 'inventions and new designs of a military character in the fields of aviation, tele-mechanics, wireless communications, and naval armaments, as well as any special task given by the NKVM'. The statute on Ostekhbiuro was signed by the chief of the Red Army staff, B.M. Shaposhnikov, and Bekauri was appointed head of Ostekhbiuro.[12]

In the mid-1930s Ostekhbiuro had become a largescale enterprise with a wide range of activities and with 3 000 employees. In official documents, for reasons of secrecy, it was called Design Bureau no. 5 (KB-5). In March 1936, 68 employees of Ostekhbiuro were awared state honours 'for arming the Red Army with new models of military technology'.[13] But clouds were already gathering over those working, apparently irreproachably, in this organisation. On 29 December 1936, V.I. Romanovskii, head of the military supervision group of the Commission of Soviet Control, sent the chairman of the commission, N.K. Antipov, a report in which the work of Ostekhbiuro was assessed as unsatisfactory. This the author of the report saw as 'a consequence of lack of organisation of the work of scientists, engineers and designers'. In the report it was said that 'the solution of the specific technical tasks assigned by the People's Commissariat for Defence is taking place intolerably slowly . . . the personnel of Ostekhbiuro, despite being checked in the past by the NKVD, none the less contained a number of dubious people'. At the beginning of January 1937 this report was sent to the NKVD. An accompanying note spoke of the necessity for a thorough check on the activity of Ostekhbiuro with regard to sabotage.

On 28 January 1937 K.I. Sokol'skii, head of a department at the Mine and Torpedo Institute, sent a letter to the Committee of Party Control about faults in the development of mines. In essence this was a political denunciation, for all the failings came down to machinations by enemies of the people, above all by those in charge of Ostekhbiuro. The Committee of Party Control at that time was headed by N.I. Ezhov, who was also the People's Commissar for Internal Affairs. On his personal order, investigation of counter-revolutionary and sabotage activity in Ostekhbiuro was handled specially by three sectors of the NKVD in co-ordination: its counter-intelligence department, its 'special' department, and the economic administration of its chief administration for state security. This was accompanied by an order to check the work of the Ostekhbiuro party organisation.[14]

On 14 February 1937 the bureau of the Smol'nyi party district committee of Leningrad devoted a special discussion to 'the situation in the Ostekhbiuro party organisation'. The leadership of the party organisation was accused of diminishing political vigilance, being cut off from the masses, and bureaucratic methods of leadership. The papers of the bureau meeting show that the reason for such a severe evaluation, and then for so severe a decision, was the friendly relations of a number of the Ostekhbiuro personnel with the family of A.L. Kamenev, who had worked in Ostekhbiuro until 1933. He was the son of the prominent party figure L.B. Kamenev executed in 1936 as a leader of the 'Trotskyist-Zinov'evist United Centre', and this relationship had served as a reason for the son's arrest in 1935. L.M. Kaganovich personally gave the order for the arrest of the younger Kamenev (a fact which was later to receive specific mention at the June 1957 plenum of the party Central Committee, when Kaganovich and other old-time Stalinists were denounced and expelled).

In spring 1937 the next reorganisation of Ostekhbiuro began. On 11 April it was transferred from NKO (the People's Commissariat of Defence, the successor to NKVM) to Narkomoboronprom (the People's Commissariat of Defence Industry). On 20 July 1937 it was renamed the 'special technical administration' of Narkomoboronprom and its headquarters were moved from Leningrad to Moscow. Bekauri remained its head, but M.P. Medvedev was left in charge of its Leningrad branch. This reorganisation was carried out without any forethought. It destroyed established links and relations between the various branches, clients, and intermediaries with which Ostekhbiuro dealt. In addition, moving a large group of scientists, designers, and engineers from Leningrad to Moscow was practically impossible from a purely technical point of view because of the complicated problems of living conditions. In practice the work of this large group was disrupted. The transfer from NKO to Narkomoboronprom itself automatically lowered the status of Ostekhbiuro.

On 8 September 1937 Bekauri was arrested and was transferred to Moscow on the same day. There began the elimination not just of cadres, but of the very structure of Ostekhbiuro. On that day People's Commissar for the Defence Industry M.L. Rukhimovich signed an order to divide Ostekhbiuro up into three independent institutes, NII-20, NII-22 and NII-36; however, their programme of work was not reviewed, and no thought was given to how the division should be carried out. On 19 September the final reorganisation of the NKOP 'special technical administration' took place: the Krizo plant was subordinated to the Voroshilov plant, the Leporso radio station was given in charge of the director of NII-20, and the Ostekhbiuro base at the Komendantskii airfield was placed under NII-22.[15]

While the structure of Ostekhbiuro was being dismantled, the interrogation of Bekauri and his colleagues took place at the Lubianka. He was arrested on the basis of a warrant signed by M.P. Frinovskii and a certificate from the NKVD dated 2 August 1937. In the latter it was stated:

> Bekauri is a participant in a counter-revolutionary organisation. On the orders of enemies of the people [Marshal M.N.] Tukhachevskii, [army commander M.N.] Orlov, and [naval commander I.M.] Ludri he carried out sabotage in the field of mine-sweeping and torpedo equipment. On this basis Bekauri is subject to immediate arrest.[16]

On the personal order of third-grade Commissar of State Security N.G. Zhurid-Nikolaev, head of the fifth (special) department of the NKVD chief administration for state security, Bekauri was transferred to Moscow and placed in the Lefortovo prison. In addition his notes and books which had been seized during a search of his flat were also sent to Moscow. Immediately after his arrest intensive interrogations began. No records of the interrogations were kept, but in the file there are two statements addressed to People's Commissar for Internal Affairs, N.I. Ezhov, dated 11 September 1937, which confirm that the interrogations began immediately after the arrest. In the first, Bekauri wrote

> After a long and stubborn silence I have decided to tell the investigation everything about my underground activity, and also about my spying for German intelligence.
>
> 1. At the time of my visit to Berlin in 1932 I made contact with German intelligence through the lawyer E.G. Prinz (a patent agent). Through him I handed over to German intelligence a number of inventions.
> 2. From 1934 I participated in an anti-Soviet plot . . . [17]

The second statement repeated the first almost word for word. The only difference is that Bekauri claimed his recruitment as a German spy was instigated by Tukhachevskii and A.S. Enukidze. However, neither of these statements was signed by Bekauri, only witnessed by Zhurid-Nikolaev. This gives every reason to suppose that they were dictated by the investigators after physical and moral pressure had been applied.

Three records of Bekauri's interrogations have been preserved; these dealt with recruitment to and co-operation with German intelligence. During the first two interrogations he told how he had transmitted evidence of the work of Ostekhbiuro through N.A. Efimov, deputy chief of the NKO department of naval administration, from 1923 to 1936. Later in 1934 Efimov himself supposedly told Bekauri of the existence of a conspiratorial organisation headed by Marshal Tukhachevskii and Army Commanders I.P. Uborevich and I.E. Iakir. The third interrogation, on 26 September 1937, was conducted by a whole group headed by Zhurid-Nikolaev. On this occasion the names of Ostekhbiuro personnel supposedly recruited by Bekauri for spying were given. Also mentioned was the 'technology of sabotage' in Ostekhbiuro: delays in the preparation of weapon prototypes as a result of endless modifications, delays in the acquisition of prototypes prepared on the basis of misleading blueprints, and presentation of the modernisation of outdated equipment as invention.

At the beginning of the 1930s Soviet military intelligence succeeded in obtaining the plans and technical documentation of an Italian torpedo. The reworking of its plans and their updating took place at the Dvigatel' factory. This was also held against Bekauri. In the interrogation record it was especially noted that in the development of torpedoes Bekauri was actively engaged in deception under the guidance of Tukhachevskii, who had been recruited by German intelligence in 1935.[18]

On 7 October 1937 Bekauri was confronted by A.V. Leonov (chief of the NKO naval armaments administration), I.M. Ludri (chief of the navy), B.I. Preobrazhenskii (chief engineer of Ostekhbiuro) and S.M. Shreiber. At the first three meetings Bekauri had completely denied the accusations of both spying and sabotage. Only at the fourth confrontation that day with Shreiber did Bekauri acknowledge all the accusations, admitting that he had lied at the previous three meetings. On the basis of the interrogations and confrontations an indictment was drawn up which was presented to him on 8 February 1938. A trial took place on the same day; it lasted 15 minutes. Bekauri conducted himself bravely. He did not acknowledge guilt, and rejected the confessions made in the investigation and the declarations addressed to Ezhov as false: 'I worked honestly, and did nothing criminal.' Despite this statement, Bekauri was sentenced to execution by shooting, the sentence being carried out on the same day.[19] Altogether 52 Ostekhbiuro personnel were arrested and sentenced, together with 76 Ostekhbiuro clients and leaders of defence industry.[20] In the course of just one day, 23 February 1938, at a session of the Military Collegium of the USSR Supreme Court in Leningrad, 18 Ostekhbiuro employees were sentenced to execution. But there was no single trial. The reason for this was probably that those arrested gave highly contradictory confessions. Some stated that sabotage had taken the form of the production of steel radio-controlled torpedo-launches. Others on the other hand defended this idea and cited as sabotage the remote-control system of the MS tank or Slon steam-engine.[21]

There were also many inconsistencies in the definition of the sabotage alleged against those in charge of Ostekhbiuro. Most of the arrested said Bekauri's theory was that 'Ostekhbiuro must have its own distinct personality'. This hardly amounted to sabotage. The situation was still worse with the allegation of spying. Here there was complete confusion not only about dates of recruitment and names of German, Italian, British and other agents, but also about the factual material which had supposedly been transmitted to them. Virtually all those repressed were accused of counter-revolutionary Trotskyist agitation. Thus in a declaration appended to the indictment of February 1938 P.A. Giliarov, head of the Ostekhbiuro laboratory, explained his actual statements in the laboratory:

1. In discussing the Stalin Constitution he asked: 'how can the dictatorship of the proletariat and democracy coexist in society?'
2. In discussing the Piatakov trial, he said: 'Whoever is against has been arrested; who can be trusted now? Surely they wanted to lead society down a different path, not necessarily an inferior one.'

It was these statements which served as a basis for the accusation of counter-revolutionary agitation.[22]

It is clear that an open trial did not take place because of the behaviour of those arrested. They all displayed stubbornness, and confessed only under physical and moral duress. The investigators could not give expert assessments of specific production and design issues, and for that reason simply falsified the records of the interrogation. Thus in 1956 during a review of accusations levelled at Ostekhbiuro personnel it was discovered that:

> At the interrogations of N.A. Giliarov and P.A. Giliarov the investigators applied physical and moral pressure, and falsified the records of the interrogations. Investigator F.G. Dubrovin confirmed that P.O. Turkov and G.I. Osipov obtained P.A. Giliarov's signature by deceit. Investigators G.M. Alashev and A.S. Mnevich confessed that P.A. Giliarov had refused to sign the record. Then P.A. Giliarov agreed to sign the record on condition that a written statement about the use of illegal methods of investigation was appended to it. F.G. Dubrovin gave P.A. Giliarov his agreement, but then destroyed the appended statement. The investigation was conducted in a situation of the most crude breaches of the USSR Criminal Code by Dubrovin, Slavin, Smirnov, and other employees of the NKVD administration, for which they were [later] charged.[23]

It was not long before many of the ideas, inventions, and projects of Ostekhbiuro personnel were applied in the defence industry. They were vindicated in World War II. In particular the BEMI-1 radio-controlled mine developed by Bekauri was actively used by partisans and saboteurs, as were radio-guided torpedoes, automation equipment for navy launches, and Port-1 and Port-2 equipment for interception of phototelegrams.

FROM THE *SHARASHKI* TO NEW BRANCHES OF THE DEFENCE COMPLEX

The idea of using the labour and knowledge of specialists who had been convicted of criminal offences arose from VSNKh and OGPU circular no. 139 of 15 May 1930 'on using specialists sentenced for sabotage on production'. In this circular in particular it was said:

> In the last two or three years the organs of OGPU have discovered counter-revolutionary organizations in a number of branches of our economy. Saboteurs have even succeeded in penetrating VSNKh, Gosplan, the health services, and production workshops . . . the elimination of the consequences of this sabotage must become a top-priority task of our industry . . . in this matter engineers who are saboteurs and have been sentenced by OGPU

must be put to use... they must be organised so that their work is done chiefly on premises of the OGPU organs... for this purpose specialists who are worthy of confidence must be selected and provided with assistance in carrying out experimental work...

Chairman of VSNKh V. Kuibyshev

Deputy Chairman of OGPU G. Iagoda[24]

So-called 'special places of imprisonment' – penal colonies for scientific workers, known in popular speech as *sharashki* – were established where such specialists were utilised according to their expertise (see also Chapter 9). At the end of the 1930s this system developed into part of the NKVD structure, and was later transferred to the MVD. In it such prisoners as the aircraft designer A.N. Tupolev, the rocket specialist S.P. Korolev, and others served their sentences (see Chapter 6).

As a rule special premises in places of imprisonment or entire buildings in Moscow, Leningrad, and other cities were earmarked for employing specialist labour – for example Tupolev's design bureau. By the second half of the 1930s the use of specialist labour had sharply increased in scale. Virtually all branches of the defence industry were paralysed as a result of the repressions and the search for saboteurs and enemies of the people. Repression affected practically all those working in the defence industry, from scientists, designers, and engineers to technicians and skilled workers. They all comprised the Gulag workforce. As a result, at the end of the 1930s the NKVD deployed the most skilled cadres of defence industry. In virtually all prisons there were special design bureaux which worked on the development of weapons, instruments, and so on. Thus, for example, in the Butyrki prison a special design bureau was engaged in the field of radio technology, where distinguished scientists such as A.L. Mints, A.G. Iarmizin, and B.I. Preobrazhenskii worked out their terms of confinement. At the request of the NKVD, they were released ahead of time by a decision of the Supreme Soviet presidium on 10 July 1941.[25]

One source of particular damage was that the reorganisation of the branches of defence industry was not thought out, and for this reason took place at heavy cost. The number of those sacked without ceremony and redeployed to other branches of industry was estimated to have been 'very large'. Normal functioning of the branches of the defence industry was disrupted and became possible again only under the supervision and with the participation of organs of the NKVD. For this reason there was a constant restructuring of the security organs themselves as new subdivisions were created. For example, at the beginning of the Great Fatherland War a serious shortage of mortars transpired. The NKVD therefore issued Order no. 001214 of 15 September 1941 to create a seventh special department of NKVD dealing with mortar production. Its chief, Senior Major of State Security P.Ia. Meshik, doubled as chief of the NKVD economic administration. Subsequently, on 10 November 1941 Major of State Security I.M. Tkachenko was appointed chief of the seventh special department; on 14 November 1942, however, the seventh special department was closed.[26]

On 5 September 1939 the 'special technical administation' was finally abolished. Its scientific-research institutes, laboratories, and experimental base were transferred to various people's commissariats. Thus, for example, NII-20 was handed over to Narkomaviaprom, and its Leningrad branch was transferred to Narkomsudprom. On 1 October 1939, by order of People's Commissar of the Shipbuilding Industry I.F. Tevosian, the Leningrad branches of NII-10 and NII-20 were merged to form an Institute of Naval Remote Control, referred to in official documents as NII-49 of Narkomsudprom.[27]

In the immediate prewar period the role of the NKVD organs grew as never before. Practically all branches of defence industry at that time were supervised by corresponding branches and sections of the NKVD. Overall leadership was provided by deputy People's Commissar A.P. Zaveniagin. Reports from virtually all defence factories were sent not only to the people's commissariats under whose jurisdiction they fell but also to Sovnarkom, to the party Central Committee – and to the NKVD. NKVD representatives were invariably present alongside scientists and designers at tests of new military equipment and instruments. In addition the NKVD could make use of its own firing ranges where experimental prototypes created in special design bureaux of prisons and camps were tested.

This situation was created after the accession of L.P. Beriia to the leadership of the NKVD. In contrast to Ezhov, his predecessor in this post, who had made the physical elimination of cadres his chief activity, Beriia had a more rational approach to the use of repressed specialists from among 'enemies of the people'. Paradoxically it was thanks to the patronage of the all-powerful People's Commissar for Internal Affairs that many technical innovations and unique scientific discoveries were able to see the light of day and then be put into production. It is only fair to note that with all the negative features of his character (cunning, rancour, cruelty, and so on), Beriia was a talented organizer with great intuition and a flair for new discoveries in the field of science and technology. Lacking specialist education, he was none the less able to grasp specialised questions and to render timely help and support. There were frequent cases when the People's Commissar himself defended so-called 'enemies of the people' from attacks by specialists within his own organisation who as a rule occupied the leading technical positions in prison and camp design bureaux, laboratories, and production establishments.

The records of his secretariat bear witness to the above. Thus, on a report of Major of State Security Ia.S. Pavlov about an unhealthy situation which had supposedly developed in a prison laboratory dealing with the development of a special technique for ensuring the secrecy of radio, telephone, and other conversations, Beriia wrote the following: 'To [chief of the NKVD administration of cadres] Comrade [B.P.] Obruchnikov! Send this fool as head of an escort unit a long way from Moscow'. The reason for such harsh punishment was the passage in his report where the zealous time-server had told his boss that 'with provocative intent the imprisoned specialists are accusing me of incompetence. Armed with the instructions of comrade Stalin, we can conquer the heights of science and technology.' A note to the report by Obruchnikov indicated that Pavlov had only had three years of schooling. Beriia underlined these passages of the report energetically and wrote in the margin one word – 'fool!' Such comments were not infrequent. The largest number relate to the period 1944–7.[28]

From 1940 Beriia also occupied the post of deputy prime minister and had responsibility, among other things, for the defence industry. It was then that, on his initiative, a Special Technical Bureau of the NKVD was created. Its staff included highly trained specialists of the defence industry who had been sentenced for sabotage. In 1939–40 special design bureaux for aircraft, aeroengines, and other fields were established on various initiatives. When its assignment had been fulfilled the group of scientists and designers involved was usually freed. Thus Petliakov, Miasishchev, Tupolev, and others were set at liberty. During the war Beriia became a member of GKO, Stalin's war cabinet, and was responsible for the production of tanks, artillery armament, and ammunition, and for transport. For this work he was awarded the title of 'Hero of Socialist Labour' in 1943.

The practice of using imprisoned specialists took on additional force during the war. Thus, in 1942–3 work of major defence significance resulted from plans drafted by imprisoned specialists of the NKVD fourth special department at factory no. 16 of Narkomaviaprom. V.P. Glushko's design led to the building of the experimental RD-16 liquid-fuelled rocket motor, intended as an aircraft booster. Prototypes of the RD-16 went through factory, flight, and ground tests simultaneously with satisfactory results. In the summer of 1944 an experimental series of rocket motors was already being manufactured in aircraft factories.[29] Similarly, on the basis of a project put forward by A.M. Dobrotvorskii, the powerful MB-100 aeroengine was built at this time by coupling two serially produced M-105 engines. In addition to the latter work, specialists provided major technical assistance to factory no. 16 of the aircraft industry while it was being built and equipped. In particular, an experimental mechanical base for aeroengine manufacture was built at the factory following a plan and guidance of specialists from the NKVD fourth special department. A large group of specialists worked at this factory in leading technical roles and assisted the successful output of its product. People's Commissar for the Aircraft Industry A.I. Shakhurin acknowledged that the contribution of imprisoned specialists of the NKVD fourth special department to resolving various complicated technical and design problems was extremely valuable.[30]

On 16 July 1944 Beriia signed a letter addressed to Stalin as chairman of GKO. The conclusion of the letter was as follows:

> In view of the importance of the work they have carried out, the NKVD of the USSR considers it appropriate to release and pardon those imprisoned specialists who have especially distinguished themselves, and thereafter to direct them to work on their speciality. A list of 35 imprisoned specialists is attached. I request your instructions.[31]

Instructions were given and the Supreme Soviet presidium on 27 July 1944 ordered the release and pardon of the 35 specialists. Among them was Korolev, technical director of the rocket aircraft project, formerly senior engineer of NII-3, who had been sentenced in 1940 by a special tribunal of the NKVD to eight years' imprisonment.

It must be noted that the general educational level of NKVD personnel remained low. In September 1944 only 4 360 employees had higher education, while 54 792 had secondary and 127 037 only primary education. At the same time there were 20 242 specialists with higher education working in the NKVD.[32] For the most part these fell into various categories of those repressed, convicted by the courts, despatched to internal exile, and so on. They comprised the basic workforce which guaranteed the fulfilment of government assignments. By these people's hands were built the Ukhtinsk combine of the oil industry, which included the Radiev plant, six major factories, and oil and gas works. Just in the war years the NKVD chief administration for highways and roads (GUSHOSDOR) built 5 000 kilometres of roads in Russia and 398 kilometres of strategic highways in the Mongolian People's Republic. A large volume of construction was carried out for electric power stations within the Volgostroi system.[33]

The NKVD organs had particular functions in providing security for railway installations, bridges, and the most important factories. In August 1941, after reorganisation, new departments for security at railway installations and industrial factories were created under the authority of the NKVD chief administration of internal troops. At the same time the NKVD chief administration of defensive works (GUOBR) was established. It was headed at first by the second-grade Commissar of State Security K.A. Pavlov, but in October 1941 it was put under the direct control of Stalin in his capacity as People's Commissar for Defence.[34]

From the beginning of the war all defence industry came under tight supervision by the NKVD. In 1942 the NKVD economic administration (EKU) had 165 employees. The first department of EKU had responsibility for the aircraft industry, the second for the production of armaments and ammunition. The seventh special department was responsible for mortar armaments and ammunition.[35]

An active search for effective forms of armaments and ammunition went on under direct NKVD supervision. This work was carried out in top-security closed special design bureaux and institutes. Some of these were attached to the corresponding people's commissariats. However, work on rocket and radio technology remained under the control of EKU NKVD. Intelligence work was significantly stepped up. During the war agents of the Foreign Department of NKVD chief administration of state security obtained 768 technical documents dealing with new military technology, all of which found full or partial application in production.[36]

The NKVD organs played a major role in facilitating the transfer of aircraft production to the eastern regions of the country. It was in these years that military aircraft factories were created in Novosibirsk, Omsk, Krasnoiarsk, and other cities. The construction of so-called satellite-towns began, closed cities totally devoted to war production (see Chapters 1 and 10). Their enterprises were placed on a martial-law footing and subjected to a tight regime of secrecy. The process of the militarisation of the economy was taken to its logical conclusion.

At the same time the subject of conversion from military to civilian production came under constant NKVD attention. In 1944 began the process of curtailing the production of obsolete and ineffective weaponry. A special Liquidation Committee directly subordinated to the GKO supervised this process. After the end of the war this committee was transferred to Sovnarkom (from 1946, the Council of Ministers). NKVD (from 1946, MVD) personnel took a direct part in its work. Production did not cease at the enterprises involved, but the product assortment changed. NKVD-MVD representatives worked alongside purchaser representatives in the factories, and exercised supervision in accordance with their competence whether trained or untrained. Documents show that the former's involvement helped to overcome narrow bureaucratic interests, though at the same time there were instances of incompetent interference resulting in muddle.

THE NKVD-MVD AND THE ATOMIC BOMB PROJECT

A special place in the interrelationship of the NKVD and the defence-industry complex is occupied by the history of the atomic bomb's creation (a subject considered more generally in Chapter 7). A proposal for its development was made by Beriia to the government in 1939 when it became known from intelligence reports that the Germans, British, and Americans were already developing proposals. However, the USSR then had neither the electronics industry nor the personnel necessary for the creation of a super-modern weapon in a short space of time. In addition there were different views among physicists at that time about the possibility of creating the bomb. As is well known, P.L. Kapitsa spoke out against its creation.[37] The situation changed sharply in 1942, when evidence was received through strategic intelligence channels about work on the atomic bomb project in the United States. At that time V.M. Zarubrin was the leading Soviet resident agent in America, and it was his network of agents which gained access to the American project.[38]

Information from foreign intelligence about the powerful development of atomic research in the United States fundamentally influenced attitudes in the Soviet Union. I.V. Kurchatov later spoke privately to a small group of his colleagues:

> ...the only way to defend our country is to make up for lost time and, unperceived by the outside world, establish atomic production on an adequate scale. If we proclaim this from the rooftops, the United States will speed up its work so much that we will never catch up.[39]

Time had been lost, and when it took the decision to build a Soviet atomic bomb the country's leadership knew the Americans were a long way ahead. All the evidence indicated that an atomic bomb could be produced in the United States before the end of the war. In the NKVD a group of young specialists was recruited. Kurchatov was appointed head of the project; others working on it included Iu.B. Khariton, Ia.B. Zeldovich, A.F. Ioffe and N.N. Semenov. All the scientific and technical information on atomic energy obtained by intelligence was addressed 'personally to comrade Kurchatov', with whom a representative of the central intelligence apparatus maintained contact.[40]

By the beginning of 1944 reliable informants were working at the various sites of the Manhattan Project, mainly in the Los Alamos laboratory. In the intelligence archives are notes analysing the progress of work on the atomic bomb in the United States. One is dated February 1945. There is also an urgent telegram from New York about the forthcoming test of the bomb and a short description of its construction. On 2 July 1945 Kurchatov was informed of this material. In August a more detailed description of the atomic bomb was received on 22 pages of English text; in October 7 pages and in December 14 more pages in English were received. This information also became known to Soviet physicists.[41]

Unquestionably the presence in Moscow of the physicist Bruno Pontecorvo significantly activated work on the Soviet atomic project. Kurchatov's laboratory was located near Moscow in Serebrianyi Bor. Officially it was called Laboratory no. 2 of the Academy of Sciences, 'a consultative scientific organ for the organisation and co-ordination of work in the field of the creation of atomic weapons'. Later a second centre was created in the town of Obninsk. More generally, whole towns began to be built in the Urals near Cheliabinsk, and in Siberia near Krasnoiarsk, by prisoners of the Gulag so as to provide Russia with a nuclear industry.

The creation of the Soviet atomic bomb was in several respects different from that of the American bomb. The basic flow of information came from outside, and the organisational work on the construction and planning of diffusion plants and on the production of enriched uranium was wholly carried out through the NKVD-MVD. According to the account of Marshal G.K. Zhukov, it was during the Potsdam Conference that US President Harry Truman told Stalin about the United States' possession of a bomb of unusually great power, though without calling it an 'atomic' bomb. When he returned from the meeting with Truman, Stalin raged at Beriia because there was not yet a Soviet bomb. When Molotov retorted that the Americans were bidding up the price (of cooperation), Stalin exclaimed: 'Let them bid up the price. We must talk with Kurchatov about accelerating our work.' (This edited passage from Zhukov's memoirs confused researchers for a considerable time. It was done deliberately to preserve the secret of the real history of the creation of the Soviet atomic bomb.)

After the bombing of Hiroshima and Nagasaki, the GKO decided on 20 August 1945 to create a Special Committee charged with direct leadership of the scientific research projects, engineering and design organisations, and industrial enterprises devoted to exploiting the atomic energy of uranium and the production of atomic weapons. (Later, in March 1953, this Committee was in addition given responsibility 'for other work of defence signficance'.) In the draft of the GKO resolution, it was proposed to appoint V.M. Molotov as chairman of the Special Committee. However this evoked a strong protest from scientists and industrialists because many of them knew all too well Molotov's style of work (indecision, slowness, unwillingness to decide difficult questions or to take responsibility on himself). For this reason the GKO opted instead for Beriia.[42] Other NKVD representatives of the special committee were deputy Commissar of Internal Affairs A.P. Zaveniagin and NKVD General V.A. Makhnev, chief of its secretariat (see Chapter 7). In March of the following year, when the people's commissariats were renamed ministries, as his other responsibilities grew, Beriia relinquished the internal affairs portfolio to S.N. Kruglov while retaining general oversight of state security as one of Stalin's deputy prime ministers.

In developing the Soviet atomic bomb co-operation began with eastern European countries for the first time. Thus an inter-governmental agreement between Czechoslovakia and the USSR on the mining of uranium ore in Czechoslovakia and its delivery to the USSR was signed on 22 November 1945. Until 1949 this ore was mined in the Jachymov mines by 5 000 German prisoners of war.[43]

On 29 August 1949 the first Soviet atomic bomb was tested. The success of the test could not be guaranteed in advance. After the test (which was successful) the atomic physicists made up a joke: 'At the tests Beriia had a list of whom to decorate and whom to put in gaol. It was the same list.'[44] On 29 October a large group of atomic scientists were decorated with Orders of the USSR. Kurchatov was given the title 'Hero of the Soviet Union', while Beriia received the Order of Lenin. The title of 'Hero of Socialist Labour' was given to the following MVD personnel: P.P. Georgievskii, A.P. Zaveniagin, A.N. Komarovskii, M.M. Mal'tsev and M.M. Tsarevskii. Besides Beriia, S.N. Kruglov, B.P. Obruchnikov and V.V. Chernyshov received the Order of Lenin.[45]

At root this signified that a new stage in the formation of the Soviet defence-industrial complex had begun. Chronologically it coincided with the period of the Cold War. The Soviet Army had begun to be equipped with new forms of armament. But Beriia did not force the pace of equipment of the armed forces with nuclear weapons. At this time the devastating significance of atomic weapons had not been sufficiently studied, and there were no adequate means of defence against them. For this reason Beriia opposed the instruction of troops on the use of atomic weapons, notwithstanding strong pressure from the Ministry of Defence. In memoranda addressed to Stalin in 1951 and to Malenkov in 1953 he justified this point of view. Later in 1957 during the June plenum of the party Central Committee he would be accused of 'hindering the process of assimilation of atomic weapons'.[46] The first training of troops in the use of atomic weapons took place only on 14 September 1954 in the region of the Totskoe settlement.[47]

'THE MVD MUST BE DECISIVELY REORGANISED'

In the late 1940s the MVD continued to broaden its range of activities. This was reflected in the establishment of the following new departments of the MVD:[48]

16 April 1949	chief administration for prospecting and developing sources of nonferrous and rare metals and the construction of factories in the Krasnoiarsk region (Eniseistroi of the MVD), headed by Major-General A.A. Paninkov
20 Sept. 1949	administration of the quartz industry
1 Nov. 1949	chief administration of camps for the construction of factories for synthetic liquid fuel, headed by chief of the MVD chief administration for industrial construction (Glavpromstroi) A.N. Komarovskii
5 Nov. 1949	Glavgidrostroi (chief administration for hydroelectric plant construction) renamed Glavgidrovolgodonstroi (i.e. for the Volga–Don basin)

25 May 1950 chief administration of labour camps for the asbestos industry

6 Oct. 1950 geological administration

Additionally, on 15 August 1949 on Beriia's proposal, the Council of Ministers voted to reorganise NII-49 of the Ministry of Shipbuilding. This scientific research institute was assigned work on the preparation and testing of automation instruments for shipbuilding. It continued to work in Leningrad and constituted the last remnant of the Ostekhbiuro group of specialists.

By 1953, by virtue of the scale of its activities, the MVD had essentially turned into 'a state within the state'. It was not only at the heart of the defence-industry complex, but it also provided its most important supporting infrastructure. Practically everything needed by the defence-industry complex was concentrated in it, from the discovery and development of sources of raw materials to the use of factories for utilising strategic raw materials, from scientific theoretical investigations to their practical application in the production of tested models of new military technology. In this system yesterday's prisoners became today's academicians and Heroes of Socialist Labour – and on the other hand, yesterday's designer and Minister of the Aviation Industry became a saboteur and a prisoner in the Gulag. A regime of strictest secrecy co-existed with the possiblity of participation in international conferences and the receipt of strictly secret information about the work of foreign scientists and designers. Those towns which arose by the will of the all-powerful MVD, like children of the defence-industry complex, provided a model for 'Cities of the Communist Future' (like Krasnoiarsk-26, the subject of Chapter 10). The *sharashki* of the 1930s had disappeared irreversibly, although much of their legacy remained. This was manifest above all in attitudes to people and the special mentality both of MVD personnel and of all those employed at enterprises of the defence-industry complex. They frequently combined forces to solve problems in the Politburo and Council of Ministers, but were burdened at the same time by the surveillance of the ubiquitous security organs.

The dismantling of the MVD system that had grown up began immediately after Stalin's death. Subsections of the structure began to be transferred wholesale from the MVD to other departments. Thus on 16 March 1953 a resolution of the Council of Ministers moved Glavpromstroi and Glavspetsstroi from the MVD to the newly created Ministry of Medium Engineering. It was the latter which became the bedrock of the modern defence-industry complex. On 26 June 1953 a decision of the Presidium of the party Central Committee abolished the Special Committee, and its apparatus was also transferred to the Ministry of Medium Engineering.[49] Future work on guiding the development of new military technology was transferred to a special organ created by a joint decision of the Supreme Soviet presidium and the Council of Ministers. Headed by B.L. Vannikov, it also included Zaveniagin, V.A. Malyshev, M.G. Pervukhin and E.P. Slavskii. Kurchatov remained the scientific director of the project. On 12 August 1953 the testing of a thermonuclear bomb took place.[50]

Much of this took place when Beriia was under arrest. Future historians will probably be able to assess his role in the creation of the defence-industry complex more successfully than is possible at present. For now it can only be noted that materials of the NKVD-MVD secretariat for the 1940s and 1950s provide much food for thought on this question. These show that the all-powerful head of the MVD was preoccupied with both political and social problems of the defence-industry complex. Thus in a number of documents addressed to the presidium of the party Central Committee and the Council of Ministers in 1952–3 he expressed concern that the unrestricted transfer of such powerful weapons as the atomic bomb into the hands of the military could have negative results in both foreign and domestic policy. He pointed to the low educational level of senior officers and generals of the Soviet Army, who had been promoted in conditions of wartime after accelerated military training. He referred with justification to the ambitions of some of the celebrated heroes of the Great Fatherland War, and in a deliberately insulting way compared giving them atomic weapons with giving with a modern machine gun to a prehistoric human being.[51]

In an unsigned draft of another memorandum, Beriia touched on the social problems of the closed cities created in the postwar period for mining raw materials and assembling weapons and testing them. Their infrastructure was more developed than in other areas. They were distinguished by a higher standard of living for the population: high pay, better social and living conditions, and material supplies. But because of the conditions of secrecy there was practically no development of other kinds of production, which threatened to have negative consequences in the future. For this reason the memorandum contained a proposal to develop purely civilian branches of industry in parallel with those of defence industry.[52] Furthermore, the memorandum raised the idea – rejected by Malenkov and Khrushchev – of freeing political prisoners. Beriia proposed providing a reasonable life in these towns to those who were amnestied and rehabilitated.

In several documents there are proposals for partial changes in the administration of the defence-industry complex. The rigidly centralised structure which had been created in the war years had, with time, become an obstacle and hindered the development of new promising branches of industry. The directors of defence-industry enterprises and establishments belonged to the *nomenklatura* of the party Central Committee and local party organs. Party committees in the defence-industry complex were subordinate both to regional and republican party organs and to the departments of the party Central Committee. Beriia proposed to review this situation and to limit the authority of party organs to the making of appointments.[53] Be that as it may, from the time of his arrest the role and significance of the MVD in the defence-industry complex was noticeably reduced, and subsequently it disappeared completely.

In the 1940s and 1950s the development of various forms of missile armament began. This was primarily connected with the development of intercontinental ballistic missiles. The launch of the first *sputnik* was followed by the establishment of a new military branch, the Strategic Missile Forces, which necessitated their equipment with weaponry and equipment. These were created by resolution of the Council of Ministers in 1960. Iurii Gagarin's flight into space was followed by the establishment of the Space Forces.[54]

In these and later years the basic functions of guaranteeing security, preserving military and state secrets, and combating spying in the defence industry were entrusted to the organs of the KGB (Committee for State Security). The latter was less powerful than the NKVD-MVD had been in the 1930s and 1940s. However, a preoccupation with top state secrets remained, and indeed may well remain to this day.

The defence-industry complex played an ever greater role in the economic and political life of the country. Its privileged funding and special prestige in many ways artificially maintained structures which needed reconstruction. The armed forces noticeably strengthened their position in 1953–7; it was they who supported Khrushchev in his struggle for power. This was particularly noticeable in the role played by Marshal Zhukov in the summer of 1957. He was the chief hero of the June Plenum of the party Central Committee. It was he, together with Minister of Internal Affairs N.P. Dudorov, and KGB Chairman I.A. Serov, who largely strengthened Khrushchev's hand in his struggle against the Molotov-Kaganovich-Malenkov group. For the first time in the history of Soviet society the 'power ministries' combined and made their strength felt (this unstable alliance would collapse before long, however, with Dudorov writing letters to Khrushchev and the party Central Committee denouncing Serov and Zhukov, the latter having already been sacked). But the decisive element was still the all-powerful party apparatus. How its relations with the defence-industry complex subsequently developed, both at the centre and in the localities, must be the subject of separate research.

NOTES

1 The Cheka (Extraordinary Commission), created on 20 December 1917, was replaced on 8 February 1922 by the GPU (State Political Administration) or OGPU (Unified State Political Administration) as it became after the formation

of the USSR. The latter's functions were absorbed in July 1934 by the NKVD (People's Commissariat of Internal Affairs), renamed MVD (Ministry of Internal Affairs) on 15 March 1946.

2 TsA FDBR ('O kontrrevoliutsionnoi vreditel'skoi organizatsii v oboronnoi promyshlennosti SSSR').

3 TsA FSBR (information concerning investigation of the Genshtabisty).

4 TsA FSBR (file of A.O. Klippel').

5 TsA FSBR (file of M.N. Orlov).

6 TsA FSBR (file of E.I. Shiptal'skii).

7 Kosheleva (1995), 172.

8 Kosheleva (1995), 174.

9 GARF, 8131, observations nos 1706–59, 37044–56.

10 Arkhiv UFSB (file of Ostekhbiuro).

11 Arkhiv UFSB (file of Ostekhbiuro).

12 Arkhiv UFSB (file of Ostekhbiuro).

13 GARF, 374/28/1238, 124–35.

14 Arkhiv UFSB (file of Ostekhbiuro, materials on political rehabilitations).

15 Arkhiv UFSB (file of Ostekhbiuro).

16 TsA FSBr (file of the investigation of B.I. Bekhauri).

17 TsA FSBr (file of the investigation of B.I. Bekhauri).

18 TsA FSBR (file of investigation of B.I. Bekhauri).

19 TsA FSBR (file of investigation of B.I. Bekhauri).

20 Arkhiv UFSB (file of Ostekhbiuro).

21 TsA FSBR (file of P.A. Bekhterev).

22 Arkhiv UNKVD (file of P.A. Giliarov).

23 Arkhiv UNKVD (rehabilitation file of P.A. Giliarov).

24 GARF, 9401/2 (orders, circulars, and directives of OGPU USSR). However, a Special Design Bureau had already been established under the NKVD's Leningrad regional administration for work of defence significance in April 1928.

25 GARF, 9401/2 (materials of the NKVD USSR secretariat).

26 GARF, 9401/2 (explanatory note about the staff structure of NKVD USSR).

27 Arkhiv UFSB (file of Ostenkhburo)

28 GARF, 9401/2 (materials of the NKVD USSR secretariat).

29 GARF, 9401/2 (materials of the NKVD USSR secretariat).

30 GARF, 9401/2 (materials of the NKVD USSR secretariat).

31 APRF, 5/2/1846, 51–2.

32 GARF, 9401/2 (materials of the NKVD USSR secretariat).

33 APRF, 5/2/1905.

34 GARF, 9401/2 (materials of the NKVD USSR secretariat).

35 GARF, 9401/2 (materials of the NKVD USSR secretariat).

36 APRF, 5/2/1905.

37 Beriia (1992).

38 Gogol' (1993), 18.

39 Astashenkov (1974), 21.

40 Gogol' (1993), 18.

41 Arkhiv sluzhby vneshnei razvedki Rossiiskoi federatsii ('Materialy o rabote nad Los-Alamosskim proektom').

42 GARF (materials of the MVD USSR secretariat).

43 Chernykh (1991).

44 Beriia (1992), 56.

45 GARF (materials of the Presidium of the USSR Supreme Soviet).

46 *Istoricheskii arkhiv* (1993), no. 3, 23.

47 Ivanov (1991), 79–86.
48 In all cases the preamble spoke of the major defence significance of the measures taken. GARF (materials of the MVD USSR secretariat).
49 GARF (materials of the MVD USSR secretariat).
50 GARF (materials of the MVD USSR secretariat).
51 GARF (materials of the MVD USSR secretariat).
52 GARF (materials of the MVD USSR secretariat).
53 GARF (materials of the MVD USSR secretariat).
54 Arkhiv Soveta Ministrov SSSR (Pravitel'stvennyi arkhiv SSSR).

References

ARCHIVES

APRF (Arkhiv Prezidenta Rossiiskoi Federatsii), Moscow.
Arkhiv Sluzhby Vneshnei Razvedki Rossiiskoi federatsii, Moscow.
Arkhiv Soveta Ministrov SSSR (Pravitel'stvennyi arkhiv SSSR), Moscow.
Arkhiv UFSB (Arkhiv Upravleniia Federal'noi Sluzhby Bezpasnosti po S-Petersburgu i Leningradskoi oblasti), St Petersburg.
Arkhiv UNKVD (Arkhiv Upravleniia Narodnogo komissariata Vnutrennykh Del po S-Peterburgu), St Petersburg.
GARF (Gosudarstvennyi arkhiv Rossiiskoi Federatsii), Moscow.
RGAE (Rossiiskii gosudarstvennyi arkhiv ekonomiki), Moscow.
RGVA (Rossiiskii gosudarstvennyi voennyi arkhiv), Moscow.
RTsKhIDNI (Rossiiskii tsentr khraneniia i izucheniia dokumentov noveishei istorii), Moscow.
TsA FSBR (Tsentral'nyi arkhiv Federal'noi Sluzhby Bezopasnosti Rossii), Moscow.
TsGA IPD (Tsentral'nyi Gosudarstvennyi arkhiv istoriko-politicheskikh dokumentov), St Petersburg.

OTHER WORKS

Abelshauser, W. (1998), 'Germany: guns, butter, and economic miracles', in Harrison, M., ed., *The economics of World War II: six great powers in international comparison*, Cambridge, 122–76.
Abramovitz, M. (1986), 'Catching up, forging ahead, and falling behind', *Journal of Economic History*, vol. 46, 385–406.
Agursky, M. (1976), 'The research institute of machine-building technology', Hebrew University of Jerusalem, Soviet Institution Series no. 8.
Agursky, M. and Adomeit, H. (1978), 'The Soviet military-industrial complex and its internal mechanism', Queen's University, Centre for International Relations, National Security Series no. 1/78, Kingston, Ontario.
Albrecht, U. (1993), *The Soviet armaments industry*, Chur (Switzerland).
Alexander, A.J. (1978), 'Decision-making in Soviet weapons procurement', *Adelphi Papers* nos. 147–8, International Institute for Strategic Studies, London.
Almquist, P. (1990), *Red forge: Soviet military industry since 1965*, New York.
Amann, R., and Cooper, J.M. (1982), *Industrial innovation in the Soviet Union*, New Haven, CT.
Amann, R., and Cooper, J.M., eds (1986), *Technical progress and Soviet economic development*, New York.
Amann, R., Cooper, J.M., and Davies, R.W., eds (1977), *The technological level of Soviet industry*, New Haven, CT.
AN SSSR (1991), *Vsesoiuznaia perepis' naseleniia 1937 g.. Kratkie itogi*, Moscow.
Aspaturian, V.V. (1973), 'The Soviet military-industrial complex: does it exist?', in Rosen, S., ed., *Testing the theory of the military-industrial complex*, Lexington, MA,103–33.

Astashenkov, P.T. (1974), *Akademik I.V. Kurchatov*, Moscow.

Barber, J., and Harrison, M. (1991), *The Soviet home front, 1941–5: a social and economic history of the USSR in World War II*, London.

Bergson, A. (1961), *The real national income of Soviet Russia since 1928*, Cambridge, MA.

Beriia, S. (1992), *Syn Lavrentiia Beriia rasskazyvaet*, Moscow.

Borisov, S.P. (1948), *Bor'ba bol'shevikov protiv voenno-promyshlennykh komitetov, 1915–1916 gg.*, Moscow.

Broadberry, S.N. (1995), 'Comparative productivity levels in manufacturing since the Industrial Revolution: lessons from Britain, America, Germany and Japan', *Structural Change and Economic Dynamics*, vol. 6, 71–95.

Budnik, V.S. (1991), 'Rakety Tret'ego Reikha', *Rabochaia tribuna*, 4 July.

Bystrova, I. (1996), 'The formation of the Soviet military-industrial complex', Centre for International Security and Arms Control, Stanford University, CA.

Bystrova, I. (1997), 'Sovetskii VPK. Teoriia, istoriia, real'nost'', *Svobodnaia mysl'*, no. 6, 30–44.

Campbell, R.W. (1972), 'Management spillovers from Soviet space and military programmes', *Soviet Studies*, vol. 23(4), 586–607.

Carr, E.H. (1971–6), *Foundations of a planned economy, 1926–1929*, vols. 2–3, London and Basingstoke.

Carr, E.H., and Davies, R.W. (1969), *A history of Soviet Russia. Foundations of a planned economy, 1926–1929*, vol. 1, parts 1, 2, London.

Chernykh, E. (1991), 'Uran pochti ne viden. Neizvestnye stranitsy sozdaniia sovetskogo iadernogo oruzhiia', *Komsomol'skaia pravda*, 9 May.

Chertok, B.E. (1992a), 'U sovetskikh raketnykh triumfov bylo nemetskoe nachalo. 1. Okhota za sekretami', *Izvestiia*, 4 March, 3; (1992b) '2. Podzemnoe khoziaistvo Tiuringii', *Izvestiia*, 5 March, 5; (1992c) '3. Institute 'Nordkhauzen'', *Izvestiia*, 6 March, 5; (1992d) '4. Iz Podlipok v Kapustin Iar', *Izvestiia*, 7 March, 3; (1992e) '5. Ostrov na Seligere', *Izvestiia*, 9 March, 3, (1992f) '6. U amerikanskikh raketnykh triumfov takzhe bylo nemetskoe nachalo', *Izvestiia*, 10 March, 7.

Cooper, J., Dexter, K., and Harrison, M. (1999), *The numbered factories and other establishments of the Soviet defence industry, 1927–1967*, Part I, *Factories and shipyards*, Occasional Paper no. 2 of the Soviet Industrialisation Project, Centre for Russian and East European Studies, University of Birmingham, available from http://www.warwick.ac.uk/Mark. Harrison/VPK/.

Cooper, J.M. (1976), 'Defence production and the Soviet economy, 1929–41', University of Birmingham, Centre for Russian and East European Studies, Soviet Industrialisation Project Series no. 3.

Cooper, J.M. (1977), 'The strategy of development of the Soviet machine tool industry, 1928–1941', University of Birmingham, Centre for Russian and East European Studies, Soviet Industrialisation Project Series no. 7.

Cooper, J.M. (1991), *The Soviet defence industry: conversion and reform*, London.

Crémieux-Brilhac, J.-L. (1981), 'La France en septembre 1939: de l'économie de crise à l'économie de guerre et l'échec de la mobilisation industrielle', in *Deutschland und Frankreich 1936–1939*, no. 15 (Deutsch-französisches Historikerkolloquium des Deutschen Historischen Instituts Paris, September 1979), Munich, 365–85.

Crowfoot, J.R., and Harrison, M. (1990), 'The USSR Council of Ministers under late Stalinism, 1945–54: its production branch composition and the requirements of national economy and policy', *Soviet Studies*, vol. 42(1), 41–60.

Danilov, B. (1981), 'Iz istorii sozdaniia reaktivnoi aviatsii', *Voenno-istoricheskii zhurnal*, no. 3, 70–5.

Davies, R.W. (1958), *The development of the Soviet budgetary system*, Cambridge.

Davies, R.W. (1989), *The industrialisation of Soviet Russia*, vol. 3, *The Soviet economy in turmoil, 1929–1930*, Basingstoke and London.

Davies, R.W. (1993), 'Soviet military expenditure and the armaments industry, 1929–33: a reconsideration', *Europe-Asia Studies*, vol. 45(4), 577–608.

Davies, R.W. (1994), 'Changing economic systems: an overview', in Davies, R.W., Harrison, M., and Wheatcroft, S.G. (1994), *The economic transformation of the Soviet Union, 1913–1945*, Cambridge, 1–23.

Davies, R.W. (1996), *The industrialization of Soviet Russia*, vol. 4, *Crisis and progress in the Soviet economy, 1931–1933*, Basingstoke and London.

Davies, R.W. and Harrison, M. (1997), 'The Soviet military-economic effort under the second five-year plan (1933–1937)', *Europe-Asia Studies*, vol. 49(3), 369–406.

Davies, R.W., Harrison, M., and Wheatcroft, S.G., eds (1994), *The economic transformation of the USSR, 1913–1945*, Cambridge.

Dmitriev, V.I. (1990), *Sovetskoe podvodnoe korablestroenie*, Moscow.

Eason, W.W. (1963), 'Labor force', in Bergson, A., Kuznets, S., eds, *Economic trends in the Soviet Union*, Cambridge MA, 38–95.

Easterly, W., Fischer, S. (1995), 'The Soviet economic decline', *World Bank Economic Review*, vol. 9(3), 341–71.

Egorov, Iu.A. (1994), 'Zarozhdenie reaktivnoi aviatsii v SSSR', in Biushgens, G.S., ed., *Samoletostroenie v SSSR. 1917–1945*, vol. 2, Moscow, 394–436

Emel'ianov, V.S. (1974), *O vremeni, o tovarishchakh, o sebe*, 2nd edn, Moscow.

Erickson, J. (1962), *The Soviet high command. a military-political history 1918–1941*, London.

Ershova, Z.V. (1988), *Vospominaniia ob Igore Kurchatove*, Moscow.

Fedotoff-White, D.D. (1944), *The growth of the Red Army*, Princeton, NJ.

Feldman, G.D. (1966), *Army, industry, and labor in Germany, 1914–1918*, Princeton, NJ.

Galenson, W. (1953), 'Industrial labor productivity', in Bergson, A., ed., *Soviet economic growth*, New York, 190–224.

Gastev, A. (1937), *Mobilizatsiia proizvodstva na voennye i predvoennye gody* (Dlia sluzhebnogo pol'zovaniia), Moscow.

Gatrell, P. (1994), *Government, industry and rearmament in Russia, 1900–1914: the last argument of Tsarism*, Cambridge.

Gatrell, P., and Harrison, M. (1993), 'The Russian and Soviet economies in two world wars: a comparative view', *Economic History Review*, vol. 46(3), 425–52.

Gibbs-Smith, C.H. (1970), *Aviation: an historical survey from its origins to the end of World War II*, London.

Girshfel'd, A.V., and Mikheev, I.M. (1928), *Ugroza voiny i nasha finansovaia samooborona*, Moscow.

Glantz, D.M. (1991), *The military strategy of the Soviet Union: a history*, London.

Gogol', V. (1993), *Bomba dlia Stalina*, Moscow.

Golovanov, Ia.K. (1994), *Korolev. Fakty i mify*, Moscow.

Goncharov, V.V. (1990), *Pervye etapy resheniia atomnoi problemy v SSSR*, Moscow.

Gowing, M. (1964), *Britain and atomic energy, 1939–1945*, London.

Gregory, P.R. (1990), *Restructuring the Soviet economic bureaucracy*, Cambridge.

Gröttrup, I. (1959), *Rocket wife*, London.

Gubarev, V., Rebrov, M., and Mosin, I. (1993), *Bomba*, Moscow.

Hardach, G. (1987), *The first World War, 1914–1918*, Harmondsworth.

Harrison, M. (1985), *Soviet planning in peace and war, 1938–1945*, Cambridge.

Harrison, M. (1990), 'A volume index of the total munitions output of the United Kingdom, 1939–1944', *Economic History Review*, vol. 43, 657–666.

Harrison, M. (1996), *Accounting for war: Soviet production, employment, and the defence burden, 1940–1945*, Cambridge.

Harrison, M. (1998a), 'The economics of World War II: an overview', in Harrison, M., ed., *The economics of World War II: six great powers in international comparison*, Cambridge.
Harrison, M. (1998b), 'Trends in Soviet labour productivity, 1928–1985: war, postwar recovery, and slowdown, *European Review of Economic History*, vol. 2(1), 1–30.
Herndon, J.S., and Baylen, J.O. (1975), 'Col. Philip R. Faymonville and the Red Army, 1934–43', *Slavic Review*, vol. 34(3), 483–505.
Holloway, D. (1977), 'Military technology', in Amann, R., Cooper, J., and Davies, R.W., eds, *The technological level of Soviet industry*, New Haven, CT, 407–89.
Holloway, D. (1982a), 'Innovation in the defence sector', in Amann, R., Cooper, J., eds, *Industrial innovation in the Soviet Union*, New Haven, CT, 276–367.
Holloway, D. (1982b), 'Innovation in the defence sector: battle tanks and ICBMs', in Amann, R., and Cooper, J., eds, *Industrial innovation in the Soviet Union*, New Haven, CT, 368–414.
Holloway, D. (1994), *Stalin and the bomb: the Soviet Union and atomic energy, 1939–1956*, New Haven, CT.
Hunter, H., and Szyrmer, J.M. (1992), *Faulty foundations: Soviet economic policies, 1928–1940*, Princeton, NJ.
Iakovlev, A.S. (1979), *Sovetskie samolety. Kratkii ocherk*, 3rd edn, Moscow.
Industrializatsiia (1973), *Industrializatsiia SSSR. 1938–1941 gg. Dokumenty i materialy*, Moscow.
Ishlinskii, A.Iu., ed. (1986), *Akademik S.P. Korolev: uchenyi, inzhiner, chelovek*, Moscow.
Isserson, G. (1963), 'Zapiski sovremennika o Tukhachevskom', *Voenno-istoricheskii zhurnal*, no. 4, 64–78.
Iurii, M.F. (1981), 'Tsentral'nyi voenno-promyshlennyi komityet (1915–18): avtoreferat dissertatsii kandidata istoricheskikh nauk', Moscow.
Ivanov, B.P. (1991), 'Atomnyi vzryv u poselka Totskoe: vospominaniia nachal'nika shtaba divizii', *Voenno-istoricheskii zhurnal*, no. 12, 79–86.
Ivkin, V.I. (1994), 'Cherez terni v kosmos', *Armeiskii sbornik*, no. 6, 72–6.
Ivkin, V.I. (1997), 'Raketnoe nasledstvo fashistskoi Germanii', *Voenno-istoricheskii zhurnal*, no. 3, 31–41.
IVMV (1973–82): *Istoriia Vtoroi Mirovoi voiny 1939–1945 gg.*, vols 1–12, Moscow.
Jacobsen, C.G., ed. (1987), *The Soviet defence enigma: estimating costs and burden*, Oxford.
Jasny, N. (1961), *Soviet industrialization, 1928–1952*, Chicago, IL.
Joint Economic Committee (1977), *Allocation of resources in the Soviet Union and China – 1977*. Hearings before the Subcommittee on Priorities and Economy in Government of the Joint Economic Committee, Congress of the United States, Part 3, Washington, DC.
Kahn, D. (1978), *Hitler's spies: German military intelligence in World War II*, London.
Kerimov, K. (1994), 'O kosmose, o podvigakh, o sebe', *Komsomol'skaia pravda*, 29 April.
Khavin, A.F. (1962), *Kratkii ocherk istorii industrializatsii SSSR*, Moscow.
Klein, B.H. (1959), *Germany's economic preparations for war*, Cambridge, MA.
Kocourek, M. (1977), 'Rocketry: level of technology in launch vehicles and manned space capsules', in Amann, R., Cooper, J., and Davies, R.W., eds, *The technological level of Soviet industry*, New Haven, CT, 490–522.
Konovalov, B. (1991), 'Iz Germanii – v Kapustin Iar', *Izvestiia*, 6 April, 3.
Korabli (1988), *Korabli i suda VMF SSSR, 1928–1945*, Moscow.
Kornai, J. (1992), *The socialist system: the political economy of communism*, Oxford.
Kosheleva, L., et al., eds (1995), *Pis'ma I.V Stalina V.M. Molotovu. 1925–1936 gg.*, Moscow.

Kostyrchenko, G.V. (1992), 'Organizatsiia aviatsionnogo krupnoseriinogo proizvodstva.)', in Biushgens, G.S., ed., *Samoletostroenie v SSSR*, vol. 1, Moscow, 413–36.

Kostyrchenko, G.V. (1994), 'Aviatsionnaia promyshlennost' nakanune i v gody Velikoi Otechestvennoi voiny (1939–1945 gg.)', in Biushgens, G.S., ed., *Samoletostroenie v SSSR*, vol. 2, Moscow, 197–238.

Kouwenhoven, R. (1996), 'A comparison of Soviet and US industrial performance, 1928–90', University of Groningen, Groningen Growth and Development Centre, Research Memorandum GD-29.

KPSS (1970), *KPSS v rezoliutsiakh i resheniakh s"ezdov, konferentsii i plenumov TsK*, vol. 4, Moscow.

Kriglov, A. (1995), *Kak sozdavalas' atomnaia promyshlennost' SSSR*, Moscow.

Kuromiya, H. (1988), *Stalin's industrial revolution: politics and workers, 1928–32*, Cambridge.

Kuvshinov, S.V., and Sobolev, D.A. (1995), 'Ob uchastii nemetskikh aviakonstruktorov v sozdanii reaktivnykh samoletov v SSSR', *Voprosy istorii estestvoznanii i tekhniki*, no. 1, 103–15.

Landes, D.S. (1969), *The unbound Prometheus: technological change and industrial development in western Europe from 1750 to the present*, Cambridge.

Liberman, P. (1996), *Does conquest pay? The exploitation of occupied industrial societies*, Princeton, NJ.

Mal'tsev, V.N. (1990), *Deiatel'nost' STO po osushchestvleniiu voennoi politiki v period sotsialisticheskogo stroitel'stva v SSSR 1920–1937 gg.*, Moscow.

Medvedev, Z.A. (1978), *Soviet science*, New York.

Meyer, A.G. (1978), 'The war scare of 1927', *Soviet Union/Union Soviétique*, 5(1), 1–25.

Milward, A.S. (1965), *The German economy at war*, London.

Mokyr, J. (1990), *The lever of riches: technical creativity and economic progress*, Oxford.

Moorsteen, R., and Powell, R.P. (1966), *The Soviet capital stock, 1928–1962*, Homewood, IL.

Nessen, G.D. (1977), *Deiatel'nost' KPSS po ukrepleniiu oboronosposobnosti SSSR v gody vtoroi piatiletki, 1933–1937*, Moscow.

Nezhinskii, L. N. (1990), 'Byla li voennaia ugroza SSSR v kontse 20-kh nachale 30–kh godov?', *Istoriia SSSR*, no. 6, 14–30.

Ocherki (1980), *Ocherki istorii Leningradskoi organizatsii KPSS 1918–1945 gg.*, Leningrad.

Ogorodnikov, F. (1931),'Mobilizatsiia promyshlennosti', *Voina i revoliutsiia*, no. 1, 110–17, no. 3, 106–12, no. 9, 94–6.

Ordway, F.I., and Sharpe, M.R. (1979), *The rocket team*, London.

Osoboe Soveshchanie (1980), *Rossiia. Osoboe Soveshchanie dlia obsuzhdeniia I ob" edineniia meropriiatii po oborone gosudarstva. Zhurnaly Osobykh Soveshchanii. 1915–1918 gg.*, Moscow, parts 1–2.

Overy, R.J. (1994), *War and economy in the Third Reich*, Oxford.

Overy, R.J. (1995a), *Why the Allies won*, London.

Overy, R.J. (1995b), 'Statistics', in Dear, I.C.B., ed., *The Oxford companion to the Second World War*, Oxford, 1059–63.

Pashkov, G.N. (1989), 'Oktiabr' – aprel' – Vselennaia', *Sovetskaia Rossiia*, 12 April, 3.

Petros'iants, A.M. (1993), *Dorogi zhizni, kotorye vybirali nas*, Moscow.

Plotnikov, K.N. (1955), *Ocherki istorii biudzheta Sovetskogo gosudarstva*, Moscow.

RAN (1992), *Vsesoiuznaia perepis' naseleniia 1939 g. Osnovnye itogi*, Moscow.

Rapoport, V., and Geller, Iu. (1995), *Izmena rodine*, Moscow.

Razvedupr RKKA (1936), *Novaia germanskaia armiia*, Moscow.

Rebrov, M. (1995), 'Poslednii argument: etiudy o konstruktore v cherno-belykh tonakh', *Krasnaia zvezda*, 25 March, 6.

Rol' razvedki (1992), 'U istokov sovetskogo atomnogo proekta: rol' razvedki, 1941–1946 gg. po materialam arkhiva vneshnei Rossii', *Voprosy istorii estestvoznaniia i tekhniki*, no. 3, 97–134.

Romanov, A. (1990), *Korolev*, Moscow.

Samuelson, L. (1998), *Plans for Stalin's war-machine: Tukhachevskii and military-economic planning, 1925–41*, London and Basingstoke (in press).

Sapir, J. (1997), 'The economics of war in the Soviet Union during World War II', in Kershaw, I. and Lewin, M., eds, *Stalinism and Nazism: dictatorships in comparison*, Cambridge.

Schneider, J.J. (1994), *The structure of strategic revolution: total war and the roots of the Soviet warfare state*, Novato, CA.

Schroder, G.W. (1955), 'How Russian engineering looked to a captured German scientist', *Aviation Week*, New York, May 9, vol. 62(19), 27–34.

Scott, H.F. and Scott, W.F. (1979), *The armed forces of the USSR*, Boulder, CO.

Semiriaga, M.I. (1995), *Kak my upravliali Germaniei. Politika i zhizn'*, Moscow.

Shavrov, V.B. (1988), *Istoriia konstruktsii samoletov v SSSR 1938–1950 gg.*, 2nd edn, Moscow.

Shoshkov, E.N. (1995), *Repressirovannoe OsTekhBiuro*, St. Petersburg.

Shteenbek, M. (1988), *Put' k prozreniiu*, Moscow.

Siegelbaum, L.H. (1983), *The politics of industrial mobilization in Russia, 1914–17: a study of the War Industries Committees*, London and Basingstoke.

Siegelbaum, L.H. (1988), *Stakhanovism and the politics of productivity in the USSR, 1935–1941*, Cambridge.

Simonov, N.S. (1996), 'Voenno-promyshlennyi kompleks SSSR v 20–50-e gody', *Svobodnaia mysl'*, no. 2, 96–114.

Simonov, N.S. (1996), *Voenno-promyshlennyi kompleks SSSR v 1920–1950-e gody: tempy ekonomicheskogo rosta, struktura, organizatsiia proizvodstva i upravlenie*, Moscow.

Sinev, N.M. (1991), *Obogashchennyi uran dlia atomnogo oruzhiia i energetiki*, Moscow.

Smit, G.D. (1946), *Atomnaia energiia dlia voennykh tselei*, Moscow.

Smyth, H.D. (1945), *Atomic energy for military purposes*, Princeton, NJ.

Sokolov, V.L. (1955), 'Soviet use of German science and technology, 1945–1946', East European Fund, Inc., Research Program on the USSR, Mimeographed Series no. 72, New York.

Sontag, J.P. (1975), 'The Soviet war scare of 1926–27', *Russian Review*, vol. 34(1), 66–77.

Sorokin, G.A. (1971), ed., *Po edinomu planu*, Moscow.

Sozdanie (1995), *Sozdanie pervoi sovetskoi iadernoi bomby*, Moscow.

Stalin, J. (1940), *Leninism*, Moscow.

Starkov, B.A. (1995), *Dela i liudi Stalinskogo vremeni*, St. Petersburg.

Stranitsy (1994), *Stranitsy istorii VNIINM. Vospominaniia sotrudnikov*, vol. 1, Moscow.

Sutton, A.C. (1968, 1971, 1973), *Western technology and Soviet development,* vol. 1, *1917–1930*, vol. 2, *1930–1945*, vol. 3, *1945–1960*, Stanford, CA.

SVE (1976–80), Grechko, A.A. *et al.*, eds, *Sovetskaia voennaia entsiklopediia*, 8 vols, Moscow.

Tokaty, G.A. (1964), 'Soviet rocket technology', in Emme, E.M., ed., *The history of rocket technology: essays on research, development, and utility*, Detroit, MI, 271–284.

Tokaty, G.A. (1968), 'Foundations of Soviet cosmonautics', *Spaceflight*, October, 335–46.

Trudy (1922), *Trudy I Vserossiiskogo s" ezda inzhinerov, rabotaiushchikh v oblasti voennoi promyshlennosti*, Moscow.

TsSU: Tsentral'noe statisticheskoe upravlenie SSSR (1959), *Narodnoe khoziaistvo SSSR v Velikoi Otechestvennoi voiny 1941–1945 gg.*, Moscow.

Tucker, R.C. (1977), 'The emergence of Stalin's foreign policy', *Slavic Review*, vol. 36(4), 563–89.

Tupper, S.M. (1982), 'The Red Army and Soviet defence industry, 1934–1941', unpub. PhD thesis, University of Birmingham.

USSBS: United States Strategic Bombing Survey (1945), *The effects of strategic bombing on the German war economy*.

Vishnev, S. (1928), 'Ekonomicheskaia podgotovka k voine za rubezhom', *Voina i revoliutsiia*, no. 7, 3–15.

Vishnev, S. (1930), 'Organizatsionnye problemy voenno-ekonomicheskoi podgotovki inostrannykh gosudarstv', in *Zapiski Kommunisticheskoi Akademii, Sektsiia po izucheniiu problem voiny*, vol. 4, Moscow.

Volpe, A. (1926), *Sovremennaia voina i rol' ekonomicheskoi podgotovki*, Moscow.

von Boetticher, M. (1979), *Industrialisierungspolitik und Verteidigungskonzeption der UdSSR 1926–1930: Herausbildung des Stalinismus und 'äussere Bedrohung'*, Düsseldorf.

von Braun, W. and Ordway, F.I. (1975), *History of rocketry and space travel*, 3rd edn, New York.

Wagenführ, R. (1933), 'Die Industriewirtschaft: Entwicklungstendenzen der deutschen und internationalen Industrieproduktion 1860 bis 1932', *Vierteljahrschafte zur Konjunkturforschung*, S. 31, Berlin.

Wagenführ, R. (1954), *Die deutsche Industrie im Kriege, 1939 bis 1945*, Berlin.

Weickhardt, G.G. (1986), 'The Soviet military-industrial complex and economic reform', *Soviet Economy*, vol. 2(3), 193–220.

Wheatcroft, S.G. and Davies, R.W. (1985), eds, *Materials for a balance of the Soviet national economy, 1928–1930*, Cambridge.

Zakharov, M. (1989), *General'nyi shtab nakanune Velikoi Otechestvennoi voiny*, Moscow.

Zaleski, E. (1971), *Planning for economic growth in the Soviet Union, 1918–1932*, Chapel Hill, NC.

Zaleski, E. (1980), *Stalinist planning for economic growth, 1933–1952*, London and Basingstoke.

Zhigur, Ia. (1930), *Razmakh budushchei imperialisticheskoi voiny*, Moscow.

Zhukov, G.K. (1970), *Vospominaniia i razmyshleniia*, Moscow.

Index